The sublime: a reader
in British eighteenth-century aesthetic theory

The sublime: a reader in
British eighteenth-century aesthetic theory

Edited by
Andrew Ashfield and Peter de Bolla

![CAMBRIDGE UNIVERSITY PRESS logo] CAMBRIDGE
UNIVERSITY PRESS

Published by the Press Syndicate of the University of Cambridge
The Pitt Building, Trumpington Street, Cambridge CB2 1RP
40 West 20th Street, New York, NY 10011-4211, USA
10 Stamford Road, Oakleigh, Melbourne 3166, Australia

First published 1996
Reprinted 1998

A catalogue record for this book is available from the British Library

Library of Congress cataloguing in publication data

The sublime: a reader in British eighteenth-century aesthetic theory
edited by Andrew Ashfield and Peter de Bolla.
p. cm.
Includes bibliographical references,
ISBN 0 521 39545 3. – ISBN 0 521 39582 8 (pbk.)
1 Sublime, The.   1 Ashfield, Andrew, 1956–   II. De Bolla, Peter, 1957–
BH301.S7S82   1996
111'.85–dc20   95-43245   CIP

ISBN 0 521 39545 3 hardback
ISBN 0 521 39582 8 paperback

Transferred to digital printing 2000

BJW

Contents

vii

Abbreviations

BJA	British Journal of Aesthetics
CI	Critical Inquiry
ECS	Eighteenth-Century Studies
ELH	Journal of English Literary History
ESQ	Emerson Studies Quarterly
JAAC	Journal of Aesthetics and Art Criticism
JBS	Journal of British Studies
JEGP	Journal of English and Germanic Philology
JHI	Journal of the History of Ideas
KCS	Kobe College Studies
MLN	Modern Language Notes
MP	Modern Philology
NLH	New Literary History
PMASAL	Publications of the Michigan Academy of Science, Arts and Letters
PMLA	Publications of the Modern Language Association
PQ	Philosophical Quarterly
QJE	Quarterly Journal of Economics
QJS	Quarterly Journal of Speech
RES	Review of English Studies
SEC	Studies in Eighteenth-Century Culture
SM	Speech Monographs
SP	Studies in Philology
SVEC	Studies on Voltaire and the Eighteenth Century
WS	Western Speech

Introduction

The history of the concept of the aesthetic has yet to be written; any such history will need to examine a number of signal moments which, it would be fairly uncontroversial to claim, must include classical discussions of representation, renaissance treatments of mimesis, nineteenth-century revaluations of aestheticism and our own postmodern defamiliarisations of the artwork. Yet, important as these moments are, modern scholarship has elevated the eighteenth-century tradition of the sublime to the principal event in this long history. Indeed it has become something of a commonplace to suggest that aesthetics began during the enlightenment. Such claims clearly beg a number of difficult questions, most importantly perhaps, the precise definition of the term 'aesthetics'. For it cannot make much sense to claim that from classical times to the eighteenth century there had been no discussion of the epistemology of the artwork, or the relationship between a representation and its representamen, or the relative values of specific art forms. Of course such discussion took place, and of course a variety of theories, some simple and some rather complex, were produced to account for that area of human activity we engage in when producing, evaluating or encountering artworks.

Consequently the claim that aesthetics began in the eighteenth century must mean something slightly different; perhaps the simplest way of conveying that difference is to call to mind the great revolutions of the enlightenment, changes in the ways in which man conceptualised himself, his relations to others and to the world outside and around him, which essentially construct the topography of modernity. Our senses of the self, society, science (in the sense of knowledge) are both derived from and dependent on models created during the eighteenth century: we are, to all intents and purposes, children of the enlightenment. More specifically in relation to the subject of aesthetics it fell to this period in particular to articulate the complexities of affective experience, and it did so in the context of an emerging new understanding of the construction of the subject. This new subject, the site of various appetites and desires, was increasingly cut loose from the old certainties, those which grounded and provided guarantees for the subject in a predominantly religious culture. It is this change from an epistemology based in theological belief and debate to one in which man must find from within himself the grounds of knowledge, which above all others distinguishes the enlightenment as the single most important moment in the history of the concept of the aesthetic.

It is, therefore, hardly surprising that the term 'aesthetics' is inextricably

1

caught up within a discursive network, a knot of distinct discourses which singly both complement and compete with each other, and collectively amount to a re-drawing of the map upon which we chart our senses of self. It is during this period that the change adverted to above, from a predominantly religious context for thought to one in which a vast range of distant branches of knowledge make competing claims for authority – we might think here of the beginnings of economics, psychology, sociology, linguistics, geology – lays the ground for the concatenation of simple concepts into complex interdependent and intertwined forms. The aesthetic, for this period, is certainly one of these complex concepts. It might be immediately pointed out that our own contemporary use of the term 'aesthetic' is also rendered problematic on account of a similar complexity, however it is nevertheless the case that the general field outlined by the term in contemporary discussion concerns the artwork. This is not so during the eighteenth century, which has no theory of 'aesthetics' in the modern sense, which is not to say that it had no views upon or theories about artworks. But what the period said and thought about artworks is bound up with what it thought and said about the nature of human experience generally. In this sense for the period in question the aesthetic is not *primarily* about art but about how we are formed as subjects, and how *as subjects* we go about making sense of our experience. 'What is it that moves me?' is, therefore, a question centrally posed to human nature, which at its furthest extreme threatens to dissolve and dissipate the human in a technology that has the potential to overmaster all sense of being. This question, the problematic of the aesthetic, was known to the period in a number of ways but it is most fully explored under the rubric of the sublime, the topic to which the following collection of materials is addressed.

One of the consequences of the argument above, and indeed of the selection of texts here presented, is a detachment from the scholarly tradition that has repeatedly told a story about the beginnings of aesthetics in eighteenth-century Britain in terms of the gradual shift towards the Kantian critique of judgment. Such a story invokes a teleology, explicitly casting the British discussion as a kind of dress rehearsal for the full-fledged philosophical aesthetics of Immanual Kant and his heirs. This tradition, in its adoption of the Kantian formula, understands the aesthetic realm as 'disinterested', which is to say it adopts and adapts Kant's thesis that judgments made about aesthetic objects are universal and without motivation. As a result of this, pre-Kantian texts are read through the lens of the third critique thereby dissolving the differences between the English and German traditions. The story ends, then, with a proclamation of the aesthetic realm as in some sense autonomous; constructed on rules internal to it, generating affective responses according to its own logic, and generally distinct from all other realms of experience. Consequently, the aesthetic, at least since Kant, has been understood as without political or ethical motivation since its *affective* registers are, according to the Kantian model, disinterested.

A case could be made that would directly counter this claim, which is to say the above sketch might be characterised as a gross misreading of the Kantian text where the political and ethical constantly impress themselves on the surface of the third critique, if only by way of example.[1] There is much to this counter-argument which underlines the fact that interpretations of the third critique over the intervening two hundred years have predominantly ignored the ideological and political grounds of the text. Be this as it may the aim of the present collection is to de-couple the British eighteenth-century tradition of the sublime from the Kantian analytic.

It was Samuel Holt Monk who first claimed with some scholarly authority that the British debate prepared for and introduced the Kantian 'autonomy of the subject', the so-called inexorable movement towards the 'subjectivism of Kant'.[2] Insofar as such arguments in part rely upon and construct specifically 'enlightenment' forms of the subject, they give an accurate sense of a general trajectory during the period towards concepts of autonomous subjectivity. However, in reading the British tradition exclusively in terms of a preparation for the Kantian description of the subject much is left out or to one side. While parts of the British tradition can be seen in terms of this gradual development of 'subjectivism', the vast bulk of discussion and debate is not exclusively concerned with 'autonomous subjectivity' at all. Indeed, it is precisely within the analytic of the sublime where we find the greatest tension between self-interest and the interest of the subject. It is this tension which provides the British tradition with its greatest difficulty, but that difficulty also leads to slightly different ways of resolving the tension from those proposed by the third critique. Where the Kantian text proposes an elegant solution to this tension in the disinterestedness of aesthetic judgment, in the British tradition there is a consistent refusal to relinquish the interconnections between aesthetic judgments and ethical conduct. This, in Kames's important contribution to the debate, results in the proposition that 'ideal presence' in its furthest extension might become 'ideal being', which is to say that the experiences we have in elevated states, precisely the affective register of the sublime, need not be divorced from those standards we invoke to govern our conduct, nor even transcend such ethical precepts, but in a concatenation of both realms, the aesthetic and the ethical, may be elevated to a form of ideal being. While in some instances this might look like the production of the autonomous subject, of the transcendent form of experience which is 'disinterested', in the most careful of the British theorists this is not so, as shall be remarked below in relation to the work of Adam Smith. Thus the aesthetic realm for British writers of the period presents a set of difficulties which must

---

[1] Recent work on the Kantian text has taken precisely this line of enquiry. See Cathy Caruth, 'The force of example: Kant's symbols', *Yale French Studies*, 74 (1988); David Lloyd, 'Kant's examples', *Representations*, 28 (Fall, 1989); and David Lloyd, 'Analogies of aesthetics: the politics of culture and the limits of critique' (unpublished paper delivered Geneva, 1987); Paul de Man, 'Phenomenality and materiality in Kant', in *The textual sublime*, eds. Hugh J. Silverman and Gary E. Aylesworth (Albany: State University of New York Press, 1990).

[2] Samuel Holt Monk, *The sublime: a study of critical theories in XVIII-century England* (Ann Arbor: University of Michigan Press, 1960), p. 4.

be solved in terms of both a convincing empirical account of the subject's affective experience and a social and ethical account of conduct. Art, as such, is therefore only one aspect of the aesthetic.

We hope that the extracts collected here demonstrate the fecundity of the British debate in its attempts to answer the question: 'what causes aesthetic pleasure?', and that the insistence made upon the discursive complexity of the concept of the sublime results in a 'thick description' of British eighteenth-century aesthetics. The collection effectively proposes an alternative way of conceiving of this tradition; we argue that far from relinquishing the inter-connections between the aesthetic and its neighbouring discourses, the British tradition insists that the affective is based in human experience and human nature, and that by necessity the aesthetic cannot, therefore, be understood as a separate realm.

This alternative suggests that the aesthetic is constantly called back to other forms of understanding and experiencing the world, to ethical or rhetorical modes, and in addition it needs to be understood as a transformational discourse. On account of this, the sublime infiltrates other forms of enquiry and works its way into discussions which are only marginal to the aesthetic. This is why the British tradition insists upon the social, ideological and finally cultural basis of the aesthetic realm. For this reason 'transcendence' and 'autonomy', as ways of explaining the commonality of taste and the affective realm of aesthetic experience respectively are not viable concepts for a writer like Adam Smith, whose *Theory of Moral Sentiments* represents the most sophisticated and elegant solution to the problem of finding and sustaining a standard of taste, that is in finding a ground for aesthetic judgments. Smith, *contra* Kant and the Kantian tradition, refuses to give up the ethical when faced with the limit experience of the sublime. This refusal insists on the ethical sustainability of sublime affect, since what he terms the superiority of achievement over virtues or talents must in the last resort be brought back to the legislation of ethical conduct.

Smith proposes this reining-in of the subject in a theoretical elaboration which is the closest the British tradition comes to the Kantian critique. It begins with an outworking of the moral sense into the aesthetic realm so that the grounds of our distinguishing between good and bad artworks are identical to our grounds for making ethical judgments. This is the first move. The second, and crucial, follow-up insists that this identity of the ethical grounds of judgment with the aesthetic can never be maintained, since the sublime continuously runs beyond the bounds of human experience. Consequently human nature is repeatedly called to account in the face of excessive or 'limit' experiences; in the ethical domain this results in the imperative to imaginatively inhibit the experiences of others. Smith, in his famous and brilliant solution to this, creates the position of the impartial spectator, a site of experience we can never directly inhabit but which we take to be the guarantor for our own experience. Being a subject in Smith's world is precisely being positioned as the spectator of oneself as one imagines another impartial spectator to gaze upon us. We are, then, in effect reined in by our own imaginative construction of the subject who sits in judgment over us; in Kames' scheme we would call this impartial spectator the outworking of ideal presence into the ideal being. Within the aesthetic realm, therefore, taste can be understood as transcendent, as going beyond the specific taste of particular individuals, once it becomes the property of the imagined spectator. In noting this, however, we are not making a Kantian argument about the transcendence of judgments of taste: it is not taste which is said to be transcendent, but the position of the ideal being. Consequently, at the point where the British tradition comes closest to the Kantian it also definitively marks off its distance from it. It is that proximity but eventual distance which in part explains why the British tradition continues to seek a solution to the problem of reconciling aesthetic affect with moral conduct, and it is in regard to these arguments and this tradition that Smith's *Theory of Moral Sentiments* can be seen as the central text of the British debate, as precisely the pathology of the sublime in contrast to Burke's symptomatology.

Where Burke, and the tradition which follows his *Enquiry*, seeks to fragment and fracture our experiences of the sublime in order to create as full a taxonomy as possible, Smith insists on the necessity for explanations of the extremes of self-interest in sublime experience which have not given up on the possibility that the sublime, or excessive, might be concatenated with the beautiful, or morally just. Consequently, Burke's catalogue of effective and affectual qualities and experiences merely draw our attention to what, according to Smith, needs to be explained.

In relation to this argument it is significant that we have singled out the topic of the sublime, since it is in and through this concatenated concept that the complexity of the British debate is manifested. Taste and genius, the two terms which function as modal concepts in the Kantian project, are present to the British debate but do not operate so clearly as transformative tropes. This is because these concepts are far more fully amenable to transcendental description: genius, in its conceptual core is hostile to the notion of historical or ideological contingency. The case with taste is slightly different, since the opposite is more commonly envisaged in which taste is precisely context bound. Discussion of taste, however, constantly returns to the transcendental in the British as well as the Continental school. Part of the reason for this concerns the vexed question over making generalisable statements about artworks: if all judgments of taste are in the final analysis solely within the domain of individual opinion then something called 'taste' cannot really be said to operate.

In the case of the sublime, however, a different set of problems arise on account of the status attained by the discourse on the sublime. For this analytic discourse is not merely concerned with ascertaining the precise location of affects – it is also productive of them. In this sense the discourse on the sublime attains the status of a technology and its appearance is coincident with a number of other discourses which similarly articulate technologies of explanation and understanding – such as economics, philology or psychology. As technology, the discourse on the sublime creates the subject of aesthetics at the same time as it legislates the aesthetic subject; it is, in a very important sense, a technique of the subject. There are large-scale changes in the epistemological grounding of the period which contribute towards this technical aspect of the sublime; we have already mentioned the crucial demise of theological certainties in the face of the new beliefs of the enlightenment. It is this general shift from a situation in which knowledge is grounded in religious belief to one in which a series of interlinked technical discourses determine, legislate and police specific forms of knowledge, that we mean to highlight in the development of the discourse on the sublime. The aim of the extracts following is to point out the ways in which the eighteenth-century tradition develops various technologies of explanation and understanding in the face of the sublime. These technologies are derived from human ratiocination, controlled by human agency and are deliberately constructed in order to account for human nature, but it does not necessarily follow that they are equally so delimited.

The discourse on the sublime, then, should be seen as a technical discourse of the subject: it bridges the incommensurable gap between aesthetic pleasure and ethical action. But, in order to function effectively as a technology of knowledge production it must become transformational, a discourse of the sublime. This is the most problematic aspect of the eighteenth-century tradition since the boundaries between distinct discourses begin to lose their definition as the sublime transforms both itself and its neighbouring discursive forms. In the extracts following we have presented some examples of precisely this kind of transformational technology. If we take the technical discourses of instruction for reading, or looking at landscape or oratorical performance, discourses legislating activities in which sublime affect may well be encountered, we find that the discourse of the sublime infiltrates these neighbouring forms and transforms both itself and the host discourse. What results in the case of these technical discourses is the fragmentation of a previously coherent set of prescriptive practices into on the one hand an ineffectual descriptive technique – oratory becomes elocution – and on the other a mixed discursive form in which oratorical performance, for example, is entwined with a whole set of somatic presentations which threaten to run away with the self, the subject that had previously provided the coherence upon which oratory was grounded.

This transformative aspect of the discourse of the sublime can be seen as generating a number of distinct symptoms, some of which it sets out to cure through the transformation of neighbouring discourses. One of these symptoms, for example, is the requirement that the subject act not only out of self-interest and self-love but also with regard to others. Smith, once again, has an elegant solution to this problem in his suggestion that we are only able to see ourselves as we imagine ourselves to be seen by others. In this sense a primary symptom of the sublime is sociology or what the period understood as anthropology, but similar symptoms arise under different guises – such as the political imperative towards national identity. This too is an outworking or transformation of the sublime, which arises in response to a neurosis deeply embedded in enlightenment descriptions of the state: the fear that one's own identity is dependent upon collective identities, names given to the state. It is for this reason that the period in question develops so many and various tropes for national identity. In the same way the transformation of economics through its confrontation with the symptom of surplus value leads to a technology which overmasters the earlier discourse of political economy. Such a transformation can be understood as a direct response to the difficulty of reconciling the sublime excess of aesthetic motivations of conduct with the civic duties that permeate political economy.

In the case of the technical discourse on the activity of reading we find two tropes which exert transformative power over the descriptive analytic, and those tropes, of ravishment and transport, effect the movement between the discussion of reading and that of the sublime. In the discourse on the sublime these tropes are first found in Dennis where they begin to exert their transformative power, thereby unravelling the legislative boundaries of their host discourse. Such tropological disturbance can also be found in the transformation of the discussion of trade and commerce into economics, or of pneumatology into psychology, of theories of the origin of society into sociology. In these and other instances of transformation there is a common effect: a trope unravels what was once a distinct boundary only in order to create, in an overplus of tropological inversion, a more effective boundary in the new legislative form. This can be noted in the technical descriptive analytic of the reading activity where the tropes of ravishment and transport begin to generate transformations at the descriptive level of the discourse. In effect the analysis of reading becomes stained by a set of discriminations which it neither knowingly inherits nor necessarily welcomes from the discourse on the sublime.

One such set of discriminations concerns the gender of the reader – perhaps a 'natural' aspect of reading. Here the transport of 'masculine' sublime affect colours the ascription of gender labels in the reading activity. Thus a trope first isolated and analysed in the discourse on the sublime is taken into another discursive environment in which it begins to generate mutations at both the surface level and within the figurative structure of the text. In this way the 'transport of the reader' comes to represent a complex figurative knot in which the possibilities for extensive tropological transformation are created.

Let us take another example: in the growing body of work produced after the mid-century which we would now term social theory or sociology – the work we associate with Adam Ferguson's *An essay on the history of civil society* for instance – a number of concepts underpin the structure of the argumentation. These concepts, such as civic duty, self-interest or the active powers of man are structured through the tropological transformations of the sublime in ways which leave the surface of the text almost entirely without reference to aesthetic affect. Ferguson, for example, sketches out a possible description of the 'progress' of society in which 'novelty', 'joy' and 'expectation' play their parts. While the use of these terms gives some indication as to their provenance in the analytic of the sublime it is not the terms themselves which point back towards their origin in discussion of the sublime but the transformation of the terms into tropes figuring Ferguson's own analysis and argumentation. Ferguson writes:

We may fancy to ourselves, that in ages of progress, the human race, like scouts gone abroad on the discovery of fertile lands, having the world open before them, are presented at every step with the appearance of novelty. They enter on every new ground with expectation and joy: They engage in every enterprise with the ardour of men, who believe they are going to arrive at national felicity, and permanent glory; and forget past disappointments amidst the hopes of future success. From mere ignorance, rude minds are intoxicated with every passion; and partial to their own condition, and to their own pursuits, they think that every scene is inferior to that in which they are placed. Roused alike by success, and by misfortune, they are sanguine, ardent, and precipitant; and leave to the more knowing ages which succeed them, monuments of imperfect skill, and of rude execution in every art; but they leave likewise the marks of a vigorous and ardent spirit, which their successors are not always qualified to sustain, or to imitate.[3]

Here the developmental narrative is structured according to the pulsation of the sublime in which the chronological trajectory implies the heights of the present, the moment at which the description and analysis is made. There is a 'natural' progress to society as much as to the argument being pursued: both end up at the point of full knowledge, of plenitude where the sublime rush of aesthetic affect has been tropologically transformed into the certitude of teleological social history. At this summit of what the modern world knows of itself we reach the sublime affect of progress.

Running concurrently with these transformations of the discourse on the sublime we find an increasingly dogged technical literature struggling to enumerate every last cause and effect of sublime affect. This is evidenced in a repetitious return to the primal scene of transport in order to refine yet further what prompts or causes it; hence the greater distinctions between vocabulary sets as the century progresses. But what had been a workable distinction for Shaftesbury or Dennis – say the distinction between the sublime and beautiful – became either too insensitive or too restrictive for a Price or Gilpin. Indeed, the picturesque theorists occasionally concatenated the sublime and beautiful thereby running against the tide of the technical literature on the sublime which ends up splitting hairs over an object it could never satisfactorily define: what I might term obscure someone else might call faint, and herein lies the problem.

If this suggests a developmental narrative in which the tradition gradually sinks into irrelevant quibbling over terms, we would like to stall such

---

[3] Adam Ferguson, *An essay on the history of civil society* (Edinburgh, 1767), p. 328.

conclusions, not least because the tradition is too complex to submit to a simplistic chronology of increasing sophistication followed by arid attempts at refinement. It is the case, however, that by the close of the century we find more than one text claiming to bring the debate to its conclusion by the simple expedient of sorting out the previous decades' worth of taxonomic errors.[4]

Of course a 'final analysis' was never likely since the relation between sub-lime affect and its cause continued to resist precise formulation. The tradition we present here developed three distinct forms of address to this relation. The first was an exclusive focus on the experiential, although the confusions between cause and affect are if anything intensified here. This approach understands the sublime in terms of a set of qualities which are presumed to be internal to a variety of objects that summon up in some shape or form notions of elevation or grandeur. The catalogue of these qualities is well rehearsed: large, distant, terrifying, of endless variety, indistinct, dignified and so on.

The second approach attends to the affect: in this case causes, such as grand objects in the world, are relegated by the attempt to describe mental effects. The question now becomes what is the peculiarity of the sensation I feel when in the presence of objects containing some or all of the above qualities? Atten-tion shifts, therefore, from the object to our mental processes which react to or register those qualities delineated by the first approach. Further questions follow from this, such as how is the feeling of the sublime different from other feelings we might experience, from the glory of war or of religious enthusiasm? Can the 'elevation' of the soul be removed from its experiential base in human conduct thereby inhabiting something like a 'purely' aesthetic realm? To what extent is the 'transport' and 'ravishment' of an encounter with the text a sexual as well as aesthetic experience? How, in sum, does the sublime take us out of ourselves, constructing in the process a kind of ideal presence of self stimulating affective experience?

The third approach turns to the analytic of the sublime itself in an attempt to understand how the analytic produces its object for enquiry, and by exten-sion the mental affect. Here attention to the discursive production of the sub-lime tends to diminish the importance of both qualities of external objects and affective reactions to them. In many ways this is the most interesting approach but it too easily leads to the conclusion that the sublime is without substance, an immaterial object; or, to put it another way, the enquiry into the sublime ends up having no subject. In this way the turn towards the dis-cursive analytic runs the risk of evacuating the object it sets out to investigate. In both the first and second approach the 'sublime' has a shape and substance, either in the outer world of vast objects or within the interior landscape of mental affect, in the third it becomes an endlessly deferred point at which the work of analysis might finally come to an end. This results in a pretty con-tinuous difficulty in ascertaining the precise limits of the analysis: once the

---

[4] Perhaps the most telling example of this is Basil Barrett, *Pretension to a final analysis of the nature and origin of sublimity, style, genius and taste* (London, 1812)

material taken for investigation is a substanceless substance anything and everything may fall within its scope, but this, it should be stressed, is the consequence of a properly transformational discourse.

The following collection of extracts sets out to map the complex interactions of these three approaches. We have grouped the extracts in sections in order to give some indication of the chronological and geo-cultural specificity of the texts. However, as we have argued above, the mutational nature of the discourse on the sublime and its tropological migrations into other discourses necessitates not merely reading across parts but also movement outside this text to others, for example to the works of Mandeville or Ferguson, to imaginative literature, travel writing, religious debate and so forth.

The first part presents the origins of eighteenth-century speculation on the sublime, and groups extracts around the central themes of what has been termed the 'Longinian tradition' (Monk). Longinus exerted an enormous influence, partly due to his classical authority and partly due to the prestige of Boileau, not only on what has been understood as the 'rhetorical sublime' but also on the later associational theorists. In this respect it is useful to distinguish between theories of sublimity which return to rhetoric for exemplification and amplification and a coherent 'Longinian tradition'. The former continues throughout the eighteenth-century debate while the latter, although primarily rhetorical in nature, in its specific connection to *Peri Hupsous* becomes less influential after mid-century. In this regard Samuel Holt Monk's thesis distorts the eighteenth-century debate through its devaluation of rhetorically centred discussions of the sublime. These discussions, to be found in what he presents as the early English tradition, are to be distinguished from what he proposes as the native tradition of English aesthetics proper, which supposedly begins with Addison's *Spectator* papers on the pleasures of the imagination.

However, the rhetorical tradition not only intertwines with this other slightly different native English tradition *throughout the course of the century*, it also provides the conceptual base for the entire development of aesthetics. Rhetoric is not just an early touchstone for the sublime, it permeates the discursive analytic through and through. One of the ways in which this is importantly manifest is the increasing attention paid to the text in discussions of the aesthetic; such 'text attentiveness' has significant ramifications within the social field, as modes of textual decorum provide models for social decorum. At the furthest extreme such attention to the text gradually comes to challenge 'real' lived experience, as if the affective experience of reading might supplant encounters with the world at large. This could be translated into Kames's terms by noting that 'ideal presence' becomes more attractive than 'real presence'; this might be one way in which we could begin to understand the period's fascination with the novel.

The first part not only introduces the Longinian tradition it also sets out to correct the impression, heretofore a commonplace of the scholarship on the sublime, that Longinus and his commentators fade from view as the century advances. We maintain that, on the contrary, this Longinian tradition repeatedly informs the *transformational* capacities of the discourse on the sublime. Without this rhetorical conceptual base to the discourse on the sublime there would be no means of getting from aesthetics to politics, or from the ethical sublime to the politics of the imagination. Furthermore, without the *techne* of rhetoric the liberating textual reading techniques of a Pope, Addison or Bysshe, which facilitated rapid movement around and through texts to arrive at sublime passages would not have been possible. For the technology of the sublime is aided by the technical development of text presentation – in the form of anthologies of the most affecting pieces of literature, such as Enfield's *Speaker* – which was firmly dependent upon rhetoric as a means of selecting extracts and constructing a taxonomy of textualised affect. The Longinian text, therefore, and its early readers in eighteenth-century Britain are absolutely crucial for an adequate understanding of the sublime tradition. It can be said, then, that the sublime begins in ethics and rhetoric, and that the history of the discourse on it describes the complex set of relations which pertain between the three overlapping domains of ethics, rhetoric and aesthetics.

Much of Part I is organised around the authority of Longinus. This is so in two distinct senses: on the one hand Longinus is invoked as an authority on the matter of elevated language, a classical source of standing and repute, while on the other the Longinian text authorises discussion of what results from such uses of language, sublimity. This is a departure from another classical authority, Aristotle, whose analysis of catharsis is to a great extent supplanted in the eighteenth-century tradition by the turn towards Longinian sublimity. In this turn away from Aristotelian reason towards Longinian rapture a new and invigorated vocabulary of the passions is developed, which includes among its terms astonishment, enthusiasm, ravishment, and transport. It is noteworthy that all four do service within both a rhetorical and an aesthetic framework, and that they participate in the beginnings of a tradition of close textual analysis – the first sustained attempts to link practical criticism of texts with an ethical description and account of human nature.

In Part II the ethical dimension to aesthetic speculation is more fully presented in Shaftesbury's theory of the moral sense. The writers presented here all fall within the mainstream of early eighteenth-century English philosophical criticism, although they should not be understood as forming a coherent school. Where Shaftesbury, for example, requires a theory of civic morality in order to ground affective response, Hartley turns to the interior psychology of the individual in order to explain why a particular response occurs in the first place. Similarly, while this English tradition looks both away from and hard at the individual, so differences in emphasis pertain around the object addressed: some writers look towards the natural world for exemplification of the sublime while others give precedence to man made forms. The latter emphasis is most exhaustively investigated in Baillie's *Essay on the Sublime* where the distinction between the rhetorical production of sublime affect and the unmediated experience of the natural sublime is systematically explored.

The individual does not disappear in this analysis since the affective sensation of the sublime is nearly always understood in terms of a raising of self-consciousness, and in these writers both the authentication and limit for such experiences is provided by moral sense theory. It is hardly surprising, then, that the interconnections between descriptions of a sublime natural world and of the feelings aroused in an encounter with that world are commonly the centre of attention in these early English discussions. It also follows from this that a particular sensitivity and attention to the language used in these descriptions becomes advantageous.

Such an attentiveness to the words we use in describing natural phenomena and our affective reactions to them is developed further in Part III which presents texts written within the context of mid-century Ireland. Here we encounter Burke for the first time and this prompts an assessment of the tradition up to this point. It might be said, for example, that with Burke's *Enquiry* the sublime finds its first major theorist. It is certainly the case that this text exerted considerable power over its successors, yet in the fuller context of the tradition here presented Burke's balancing act between psychological explanations of sublime affect and associational descriptions of the qualities of external objects comes to feel unsatisfactory. Nevertheless the terms of the debate are clearly articulated by mid-century: the first two approaches sketched out above represent the most efficacious means of beginning an enquiry into the sublime, hence the precision with which Burke is able to delineate both causes and qualities. It remains largely for Burke's successors to press the limits of these approaches and, in the wake of the *Enquiry* to develop the third approach outlined above. But Burke himself found good cause to adopt a more discursively centred analysis of the sublime in the face of the event which above all others brought home the political ramifications of sublime excess: the French Revolution, an event which for Burke not only could not but also should not be described as sublime.

Parts IV and V print extracts from works produced in the context of the 'Aberdonian Enlightenment' between 1759 and 1785, and those produced in the context of Edinburgh and Glasgow. We have come to associate these contexts with the Scottish Enlightenment, although recent studies have taken great pains to dissociate the Aberdonian school from those in Edinburgh and Glasgow. Such distinctions are less important for the present anthology than the differences between the thriving intellectual milieu of Scotland generally and the English tradition. The Scottish context gave a slightly different spin to the question of sublimity, represented in our extracts by Duff's *Essay*, which sets out to inquire into the poetic base of heightened response. The most important feature of this account is Duff's willingness to embrace the excessive in his formulation of the original genius as going beyond the 'legal restraints of criticism'. In this sense an original genius is 'lawless'. Here the third approach which sees the discourse on the sublime in terms of its own analytic powers reaps its rewards: it is now possible to understand the sublime analogically, as a scheme or technology which constantly 'goes beyond' the limits assigned it. Thus the topic of enquiry for Duff, like many of his Scottish compatriots, slightly alters as attention shifts away from the natural world and our mental processes prompted by encounters with it towards the transformational power of the analytic of the sublime.

Duff also makes the point that the genius must himself be enraptured if the audience is to be similarly moved. This mimetic focus to the analysis of the sublime permeates the associationist account and will be interestingly extended within the domain of the reader's response by Beattie. It is also subjected to some investigation in Reid's account who, in common with the other writers in Part IV, wishes to bring the analysis of heightened experience to bear on ethical protocols of action.

In the extracts from Hume we find a similar base in the ethical but in this case the analysis is turned towards the passions and the imagination. His approach has clear connections to Smith's account of wonder and surprise, and we find common to the two an emphasis on both the effectivity and affectivity of the experience of unusual objects, be they large, distinct, distant and so on. It is this slant to the discussion which will become a founding principle of the post-Kantian tradition in which aesthetic affect stems directly from the disinterestedness of the experiencing subject. Both Smith and Hume investigate this interplay between the effect and the affect through their concentration on the relations between internal sensation and external stimulus.

As with Duff, both Blair and Kames work out of the Longinian rhetorical tradition in which the sublime is understood via reference to the arts of oratory and efficacious expression. Blair however takes issue with the Longinian analysis arguing that the five principal sources of the sublime identified in *Peri Hupsous* should be more correctly understood as properties of writing not of the sublime proper. Blair, in common with Hume and Smith, wishes to ground his analysis of the sublime on the materiality of forms.

The extension of this mode of analysis into the realm of language represents a renewed attempt to describe the complexity of figurative expression. In this respect Blair prefigures much contemporary work on the nature of figural language in his insistence on the division between words and the thoughts they are taken to convey. This leads to his perception that sublimity does not lay in the words themselves, or even in the 'expression' as in the Longinian tradition, but in something 'material' to language itself. That materiality is usually taken to be the 'thought'.

This division of word and thought predates Blair by a very long time, but it is the renewed interest in the effects of elevated language which begins to generate more sophisticated accounts of how figural language operates. This can be seen most clearly in Kames's proposal that the sublime is essentially the product of a 'double signification': it denotes both a quality found in objects as well as the affect experienced in the perceiving subject. The identification of this dual denotation is a crucial step forward and allows a far more supple analysis the aesthetic realm: we need no longer worry about whether the cause of the elevated experience is out there in the world or in here, in our own internal responses to that world. Now, with Kames's 'doubling' it can be seen to be in both places and work can begin to be focussed on the mediation between the two.

The ramifications of this are extremely important; attention moves away from the obsessive drive to locate sublime affect and effect towards the construction of a descriptive model which can account for the transactions between inner mental states and the qualities of objects in the world. Consequently the analysis of the sublime begins to change from something centred upon instances of it, whether they be in the natural world, in the text or in the mind of the viewer, to an investigation of the mechanism or technology by which one comes to know of the sublime at all. Interest in the object – say mountainous scenery – therefore diminishes as writers begin to become increasingly occupied with the discursive production of sublimity. Accordingly a greater concentration on the procedures and protocols of the analysis itself begins to emerge and this results in the severance of the sublime from any material forms at all. The sublime is precisely that which has no object, no analogue in the world of forms.

Smith embraces this insight in his implication that philosophy should be primarily addressed to the imagination. This is developed by Smith into a theory of conscience that, as we have already noted above, is based upon an imagined impartial spectator. The aesthetic and ethical come together in Smith's formulation as the excessive production of the one is brought to the law of the other. This produces a third object of enquiry, an imaginary object which is the direct result of the analytic discourse itself.

In Part VI we present extracts from two slightly different aspects of later eighteenth-century speculation on the sublime. The first concerns the debate around the picturesque, while the second is animated by the events in France following the revolution. This final part differs from the previous five since it does not set out to be representative of a relatively coherent segment of the larger tradition. In this case our aim has been to suggest two ways in which the eighteenth-century tradition fractures and fragments into distinct areas of enquiry, and in suggesting this we have made no attempt to be exhaustive in our selections.

This last part also prompts a brief comment on the chronological bookends of the anthology. We open fairly uncontroversially with the early eighteenth-century interest in Longinus, since this is where British writers made their start. Our concluding point, however, is more problematic since, as the entire collection sets out to argue, the discourse on the sublime is transformational. While it begins with the Longinian rhetorical tradition it ends in a fractured multiplicity of distinct discursive domains which untidily permeate a number of different disciplines and discussions. Some of these discussions remain coherent well into the nineteenth century whereas others have virtually become moribund by the 1790s. In order to give a sense of the quite different interests and priorities that develop as the discourse on the sublime fragments we have chosen to extract texts from two unconnected areas of discussion and debate.

The first of these areas is most often understood as a critique of taxonomy within the tradition of the sublime, but this does not relegate it to a mere addendum to the Burkean inquiry: the picturesque sets out to articulate an aesthetics of reaction and fantasy based in an entirely different social and class milieu from the elite patrician culture of the earlier debate. Gilpin or Marshall do not only speak for a different aesthetic they also give voice to a new class of citizen within the republic of culture. The second area of discussion can be characterised as the English response to the French Revolution.

In the case of the picturesque the transformational power of the analytic of the sublime can be clearly observed. The picturesque developed not only as a response to changing attitudes to the landscape but also to what it perceived as the bankruptcy of a specific form of the analysis of the sublime – namely the attempt to map causes onto affects precisely, to claim for example that a large and massy object *necessarily* produces an affect of sublimity. The picturesque saw the world differently, its encounter with 'landscape' was inflected through nearly a century's worth of contest and conflict over the right to use, see and picture the land. Within the mainstream of eighteenth-century discussion of the sublime landscape-aesthetics were fundamentally preoccupied with the pleasures of the eye. This aesthetic was indifferent to the needs of both the land and its users, to the productive capacity of the land to yield sustenance or organise social relations: it was content for the land to look like a picture, and when it did not conform to its idealised forms it usually re-arranged both land and dwellings in order to make it conform.

The picturesque developed an alternative address to the landscape in its embrace of fantasmic models of perception. It did not seek to turn the real world into its idealised projections; on the contrary it enjoyed the friction caused between the real and the imaginary and sought to occupy the terrain between them. Where the early eighteenth-century sublime is all blasting waterfalls and dizzying declivities, the picturesque softens the focus in its domestication of the landscape. This impulse towards domestication can be understood in two senses: firstly the picturesque promoted domestic tourism thereby revaluing the topographical arrangements of the British countryside in an explicit rejection of the grandeur of European topography. Secondly it adapts the analytic of the sublime to a new social and political environment, predominantly middle class, with a whole new set of priorities and assumptions – regarding among other things gender and class – that challenge the hegemony of elitist cultural aspiration. The domestication of the landscape is a cover for an attempt at dismantling the culture of land ownership, but, and this is the point, the sublime reappears in the picturesque, which should be seen as a tropological transformation of the discourse of the sublime, another answer to the question: 'what causes and sustains aesthetic pleasure, and in what does that pleasure consist?'

The second example we present in the concluding part is organised around explicit political issues. Here we hope to demonstrate some of the ways in which the analytic of the sublime is carried out in more overtly political

Eighteenth-century readers of Longinus were particularly impressed by the style and verbal resonance of the text. A number of passages became almost conventional topoi for the display of a commentator's learning and appreciation, many of which were known in the fine English translations.[1]

Longinus suggests that there are five sources of the sublime [Longinus], and these are much discussed and debated throughout the eighteenth century. See below part V in which Blair's comments represent one of the critical strands of this debate in which all but the first two sources are diminished as of real importance in the analytic of the sublime. There is, however, another strand to this discussion in which the rhetorical analysis of tropes and figures takes on far greater importance thereby creating an understanding of the sublime in terms of its discursive and figurative formation.[2]

Another topos in the Longinian text for extensive commentary begins 'So the space between Heaven and Earth' in section IX. This distinction in conjunction with images of terror leads Smith to cite Milton's sublimity:

There is a serious turn, an inborn Sedateness in the Mind, which renders Images of Terror grateful and engaging. Agreeable Sensations are not only produced by bright and lively Objects, but sometimes by such as are gloomy and solemn. It is not the blue Sky, the chearful Sun-shine, or the smiling Landscape, that give us all our Pleasure, since we are indebted for no little share of it to the silent Night, the distant howling Wilderness, the melancholy Grot, the dark Wood, and hanging Precipice.[3]

We find already in this early eighteenth-century borrowing from Longinus a comparison of the poet's capacities to rouse sublime sensation with those of natural phenomena [Longinus]. The period will go on to develop this idea in connection with the concept of original genius [Dennis], which can be understood as an outworking of the discourse on the sublime. Welsted, for example, in his commentary on the Longinian text writes:

if these great men are at some times as the Ocean in its exaltations, or as the Sun in his meridian, they must be allowed at others to resemble him in his decline;...There is a kind of inconstancy in the productions of great Geniuses. Now you shall see them

[1] See for example Anthony Blackwall's translation of the Longinian text: 'The Sublime is a just grand, and marvellous thought. It strikes like lightning with a conquering and resistless flame. It appears beautiful either in the plain or figurative style; it admits all the ornaments of language; yet needs none of 'em; but commands and triumphs in its own native majesty. The true Sublime will bear translation into all languages, and will be great and surprising in all languages, and to all persons of understanding and judgment, notwithstanding the difference of their country, education, interest and party. It carries all before it by its own strength; and does not so much raise persuasion in the hearer or reader, as throw him into an ecstasy, and transport him out of himself. We admire it at first without considering; and upon mature consideration we are convinc'd that we can never admire it too much. It defies opposition, envy, and time; and is infinitely advanced above cavil and criticism.' *The sacred classics defended and illustrated*, 2 vols, 3rd edn corr (London, 1737), I, 247-8.

[2] The energies surrounding these issues are commented upon by Neil Hertz in his essay on Longinus; see *The end of the line: essays on psychoanalysis and the sublime* (New York: Columbia University Press, 1985), pp. 1-20.

[3] William Smith, *Dionysius Longinus on the sublime* 2nd edn corr. (London, 1743), p. 124.

striking the clouds with their heads; now touching the lowest ground; they have their risings, and they have their wanes[4]: ...

One of the most important aspects of the Longinian text for the eighteenth-century tradition is the link made between the aesthetic realm and ethics. In the tradition that has come to be known as civic humanism this connection was most obviously made in moral sense theory (see below part II) where the philosophical justification of sublime rhapsodies is to be found in the limiting criteria of ethical conduct. In this regard sections of the ancient treatise became particularly troublesome, such as that beginning 'What then we can suppose...' (section XXXV) [Longinus] since the Longinian text at points suggests that the highest flights of sublime fantasy have no need for accuracy or ethical limits.

Indeed the moral sense theory of Shaftesbury and Hutcheson can be seen as precisely a counter to the potentially licentious theory of their classical forebears. In this way early eighteenth-century commentators constructed an image of modernity that improved upon ancient culture, enabling them to recognise in the texts of antiquity aspects of that culture which might provide grounds upon which their own sense of the modern was to be founded. Thus, while Longinus suggests that nature implants a harmony in the voice of man (section XXXIX) eighteenth-century readers adopt this as a specifically modern form in which the natural world is taken as emblematic of the higher harmonies of moral sense. Consequently Longinus not only speaks to the contemporary eighteenth-century reader but also on behalf of him; it is this which gives a specific authority to the Longinian text.

Such strategies of authentication were not only employed in relation to the philosophical treatises of antiquity, they were also a pretty constant feature of religious commentary and speculation. The most significant link between the nascent tradition of the sublime and christian doctrine is made in the common use of the term 'enthusiasm' [Dennis]. It is common to find a connection between an 'angry God' who is thought to instill the greatest terror and the 'loftiness of conception' aroused in states of enthusiasm. Dennis goes on to argue that the sublime may often be without common passion but it is never without enthusiastic passion, thereby strengthening the link that persists between states of religious ecstasy or enlightenment and sublime experience.[5]

This line of argument leads Dennis towards a set of variations on the Longinian sources of the sublime. Where Longinus noted five such sources Dennis gives us four omitting the fifth on the structure or composition of

---

[4] 'Remarks on Longinus' in *The works in verse and prose of Leonard Welsted*, ed. John Nichols (London, 1787), pp. 422-3. Welsted also compared Milton to sublime natural phenomena: 'When I see him thus, in his most exalted flights, piercing beyond the boundaries of the universe, he appears to me as a vast comet, that for want of room is ready to burst its orb and grow eccentric...'. Welsted, p. 405. Joseph Addison also applied this idea to *Paradise Lost* itself; see *The Spectator*, no. 339, 29 March 1712.

[5] See Susie L. Tucker, *Enthusiasm, a study in semantic change* (Cambridge: Cambridge University Press, 1972).

periods, partly because it is partially redundant in Longinus, and partly because it lacks the connection Dennis is trying to establish with Enthusiasm. The six marks Dennis subsequently gives are probably a reconfiguration of Longinus realigned to French writings on the passions. Descartes, for example, enumerates six primitive passions – Wonder, Love, Hatred, Desire, Joy and Sadness. Malebranche produced a sixfold division of passions based on Love and Hatred subdivided according to circumstance – present, expected or removed, and Hutcheson was later to derive six passions from the sense of Honour. Given that Dennis had earlier divided the 'Enthusiastick Passions' into six (in *The Grounds of Criticism*) – Admiration, Terror, Horror, Joy, Sadness, Desire 'caus'd by Ideas occurring to us in Meditation' – a list which deviates significantly from Descartes and embraces part of Malebranche's refinement – such an emphasis on Religion and its relation to the Passions can be seen as an amalgamation of Longinus and the French tradition.

It falls to Dennis to coin the phrase which will reverberate through the eighteenth-century discussion of the transporting effects of reading: 'the pleasing rape upon the very soul of the reader' [Dennis]. While Dennis is reluctant to explore the full sexual connotations of the reading scene later theorists will not only be troubled by its violence they will also enjoy its 'ravishment' and 'transport'.

We also find in these first extracts an extremely common tendency to link the sublime with the beautiful. Indeed the eighteenth-century tradition is as vigorous in its attempts to distinguish the two terms in precise correlation to the frequency with which the two are compounded. Burke's attempts to distinguish the one from the other are perhaps best known in which the sublime comes attached to a number of qualifiers that preclude the possibility of something's being *both* sublime and beautiful.

The connection between what elevates (the sublime) and what astonishes (the marvellous) is more uniformly respected throughout the period [Blackmore, Stackhouse, Reresby]. This connection is important because once again the bridge is made between rhetorical phenomena, the principal cause of elevation, and natural phenomena, the principal cause of astonishment, thereby enabling analyses of sublimity in terms of both effects and causes. It is, of course, the text of Longinus which primarily effects this bridge-making.

In the service of such analyses the trope of translatio is consistently employed and even commented upon [Blackmore] when something is seen in 'uncommon Circumstances'. Precisely the same trope can be found at work in Reresby when he makes the distinction between the 'sublime of ordinary' and of 'extraordinary Things' [Reresby]. The trope of translatio could be said to be the founding figure for the Longinian tradition since it establishes the grounding of rhetorical power in raising heightened response, and it is precisely this same trope which will determine the necessity of original genius in the production of art: make it new is the imperative of the sublime.

Such gifted individuals are to be distinguished from mere orators whose imitative powers are mechanical in comparison to the original genius [Reresby]. The poet, therefore, in a tradition stretching back to antiquity and the vates of classical culture, is to be understood as embodying special gifts which are now to be marshalled in the context of a secularised neoclassical society. These individuals – the original geniuses of augustan culture – surpass mere mortals who inhabit the realm of the natural in their ability to move into the supernatural [Stackhouse].

1

from *Dionysius Longinus on the sublime*
tr. William Smith (1743)

Section I

...But I request you, my dear friend, to give me your opinion on whatever I advance, with that exactness which is due to truth, and that sincerity, which is natural to yourself. For well did the sage answer the question, *in what do we most resemble the gods?* when he replied, *in doing good and speaking truth.* But since I write, my dear friend, to you, who are versed in every branch of polite learning, there will be little occasion to use many previous words in proving, that the sublime is a certain eminence or perfection of language, and that the greatest writers, both in verse and prose, have by this alone obtained the prize of glory, and filled all time with their renown. For the sublime not only persuades, but even throws an audience into transport. The marvellous always works with more surprising force, than that which barely persuades or delights. In most cases, it is wholly in our own power, either to resist or yield to persuasion. But the sublime, endued with strength irresistible, strikes home, and triumphs over every hearer. Dexterity of invention, and good order and economy in composition, are not to be discerned from one or two passages, nor scarcely sometimes from the whole texture of a discourse; but the sublime, when seasonably addressed, with the rapid force of lightning has borne down all before it, and shown at one stroke the compacted might of genius....

Section VII

You cannot be ignorant, my dearest friend, that in common life there is nothing great, a contempt of which shows a greatness of soul. So riches, honours, titles, crowns, and whatever is veiled over with a theatrical splendour, and a gaudy outside, can never be regarded as intrinsically good, in the opinion of a wise man, since by despising such things no little glory is acquired. For those persons, who have ability sufficient to acquire, but through an inward generosity scorn such acquisitions, are more admired than those, who actually possess them.

In the same manner we must judge of whatever looks great both in poetry and prose. We must carefully examine whether it be not only appearance. We must divest it of all superficial pomp and garnish. If it cannot stand this trial, without doubt it is only swelled and puffed up, and it will be more for our honour to condemn than to admire it. For the mind is naturally elevated by the true sublime, and so sensibly affected with its lively strokes, that it swells in transport and an inward pride, as if what was only heard had been the product of its own invention.

He therefore, who has a competent share of natural and acquired taste, may easily discover the value of any performance from a bare recital of it. If he finds, that it transports not his soul, nor exalts his thoughts; that it calls not up into his mind ideas more enlarged than what the mere sounds of the words convey, but on attentive examination its dignity lessens and declines; he may conclude, that whatever pierces no deeper than the ears, can never be the true sublime. That on the contrary is grand and lofty, which the more we consider, the greater ideas we conceive of it; whose force we cannot possibly withstand; which immediately sinks deep, and makes such impressions on the mind, as cannot be easily worn out or effaced. In a word, you may pronounce that sublime beautiful and genuine, which always pleases, and takes equally with all sorts of men. For when persons of different humours, ages, professions, and inclinations, agree in the same joint approbation of any performance, then this union of assent, this combination of so many different judgments, stamps an high and indisputable value on that performance, which meets with such general applause.

Section VIII

There are, if I may so express it, five very copious sources of the sublime, if we presuppose an ability of speaking well, as a common foundation for these five sorts, and indeed without it, any thing besides will avail but little.

I. The first and most excellent of these is a boldness and grandeur in the thoughts, as I have shewn in my essay on Xenophon.

II. The second is called the pathetic, or the power of raising the passions to a violent and even enthusiastic degree; and these two being genuine constituents of the sublime, are the gifts of nature, whereas the other sorts depend in some measure upon art.

III. The third consists in a skilful application of figures, which are two-fold, of sentiment and language.

IV. The fourth is a noble and graceful manner of expression, which is not only to choose out significant and elegant words, but also to adorn and embellish the style, by the assistance of tropes.

V. The fifth source of the sublime, which completes all the preceding, is the structure or composition of all the periods, in all possible dignity and grandeur....

Section IX

But although the first and most important of these divisions, I mean, elevation of thought, be rather a natural than an acquired qualification, yet we ought to spare no pains to educate our souls to grandeur, and impregnate them with generous and enlarged ideas.

"But how, it will be asked, can this be done?" Why, I have hinted in another place, that the sublime is an image reflected from the inward greatness of the soul. Hence it comes to pass, that a naked thought without words challenges admiration, and strikes by its grandeur. Such is the silence of Ajax in the *Odyssey*, which is undoubtedly noble, and far above expression.

To arrive at excellence like this, we must needs suppose that, which is the cause of it, I mean, that an orator of the true genius must have no mean and ungenerous way of thinking. For it is impossible for those, who have grovelling and servile ideas, or are engaged in the sordid pursuits of life, to produce any thing worthy of admiration, and the perusal of all posterity. Grand and sublime expressions must flow from them, and them alone, whose conceptions are stored and big with greatness. And hence it is, that the greatest thoughts are always uttered by the greatest souls. When Parmenio cried, "I would accept these proposals, if I was Alexander;" Alexander made this noble reply, "And so would I, if I was Parmenio." His answer showed the greatness of his mind.

So the space between heaven and earth marks out the vast reach and capacity of Homer's ideas, when he says,

> While scarce the Skies, her horrid Head can bound;
> She stalks on Earth. –   Mr. Pope.

This description may with more justice be applied to Homer's genius than the extent of discord....

How grand also and pompous are those descriptions of the combat of the gods!

> Heav'n in loud Thunders bids the Trumpet sound,
> And wide beneath them groans the rending Ground.
> Deep in the dismal Regions of the Dead
> Th'infernal Monarch rear'd his horrid Head;
> Leap'd from his Throne, lest Neptune's Arm should lay
> His dark Dominions open to the Day,
> And pour in Light on Pluto's drear Abodes,
> Abhorr'd by Men, and dreadful ev'n to Gods.   Mr. Pope.

...What a prospect is here, my friend! The Earth laid open to its centre; Tartarus itself disclosed to view; the whole world in commotion, and tottering on its basis! and what is more, heaven and hell, things mortal and immortal, all combating together, and sharing the danger of this important battle. But yet, these bold representations, if not allegorically understood, are downright blasphemy, and extravagantly shocking. For Homer, in my opinion, when he gives us a detail of the wounds, the seditions, the punishments, imprisonments, tears of the deities, with those evils of every kind, under which they languish, has to the utmost of his power exalted his heroes, who fought at Troy, into gods, and degraded his gods into men....

And how far does he excel those descriptions of the combats of the gods, when he sets a deity in his true light, and paints him in all his majesty, grandeur, and perfection; as in that description of Neptune, which has been already applauded by several writers:

> Fierce as he past the lofty Mountains nod,
> The Forests shake, Earth trembled as he trode,
> And felt the Footsteps of th'immortal God.
> His whirling Wheels the glassy Surface sweep;
> Th' enormous Monsters rolling o'er the Deep
> Gambol around him on the watry Way,
> And heavy Whales in awkward Measures play:
> The Sea subsiding spreads a level Plain,
> Exalts, and owns the Monarch of the Main:
> The parting Waves before his Coursers fly;
> The wond'ring Waters leave the Axle dry.
>
> Mr. Pope.

So likewise the jewish legislator, no ordinary person, having conceived a just idea of the power of god, has nobly expressed it in the beginning of his law. "*And god said, – what? – Let there be light, and there was light. Let the earth be, and the earth was.*"

I hope my friend will not think me tedious, if I add another quotation from the poet, in regard to his mortals; that you may see, how he accustoms us to mount along with him to heroic grandeur. A thick and impenetrable cloud of darkness had on a sudden enveloped the Grecian army, and suspended the battle. Ajax, perplexed what course to take, prays thus,

> Accept a Warrior's Pray'r, eternal Jove;
> This Cloud of Darkness from the Greeks remove;
> Give us but Light, and let us see our Foes,
> We'll bravely fall, tho' Jove himself oppose.

The sentiments of Ajax are here pathetically expressed: it is Ajax himself. He begs not for life: a request like that would be beneath a hero. But because in that darkness he could display his valour in no illustrious exploit, and his great heart was unable to brook a sluggish inactivity in the field of action, he only prays for light, not doubting to crown his fall with some notable performance, although Jove *himself* should oppose his efforts. Here Homer, like a brisk and favourable gale, renews and swells the fury of the battle; he is as warm and impetuous as his heroes are, or (as he says of Hector)

> With such a furious Rage his Steps advance,
> As when the God of Battles shakes his Lance,
> Or baleful Flames on some thick Forest cast,
> Swift marching lay the wooded Mountain waste:
> Around his Mouth a foamy Moisture stands.

Yet Homer himself shews in the *Odyssey* (what I am going to add is neces-sary on several accounts) that when a great genius is in decline, a fondness for the fabulous clings fast to age....

It proceeds, I suppose, from the same reason, that having wrote the *Iliad* in the youth and vigour of his genius, he has furnished it with continued scenes of action and combat; whereas, the greatest part of the *Odyssey* is spent in narration, the delight of old-age. So that, in the *Odyssey*, Homer may with justice be resembled to the setting sun, whose grandeur still remains, without the meridian heat of his beams. The style is not so grand and majestic as that of the *Iliad*; the sublimity not continued with so much spirit, nor so uniformly noble; the tides of passion flow not along with so much profusion, nor do they hurry away the reader in so rapid a current. There is not the same volu-bility and quick variation of the phrase; nor is the work embellished with so many strong and expressive images. Yet like the ocean, whose very shores when deserted by the tide, mark out how wide it sometimes flows, so Homer's genius, when ebbing into all those fabulous and incredible ramblings of Ulys-ses, shows plainly how sublime it once had been. Not that I am forgetful of those storms, which are described in so terrible a manner, in several parts of the *Odyssey*; of Ulysses's adventures with the Cyclop, and some other instances of the true sublime. No; I am speaking indeed of old-age, but it is the old-age of Homer. However it is evident from the whole series of the *Odys-sey*, that there is far more narration in it, than action....

I have digressed thus far, for the sake of showing, as I observed before, that a decrease of the pathetic in great orators and poets often ends in the moral kind of writing. Thus the *Odyssey* furnishing us with rules of morality, drawn from that course of life, which the suitors lead in the palace of Ulysses, has in some degree the air of a comedy, where the various manners of men are ingeniously and faithfully described.

Section X

Let us consider next, whether we cannot find out some other means, to infuse sublimity into our writings. Now, as there are no subjects, which are not attended by some adherent circumstances, an accurate and judicious choice of the most suitable of these circumstances, and an ingenious and skilful con-nection of them into one body, must necessarily produce the sublime. For what by the judicious choice, and what by the skilful connection, they cannot but very much affect the imagination.

Sappho is an instance of this, who having observed the anxieties and tor-tures inseparable to jealous love, has collected and displayed them all with the most lively exactness. But in what particular has she shown her excellence? In selecting those circumstances, which suit best with her subject, and after-wards connecting them together with so much art.

Blest as th'immortal Gods is he,
The Youth who fondly sits by thee,
And hears, and sees thee all the while
Softly speak, and sweetly smile.

'Twas this depriv'd my Soul of Rest,
And rais'd such Tumults in my Breast;
For while I gaz'd, in Transport tost,
My Breath was gone, my Voice was lost.

My Bosom glow'd; the subtle Flame
Ran quick thro' all my vital Frame;
O'er my dim Eyes a Darkness hung;
My Ears with hollow Murmurs rung.

In dewy Damps my Limbs were chill'd;
My Blood with gentle Horrors thrill'd;
My feeble Pulse forgot to play,
I fainted, sunk, and dy'd away.　　　　　　　　　Philips.

Are you not amazed, my friend, to find how in the same moment she is at a loss for her soul, her body, her ears, her tongue, her eyes, her colour, all of them as much absent from her, as if they had never belonged to her? And what contrary effects does she feel together? She *glows*, she *chills*, she *raves*, she *reasons*; now she is in *tumults*, and now she is *dying away*. In a word, she seems not to be attacked by one alone, but by a combination of the most violent passions....

Section XIV

If ever therefore we are engaged in a work, which requires a grandeur of style and exalted sentiments, would it not then be of use to raise in ourselves such reflections as these? – How in this case would Homer, or Plato, or Demosthenes, have raised their thoughts? Or if it be historical, – How would Thucydides? For these celebrated persons, being proposed by us for our pattern and imitation, will in some degree lift up our souls to the standard of their own genius. It will be yet of greater use, if to the preceding reflections we add these – What would Homer or Demosthenes have thought of this piece? or, what judgment would they have passed upon it? It is really a noble enterprise, to frame such a theatre and tribunal, to sit on our own compositions, and submit them to a scrutiny, in which such celebrated heroes must preside as our judges, and be at the same time our evidence. There is yet another motive, which may yield most powerful incitements, if we ask ourselves, – what character will posterity form of this work, and of me the author? For if any one, in the moments of composing, apprehends that his performance may not be able to survive him, the productions of a soul, whose views are so short and confined, that it cannot promise itself the esteem and applause of succeeding ages, must needs be imperfect and abortive.

Section XXXV

The parallel between Plato and his opponent must be drawn in a different light. For Lycias not only falls short of him in the excellence, but in the number also, of his beauties. And what is more, he not only falls short of him in the number of his beauties, but exceeds him vastly in the number of his faults.

What then can we suppose that those god-like writers who had in view, who laboured so much in raising their compositions to the highest pitch of the sublime, and looked down with contempt upon accuracy and correctness? – Amongst others, let this reason be accepted. Nature never designed man to be a grovelling and ungenerous animal, but brought him into life, and placed him in the world, as in a crowded theatre, not to be an idle spectator, but spurred on by an eager thirst of excelling, ardently to contend in the pursuit of glory. For this purpose, she implanted in his soul an invincible love of grandeur, and a constant emulation of whatever seems to approach nearer to divinity than himself. Hence it is, that the whole universe is not sufficient, for the extensive reach and piercing speculation of the human understanding. It passes the bounds of the material world, and launches forth at pleasure into endless space. Let any one take an exact survey of a life, which, in its every scene, is conspicuous on account of excellence, grandeur, and beauty, and he will soon discern for what noble ends we were born. Thus the impulse of nature inclines us to admire, not a little clear transparent rivulet that ministers to our necessities, but the Nile, the Ister, the Rhine, or still much more, the ocean. We are never surprised at the sight of a small fire that burns clear, and blazes out on our own private hearth, but view with amaze the celestial fires, although they are often obscured by vapours and eclipses. Nor do we reckon any thing in nature more wonderful than the boiling furnaces of Etna, which cast up stones, and sometimes whole rocks, from their labouring abyss, and pour out whole rivers of liquid and unmingled flame. And from hence we may infer, that whatever is useful and necessary to man, lies level to his abilities, and is easily acquired; but whatever exceeds the common size, is always great, and always amazing.

Section XXXIX

We have now, my friend, brought down our enquiries to the fifth and last source of sublimity, which, according to the divisions premised at first, is the composition or structure of the words. And although I have drawn up, in two former treatises, whatever observations I had made on this head, yet the present occasion lays me under a necessity of making some additions here.

Harmonious composition has not only a natural tendency to please and to persuade, but inspires us, to a wonderful degree, with generous ardour and passion. Fine notes in music have a surprising effect on the passions of an audience. Do they not fill the breast with inspired warmth, and lift up the heart into heavenly transport? The very limbs receive motion from the notes, and the hearer, although he has no skill at all in music, is sensible however, that all its turns make a strong impression on his body and mind. The sounds of any musical instrument are in themselves insignificant, yet by the changes of the air, the agreement of the chords, and symphony of the parts, they give extraordinary pleasure, as we daily experience, to the minds of an audience. Yet these are only spurious images and faint imitations of the persuasive voice of man, and far from the genuine effects and operations of human nature.

What an opinion therefore may we justly form of fine composition, the effect of that harmony, which nature has implanted in the voice of man? It is made up of words, which by no means die upon the ear, but sink within, and reach the understanding. And then, does it not inspire us with fine ideas of sentiments and things, of beauty and of order, qualities of the same date and existence with our souls? Does it not, by an elegant structure and marshalling of sounds, convey the passions of the speaker into the breasts of his audience? Then, does it not seize their attention, and by framing an edifice of words to suit the sublimity of thoughts, delight, and transport, and raise those ideas of dignity and grandeur, which it shares itself, and was designed, by the ascendent it gains upon the mind, to excite in others? But it is folly to endeavour to prove what all the world will allow to be true. For experience is an indisputable conviction....

Section XL

But amongst other methods, an apt connection of the parts conduces as much to the aggrandising discourse, as symmetry in the members of the body to a majestic mien. If they are taken apart, each single member will have no beauty or grandeur, but when skilfully knit together, they produce what is called a fine person. So the constituent parts of noble periods, when rent asunder and divided, in the act of division fly off and lose their sublimity; but when united into one body, and associated together by the bond of harmony, they join to promote their own elevation, and by their union and multiplicity bestow a more emphatical turn upon every period. Thus several poets, and other writers, possessed of no natural sublimity, or rather entire strangers to it, have very frequently made use of common and vulgar terms, that have not the least air of elegance to recommend them, yet by musically disposing and artfully connecting such terms, they clothe their periods in a kind of pomp and exaltation, and dextrously conceal their intrinsic lowness....

2

John Dennis, from *Remarks on a book entitled, Prince Arthur* (1696)

The Preface

...I designed to have inserted a discourse concerning poetical genius, of which no one that I know of has hitherto treated. I designed to show that this extraordinary thing in poetry which has been hitherto taken for something supernatural and divine, is nothing but a very common passion, or a complication of common passions. That felicity in writing has the same effect upon us that happiness in common life has: that in life when any thing lucky arrives to us, upon the first surprise we have a transport of joy, which is immediately followed by an exaltation of mind: *ut res nostræ sint ita nos magni atque humiles sumus*; and that both these, if the thing that happens be beyond expectation fortunate, are accompanied with astonishment: we are amazed at our own happiness: that the very same thing befalls us upon the conception of an extraordinary hint. The soul is transported upon it, by the consciousness of its own excellence, and it is exalted, there being nothing so proper to work on its vanity; because it looks upon such a hint as a thing peculiar to itself, whereas what happens in life to one man, might as well have happened to another; and lastly, if the hint be very extraordinary, the soul is amazed by the unexpected view of its own surpassing power. Now it is very certain that a man in transport, and one that is lifted up with pride and astonished, expresses himself quite with another air, than one who is calm and serene. Joy in excess as well as rage is furious. And the pride of soul is seen in the expression as well as in the mien and actions, and is the cause of that elevation, which Longinus so much extols, and which, he says, *is the image of the greatness of the mind.* Now it is certain that greatness of mind is nothing but pride well regulated. Now as joy causes fury, and pride elevation, so astonishment gives vehemence to the expression.

This was the doctrine which I designed to deliver, of which I had the first hint from the following verses,

> Rapture and Fury carried me thus far
> Transported and Amaz'd.

Which are in an admirable poem written by a very great man, who with all that wonderful fire which is so conspicuous in him, has all the discernment and the fine penetration, which is necessary for the reflecting upon the most secret motions of his own mind, and upon those of others.

After that I had done this, I designed to lay down this definition of genius, that it was the expression of a furious joy, or pride, or astonishment, or all of them caused by the conception of an extraordinary hint. Then I intended to show, that a great many men have extraordinary hints, without the forementioned motions, because they want a degree of fire sufficient to give their animal spirits a sudden and swift agitation. And these are called cold-writers. On the other side, if men have a great deal of fire and have not excellent organs, they feel the forementioned motions in thinking without extraordinary hints. And these we call fustian-writers. When I had done this I intended to show that Mr Blackmore had very seldom either the hints or the motions. In order to which I designed to consider the several sorts of hints that might justly transport the soul by a conscious view of its own excellency. And to divide them into hints of *thoughts* and hints of *images*. That the *thoughts* which might justly cause these motions of spirits were of three sorts, such as discover a greatness of mind, or a reach of soul, or an extent of capacity. That *images* were either of *sounds* or of *things*, that *images* of *things* were either *mighty* or *vast* ones. I designed to give examples of all these from Homer and Virgil, and from Milton and Tasso; and to have compared them with several passages in Mr Blackmore's poem. I designed particularly to have treated of the clearness, and justness, and of the energy of *images*....

3

John Dennis,
from *The advancement and reformation of modern poetry* (1701)

Part I. Chapter V
That Passion is the chief Thing in Poetry, and that all Passion is either ordinary Passion, or Enthusiasm

But before we proceed, let us define poetry; which is the first time that a definition has been given of that noble art: for neither ancient nor modern critics have defined poetry in general.

Poetry then is an imitation of nature, by a pathetic and numerous speech. Let us explain it.

As poetry is an art, it must be an imitation of nature. That the instrument with which it makes its imitation, is speech, need not be disputed. That that speech must be musical, no one can doubt: for numbers distinguish the parts of poetic diction, from the periods of prose. Now numbers are nothing but articulate sounds, and their pauses measured by their proper proportions of time. And the periods of prosaic diction are articulate sounds, and their pauses unmeasured by such proportions. That the speech, by which poetry makes its imitation, must be pathetic, is evident; for passion is still more necessary to it than harmony. For harmony only distinguishes its instrument from that of prose, but passion distinguishes its very nature and character. For, therefore, poetry is poetry, because it is more passionate and sensual than prose. A discourse that is writ in very good numbers, if it wants passion, can be but measured prose. But a discourse that is every where extremely pathetic, and, consequently, every where bold and figurative, is certainly poetry without numbers.

Passion then, is the characteristical mark of poetry, and, consequently, must be every where: for wherever a discourse is not pathetic, there it is prosaic. As passion in a poem must be every where, so harmony is usually diffused throughout it. But passion answers the two ends of poetry better than harmony can do, and upon that account is preferable to it: for, first, it pleases more, which is evident: for passion can please without harmony, but harmony tires without passion. And in tragedy, and in epic poetry, a man may instruct without harmony, but never without passion: for the one instructs by admiration, and the other by compassion and terror. And as for the greater ode, if it wants passion, it becomes hateful and intolerable, and its sentences grow contemptible.

32

Passion is the characteristical mark of poetry, and therefore it must be every where; for without passion there can be no poetry, no more than there can be painting. And although the poet and the painter describe action, they must describe it with passion. Let any one who beholds a piece of painting, where the figures are shown in action, conclude, that if the figures are without passion, the painting is contemptible. There must be passion every where, in poetry and painting, and the more passion there is, the better the poetry and the painting, unless the passion is too much for the subject; and the painter, and the poet, arrive at the height of their art, when they describe a great deal of action, with a great deal of passion. It is plain then, from what has been said, that passion in poetry must be every where, for where there is no passion, there can be no poetry; but that which we commonly call passion, cannot be every where in any poem. There must be passion then, that must be distinct from ordinary passion, and that must be enthusiasm. I call that ordinary passion, whose cause is clearly comprehended by him who feels it, whether it be admiration, terror or joy; and I call the very same passions enthusiasms, when their cause is not clearly comprehended by him who feels them. And those enthusiastic passions, are sometimes simple, and sometimes complicated, all of which we shall show examples lower. And thus I have shown, that the chief thing in poetry, is passion: but here the reader is desired to observe, that by poetry, we mean poetry in general, and the body of poetry; for as for the form or soul of particular poems, that is allowed by all to be a fable. But passion is the chief thing in the body of poetry; as spirit is in the human body. For without spirit the body languishes, and the soul is impotent: now every thing that they call spirit, or genius in poetry, in short, every thing that pleases, and consequently, moves, in the poetic diction, is passion, whether it be ordinary or enthusiastic.

And thus we have shown, what the chief excellence in the body of poetry is, which we have proved to be passion. Let us now proceed, to the proofs of what we propounded. That sacred subjects, are more susceptible of passion, than profane ones; and that the subjects of the ancients, were sacred in their greater poetry, I mean either sacred in their own natures, or by their manner of handling them.

Part I. Chapter VII
The causes of poetical enthusiasm, shown by examples

...And thus we have endeavoured to show, how the enthusiasm proceeds from the thoughts, and consequently from the subject. But one thing we have omitted, that as thoughts produce the spirit, the spirit produces and makes the expression; which is known by experience to all who are poets: for never any one, while he was rapt with enthusiasm, wanted either words or harmony; and is self evident to all who consider, that the expression conveys and shows the spirit, and therefore must be produced by it. So that from what we have said, we may venture to lay down this definition of poetical genius: poetical genius, in a poem, is the true expression of ordinary or enthusiastic passions proceeding from ideas to which it naturally belongs; and poetic genius, in a poet, is the power of expressing such passion worthily: and the sublime is a great thought, expressed with the enthusiasm that belongs to it, which the reader will find agreeable to the doctrine of Cecilius. Longinus, I must confess, has not told us what the sublime is, because Cecilius, it seems, had done that before him. Though methinks, it was a very great fault, in so great a man as Longinus, to write a book which could not be understood, but by another man's writings; especially when he saw that those writings were so very defective, that they were not likely to last. But although Longinus does not directly tell us what the sublime is, yet in the first six or seven chapters of his book, he takes a great deal of pains to set before us the effects which it produces in the minds of men; as for example, that it causes in them admiration and surprise; a noble pride, and a noble vigour, an invincible force, transporting the soul from its ordinary situation, and a transport, and a fulness of joy mingled with astonishment. These are the effects that Longinus tells us, the sublime produces in the minds of men. Now I have endeavoured to show, what it is in poetry that works these effects. So that, take the cause and the effects together, and you have the sublime.

4

John Dennis,
from *The grounds of criticism in poetry* (1704)

Chapter IV
What the greater Poetry is, what Enthusiasm is.

The greater poetry then, is an art by which a poet justly and reasonably excites great passion, in order to please and instruct, and make mankind better and happier; so that the first and grand rule in the greater poetry is, that a poet must every where excite great passion: but in some branches of the greater poetry, it is impossible for a poet every where to excite in a very great degree, that which we vulgarly call passion: as in the ode, for example, and in the narration of the epic poem. It follows then, that there must be two sorts of passion: *first*, that which we call vulgar passion; and *secondly*, enthusiasm.

First, vulgar passion, or that which we commonly call passion, is that which is moved by the objects themselves, or by the ideas in the ordinary course of life; I mean, that common society which we find in the world. As for example, anger is moved by an affront that is offered us in our presence, or by the relation of one; pity by the sight of a mournful object, or the relation of one; admiration or wonder, (the common passion, I mean; for there is an enthusiastic admiration, as we shall find anon) by the sight of a strange object, or the relation of one.

But, *secondly*, enthusiastic passion, or enthusiasm, is a passion which is moved by the ideas in contemplation, or the meditation of things that belong not to common life. Most of our thoughts in meditation are naturally attended with some sort and some degree of passion; and this passion, if it is strong, I call enthusiasm. Now the enthusiastic passions are chiefly six, admiration, terror, horror, joy, sadness, desire, caused by ideas occurring to us in meditation, and producing the same passions that the objects of those ideas would raise in us, if they were set before us in the same light that those ideas give us of them. And here I desire the reader to observe, that ideas in meditation are often very different from what ideas of the same objects are, in the course of common conversation. As for example, the sun mentioned in ordinary conversation, gives the idea of a round flat shining body, of about two foot diameter. But the sun occurring to us in meditation, gives the idea of a vast

35

and glorious body, and at the top of all the visible creation, and the brightest material image of the divinity. I leave the reader therefore to judge, if this idea must not necessarily be attended with admiration; and that admiration I call enthusiasm. So thunder mentioned in common conversation, gives an idea of a black cloud, and a great noise, which makes no great impression upon us. But the idea of it occurring in meditation, sets before us the most forcible, most resistless, and consequently the most dreadful phænomenon in nature: so that this idea must move a great deal of terror in us, and it is this sort of terror that I call enthusiasm. And it is this sort of terror, or admiration, or horror, and so of the rest, which expressed in poetry make that spirit, that passion, and that fire, which so wonderfully please....

...It is now our business to show two things: first, what this enthusiastic terror is; and, secondly, from what ideas it is chiefly to be derived.

First, let us show what this sort of enthusiasm is; and in order to do that, let us show as briefly as we can, what the common passion is, which we call terror. Fear then, or terror, is a disturbance of mind proceeding from an apprehension of an approaching evil, threatening destruction or very great trouble either to us or ours. And when the disturbance comes suddenly with surprise, let us call it terror; when gradually, fear. Things then that are power-ful, and likely to hurt, are the causes of common terror; and the more they are powerful and likely to hurt, the more they become the causes of terror: which terror, the greater it is, the more it is joined with wonder, and the nearer it comes to astonishment. Thus we have shown what objects of the mind are the causes of common terror, and the ideas of those objects are the causes of enthusiastic terror.

Let us now show from what ideas this enthusiastic terror is chiefly to be derived. The greatest enthusiastic terror then must needs be derived from religious ideas: for since the more their objects are powerful, and likely to hurt, the greater terror their ideas produce; what can produce a greater terror, than the idea of an angry god? Which puts me in mind of that admirable passage of Homer, about the fight of the gods, in the twentieth of the Iliads, cited by Longinus in his chapter of the loftiness of the conception....

I now come to the precepts of Longinus, and pretend to show from them, that the greatest sublimity is to be derived from religious ideas. But why then, says the reader, has not Longinus plainly told us so? He was not ignorant that he ought to make his subject as plain as he could. For he has told us in the beginning of his treatise, that every one who gives instruction concerning an art, ought to endeavour two things: the first is to make his reader clearly understand what that is which he pretends to teach: the second is to show him how it may be attained. And he blames Cecilius very severely for neglecting the last; how then, says the objector, comes he himself to have taken no care of the first? Is it because Cecilius had done it before him? If so, it was a very great fault in Longinus to publish a book which could not be understood but by another man's writings; especially when he saw that those writings were so very defective, that they would not probably last. But what, continues the objector, if Cecilius had not done it before him? For Longinus tells us, that Cecilius makes use of a multitude of words to show what it is; now he who knows any thing clearly, may in a few words explain it clearly to others; and he who does not, will make it obscure by many.

To this I answer, that although Longinus did by long study and habitude know the sublime when he saw it, as well as any man, yet he had not so clear a knowledge of the nature of it, as to explain it clearly to others. For if he had done that, as the objector says, he would have defined it; but he has been so far from defining it, that in one place he has given an account of it that is contrary to the true nature of it. For he tells us in that chapter which treats of the fountains of sublimity, that loftiness is often without any passion at all; which is contrary to the true nature of it. The sublime is indeed often without common passion, as ordinary passion is often without that. But then it is never without enthusiastic passion: for the sublime is nothing else but a great thought, or great thoughts moving the soul from its ordinary situation by the enthusiasm which naturally attends them. Now Longinus had a notion of enthusiastic passion, for he establishes it in that very chapter for the second source of sublimity. Now Longinus, by affirming that the sublime may be without not only that, but ordinary passion, says a thing that is not only contrary to the true nature of it, but contradictory to himself. For he tells us in the beginning of the treatise, that the sublime does not so properly persuade us, as it ravishes and transports us, and produces in us a certain admiration, mingled with astonishment and with surprise, which is quite another thing than the barely pleasing, or the barely persuading; that it gives a noble vigour to a discourse, an invincible force, which commits a pleasing rape upon the very soul of the reader; that whenever it breaks out where it ought to do, like the artillery of Jove, it thunders, blazes, and strikes at once, and shows all the united force of a writer. Now I leave the reader to judge, whether Longinus has not been saying here all along that sublimity is never without passion....

But to return to terror, we may plainly see by the foregoing precepts and examples of Longinus, that this enthusiastic terror contributes extremely to the sublime; and, secondly, that it is most produced by religious ideas.

First, ideas producing terror, contribute extremely to the sublime. All the examples that Longinus brings of the loftiness of the thought, consist of terrible ideas. And they are principally such ideas that work the effects, which he takes notice of in the beginning of his treatise, *viz.* that ravish and transport the reader, and produce a certain admiration, mingled with astonishment and with surprise. For the ideas which produce terror, are necessarily accompanied with admiration, because every thing that is terrible, is great to him to whom it is terrible; and with surprise, without which terror cannot subsist; and with astonishment, because every thing which is very terrible, is wonderful and astonishing: and as terror is perhaps the violentest of all the passions, it consequently makes an impression which we cannot resist, and which is hardly to be defaced: and no passion is attended with greater joy than enthusiastic terror, which proceeds from our reflecting that we are out of danger at the very time that we see it before us. And as terror is one of the violentest of all passions, if it is very great, and the hardest to be resisted, nothing gives more force, nor more vehemence to a discourse.

But, secondly, it is plain from the same Longinus, that this enthusiastic terror is chiefly to be derived from religious ideas. For all the examples which he has brought of the sublime, in his chapter of the sublimity of the thoughts, consists of most terrible and most religious ideas; and at the same time every man's reason will inform him, that every thing that is terrible in religion, is the most terrible thing in the world.

But that we may set this in a clearer light, let us lay before the reader the several ideas which are capable of producing this enthusiastic terror; which seem to me to be those which follow, *viz.* gods, dæmons, hell, spirits and souls of men, miracles, prodigies, enchantments, witchcrafts, thunder, tempests, raging seas, inundations, torrents, earthquakes, volcanoes, monsters, serpents, lions, tigers, fire, war, pestilence, famine, &c.

Now of all these ideas none are so terrible as those which show the wrath and vengeance of an angry god; for nothing is so wonderful in its effects: and consequently the images or ideas of those effects must carry a great deal of terror with them, which we may see was Longinus's opinion, by the examples which he brings in his chapter of the sublimity of the thoughts. Now of things which are terrible, those are the most terrible which are the most wonderful; because that seeing them both threatening and powerful, and not being able to fathom the greatness and extent of their power, we know not how far and how soon they may hurt us.

But further, nothing is so terrible as the wrath of infinite power, because nothing is so unavoidable as the vengeance designed by it. There is no flying nor lying hid from the great universal monarch. He may deliver us from all other terrors, but nothing can save and defend us from him. And therefore reason, which serves to dissipate our terrors in some other dangers, serves but to augment them when we are threatned by infinite power; and that fortitude, which may be heroic at other times, is downright madness then.

For the other ideas, which we mentioned above, they will be found to be more terrible as they have more of religion in them. But we shall have so many necessary occasions of giving examples of them, in the sequel of this treatise, that it will be altogether needless to do it now. But here it will be convenient to answer an objection: for how come some of the forementioned ideas, which seem to have but little to do with religion, to be terrible to great and to wise men? as it is plain that such, when they read the descriptions of them in Homer and Virgil, are terrified.

To which we answer, that the care, which nature has inrooted in all, of their own preservation, is the cause that men are unavoidably terrified with any thing that threatens approaching evil. It is now our business to show how the ideas of serpents, lions, tigers, &c. were made by the art of those great poets, to be terrible to their readers, at the same time that we are secure from their objects.

It is very plain that it is the apprehension of danger which causes that emotion in us which we call terror, and it signifies nothing at all to the purpose whether the danger is real or imaginary; and it is as plain too, that the soul never takes the alarm from any thing so soon as it does from the senses, especially those two noble ones of the eye and the ear, by reason of the strict affinity which they have with the imagination; and the evil always seems to be very near, when those two senses give notice of it; and the nearer the evil is, the greater still is the terror. But now let us see how those two poets did, by virtue of their ideas, bring even absent terrible objects within the reach of those two noble senses. First then, to bring an absent terrible object before our sight, they drew an image or picture of it; but to draw an image or picture of a terrible object, so as to surprise and astonish the soul by the eye, they never failed to draw it in violent action or motion; and in order to that, they made choice of words and numbers, which might best express the violence of that action or motion. For an absent object can never be set before the eye in a true light, unless it be shown in violent action or motion; because unless it is shown so, the soul has leisure to reflect upon the deceit. But violent motion can never be conceived without a violent agitation of spirit, and that sudden agitation surprises the soul, and gives it less time to reflect; and at the same time causes the impressions that the objects make to be so deep, and their traces to be so profound, that it makes them in a manner as present to us, as if they were really before us. For the spirits being set in a violent emotion, and the imagination being fired by that agitation; and the brain being deeply penetrated by those impressions, the very objects themselves are set as it were before us, and consequently we are sensible of the same passion that we should feel from the things themselves. For the warmer the imagination is, the less able we are to reflect, and consequently the things are the more present to us of which we draw the images; and therefore when the imagination is so inflamed, as to render the soul utterly incapable of reflecting, there is no difference between the images and the things themselves; as we may see, for example, by men in raging fevers. But those two great poets were not satisfied with setting absent objects before our eyes, by showing them in violent motion; but if their motion occasioned any extraordinary sounds that were terrifying, they so contrived their numbers and expressions, as that they might be sure to ring those sounds in the very ears of their readers....

5

Sir Richard Blackmore,
from *Essays upon several subjects* (1716)

An essay on the nature and constituion of epic poetry.
Of the marvellous

Another thing indispensably required to the constitution of an epic poem is, that the narration be marvellous; and the reason is, that when the poet intends to give delight and convey instruction, as admiration engages attention, so it prepares and opens the mind to admit the force of the poet's sentiments, and receive from them deep impressions. Hence the beautiful and surprising turns, as well in the diction as the incidents of a noble poem, strike the imagination with resistless force, break in upon the soul and excite generous and divine passions suitable to the subject. This therefore is a necessary property, by which the poet is qualified to gain his principal end, which is to afford pleasure and instruction; and is a peculiar and inseparable character, that limits the general nature of poetry, and makes the epic differ from the tragic, to which however it is more nearly allied than to any other species.

All things excite admiration that either transcend the sphere of finite activity, or that break the usual series of natural causes and events. The first sort, which proceed from almighty power, are styled miracles: I shall not here by a strict disquisition, enter into the nature and definition of a miracle, which some look upon as an immediate effect of unlimited might, and others as an action which the spectators believe the supreme being to be the author of, while they are unable to account for any natural cause, from whence it should arise. It is enough, that in this place, I give this idea of it, that it is a presumptive, immediate operation of divine power. The other sort of effects that move admiration, do not surmount the limits of created activity, but proceed from second subordinate causes; yet then they interrupt the ordinary course of things, and deviate from the established custom or laws of nature.

Some of these irregular productions are monstrous and frightful, and strike the imagination with disgust and terror, and others are sports of nature, which are often pleasing and beautiful errors: other things raise our admiration by their singular and extraordinary perfection; so exquisite and consummate beauty, extraordinary strength and agility of body, as well as the finished pieces and inventions of the most excellent masters in painting, building, and polite literature, because they surpass their own ordinary performances and those of other artists, fill the mind with agreeable amazement. Other objects,

40

although not irregular, nor more or less perfect than the ordinary individuals of their species, are marvellous, because they seldom come to pass. We view a planet or a star without concern or emotion of mind, while the sight of a comet raises our admiration; not by its being a more excellent luminary, but by its infrequent appearance. Our wonder is likewise moved by common objects represented in uncommon circumstances; as for instance, the sun when eclipsed, foreigners in a strange habit, the shells of fishes found on the tops of mountains, and trees and nutshells discovered in the bowels of the earth.

It is in the novelty of these appearances, that the essential idea of marvellous does consist. Any thing is therefore admirable, because it is surprising, and therefore surprising because extraordinary and unexpected. All unusual occurrences, especially the excursions and transgressions of nature in her operations, move the imagination with great force, agitate the spirits, and raise in the soul strong emotions, which by degrees diminish after long acquaintance; and as familiarity wears off our abhorrence and reconciles us to frightful objects, so it abates the pleasure of constant enjoyments, and by degrees creates satiety. Exquisite music, delicious gardens, magnificent buildings, and ravishing prospects, after long possession, do not excite that delightful wonder which it produces in those who are unaccustomed to them. Novelty, as before asserted, is the parent of admiration; and it is for this reason, that the sentiments in epic poetry, which by their beauty, strength and dignity, are raised above the level of vulgar conceptions, and are always new, either in themselves or the uncommon turn given to them by the poet, act powerfully upon the imagination, and surprise the soul with pleasing astonishment. And hence likewise it is, that the rich, splendid, and figurative diction, which is proper to that species of poetry, like the magnificence and pomp of princes on solemn occasions, excites the wonder of the people not inured to such prospects....

Of the sublimity of the thoughts

Thoughts are then sublime, when they are conceived in an extraordinary manner, and are elevated above obvious and familiar sentiments; and this sublimity of the ideas imparts internal heat, vigour and majesty to the narration, as the judicious and happy choice of pure, proper and expressive words, and splendid and polite diction, give outward richness, elegance, and magnificence.

That a poet of this kind may raise his thoughts to a just sublimity for matters of such dignity and excellence as those which he is conversant about, it is necessary he should fix his mind upon them, that by familiarity and long acquaintance with them, he may stock his imagination with splendid and beautiful images. It is the remark of Longinus, that it is impossible for a man inured only to base and vulgar thoughts, to reach that elevation of mind which is necessary for an orator of the first rank; such a man, says he, will never speak any thing worthy of posterity; and therefore he advises men to nourish in their minds a generous temper, that will always incline them to form high and noble ideas: and if it be so necessary for an orator, it is yet much more required of an epic poet, whose subject is always great and illustrious. If it be his ambition to write extraordinary things, becoming the height and importance of his subject, worthy of his character, and fit to be transmitted to future times, he should not grovel in the dust, nor breathe in thick impure air, but keep above, and inure himself to lofty contemplation, till by a constant correspondence and intercourse with superior objects, he gets a habit of thinking in the great and elevated manner, peculiar to the heroic poet. By this he will be enabled to rise to the heights of heaven, and from thence to cast himself down with a generous freedom and resolution, and plunge amidst the depths of nature, to discover the secret springs of her wonderful operations; and by the same principle he will be capable of penetrating the dark walks and mysterious labyrinths of divine providence, in the administration of humane affairs; by which means he will collect rich materials, and proper ornaments to embellish his work, and make it marvellous.

And this power of forming great and extraordinary conceptions and laying up hoards of lively and wonderful ideas, is so necessary to inspire the narration with life and ardour, that it is impossible by any means to supply its absence. Where this is wanting, all artificial decoration is idle and ridiculous; but this alone gives such force and lustre, that without the additions of art, it will attract our esteem and raise our admiration. This is remarkable not only in poetical eloquence, but in that of the pulpit, where some preachers, though not curious in the choice of their words, nor correct and musical in their diction, by the sublimity of their thoughts and divine expression, accompanied with an awful gravity, a becoming zeal, and the serious air of one in earnest, succeed far better than many who are more polite and regular in their style. It is the majesty, strength, and vivacity of the images, the solidity and loftiness of the sentiments, that chiefly penetrate and melt the audience; and the various precepts of rhetoric, which of themselves have no force, can only assist their operation: notwithstanding great poets, as well as orators, may be defective in some points that relate to external embellishments, they abundantly atone for all their faults by the admirable and excellent sense which they every where abound with; and as Longinus says of Demosthenes and Plato, one or two of their wonderful thoughts make amends for all their errors. Extraordinary minds, as that critic remarks, are so taken up with great objects, that they have no time or inclination to attend to the low and minute affairs of rhetoric, and therefore their omissions are not so much to be imputed to want of skill, as to inadvertency; not to the weakness of their judgments, but to the strength and elevation of their conceptions.

6

Tamworth Reresby, from *A miscellany of ingenious thoughts and reflections* (1721)

Concerning sublimity of style and discourse

What is generally amongst orators and poets called sublime, will be found, upon enquiry, to be the simple effect of energy and number: so that having proved that all languages are capable of the one, there need no arguments to prove them capable of the other: or that they are all equally entitled to every prerogative of eloquence. Any discourse is more or less excellent, according as his ideas are more or less clear, brilliant, and exalted, who composes it; and it will not be denied, I suppose, that extraordinary geniuses may be met with in all languages.

What bears the title of sublime, or marvellous, has been at all times so much in request, that the ancients, as well as some modern critics, have bestowed large treatises upon it: and I suppose, some of them, who have writ abundantly upon this matter, affected to recommend their own works for pieces of elaborate eloquence, whilst they showed by their criticisms, that they understood the rules of art; but the difference is vastly wide between theory and practice.

Longinus is the most ancient author that is to be found upon this subject; and he tells us, that the *sublime is that which forms the excellency and the sovereign perfection of discourse...That which transports...That which produces a certain admiration mixed with wonder and surprise....That which raises the soul, and inspires her with a more exalted opinion of herself.* These expressions we see give a true notion to the surprising effects of the *sublime*; but we are still to seek for the true cause of these effects: we are by this means apprised, indeed, that when we feel ourselves pleased and ravished with some noble expressions, or an ingenious elaborate discourse, that it must be somewhat *marvellous*, which in so particular a manner affects us; but we remain still ignorant as to the nature of the marvellous, or sublime. I shall therefore endeavour to supply this defect, with some conjectures of my own; and shall always leave room enough to the reader to improve these by his greater judgment and penetration.

The *sublime* then, in my opinion, consists in a complete and lively imitation of nature, or of that which surpasses nature. I suppose, that a bare imitation of nature constitutes the sublime of orators; and the imitation of what is

43

above nature, the sublime of poets. For it will not be disputed, I believe, that there goes into the composition of poetry, something supernatural and divine.

As there is nothing more noble, or worthy of admiration, than nature; so whatever is found to represent her to the life, cannot fail, at the same time, to appear truly great and sublime. And as nature is not ever uniform in her operations, does not ever proceed in the same method, and has her prodigies and miracles; so does this marvellous display itself in a vigorous and sinewy expression of nature's wonders. But if we look a little nearer into this matter, we shall find that it is man's vanity alone that prompts him to look out for the surprising works of nature, upon which to exercise his most improved faculties; for there is nothing in her so vile and contemptible, in his opinion, which, if well examined and represented, would not produce the sentiments of admiration and surprise. When the prophet says, *how glorious are thy works, O Lord! Thou has made them all with wisdom*: this ejaculation comprehends as well the worms of the earth, the leaves of trees, the hair of the head, as the elements, the heavens, and the planets. God is wonderful in all his works; nor can we contemplate any of them with attention, and not pay him, at the same time, a tribute of wonder, as well as praise: and there will be found ever a little more only, or a little less, between the sublime of ordinary and the most extraordinary things of nature....

7

Jonathan Richardson, the elder, from *An Essay on the theory of painting* (1725)

Of the sublime

...By the sublime in general I mean the most excellent of what is excellent, as the excellent is the best of what is good. The dignity of a man consists chiefly in his capacity of thinking, and of communicating his ideas to another; *the greatest, and most noble thoughts, images, or sentiments, conveyed to us in the best chosen words*, I take therefore to be the perfect sublime in writing; the admirable, the marvellous.

But as there may be degrees even in the sublime, something short of the utmost may be also sublime.

Thought, and language are two distinct excellencies: there are few that are capable of adding dignity to a great subject, or even of doing right to such a one; in some cases none: the bulk of mankind conceive not greatly, nor do they know how to utter the conceptions they have to the best advantage; and those that have higher capacities exert them but rarely, and on few occasions: hence it is that we so justly admire what is so excellent, and so uncommon.

The great manner of thinking (as thought in general) is either pure invention, or what arises upon hints suggested from without....

As the thoughts, so the language of the sublime must be the most excellent; what that is is the question: whether it be confined to the florid, to magnificent, and sonorous words, tours, figures, &c. or whether brevity, simplicity, or even common, and low words are the best on some occasions.

Poetry, history, declamation, &c. have their peculiar styles, but the sublime (as our high court of parliament is not under the restrictions which inferior courts are) is not limited to any particular style: the best is the sublime language, and that is best that sets the idea in the strongest light; that is the great end, and use of words; but if those that please the ear do equally serve that purpose, no doubt they are preferable, but not otherwise. Plain and common words paint a great image sometimes stronger than any other....

The only reasons that can be given for a peculiarity of style in the sublime are, that as the thought must be great, the language must be so too as best expressing such thought; and because the music of the words serve to the same purpose, and moreover please. I own all this is generally true: why do we use the term *sublime*, and not *the very best*, both which express the same

45

thing, only that one raises, and the other depresses the idea? But I deny that it is always thus; and only contend that when low, common words, and a plain style best serves the main end of language, it is then, and only then the sublime style. And when this happens the pleasure that is wanting in the sound is abundantly recompensed by observing the judgment of him who made so wise a choice....

But the sublime, as the crown in the state hides all defects; it fills and satisfies the mind, nothing appears to be wanting; nothing to be amiss, or if it does it is easily forgiven. All faults die, and vanish in presence of the sublime, which when it appears is as *the sun traversing the vast desert of the sky.*

Longinus rightly accounts for the defects that are seen in men that have attained sublimity, their minds (he says) intent upon what is great cannot attend to little things; and indeed the life, and capacity of a man are insufficient for both, and even for all that is great in painting. But who would not rather be Demosthenes, than Hyperides, though one of these had no faults, and the other many? This other had the sublime! He was admirable, not merely irreproachable: (I am still speaking after Longinus.) When we see the sublime it elevates the soul, gives her a higher opinion of her self, and fills her with joy, and a noble kind of pride, as if her self had produced what she is admiring. It ravishes, it transports, and creates in us a certain admiration, mixed with astonishment. And like a tempest drives all before it.

> – And must confess to find
> In all things else Delight indeed, but such
> As us'd, or not works in the Mind no Change,
> Nor Vehement Desire: –
> – But Here
> Far Otherwise transported I behold.
> – Here Passion first I felt,
> Commotion strange, in all Enjoyments else
> Superiour and Unmov'd.   Milton.

In the foregoing treatise I have been showing what I take to be the rules of painting, and although any one had understood, and practised them all, I must yet say one thing is wanting, go, and endeavour to attain the sublime. For a painter should not please only, but surprise.

Plus ultra was the motto of the emperor Charles V whose actions were of the sublime kind, and as monsieur St Evremont finely distinguishes, rather vast, than great: and this should be the motto of all that apply themselves to any noble art, particularly of a painter; he must not propose like Pyrrhus to conquer such a country, then such a one, then another, and then rest, he must resolve like time to be always going on, or

> – Like the Pontick Sea
> Whose Icy Current, and Compulsive Course
> Ne'er knows retiring Ebb, but keeps due on
> To the Propontick, and the Hellespont   Shakespeare.

He must be perpetually advancing. And whatever rules are given as fundamental of the art *plus ultra* like a golden thread should be woven in, and run
throughout the whole piece.

To be contented with mediocrity in art, is an argument of a meanness of
spirit incapable even of that; and though it be attained it is a state of insipidity,
a kind of non-entity: to be remarkable for nothing, is not to be at all; and less
eligible than to be remarkably a blockhead.

– For who would lose
Though full of Pain this Intellectual Being,
Those Thoughts that wander through Eternity,
To perish rather, swallow'd up, and lost
In the wide Womb of Uncreated night.   Milton.

He that upon trial finds himself incapable of any science may turn to something else until he lights upon that in which he may excel, as there is none but
may in one thing or other; but he that does just tolerably well, stops there, and
never gets higher in any thing; he is of a sort of species of animals that makes
the transition from men to brutes easy.

When we propose only an exact imitation of nature we shall certainly fall
short of it; so when we aim no higher than what we find in any one, or more
masters, we shall never reach their excellence: he that would rise to the sublime must form an idea of something beyond all we have yet seen; or which
art, or nature has yet produced; painting, such as when all the excellencies of
the several masters are united, and their several defects avoided....

Nor must he stop here, but create an original idea of perfection. The utmost
that the best masters have done, is not to be supposed the utmost it is possible
for humane nature to arrive at; Leonardo da Vinci, or Michelangelo might
have been thought to have carried the art as far as it could go had not Rafaëlle
appeared; as Cimabue, and Giotto were probably thought to have done in
their times:

Credette Cimabue nella Pittura
Tener lo Campo, & ora ha Giotto il Grido
Si che la fama di colui oscura.   Dante.

Who knows what is hid in the womb of time! Another may eclipse Rafaëlle;
a new Columbus may cross the Atlantic ocean, and leave the pillars of that
Hercules far behind. The outlines, and airs of the best antique, with the best
colouring of the moderns united would do this; but more yet than this is not
impossible. And this more, should be attempted.

As God no Model for the Worlds could find,
But form'd them in his Own Eternal Mind;
So should the Artist, warm'd with Heav'nly Fire,
To a perfection yet Unknown aspire.   Pope.

This is the great rule for the sublime; not to be given however until those fundamentals of the art have been well known, and practised; it is to be opened when a man has got far on his way, as the commissions of admirals, or generals going on some great expedition frequently are. The sublime disdains to be trammelled, it knows no bounds, it is the sally of great geniuses, and the perfection of humane nature; but like Milton's paradise

> Wild, above Rule, or Art, Enormous Bliss!
> Return me to my Native Element
> Lest from this flying Steed, unrein'd (as once
> Bellerophon tho' from a lower Clime)
> Dismounted, on the Aleian field I fall
> Erroneous, there to wander, and forlorn.   Milton.

8

Thomas Stackhouse, from *Reflections on the nature and property of languages* (1731)

Chapter XVIII
Of sublimity or loftiness

Sublimity or loftiness is one of the principal effects of the energy and number of a language; so that to have proved that all languages have their number and energy, is enough, one would think, to show that they have all likewise their sublime, and that there is nothing in eloquence so magnificent, that may not be attained in one tongue as well as another. Or if it be true that the nobleness of thought is the true cause of the sublimity of style, may not men of all languages have equally great thoughts and conceptions?

But because this sublime is of so great estimation in eloquence, that some of the most famous rhetoricians of antiquity have thought it worth while to make entire treatises about it, it may not undeserve a chapter by itself. One of these treatises that has escaped the injuries of time is that of Longinus, although it be somewhat defective. This excellent piece has been given us in French by an author every way capable to compose the original, and one may say that his translation and reflections are enough to convince us that the sublime belongs no more to the genius of particular tongues than particular men.

I have several times read over this work; and how excellent soever it may be, it does not in my opinion give us any precise ideas wherein this sublime consists. He tells us indeed in the first place what are its effects, then what are its causes, and comes at last to give us examples of the true and false sublime, but in all this it does not appear to me that he determines wherein it consists.

For to say that the sublime is *that which constitutes the excellence and sovereign perfection of discourse – that which ravishes – that which transports, and produces in us a certain admiration mixed with wonder and surprise – that which elevates the soul, and makes it conceive a greater opinion of itself*: all these expressions give us a full conception of the wonderful effects of it, but they leave us still to seek what is the cause of these effects. They give us to understand, that when we feel ourselves ravished and transported with some masterly strokes in a discourse, there must be something marvellous in it, but this is not showing us what the nature of that marvellous thing is; so that in what Longinus has said, he has not sufficiently instructed our reason, and yet it is by the light of reason, that we are to become learned and wise.

But who dare undertake to supply what is wanting in a work of so great a reputation? Until some abler hand than mine shall do it, I hope I may be allowed to propose my conjectures, only so far as they may be necessary for the execution of my design.

What we call the sublime then I take to be nothing else, but a lively and perfect imitation either of nature, or of what surpasses it. The imitation of nature is the sublime of orators, the imitation of what is above nature the sublime of poets; and I shall hereafter have occasion to show, why poetry requires something divine and supernatural in it.

As nothing is more grand and admirable than nature, that which imitates it perfectly, and presents us with lively and resemblant images, will always appear truly great and sublime: and as nature is not uniform in her operations, does not always proceed in the same method, but has sometimes her prodigies and miracles; a lively expression of these prodigies is that, wherein the sublime and marvellous principally appears.

Herein, as I conceive, does the sublime consist, which produces all the wonderful effects that Longinus speaks of, and this idea, in my opinion, agrees exactly with all the precepts that he hath laid down to attain it. Nay, this idea is consonant to his own thoughts of the matter: for when he says that in the works of art we consider the labour and finishing, but in those of nature, the sublime and wonderful, he plainly means that the sublime and wonderful in discourse, is that which rightly represents the sublime and wonderful in nature, and although he here mentions the extraordinary effects of nature only, and seems to insinuate that there can be nothing sublime in the representation of common things, it is nevertheless certain, that an excellent picture even of the most common things, will always touch and ravish the soul, for what is there in nature so vile and despicable, that when thoroughly examined and truly represented, does not produce an admiration mixed with astonishment and surprise? When the royal prophet says, *how wonderful are thy works, O, Lord, in wisdom hast thou made them all*, he includes therein the works of the earth, the leaves of the trees, and the hairs of our head, as well as the elements, the heavens, and the plants. God is wonderful in all things, and the least of his works cannot be attentively beheld without astonishment, nor does the sublime of things ordinary and extraordinary in nature differ, but in the degree of being more or less so.

Nay even those passions that have nothing great in them, and are rather indications of a littleness and weakness of spirit, such as affliction, fear, sadness, &c. may be so well painted and set forth, that the soul may feel itself as much moved and transported thereby, as by the representation of what we account the greatest things. Nor is there any reason to say, there can be nothing great and sublime in a lively description of the fright and astonishment men will be seized with at the great solemnity of the last judgment, and this I verily believe is what Longinus intended by these words, that *art is never in so high a point of perfection, as when it resembles nature so strongly, that it may be taken for nature itself*.

Now if according to this notion this sublime be able to produce all the effects that Longinus ascribes to it, it may likewise be taken from those causes that he remarks: and the first of these is a certain elevation of mind that makes us think happily of things: for in truth what is it to think happily of things but to conceive them just as they are, or to speak sublimely of them, but to express them just as we think them.

The second cause is the pathetic, that is, as he explains it, that enthusiam and natural vehemence that moves and affects us, but now no orator that has received the vehemence from the author of nature, ever uses it well but when he speaks according to just and natural ideas; when he goes beyond these he turns obscure and bombast, and becomes ridiculous.

The third cause proceeds from figures turned after a certain manner. Now to turn these figures well, we must always make them natural, *i.e.* take them from objects that have a natural relation to the subject we are treating of, otherwise instead of showing the greatness, they will only discover the littleness of an imagination.

The fourth cause is nobleness of expression, but this comes much to the same thing with what I have said before, *viz.* that if a man thinks a thing happily, and expresses it as he thinks it, he cannot but express it nobly.

The fifth and principal cause is in the composition and order of words, in all their magnificence and glory, which is the same with number that I have already treated of. But this composition consists in following the order, wherein the thoughts and ideas we conceive of things are most naturally painted. So that all we can learn from what Longinus has told us about causes of sublime tends only to instruct us in this, *that to speak in a great and exalted manner is to represent either natural or supernatural things as beautiful, as great and marvellous as they really are.*

The examples that he produces, confirm the same thing. There is not indeed any thing great and magnificent in these examples, but as they represent nature in such lively characters, that one would think it were nature itself that speaks. The answer of Alexander to Parmenio has something very great in it, because it perfectly paints the bold and ambitious nature of that prince Parmenio, whose heart had not conceived so great designs as that of Alexander, would have been content to have married Darius's daughter, and had part of Asia for her dower. But Alexander, whom the whole world could not satisfy, would not hearken to the proposal, and his answer to Parmenio could not well have more grandeur in it, because it represents to us, in a very delicate and lively manner, the unbounded ambition of that conqueror, for it is in ambition that the ignorant and corrupted world places all greatness of soul. *If I were Alexander says Parmenio to him, I would accept of the offer that Darius makes me, and I too if I were Parmenio, says Alexander.*

The expressions he quotes from Homer, derive their loftiness from their representing nature as great as it really is. But the words of Moses are the most stately and magnificent that can be pronounced by the mouth of man, because they carry a true and most sensible character of God's omnipotence, by showing that his word was enough to make all things arise out of nothing, and if Longinus had made all the reflections upon this expression of Moses that it deserved, and a person of his sagacity should have done, he would not have ascribed it to the invention of this great legislator; he might have perceived that man could not have invented such an expression of himself, and that he must necessarily be inspired by the divine wisdom to do it. Since if there was required an infinite power to give fruitfulness to nothing, and man having no natural conception how nothing could become fruitful, he could not have expressed it so worthily, had not the being, in whom this power resides, suggested it. But this is not a place to show at large what knowledge a thinking man may draw from these words, *he spoke and all things were made, he said let there be light and there was light.*

These, in my opinion, are the clearest and most precise ideas of what we call the sublime, and if they are true in fact, I can see no reason why every tongue should not be furnished with proper materials to draw the most resemblant pictures of every thing that nature can produce; of every great and wonderful thing that men can say or do; nay of every thing that God has revealed to them, either as an object of their faith, or a rule for their practice. Why, for example, might not a Demosthenes or a Cicero thunder and lighten in our language as well as they did in theirs? Why might not Moses have spoke in French what he did in Hebrew, and with the same dignity and majesty: let men labour the point as much they please, they will never be able, I believe, to find out any sufficient reasons why there should be any difference.

The admirers of Greek and Latin perhaps may imagine, that some tongues are not so proper to keep up all this elevation of thought, because the nations that speak them may not have the hardiness perhaps that the Greeks and Romans had, to make use of such bold figures and expressions, as sometimes transcend the truth. But if these nations are more modest in their style, their sublime is therefore truer and less liable to become bombast. We, for instance, in this nation, are not near so hardy, in our manner of speaking; but our chaste and modest eloquence is more regular, and should therefore please men of exquisite tastes better. For if it be true that our tongue values itself upon its moderation and chastity; if it does not love to make use of such expressions, as please none but men of irregular imaginations, and such as are blinded with self-conceit, then is it preferable in this respect both to the Greek and Latin.

In short, all those that have taste good enough not to take bombast and nonsense for sublime, will find, that the French will admit of all sorts of figures which are contained in the rules of true eloquence, from whence true greatness of expression comes; for therein we treat of such subjects as requite the sublime and marvellous with all imaginable success. That which constituted the eloquence of the pagans, related to temporal things only, but Christians have subjects that have no other bounds than eternity, and if it has been said of the princes of the Greek and Roman eloquence, that *they stormed, they thundered, they lightened, that it was all a consuming fire, and a torrent that overwhelmed every thing*; the same may be said with more reason and truth of some of our preachers, who change wolves into lambs, and vultures into doves, and do greater wonders by the power of the word, than what fabulous poets have imputed to the power of their gods.

9

Hildebrand Jacob,
from *The works* (1735)

How the mind is raised to the sublime

They who never felt that kind of enthusiasm, which Aristotle, and Longinus mention, as necessary to succeed in poetry, and produce the sublime in writing, will be little the better informed, from what may be said, to give an idea of it. He, who can behold without emotion, and surprise the more noble works of nature, and of art, will gain, even from the most expressive words, and strongest terms, but a very faint notion of what is not so easily described, or taught, as conceived by a mind truly disposed for the perception of that, which is great and marvellous.

All the vast, and wonderful scenes, either of delight, or horror, which the universe affords, have this effect upon the imagination, such as unbounded prospects, particularly that of the ocean, in its different situations of agitation, or repose; the rising and setting sun; the solemnity of moon light; all the phænomena in the heavens, and objects of astronomy. We are moved in the same manner by the view of dreadful precipices; great ruins; subterraneous caverns, and the operations of nature in those dark recesses. The like is often produced by that greatness, which results from the ornaments, and magnificence of architecture; the sight of numerous armies, and assemblies of people. We are no less inspired, if it may be so called, by that kind of ardour from the charms of beauty, or the resemblance of beautiful persons, and things in fine statues, or paintings.

We are almost equally obliged to the sense of hearing for working on our imaginations much after the same way, as when we are lulled by the whispering of winds; the fall of waters in cataracts, or heavy showers; the roaring of the sea; the noise of tempests amongst lofty trees; thunder; the clash of arms, and voice of war. Few can read in Milton the following description, which he has given, of the opening of the infernal gates without some emotion,

> – On a sudden open fly
> With impetuous Recoil, and jarring Sound
> Th' infernal Doors, and on their Hinges' grate
> Harsh Thunder, that the lowest Bottom shook
> Of Erebus –

Or the applause of Satan's reply in council to Abdiel,

53

> He said, and as the Sound of Waters deep
> Hoarse Murmur eccho'd to his Words Applause
> Thro' th' infinite Host –

Or that of Mammon's speech,

> He scarce had finish'd, when such Murmur fill'd
> Th' Assembly, as when hollow Rocks retain
> The Sound of blustring Winds, which all Night long
> Had rouz'd the Sea –

Or his comparison of the noise, which was heard at the breaking up of the infernal council, to the sound of distant thunder.

The *Il Pensoroso* of this great poet might alone suffice to show, how easily his imagination was warmed by every little circumstance capable of throwing the mind into this cast. Shakespeare was no less susceptible of this poetic enthusiasm, as his enchantments, fairy way of writing, spirits, and creatures of his own formation may testify. The easterns swore by the coming on of night; by the whistling of the winds; by the hour of evening, &c. and by their bold metaphors, and figurative style, we find, they were more than any other people addicted to sublimity of expression.

The force of numbers; the power of music, and oratory; the passion of love, and influence of wine are very efficacious in giving this elevation of thought.

> Quo me, Bacche, rapis tui
> Plenum? quæ in Nemora, aut quos agor in specus,
> Velox Mente nova?

Says Horace, full of this ardour. Devotion, with intense prayer; some kinds of superstition; and the strange convulsions in nature, which have been thought to portend great, and extraordinary events, will put the imagination into this way; as may be found upon reading * Virgil's description of those prodigies, which followed the death of J. Cæsar, and were said, to presage the civil war between Brutus, and Cassius.

These, and many things of the like nature produce that enthusiasm, which is so requisite to succeed in poetry, and cause the sublime; to which may be added terror, and compassion, with all that relates to the pathetic; the consideration of the heroic deeds, and great sentiments of illustrious men; reflections on the various revolutions which have happened in different ages to the nations of the earth; the contemplation on death itself, and on the formation and final dissolution of all things.

---

* *Georgics.* Bk i.

10

Joseph Trapp,
from *Lectures on Poetry* (1742)

Lecture IX
Of the beauty of thought in poetry; or of elegance and sublimity

...Beauty in writing may be considered as twofold: either the elegant, or sublime. The latter is manifestly distinct from the former; for there may be elegance
often where there is no sublimity; but it may be questioned, on the other hand,
whether everything sublime is not elegant. To me, indeed, it seems not so; or,
if we must determine otherwise, it must be said that elegance joined with sublimity is often a different species of elegance. Whatever, indeed, is sublime, is
beautiful. So Pallas is described by the poets, but with a beauty peculiar to herself, awful, majestic, surrounded with an amiable grandeur, quite different from
the charms of Venus, who is possessed with all the soft attractives, who is all
over elegant but very little sublime. But however this question be determined,
in the sequel of this discourse I shall examine into the properties of each of
these beauties distinctly, and afterwards joined together.

That noble and happy sublimity of thought which by Longinus is termed τὸ
περὶ τὰς νοήσεις ἁδρεπήβολον, is impossible to be learned by precept; it is
the gift of nature only, though it may be much assisted by art....

What Longinus calls φαντασίαι, and others, as he tells us, εἰδωλοποιίας,
the Roman writers style visions, or imaginations, and the modern images.
These, then, operate, "when (as Longinus speaks) a man has so strong an
imagination of the things he describes that he seems to be in transport, as it
were, to behold them with his own eyes, and places them before those of his
hearers." What Longinus adds immediately afterwards, in relation to these
images, I must confess I do not rightly comprehend, or (with all deference to
so great authority) I cannot assent to. ὡς δ'ἕτερόν τι ῥητορικὴ φαντασία
βούλεται καὶ ἕτερον ἡ παρὰ ποιηταῖς, οὐκ ἂν λάθοι σε, οὐδ᾽ ὅτι τῆς μὲν ἐν
ποιήσει τέλος ἐστὶν ἔκπληξις, τῆς δ᾽ ἐν λόγοις ἐνάργεια. Which Tollius thus
paraphrastically translates: "You cannot be ignorant, I suppose, that oratorical visions intend one thing, and poetical another; that the aim of the latter
is to affect the hearers with terror, of the former, to express everything so
strongly that it may be rather seen than heard by the audience. The one we
may properly call evidence, or illustration; the other consternation, or amazement." I own, I say, this is what I cannot well digest; for neither is it true that
the images which poetry impresses affect us with terror only, for all sorts of

55

images are impressed by poetry; nor is it the peculiar property of oratory "to express everything so strongly, that it may be rather seen, than heard by the audience," since poetry has a much larger share in this province than oratory. The only difference between them in this particular is that all images are impressed more strongly by the one; but all are truly impressed by both. This is a difficulty in Longinus which not one of his numerous commentators has touched upon. If, therefore, I am fallen into any mistake, I hope I shall be the easier pardoned, as I have none of the helps of the learned to conduct me out of it. But however that be, all are agreed that the images excited, both by oratory and poetry, strike the mind with a sudden force. . . .

Lecture XI
[The same continued]

I have little occasion to enlarge distinctly upon the sublime, because many things relating to it fell in with what I have before advanced. However, as this was one of the topics I proposed to treat of, it is necessary I should say somewhat to it, before I conclude this dissertation. I cannot better explain to you the nature of the sublime, and the manner of its affecting us, than by giving you the sense of Longinus upon it, not in a literal version, but by representing the substance of him in a few words. Whence is it that writers of this class, in a divine impetuosity seem regardless of accuracy, and scorn to be confined within the vulgar rules of exactness? The truth is, nature has formed man of an inquisitve genius, and placed him in the world to behold and admire the wonders of it, not as an idle spectator, but as one concerned in its busiest scenes, eager for action, and panting after glory. To this end, he is strongly actuated by a love and desire of every thing that is great and divine. The vast expanse of the universe cannot bound his imagination; he extends his thoughts into other worlds, and is lost only in infinity.

> – *Vivida vis animi pervincit, & extra*
> *Procedit longe flammantia mœnia mundi.*
> His vigorous and active Mind is hurl'd
> Beyond the seeming Limits of the World.   Creech.

And, in truth, if we contemplate a hero, whose life is one continued series of great actions, we then may make some estimate of what we were born to. Hence, then, it is, that fountains and rivulets, which answer all the common conveniences of life, never in a great degree awaken our attention. But when we view the Rhine, the Nile, the Danube, but, above all, the ocean, we stand fixed at once with awe and wonder. So again, without any emotion, we behold the daily fires, of our own making, how long soever they continue burning: but we gaze with astonishment at any sudden light in the heavens, although it vanishes, perhaps, as soon as it appears. Nor is there any thing more wonderful in nature than the eruptions of Mount Ætna, which sometimes discharges from its caverns stones, and deluges of fire: . . .

Towards the end of the seventeenth century Novelty [Addison] acquired enhanced status as the role of domestic consumption and the psychology of appetites began to feature prominently in economic debates. The concept was further augmented through the recognition of the function of novelty in the exercise of the Passions, found pre-eminently in moral sense theory. Augustan culture placed a premium on Wit and Invention and was particularly attracted to metaphorical usage based on novel turns of thought. Throughout the century Novelty continued to maintain an important role, reaching a high point of interest in Adam Smith's enquiry into its role in the origin and growth of the arts and sciences. Its value, however, diminished with the recognition that unlike the sublime or beautiful there was no intrinsic value to Novelty.

The concept of Novelty was further tarnished in its association with the new literary form of the novel, which increasingly came under attack for both its emasculating properties and as a corrupter of female morals. By the end of the century Novelty began to lose its role as a cypher in moral theory and began to attract hostile criticism. From this vantage point Novelty began to be linked to human caprice, inconstancy and superficial sentimentality.[1] While in romanticism the value of Novelty began to be overtaken by a formidable investment in the concept of originality.[2]

Early discussions of Romance are intrigued by the enchantments of the hero [Addison] who often comes to the rescue of distressed damsels. This fascination lends itself to the developing account of the structure of the sublime which is framed within the same discursive environment as the discussion of Romance. Hume, for example, distinguished two affections, 'aversion to all giants' and 'submission to all damsels' as characteristic of Romance, and these two affections come together in the hero who 'unites in all Adventures, which are alwise design'd to rescue distrest Damsels from the Captivity & Violence of Giants'.[3] This narrative model lends to the analytic of the sublime a structure of aversion to anything threatening coupled to a curiosity in the threat which leads to submission. The damsel who is rescued in the Romance narrative is, however, in the analytic of the sublime transformed into the inquiring subject itself. Consequently the narrative structure of Romance is figured into the pulsation of the sublime in which aversion gives way to submission in the attempt to rescue the self from itself. The moral of the story becomes, therefore, rescuing damsels in distress is equivalent to rescuing oneself from the threat of being threatening (to oneself).

Mountainous scenery is frequently invoked in discussion of the sublime [Addison] and has led to a number of commonplace assertions concerning

---

[1] Richard Payne Knight attacks the love of novelty in terms of the degeneration into 'morbid restlessness' which was taken to be destructive of the deep moral impressions literature ought to inculcate through taste. See on this *An analytical inquiry into the principles of taste*, 4th edn (London, 1808), pp. 447-56.

[2] On Addison and novelty see C.D. Thorpe, 'Addison and some of his predecessors on "Novelty"', *PMLA*, 52 (1937), 1114-29.

[3] David Hume, *An historical essay on chivalry and modern honour*, ed. E.C. Mossner, *MP*, 45 (1947), 54-60; 60.

change in taste for terrifying and extreme landscape over the course of the century. It is generally held, for example, that early eighteenth-century travellers were either uninterested in or positively dismissive of alpine scenery. In point of fact the story is more varied than this suggests; Addison, for example, wrote a dream allegory on Liberty set in the Alps, [*Tatler*, no. 161, 20 April 1710] which Bishop Hurd thought picturesque and sublime. He also thought that it might have been improved 'if the author [had] fallen asleep over a canto of Spenser'.[4]

Even earlier in the late seventeenth century Dennis had commented upon an alpine crossing:

On the other side of that Torrent, was a Mountain...Its craggy Clifts, which we half discern'd, thro the misty gloom of the Clouds that surrounded them, sometimes gave us a horrid Prospect. And sometimes its face appear'd Smooth and Beautiful, as the most even and fruitful Vallies. So different from themselves were the different parts of it: In the very same place Nature was seen Sever and Wanton. In the mean time we walk'd upon the very brink, in a literal sense, of Destruction; one Stumble, and both Life and Carcass had been at once destroy'd. The sense of this produc'd different motions in me, viz, a delightful Horrour, a terrible Joy, and at the same time, that I was infinitely pleas'd, I trembled...For the Alpes are works which she [Nature] seems to have design'd, and executed too in Fury. Yet she moves us less, where she studies to please us more. I am delighted, 'tis true at the prospect of Hills and Valleys, of flowry Meads, and murmuring Streams, yet it is a delight that is consistent with Reason, a delight that creates or improves Meditation. But transporting Pleasures follow'd the sight of the Alpes, and what unusual transports think you were those, that were mingled with horrours, and sometimes almost with despair? But if these Mountains were not a Creation, but form'd by universal Destruction...than are these Ruines of the old World the greatest Wonders of the New.[5]

The notion of the genius of the place [Shaftesbury] was much invoked in eighteenth-century landscape aesthetics as one of the ways in which correct taste might be adhered to and invention regulated. Pope placed great stress upon the term and on the principle of consulting the genius of the place in any form of landscape construction.[6]

[4] Hurd was, in fact, an early afficionado of alpine scenery, writing: 'a near prospect of the Alps, which are broken into so many steps and precipices, that they fill the mind with an agreeable kind of horror, and form one of the most irregular, misshapen scenes in the world'. *Works*, 8 vols. (London, 1811), I, 510-11.
[5] *The critical works of John Dennis*, ed. E.N. Hooker, 2 vols. (Baltimore: Johns Hopkins University Press, 1939), II, 380-1. See on this C.D. Thorpe, 'Two Augustans cross the Alps', *SP* 32 (1935), 463-8; F.E. Litz, 'Richard Bentley on beauty, irregularity, and mountains', *ELH*, 22 (1945), pp. 327-32; H.V.S. Ogden, 'Thomas Burnet's Telluris theoria sacra and mountain scenery', *ELH*, 14 (1947), 139-50; and Marjorie Hope Nicholson, *Mountain gloom and mountain glory: the development of the aesthetics of the infinite* (Ithaca: Cornell University Press, 1959).
[6] See also Joseph Spence: 'When you set me to write about gardening, you set me upon a thing that I love extremely; but as to any large tract of ground, there is no saying anything in particular without being upon the spot; and having considered it well and often. Some general rules one might mention, but, after all, nine parts on ten depend upon the application. Yet I will just mention some that I followed myself....The first and most material is to consult the Genius of the place. What is, is the great guide as to what ought to be.' *Observations, anecdotes, and characters of books and men*, ed. James M. Osborn, 2 vols. (Oxford: Clarendon Press, 1966), II, 646.

The early encounter of moral sense theory with the discourse on the sublime leads to a number of terms being drawn up in various alignments. The 'fair, beautiful and good' [Shaftesbury], for example, constitute a pretty constant Platonic cluster at the heart of moral-sense philosophy and can be found in the works of Hutcheson, Turnbull, Fordyce, Coventry, Akenside and Gilbert Cooper as well as Shaftesbury. The sublime and beautiful begin to exercise their power as the most obvious binary pairing thereby rendering other connections, between the beautiful and the good for example, slightly marginalised in the discussion. Such reliance upon Platonic concepts and arguments forms the basis of early eighteenth-century philosophical discourse; the period, however, wished to constitute this classical tradition in its own terms, hence the connection between stoicism and Platonism [Akenside] as a proclaimed project.[7]

This particular strand to early aesthetic speculation depends upon the technique of representing ideas emblematically [Akenside], and this began to be eroded by developments which saw passion in opposition to precept, and then further displaced by the shift towards Ideal Presence [Kames]. It was an axiom of moral sense philosophy after Shaftesbury 'That moral ideas could not at all be expressed by words, if they could not be pictured to us by means of analogous sensible objects.'[8] This sums up very succinctly the entire project of the discourse on the sublime: to construct via analogy a structure to the sublime experience which relates affects to causes.

In the later development of ideal presence in Kames's theory the project became more associated with specifically textual analogies, thereby overshadowing moral-sense philosophy by a growing interest in close literary analysis. In this way emblematical modes of thinking give way to textual; this will also result in the undermining of many classical poetic tropes, such as personification, since ideal presence does not require figurative expression. In the scene of reading which results from this readers become spectators of their own self-dramatisation: the experience of the reading activity itself generates sublime affect in a kind of 'look, no hands! I am reading myself reading'.

There is, nevertheless, a continuing investigation into the link between the moral powers and the imagination [Akenside]. This is necessary in order to remove imagination from the realm of wayward fancy and disordered passion. It also prepares for the promotion of the moral value of imaginative literature in the formation of a republic of taste thus enabling the presentation of imaginative writing as a unique site of moral awakening. Consequently taste and morality become inextricably linked in a new union that short-circuits the inculcation of precept. Finally, although moral sense theory

[7] For the treatment of Stoic and Platonic thought in the formative stages of British moral philosophy see: Esther Tiffany, 'Shaftesbury as Stoic', *PMLA*, 38 (1923), 642-84; Ernst Cassirer, *The Platonic renaissance in England*, tr. J.P. Pettegrove (Austin: The University of Texas Press, 1953).

[8] George Turnbull, *The principles of moral philosophy*, 2 vols. (London, 1740), I, 54. Hutcheson similarly advanced the view that 'we are not content with a bare Narration, but endeavour, if we can, to present the Object itself, or the most lovely Image of it'. *An inquiry into the original of our ideas of beauty and virtue*, 4th edn (London, 1738), p. 216.

stressed the Platonic concepts of beauty, order and decency above the vast, grand and novel, the empirical analysis of passion into two distinct and gender-based forms brought sublime, 'masculine' virtues into play, leading to a further offshoot of gender-based 'aesthetic' passions developed out of the identification of moral powers with the imagination. Thus we find initial emphases on beauty, decency and order being displaced by the emergence of 'masculine' qualities such as the vast and magnificent.

Perhaps the central question animating early discussion of the sublime is the connection between rhetorical and natural causes of sublime affect [Baillie]. This comes down to the requirement that one distinguish between qualities taken to inhere in objects which arouse the sublime and descriptions of those objects. Baillie believed that a complete catalogue of natural qualities would eventually define the limits of sublimity.

Natural qualities have particular affective registers which lead to a raising of self-consciousness; this is taken to be equivalent to 'vastness' in the natural world [Baillie]. With the introduction of association, however, objects which do not 'naturally' embody particular qualities may take on those associated with other objects. Consequently, the picture becomes far more complex since through association any object may become like any other.

Aside from natural qualities there are emotive aspects to our experience which may also raise sublime affect. The desire for power [Baillie], for example, is one such emotive drive. Political power is very often associated with heroism, which as noted above finds its primary discursive analytic in discussions of romance. Where Baillie has in mind power in a social or political setting Burke will take the same concept and abstract it into power in general.

Baillie is also close to Burke in his analysis of pain and pleasure, and their instructive registers [Baillie]. This can be said to be one of the initiating moments of the study of psychology within the sublime tradition, as the pulsation of pain and pleasure alternate in the development of models of consciousness.

Power is also understood in worldly terms as an attribute that might be gained through wealth [Priestley]. The integration of economic models with aesthetic will develop in the Scottish school into political economy.

Perhaps the most productive and potentially powerful analysis of the sublime is presented by Priestley in his suggestion concerning 'transferred sublimity' [Priestley]. One way of looking at this is to see it as a slight variant on the associational hypothesis: objects take on qualities they do not possess themselves via association. Priestley, however, strikes to the very heart of the discourse of the sublime which is structured around the concept of discursive transformation. Consequently the transfer of sublimity from one thing to another, or one kind of experience to another, opens up the possibility of initiating an investigation of the means by which discursive transformation is effected. This will conclude in the analytic of the sublime becoming a self-investigative project in which the discursive analytic produces from within itself its own modes and methods of enquiry.

11

Joseph Addison, from *The Spectator* (1712-14)

The Spectator No. 412 Monday, June 23, 1712

...Divisum sic breve fiet Opus.   Martial.

I shall first consider those pleasures of the imagination, which arise from the actual view and survey of outward objects: and these, I think, all proceed from the sight of what is *great, uncommon,* or *beautiful.* There may, indeed, be something so terrible or offensive, that the horror or loathsomeness of an object may overbear the pleasure which results from its *greatness, novelty,* or *beauty*; but still there will be such a mixture of delight in the very disgust it gives us, as any of these three qualifications are most conspicuous and prevailing.

By *greatness,* I do not only mean the bulk of any single object, but the largeness of a whole view, considered as one entire piece. Such are the prospects of an open champian country, a vast uncultivated desert, of huge heaps of mountains, high rocks and precipices, or a wide expanse of waters, where we are not struck with the novelty or beauty of the sight, but with that rude kind of magnificence which appears in many of these stupendous works of nature. Our imagination loves to be filled with an object, or to grasp at any thing that is too big for its capacity. We are flung into a pleasing astonishment at such unbounded views, and feel a delightful stillness and amazement in the soul at the apprehension of them. The mind of man naturally hates every thing that looks like a restraint upon it, and is apt to fancy itself under a sort of confinement, when the sight is pent up in a narrow compass, and shortened on every side by the neighbourhood of walls or mountains. On the contrary, a spacious horizon is an image of liberty, where the eye has room to range abroad, to expatiate at large on the immensity of its views, and to lose itself amidst the variety of objects that offer themselves to its observation. Such wide and undetermined prospects are as pleasing to the fancy, as the speculations of eternity or infinitude are to the understanding. But if there be a beauty or uncommonness joined with this grandeur, as in a troubled ocean, a heaven adorned with stars and meteors, or a spacious landskip cut into rivers, woods, rocks, and meadows, the pleasure still grows upon us, as it arises from more than a single principle.

Everything that is *new* or *uncommon* raises a pleasure in the imagination, because it fills the soul with an agreeable surprise, gratifies its curiosity, and gives it an idea of which it was not before possessed. We are, indeed, so often conversant with one set of objects, and tired out with so many repeated shows of the same things, that whatever is *new* or *uncommon* contributes a little to vary human life, and to divert our minds, for a while, with the strangeness of its appearance: it serves us for a kind of refreshment, and takes off from that satiety we are apt to complain of in our usual and ordinary entertainments. It is this that bestows charms on a monster, and makes even the imperfections of nature please us. It is this that recommends variety, where the mind is every instant called off to something new, and the attention not suffered to dwell too long, and waste itself on any particular object. It is this, likewise, that improves what is great or beautiful, and makes it afford the mind a double entertainment. Groves, fields, and meadows, are at any season of the year pleasant to look upon, but never so much as in the opening of the spring, when they are all new and fresh, with their first gloss upon them, and not yet too much accustomed and familiar to the eye. For this reason there is nothing that more enlivens a prospect than rivers, jetteaus, or falls of water, where the scene is perpetually shifting, and entertaining the sight every moment with something that is new. We are quickly tired with looking upon hills and valleys, where every thing continues fixed and settled in the same place and posture, but find our thoughts a little agitated and relieved at the sight of such objects as are ever in motion, and sliding away from beneath the eye of the beholder.

But there is nothing that makes its way more directly to the soul than *beauty*, which immediately diffuses a secret satisfaction and complacency through the imagination, and gives a finishing to any thing that is great or uncommon. The very first discovery of it strikes the mind with an inward joy, and spreads a cheerfulness and delight through all its faculties. There is not perhaps any real beauty or deformity more in one piece of matter than another, because we might have been so made, that whatsoever now appears loathsome to us, might have shown it self agreeable; but we find by experience, that there are several modifications of matter which the mind, without any previous consideration, pronounces at first sight beautiful or deformed....

No. 413 Tuesday, June 24, 1712

...Causa latet, vis est notissima...   Ovid.

...One of the final causes of our delight, in any thing that is *great*, may be this. The supreme author of our being has so formed the soul of man, that nothing but himself can be its last, adequate, and proper happiness. Because, therefore, a great part of our happiness must arise from the contemplation of his being, that he might give our souls a just relish of such a contemplation, he has made them naturally delight in the apprehension of what is great or unlimited.

Our admiration, which is a very pleasing motion of the mind, immediately rises at the consideration of any object that takes up a great deal of room in the fancy, and, by consequence, will improve into the highest pitch of astonishment and devotion when we contemplate his nature, that is neither circumscribed by time nor place, nor to be comprehended by the largest capacity of a created being.

He has annexed a secret pleasure to the idea of any thing that is *new* or *uncommon*, that he might encourage us in the pursuit after knowledge, and engage us to search into the wonders of his creation; for every new idea brings such a pleasure along with it, as rewards any pains we have taken in its acquisition, and consequently serves as a motive to put us upon fresh discoveries....

In the last place, he has made every thing that is beautiful in all other objects pleasant, or rather has made so many objects appear beautiful, that he might render the whole creation more gay and delightful. He has given almost every thing about us the power of raising an agreeable idea in the imagination: so that it is impossible for us to behold his works with coldness or indifference, and to survey so many beauties without a secret satisfaction and complacency. Things would make but a poor appearance to the eye, if we saw them only in their proper figures and motions: and what reason can we assign for their exciting in us many of those ideas which are different from any thing that exists in the objects themselves, (for such are light and colours) were it not to add supernumerary ornaments to the universe, and make it more agreeable to the imagination? We are every where entertained with pleasing shows and apparitions, we discover imaginary glories in the heavens, and in the earth, and see some of this visionary beauty poured out upon the whole creation; but what a rough unsightly sketch of nature should we be entertained with, did all her colouring disappear, and the several distinctions of light and shade vanish? In short, our souls are at present delightfully lost and bewildered in a pleasing delusion, and we walk about like the enchanted hero of a romance, who sees beautiful castles, woods and meadows; and at the same time hears the warbling of birds, and the purling of streams; but upon the finishing of some secret spell, the fantastic scene breaks up, and the disconsolate knight finds himself on a barren heath, or in a solitary desert. It is not improbable that something like this may be the state of the soul after its first separation, in respect of the images it will receive from matter; though indeed the ideas of colours are so pleasing and beautiful in the imagination, that it is possible the soul will not be deprived of them, but perhaps find them excited by some other occasional cause, as they are at present by the different impressions of the subtle matter on the organ of sight....

The Spectator No. 414 Wednesday, June 25, 1712

...Alterius sic
Altera poscit opem res & conjurat amicè.   Horace.

If we consider the works of *nature* or *art*, as they are qualified to entertain the imagination, we shall find the last very defective, in comparison of the former; for though they may sometimes appear as beautiful or strange, they can have nothing in them of that vastness and immensity, which afford so great an entertainment to the mind of the beholder. The one may be as polite and delicate as the other, but can never show herself so august and magnificent in the design. There is something more bold and masterly in the rough careless strokes of nature, than in the nice touches and embellishments of art. The beauties of the most stately garden or palace lie in a narrow compass, the imagination immediately runs them over, and requires something else to gratify her; but, in the wide fields of nature, the sight wanders up and down without confinement, and is fed with an infinite variety of images, without any certain stint or number. For this reason we always find the poet in love with a country-life, where nature appears in the greatest perfection, and furnishes out all those scenes that are most apt to delight the imagination....

But although there are several of these wild scenes, that are more delightful than any artificial shows; yet we find the works of nature still more pleasant, the more they resemble those of art: for in this case our pleasure arises from a double principle; from the agreeableness of the objects to the eye, and from their similitude to other objects: we are pleased as well with comparing their beauties, as with surveying them, and can represent them to our minds, either as copies or originals. Hence it is that we take delight in a prospect which is well laid out, and diversified with fields and meadows, woods and rivers, in those accidental landskips of trees, clouds and cities, that are sometimes found in the veins of marble, in the curious fret-work of rocks and grottoes, and, in a word, in any thing that hath such a variety or regularity as may seem the effect of design, in what we call the works of chance....

We have before observed, that there is generally in nature something more grand and august, than what we meet with in the curiosities of art. When, therefore, we see this imitated in any measure, it gives us a nobler and more exalted kind of pleasure than what we receive from the nicer and more accurate productions of art. On this account our English gardens are not so entertaining to the fancy as those in France and Italy, where we see a large extent of ground covered over with an agreeable mixture of garden and forest, which represent every where an artificial rudeness, much more charming than that neatness and elegancy which we meet with in those of our own country....

No. 417 Saturday, June 28, 1712

...It would be in vain to enquire, whether the power of imagining things strongly proceeds from any greater perfection in the soul, or from any nicer texture in the brain of one man than of another. But this is certain, that a noble writer should be born with this faculty in its full strength and vigour, so as to be able to receive lively ideas from outward objects, to retain them long, and to range them together, upon occasion, in such figures and representations as are most likely to hit the fancy of the reader. A poet should take as much pains in forming his imagination, as a philosopher in cultivating his understanding. He must gain a due relish of the works of nature, and be thoroughly conversant in the various scenery of a country life.

When he is stored with country images, if he would go beyond pastoral, and the lower kinds of poetry, he ought to acquaint himself with the pomp and magnificence of courts. He should be very well versed in every thing that is noble and stately in the productions of art, whether it appear in painting or statuary, in the great works of architecture which are in their present glory, or in the ruins of those which flourished in former ages.

Such advantages as these help to open a man's thoughts, and to enlarge his imagination, and will therefore have their influence on all kinds of writing, if the author knows how to make right use of them. And among those of the learned languages who excel in this talent, the most perfect in their several kinds, are perhaps Homer, Virgil, and Ovid. The first strikes the imagination wonderfully with what is great, the second with what is beautiful, and the last with what is strange. Reading the *Iliad* is like travelling through a country uninhabited, where the fancy is entertained with a thousand savage prospects of vast deserts, wide uncultivated marshes, huge forests, misshapen rocks and precipices. On the contrary, the *Æneid* is like a well-ordered garden, where it is impossible to find out any part unadorned, or to cast our eyes upon a single spot, that does not produce some beautiful plant or flower. But when we are in the *Metamorphosis*, we are walking on enchanted ground, and see nothing but scenes of magic lying round us.

Homer is in his province, when he is describing a battle or a multitude, a hero or a god. Virgil is never better pleased, than when he is in his Elysium, or copying out an entertaining picture. Homer's epithets generally mark out what is great, Virgil's what is agreeable. Nothing can be more magnificent than the figure Jupiter makes in the first *Iliad*, nor more charming than that of Venus in the first *Æneid*....

Homer's persons are most of them god-like and terrible; Virgil has scarce admitted any into his poem, who are not beautiful, and has taken particular care to make his hero so....

No. 418 Monday, June 30, 1712

...ferat & rubus asper amomum.   Virgil.

The pleasures of these secondary views of the imagination, are of a wider and more universal nature than those it has, when joined with sight; for not only what is great, strange or beautiful, but any thing that is disagreeable when looked upon, pleases us in an apt description. Here, therefore, we must enquire after a new principle of pleasure, which is nothing else but the action of the mind, which *compares* the ideas that arise from words, with the ideas that arise from the objects themselves; and why this operation of the mind is attended with so much pleasure, we have before considered. For this reason therefore, the description of a dung-hill is pleasing to the imagination, if the image be represented to our minds by suitable expressions; although, perhaps, this may be more properly called the pleasure of the understanding than of the fancy, because we are not so much delighted with the image that is contained in the description, as with the aptness of the description to excite the image.

But if the description of what is little, common or deformed, be acceptable to the imagination, the description of what is great, surprising or beautiful, is much more so; because here we are not only delighted with *comparing* the representation with the original, but are highly pleased with the original itself. Most readers, I believe, are more charmed with Milton's description of paradise, than of hell; they are both, perhaps, equally perfect in their kind, but in the one the brimstone and sulphur are not so refreshing to the imagination, as the beds of flowers, and the wilderness of sweets in the other.

There is yet another circumstance which recommends a description more than all the rest, and that is, if it represents to us such objects as are apt to raise a secret ferment in the mind of the reader, and to work, with violence, upon his passions. For, in this case, we are at once warmed and enlightened, so that the pleasure becomes more universal, and is several ways qualified to entertain us. Thus, in painting, it is pleasant to look on the picture of any face, where the resemblance is hit, but the pleasure increases, if it be the picture of a face that is beautiful, and is still greater, if the beauty be softened with an air of melancholy or sorrow. The two leading passions which the more serious parts of poetry endeavour to stir up in us, are terror and pity. And here, by the way, one would wonder how it comes to pass, that such passions as are very unpleasant at all other times, are very agreeable when excited by proper descriptions. It is not strange, that we should take delight in such passages as are apt to produce hope, joy, admiration, love, or the like emotions in us, because they never rise in the mind without an inward pleasure which attends them. But how comes it to pass, that we should take delight in being terrified or dejected by a description, when we find so much uneasiness in the fear or grief which we receive from any other occasion?

If we consider, therefore, the nature of this pleasure, we shall find that it does not arise so properly from the description of what is terrible, as from the reflection we make on our selves at the time of reading it. When we look on such hideous objects, we are not a little pleased to think we are in no danger of them. We consider them at the same time, as dreadful and harmless; so that the more frightful appearance they make, the greater is the pleasure we receive from the sense of our own safety. In short, we look upon the terrors of a description, with the same curiosity and satisfaction that we survey a dead monster.

> ...Informe cadaver
> Protrahitur, nequeunt expleri corda tuendo
> Terribiles oculos: vultum, villosaque setis
> Pectora semiferi, atque extinctos faucibus ignes.   Virgil.

It is for the same reason that we are delighted with the reflecting upon dangers that are past, or in looking on a precipice at a distance, which would fill us with a different kind of horror, if we saw it hanging over our heads.

In the like manner, when we read of torments, wounds, deaths, and the like dismal accidents, our pleasure does not flow so properly from the grief which such melancholy descriptions give us, as from the secret comparison which we make between our selves and the person who suffers. Such representations teach us to set a just value upon our own condition, and make us prize our good fortune which exempts us from the like calamities. This is, however, such a kind of pleasure as we are not capable of receiving, when we see a person actually lying under the tortures that we meet with in a description; because, in this case, the object presses too close upon our senses, and bears so hard upon us, that it does not give us time or leisure to reflect on our selves. Our thoughts are so intent upon the miseries of the sufferer, that we cannot turn them upon our own happiness. Whereas, on the contrary, we consider the misfortunes we read in history or poetry, either as past, or as fictitious, so that the reflection upon our selves rises in us insensibly, and overbears the sorrow we conceive for the sufferings of the afflicted.

But because the mind of man requires something more perfect in matter, than what it finds there, and can never meet with any sight in nature which sufficiently answers its highest ideas of pleasantness; or, in other words, because the imagination can fancy to itself things more great, strange, or beautiful, than the eye ever saw, and is still sensible of some defect in what it has seen; on this account it is the part of a poet to humour the imagination in its own notions, by mending and perfecting nature where he describes a reality, and by adding greater beauties than are put together in nature, where he describes a fiction....

No. 489 Saturday, September 20, 1712

…Βαθθρρείταο μέγα σθένος ᾿Ωκεανοῖο.   Homer.

Sir,

'Upon reading your *Essay*, concerning the pleasures of the imagination, I find, among the three sources of those pleasures which you have discovered, that *greatness* is one. This has suggested to me the reason why, of all objects that I have ever seen, there is none which affects my imagination so much as the sea or ocean. I cannot see the heavings of this prodigious bulk of waters, even in a calm, without a very pleasing astonishment; but when it is worked up in a tempest, so that the horizon on every side is nothing but foaming billows and floating mountains, it is impossible to describe the agreeable horror that rises from such a prospect. A troubled ocean, to a man who sails upon it, is, I think, the biggest object that he can see in motion, and consequently gives his imagination one of the highest kinds of pleasure that can arise from greatness. I must confess, it is impossible for me to survey this world of fluid matter, without thinking on the hand that first poured it out, and made a proper channel for its reception. Such an object naturally raises in my thoughts the idea of an almighty being, and convinces me of his existence, as much as a metaphysical demonstration. The imagination prompts the understanding, and by the greatness of the sensible object, produces in it the idea of a being who is neither circumscribed by time nor space.

'As I have made several voyages upon the sea I have often been tossed in storms, and on that occasion have frequently reflected on the descriptions of them in ancient poets. I remember Longinus highly recommends one in Homer, because the poet has not amused himself with little fancies upon the occasion, as authors of an inferior genius, whom he mentions, had done, but because he has gathered together those circumstances which are the most apt to terrify the imagination, and which really happen in the raging of a tempest. It is for the same reason, that I prefer the following description of a ship in a storm, which the psalmist has made, before any other I have ever met with. *They that go down to the sea in ships, that do business in great waters: these see the works of the Lord, and his wonders in the deep. For he commandeth and raiseth the stormy wind, which lifteth up the waters thereof. They mount up to the heaven, they go down again to the depths, their soul is melted because of trouble. They reel too and fro, and stagger like a drunken Man, and are at their wits end. Then they cry unto the Lord in their trouble, and he bringeth them out of their distresses. He maketh the storm a calm, so that the waves thereof are still. Then they are glad, because they be quiet; so he bringeth them unto their desired haven.*

'By the way, how much more comfortable, as well as rational, is this system of the psalmist, than the pagan scheme in Virgil, and other poets, where one deity is represented as raising a storm, and another as laying it. Were we only to consider the sublime in this piece of poetry, what can be nobler than the idea it gives us, of the supreme being thus raising a tumult among the elements, and recovering them out of their confusion; thus troubling and becalming nature?…

12

Joseph Addison, from *A discourse on ancient and modern learning* (1734)

...Another great pleasure the ancients had beyond us, if we consider them as the poet's countrymen, was, that they lived as it were on the spot, and within the verge of the poem; their habitations lay among the scenes of the *Æneid*; they could find out their own country in Homer, and had every day perhaps in their sight the mountain or field where such an adventure, or such a battle was fought. Many of them had often walked on the banks of Helicon, or the sides of Parnassus, and knew all the private haunts and retirements of the muses: so that they lived as it were on *fairy ground*, and conversed in an enchanted region, where every thing they looked upon appeared romantic, and gave a thousand pleasing hints to their imaginations. To consider Virgil only in this respect: how must a Roman have been pleased that was well acquainted with the capes and promontories, to see the original of their names, as they stand derived from Misenus, Palinurus and Cajeta? That could follow the poet's motions, and attend his hero in all his marches from place to place? That was very well acquainted with the lake Amsanctus, where the fury sunk, and could lead you to the mouth of the cave where Æeneas took his descent for hell? Their being conversant with the place where the poem was transacted, gave them a greater relish than we can have at present of several parts of it; as it affected their imaginations more strongly, and diffused through the whole narration a greater air of truth. The places stood as so many marks and testimonies to the veracity of the story that was told of them, and helped the reader to impose upon himself in the credibility of the relation. To consider only that passage in the 8th *Æeneid*, where the poet brings his hero acquainted with Evander, and gives him a prospect of that circuit of ground, which was afterwards covered with the metropolis of the world. The story of Cacus, which he there gives us at large, was probably raised on some old confused tradition of the place, and if so, was doubly entertaining to a Roman, when he saw it worked up into so noble a piece of poetry, as it would have pleased an Englishman, to have seen in prince Arthur any of the old traditions of Guy varied and beautified in an episode, had the chronology suffered the author to have led his hero into Warwickshire on that occasion. The map of the place, which was afterwards the seat of Rome, must have been wonderfully pleasing to one that lived upon it afterwards, and saw all the alterations that happened in such a compass of ground....

There is another engaging circumstance that made Virgil and Homer more particularly charming to their own countrymen, than they can possibly appear to any of the moderns; and this they took hold of by choosing their heroes out of their own nation: for, by this means, they have humoured and delighted the vanity of a Grecian or Roman reader, they have powerfully engaged him on the hero's side, and made him, as it were, a party in every action; so that the narration renders him more intent, the happy events raise a greater pleasure in him, the passionate part more moves him, and in a word, the whole poem comes more home, and touches him more nearly, than it would have done, had the scene lain in another country, and a foreigner been the subject of it. No doubt but the inhabitants of Ithaca preferred the *Odyssey* to the *Iliad*, as the Myrmidons, on the contrary were not a little proud of their Achilles. The men of Pylos probably could repeat word for word the wise sentences of Nestor; and we may well suppose Agamemnon's countrymen often pleased themselves with their prince's superiority in the Greek confederacy. I believe therefore, no Englishman, reads Homer or Virgil, with such an inward triumph of thought, and such a passion of glory, as those who saw in them the exploits of their own countrymen or ancestors. And here by the way, our Milton, has been more universally engaging in the choice of his persons, than any other poet can possibly be. He has obliged all mankind; and related the whole species to the two chief actors in his poem. Nay, what is infinitely more considerable; we behold in him, not only our ancestors, but our representatives. We are really engaged in their adventures, and have a personal interest in their good or ill success. We are not only their offspring, but sharers in their fortunes; and no less than our own eternal happiness, or misery, depends on their single conduct: so that every reader will here find himself concerned, and have all his attention and solicitude raised, in every turn and circumstance of the whole poem.

13

Anthony Ashley Cooper, Third Earl of Shaftesbury, from *Characteristics* (1714)

Treatise V. The moralists. A philosophical rhapsody
Part III. Section 1

...Here, Philocles, we shall find our sovereign genius; if we can charm the genius of the place (more chaste and sober than your Silenus) to inspire us with a truer song of nature, teach us some celestial hymn, and make us feel divinity present in these solemn places of retreat.

Haste then, I conjure you, said I, good Theocles, and stop not one moment for any ceremony or rite. For well I see, methinks, that without any such preparation, some divinity has approached us, and already moves in you. We are come to the sacred groves of the Hamadryads, which formerly were said to render oracles. We are on the most beautiful part of the hill; and the sun, now ready to rise, draws off the curtain of night, and shows us the open scene of nature in the plains below. Begin: for now I know you are full of those divine thoughts that meet you ever in this solitude. Give them but voice and accents: you may be still as much alone as you are used, and take no more notice of me than if I were absent.

Just as I had said this, he turned away his eyes from me, musing a while by himself; and soon afterwards, stretching out his hand, as pointing to the objects round him, he began.

"Ye fields and woods, my refuge from the toilsome world of business, receive me in your quiet sanctuaries, and favour my retreat and thoughtful solitude. Ye verdant plains, how gladly I salute ye! Hail all ye blissful mansions! known seats! delightful prospects! majestic beauties of this earth, and all ye rural powers and graces! Blessed be ye chaste abodes of happiest mortals, who here in peaceful innocence enjoy a life unenvied, although divine; whilst with its blessed tranquillity, it affords a happy leisure and retreat for man; who, made for contemplation, and to search his own and other natures, may here best meditate the cause of things; and placed amidst the various scenes of Nature, may nearer view her works.

O glorious nature! supremely fair, and sovereignly good! All-loving and all-lovely, all-divine! Whose looks are so becoming, and of such infinite grace; whose study brings such wisdom, and whose contemplation such delight; whose every single work affords an ampler scene, and is a nobler spectacle than all which ever art presented! O mighty nature! Wise substitute of providence! impowered creatress! Or thou impowering divinity, supreme creator! Thee I invoke, and thee alone adore. To thee this solitude, this place, these rural meditations are sacred; whilst thus inspired with harmony of thought, although unconfined by words, and in loose numbers, I sing of nature's order in created beings, and celebrate the beauties which resolve in thee, the source and principle of all beauty and perfection.

Thy being is boundless, unsearchable, impenetrable. In thy immensity all thought is lost; fancy gives over its flight: and wearied imagination spends itself in vain; finding no coast nor limit of this ocean, nor, in the widest tract through which it soars, one point yet nearer the circumference than the first center whence it parted. Thus having oft essayed, thus sallied forth into the wide expanse, when I return again within myself, struck with the sense of this so narrow being, and of the fulness of that immense one; I dare no more behold the amazing depths, nor sound the abyss of *Deity*.

Yet since by thee (O sovereign mind!) I have been formed such as I am, intelligent and rational; since the peculiar dignity of my nature is to know and contemplate thee; permit that with due freedom I exert those faculties with which thou hast adorned me. Bear with my venturous and bold approach. And since nor vain curiosity, nor fond conceit, nor love of ought save thee alone, inspires me with such thoughts as these, be thou my assistant, and guide me in this pursuit; whilst I venture thus to tread the labyrinth of wide nature, and endeavour to trace thee in thy works."

Here he stopped short, and starting, as out of a dream; now, Philocles, said he, inform me, how have I appeared to you in my fit? Seemed it a sensible kind of madness, like those transports which are permitted to our poets? or was it downright raving? ...

Thus I continue then, said Theocles, addressing myself, as you would have me, to that Guardian-Deity and inspirer, whom we are to imagine present here; but not here only. For "O mighty *genius*! sole-animating and inspiring power! Author and subject of these thoughts! Thy influence is universal: and in all things thou art inmost. From thee depend their secret springs of action. Thou movest them with an irresistible unwearied force, by sacred and inviolable laws, framed for the good of each particular being; as best may suit with the perfection, life, and vigour of the whole. The vital principle is widely shared, and infinitely varied: dispersed throughout; nowhere extinct. All lives: and by succession still revives. The temporary beings quit their borrowed forms, and yield their elementary substance to new-comers. Called in their several turns, to life, they view the light, and viewing pass; that others too may be spectators of the goodly scene, and greater numbers still enjoy the privilege of nature. Munificent and great, she imparts herself to most; and makes the subjects of her bounty infinite. Nought stays her hastening hand. No time nor substance is lost or unimproved. New forms arise: and when the old dissolve, the matter whence they were composed is not left useless, but wrought with equal management and art, even in corruption, nature's seeming waste, and vile abhorrence. The abject state appears merely as the way or passage to some better. But could we nearly view it, and with indifference, remote from the antipathy of sense; we then perhaps should highest raise our admiration: convinced that even the way itself was equal to the end. Nor can we judge less favourably of that consummate art exhibited through all the works of nature; since our weak eyes, helped by mechanic art, discover in these works a hidden scene of wonders; worlds within worlds, of infinite minuteness, though as to art still equal to the greatest, and pregnant with more wonders than the most discerning sense, joined with the greatest art, or the acutest reason, can penetrate or unfold.

But it is in vain for us to search the bulky mass of *matter*: seeking to know its nature; how great the whole itself, or even how small its parts.

If knowing only some of the rules of *motion*, we seek to trace it further, it is in vain we follow it into the bodies it has reached. Our tardy apprehensions fail us, and can reach nothing beyond the body itself, through which it is diffused. Wonderful being! (if we may call it so) which bodies never receive, except from others which lose it; nor ever lose, unless by imparting it to others. Even without change of place it has its force: and bodies big with motion labour to move, yet stir not; whilst they express an energy beyond our comprehension.

In vain too we pursue that phantom *time*, too small, and yet too mighty for our grasp; when shrinking to a narrow point, it escapes our hold, or mocks our scanty thought by swelling to eternity: an object unproportioned to our capacity, as is thy being, O thou ancient cause! older than time, yet young with fresh eternity.

In vain we try to fathom the abyss of *space*, the seat of thy extensive being; of which no place is empty, no void which is not full.

In vain we labour to understand that principle of *sense* and *thought*, which seeming in us to depend so much on motion, yet differs so much from it, and from matter itself, as not to suffer us to conceive how thought can more result from this, than this arise from thought. But thought we own pre-eminent, and confess the reallest of beings; the only existence of which we are made sure, by being conscious. All else may be but dream and shadow. All which even sense suggests may be deceitful. The *sense* itself remains still: *reason* subsists: and *thought* maintains its eldership of being. Thus are we in a manner conscious of that original and eternally existent *thought* whence we derive our own. And thus the assurance we have of the existence of beings above our sense, and of *thee* (the great exemplar of thy works) comes from thee, the *all-true*, and perfect, who hast thus communicated thyself more immediately to us, so as in some manner to inhabit within our souls; thou who art original *soul* diffusive, vital in all, inspiriting the whole!

All Nature's wonders serve to excite and perfect this idea of their author. It is here he suffers us to see, and even converse with him, in a manner suitable to our frailty. How glorious is it to contemplate him, in this noblest of his works apparent to us, the system of the bigger world!

Here I must own, it was no small comfort to me, to find that, as our meditation turned, we were likely to get clear of an entangling abstruse philosophy. I was in hopes Theocles, as he proceeded, might stick closer to Nature, since he was now come upon the borders of our world. And here I would willingly have welcomed him, had I thought it safe at present to venture the least interruption.

"Besides the neighbouring plants (continued he, in his rapturous strain) what multitudes of fixed *stars* did we see sparkle, not an hour ago, in the clear night, which yet had hardly yielded to the day? How many others are discovered by the help of art? Yet how many remain still, beyond the reach of our discovery! Crowded as they seem, their distance from each other is as unmeasurable by art, as is the distance between them and us. Whence we are naturally taught the immensity of that *being*, who through these immense spaces has disposed such an infinite of bodies, belonging each (as we may well presume) to systems as complete as our own world: since even the smallest spark of this bright galaxy may vie with this our sun; which shining now full out, gives us new life, exalts our spirits, and makes us feel *divinity* more present.

Prodigious orb! Bright source of vital heat, and spring of day! – soft flame, yet how intense, how active! How diffusive, and how vast a substance; yet how collected thus within itself, and in a glowing mass confined to the center of this planetary world! – mighty Being! Brightest image, and representative of the Almighty! Supreme of the corporeal world! Unperishing in grace, and of undecaying youth! Fair, beautiful, and hardly mortal creature! By what secret ways dost thou receive the supplies which maintain thee still in such unwearied vigour, and unexhausted glory; notwithstanding those eternally emitted streams, and that continual expense of vital treasures which inlighten and invigorate the surrounding worlds?

Around him all the *planets*, with this our earth, single, or with attendants, continually move; seeking to receive the blessing of his light, and lively warmth! Towards him they seem to tend with prone descent, as to their center; but happily controlled still by another impulse, they keep their heavenly order and just numbers, and exactest measure, go the eternal rounds.

But, O thou who art the author and modifier of these various motions! O sovereign and sole mover, by whose high art the rolling spheres are governed, and these stupendous bodies of our world hold their unrelenting courses! O wise economist, and powerful chief, whom all the elements and powers of nature serve! How hast thou animated these moving worlds? What spirit or soul infused? What bias fixed? Or how encompassed them in liquid ether, driving them as with the breath of living winds, thy active and unwearied ministers in this intricate and mighty work?

Thus powerfully are the systems held entire, and kept from fatal interfering. Thus is our ponderous *globe* directed in its annual course; daily revolving on its own centre: whilst the obsequious *moon* with double labour, monthly surrounding this our bigger orb, attends the motion of her sister-planet, and pays in common her circular homage to the sun.

Yet is this mansion-*globe*, this man-container, of a much narrower compass even than other its fellow-wanderers of our system. How narrow then must it appear, compared with the capacious system of its own sun? And how narrow, or as nothing, in respect of those innumerable systems of other apparent suns? Yet how immense a body it seems, compared with ours of human form, a borrowed remnant of its variable and oft-converted surface? although animated with a sublime celestial spirit, by which we have relation and tendency to thee our heavenly sire, centre of souls; to whom these spirits of ours by nature tend, as earthly bodies to their proper centre. O did they tend as unerringly and constantly! But thou alone composest the disorders of the corporeal world, and from the restless and fighting elements raisest that peaceful concord, and conspiring beauty of the ever-flourishing creation. Even so canst thou convert these jarring motions of intelligent beings, and in due time and manner cause them to find their rest; making them contribute to the *good* and perfection of the *universe*, thy all-good and perfect work." ...

...The wildness pleases. We seem to live alone with nature. We view her in her inmost recesses, and contemplate her with more delight in these original wilds, than in the artificial labyrinths and feigned wildernesses of the palace. The objects of the place, the scaly serpents, the savage beasts, and poisonous insects, how terrible soever, or how contrary to human nature, are beauteous in themselves, and fit to raise our thoughts in admiration of that divine wisdom, so far superior to our short views. Unable to declare the use or service of all things in this universe, we are yet assured of the perfection of all, and of the justice of that economy, to which all things are subservient, and in respect of which, things seemingly deformed are amiable; disorder becomes regular; corruption wholesome; and poisons (such as these we have seen) prove healing and beneficial.

But behold! through a vast tract of sky before us, the mighty Atlas rears his lofty head, covered with snow, above the clouds. Beneath the mountain's foot, the rocky country rises into hills, a proper basis of the ponderous mass above: where huge embodied rocks lie piled on one another, and seem to prop the high arch of heaven. See! with what trembling steps poor mankind treads the narrow brink of the deep precipices! From whence with giddy horror they look down, mistrusting even the ground which bears them; whilst they hear the hollow sound of torrents underneath, and see the ruin of the impending rock; with falling trees which hang with their roots upwards, and seem to draw more ruin after them. Here thoughtless men, seized with the newness of such objects, become thoughtful, and willingly contemplate the incessant changes of this earth's surface. They see, as in one instant, the revolutions of past ages, the fleeting forms of things, and the decay even of this our globe; whose youth and first formation they consider, whilst the apparent spoil and irreparable breaches of the wasted mountain show them the world itself only as a noble ruin, and make them think of its approaching period. – But here mid-way the mountain, a spacious border of thick wood harbours our wearied travellers: who now are come among the evergreen and lofty pines, the firs, and noble cedars, whose towering heads seem endless in the sky; the rest of trees appearing only as shrubs beside them. And here a different horror seizes our sheltered travellers, when they see the day diminished by the deep shades of the vast wood; which closing thick above, spreads darkness and eternal night below. The faint and gloomy light looks horrid as the shade itself: and the profound stillness of these places imposes silence upon men, struck with the hoarse echoings of every sound within the spacious caverns of the wood. Here space astonishes. Silence itself seems pregnant; whilst an unknown force works on the mind, and dubious objects move the wakeful sense. Mysterious voices are either heard or fancied: and various forms of deity seem to present themselves, and appear more manifest in these sacred sylvan scenes; such as of old gave rise to temples, and favoured the religion of the ancient world. Even we ourselves, who in plain characters may read *divinity* from so many bright parts of earth, choose rather these obscurer places, to spell out that mysterious being, which to our weak eyes appears at best under a veil of cloud."

Here he paused a while, and began to cast about his eyes, which before seemed fixed. He looked more calmly, with an open countenance and free air; by which, and other tokens, I could easily find we were come to an end of our descriptions; and that whether I would or no, Theocles was now resolved to take his leave of the sublime: the morning being spent, and the forenoon by this time well advanced.

Part III
Section II

...O Theocles! said I, well do I remember now the terms in which you engaged me, that morning when you bespoke my love of this mysterious beauty. You have indeed made good your part of the condition, and may now claim me for a proselyte. If there by any seeming extravagance in the case, I must comfort myself the best I can, and consider that all sound love and admiration is *enthusiasm*: "The transports of poets, the sublime of orators, the rapture of musicians, the high strains of the virtuosi; all mere *enthusiasm*! Even learning itself, the love of arts and curiosities, the spirit of travellers and adventurers; gallantry, war, heroism; all, all *enthusiasm*!" It is enough: I am content to be this new enthusiast, in a way unknown to me before.

And I, replied Theocles, am content you should call this love of ours *enthusiasm* allowing it the privilege of its fellow-passions. For is there a fair and plausible enthusiasm, a reasonable ecstasy and transport allowed to other subjects, such as architecture, painting, music; and shall it be exploded here? Are there senses by which all those other graces and perfections are perceived? and none by which this higher perfection and grace is comprehended? Is it so preposterous to bring that enthusiasm hither, and transfer it from those secondary and scanty objects, to this original and comprehensive one? Observe how the case stands in all those other subjects of art or science. What difficulty to be in any degree knowing! How long e'er a true taste is gained! How many things shocking, how many offensive at first, which afterwards are known and acknowledged the highest beauties! For it is not instantly we acquire the sense by which these beauties are discoverable. Labour and pains are required, and time to cultivate a natural genius, ever so apt or forward. But who is there once thinks of cultivating this soil, or of improving any sense or faculty which nature may have given of this kind? And is it a wonder we should be dull then, as we are, confounded, and at a loss in these affairs, blind as to this higher sense, these nobler representations? Which way should we come to understand better? which way be knowing in these beauties? Is study, science, or learning necessary to understand all beauties else? And for the sovereign *beauty*, is there no skill or science required? In painting there are shades and masterly strokes which the vulgar understand not, but find fault with: in architecture there is the rustic, in music the chromatic kind, and skilful mixture of dissonancies: and is there nothing which answers to this, in the *whole*?

I must confess, said I, I have hitherto been one of those vulgar, who could never relish the shades, the rustic, or the dissonancies you talk of. I have never dreamt of such master-pieces in nature. It was my way to censure freely on the first view. But I perceive I am now obliged to go far in the pursuit of beauty; which lies very absconded and deep: and if so, I am well assured that my enjoyments hitherto have been very shallow. I have dwelt, it seems, all this while upon the surface, and enjoyed only a kind of slight superficial beauties; having never gone in search of beauty itself, but of what I fancied such. Like the rest of the unthinking world, I took for granted that what I liked was beautiful; and what I rejoiced in, was my good. I never scrupled loving what I fancied; and aiming only at the enjoyment of what I loved, I never troubled myself with examining what the subjects were, nor ever hesitated about their choice.

Begin then, said he, and choose. See what the subjects are; and which you would prefer; which honour with your admiration, love, and esteem. For by these again you will be honoured in your turn. Such, Philocles, as is the worth of these companions, such will your worth be found. As there is emptiness or fulness here, so will there be in your enjoyment. See therefore where fulness is, and where emptiness. See in what subject resides the chief excellence: where *beauty* reigns: where it is entire, perfect, absolute; where broken, imperfect, short. View these terrestrial beauties, and whatever has the appearance of excellence, and is able to attract. See that which either really is, or stands as in the room of fair, beautiful, and good: "A mass of metal; a tract of land; a number of slaves; a pile of stones; a human body of certain lineaments and proportions:" Is this the highest of the kind? Is *beauty* founded then in body only; and not in action, life, or operation?

Hold! hold! said I (good Theocles!) you take this in too high a key, above my reach. If you would have me accompany you, pray lower this strain a little; and talk in a more familiar way.

Thus then, said he, (smiling) whatever passion you may have for other beauties; I know, good Philocles, you are no such admirer of wealth in any kind, as to allow much beauty to it; especially in a rude heap or mass. But in medals, coins, embossed work, statues, and well-fabricated pieces, of whatever sort, you can discover beauty, and admire the kind. True, said I; but not for the metal's sake. It is not then the metal or matter which is beautiful with you. No. But the art. Certainly. The art then is the beauty. Right. And the art is that which beautifies. The same. So that the beautifying, not the beautified, is the really beautiful. It seems so. For that which is beautified, is beautiful only by the accession of something beautifying: and by the recess or withdrawing of the same, it ceases to be beautiful. Be it. In respect of bodies therefore, beauty comes and goes. So we see. Nor is the body itself any cause either of its coming or staying. None. So that there is no principle of beauty in body. None at all. For body can no way be the cause of beauty to itself. No way. Nor govern nor regulate itself. Nor yet this. Nor mean nor intend itself. Nor this neither. Must not that therefore, which means and intends for it, regulates and orders it, be the principle of beauty to it? Of necessity. And what must that be? *Mind*, I suppose; for what can it be else?

Here then, said he, is all I would have explained to you before: "That the beautiful, the fair, the comely, were never in the matter, but in the art and design; never in body itself, but in the form or forming power." Does not the beautiful form confess this, and speak the beauty of the design, whenever it strikes you? What is it but the design which strikes? What is it you admire but *mind*, or the effect of mind? It is mind alone which forms. All that is void of mind is horrid: and matter formless is deformity itself....

14

Henry Needler,
from *The works* (1724)

On the excellency of divine contemplation

The mind of man is naturally delighted with the contemplation of whatever is beautiful and excellent; and the greater and more sublime those perfections are, wherewith any object is endued, the more exalted and refined is the pleasure, which the soul conceives from the contemplation of it. Now God is a being of infinite perfection and excellence, in whom all the rays of goodness and beauty which are scattered and dispersed among the creatures, concentre and are united. It cannot therefore be imagined, but that the contemplation of so lovely and excellent an object must be highly grateful and pleasing to the soul. That infinity of the divine attributes and perfections, which by puzzling and embarrassing the understanding, might be thought to lessen this pleasure, does really increase it. For the mind is naturally pleased with the speculation of what is infinite, and loves to lose itself, as it were, in an unfathomable depth.

The grandeur and magnificence of an infinite object affect it with an ineffable complacency; somewhat like that we take in beholding the vast expanse of the firmament, or the spacious surface of the ocean. Thus we find that those theorems in geometry, which have a relation to infinity, afford the greatest delight and satisfaction to curious minds: such, for example, as that of Torricellius, that a solid of infinite length, may be equal to a finite quantity: or those wonderful theorems about the proportions of infinite quantities, which Dr Halley has published in the *Philosophical Transactions*. But now, as the most excellent creatures with all their attributes and perfections are but finite, so it is impossible that the mind should find this sort of pleasure in the contemplation of them. It is only in the all-glorious essence of the creator, that it can entertain itself with these unbounded prospects, and be ravished with the speculation of these infinite grandeurs.

But farther; as the contemplation of the divine attributes in themselves, cannot but be very grateful and entertaining; so that delight must needs be exceedingly increased, when we consider them with the relation they bear to us, and how they all, as it were, conspire to render us happy, as well as that adorable being to whose essence they belong. The goodness of God makes all his attributes in some sense our own; in as much as it moves him to communicate such a share of them to us, as the narrowness of our created capacities can receive, and engages him to employ them all for our advantage.

What joy must it give a man, to consider that he is the creature of a being of infinite wisdom, power, goodness, and all other perfections; who made him with no other view, than that he might make him happy in the enjoyment of himself; and will certainly one day deliver him for ever from all the miseries and imperfections under which he now labours, and admit him to a participation of his own infinite wisdom and happiness!

What wound of affliction can be so deep, as that this sovereign balsam will not heal it? What weight of sorrow so heavy, as this strong consolation will not enable a man to bear? What though at present we live in a state of ignorance and misery, banished from our native country above, the region of beatified spirits, into this barren and uncomfortable world; when in a few days we shall return thither again; and live there in bliss and security for ever.

The soul thirsts after an infinite good, nor can any thing less fully satisfy its desires. Were there nothing for us to enjoy beyond what this world can afford, we might justly deplore the unhappy frame of our natures, which would subject us to a fatal necessity of being miserable, merely through the disproportion of our desires to our enjoyments. Our own unsatisfied longings after farther good would become our torment; and to be immortal, would be to be condemned to pine away eternity in the anguish of a hopeless, yet fervent and unextinguished love. It is God only, who can give such perfect repose and contentment to the soul; who can fill all its capacities, and satisfy all its most enlarged desires! In him is an immense ocean of good! an infinite treasure of beauty and perfection! a never-failing spring of bliss, which the soul will never be able to exhaust throughout all the ages of eternity! Since therefore the soul is conscious to herself, that she desires an infinite good, and that she cannot be happy but in the fruition of it; how is it possible that she should duly contemplate the glorious attributes and perfections of the deity, without feeling herself transported with the most ravishing joy! In him she finds something really existing, sufficient to satisfy all her most craving appetites, and commensurate to her largest wishes; and is pleasingly convinced, that that unquenchable thirst which she feels in herself after good, was not given to make her miserable, but to render her capable of the sublimest happiness. She looks upon God as her natural portion and inheritance; and upon every perfection and excellence she discovers in him, as a treasure, in the possession and enjoyment of which, by contemplation and love, she shall one day become happy.

But, besides the delight and consolation, which the mind receives from a due contemplation of God, and the divine attributes, there is still a farther advantage to be reaped from this angelical exercise; and that is the moralising our souls, and regulating our wills and affections. Nothing has a more direct tendency to this, than divine contemplation. This refines and elevates our affections; and inspires us with a certain dignity of mind and virtuous pride, which makes us despise the low pleasures of sense, and raises us above this transitory scene of things. This teaches us, that those divine faculties of our souls, reason and understanding, were not given us merely to purvey for the pleasures and necessities of the body, and to contrive the means of supporting for a while a wretched perishing being; but to render as capable of contemplating and enjoying him, whom to know is eternal life!

It is the opinion of many divines, that the clear vision of God, which beatified souls shall enjoy, will have so powerful an influence upon them, as to constrain them, by a certain happy necessity, to goodness. If this be true, we ought in reason to conclude, that an assiduous contemplation of God must have a proportionable effect upon the soul, and at least very strongly incline, although not absolutely necessitate it, to be virtuous. And indeed, it cannot well be otherwise; for, as he that keeps continually in view both his duty itself, and the reasons and motives of it, can scarcely do otherwise than perform it; so it is impossible that a man should attentively contemplate the divine nature and attributes, and yet be ignorant either of his duty, or the motives to it. How should he, who keeps up in his mind a lively sense of his living and acting under the eye, and in the continual presence of a just and powerful God, who will not suffer the transgressors of his righteous laws to go unpunished, nor let the observers of them pass unrewarded, find in his heart to sin against him? It is only because we do not attend to these weighty truths as we ought, that they have so little influence on our hearts and lives. If we never reflect on these things, they will have no more effect upon us, than if they were not at all; and the only way to make them of real use to the purifying our hearts, and reforming our lives, is to fix and rivet them in our minds, by frequent and serious contemplation.

On the beauty of the universe

There is nothing that affords a more sensible proof both of the existence and goodness of God, than the beauty of the universe, those innumerable gay appearances and delightful spectacles, which are scattered through all the scenes of the visible creation. Thunder, lightning, earthquakes and such like astonishing phænomena of Nature, may perhaps terrify us into an apprehension of a superior power; but this is a proof which works upon us in the most sweet and agreeable, though at the same time forcible and convincing manner. This gives us the most lovely and amiable view of our maker, and whilst it persuades our understandings of his being, engages our affections to rejoice in, adore and love him.

The superstitious among the Romans imagined, that the places in the country, which were more than commonly pleasant, such as the openings of woods and the flowery margins of fountains, were haunted by certain rural deities. This fancy of theirs has often given me occasion to reflect, at the sight of such places, that although there are indeed no marks to be seen in them of the presence of their chimerical divinities, yet that an attentive and considering mind may find there many tokens and signatures of the real presence and operation of the true God.

The beauty of the universe plainly shows, that it is neither the work of fate nor chance, but of a powerful and munificent intelligence, who considered, in the framing of it, not only what was needful for the preservation, but likewise the ornament of nature; and provided not only for the necessity, but even for the innocent delight and entertainment of all his sensible creatures. With how many charms and graces has he adorned every part of the universe? as if he designed that nature should represent to us the beauty and loveliness, as well as the wisdom and beneficence, of its author.

The ample arch of heaven, which hangs over our heads, is tinctured with a sprightly azure. In a clear night it appears like a vast roof of sapphire, studded with innumerable glowing spangles, or illumined with ten thousand shining lamps. The sun is so glorious and splendid a body, that he has attracted the devotion, as well as the admiration of many nations. With what variety of colours do his beams adorn the wandering clouds? He dyes some with scarlet or purple, and paints the skirts of others with silver or tinctures them with gold. How many beautiful and entertaining scenes do we behold in the heavens? What wild and rude, yet pleasing and agreeable prospects of craggy rocks and steep mountains, do they often present to our view? How beauteous as well as useful is that nightly substitute of the sun, the moon, who cheers us in his absence with her borrowed beams? In how many several forms, in how many various dresses of light does she appear to our eyes? Sometimes she shines over us in a perfect silver orb, or, approaching to the horizon, extends her bulk into a large bloody beamless globe; at other times (when newly returned from her dark retirement) she appears horned, or, like a sickle, edged only on one side with a narrow border of light.

From contemplating the beauties of the heavens, let us now descend to those of the earth. Here we have a new scene of delightful objects opened to our view. Although that paradise within, which consisted in a constant joy and inward tranquillity of mind, be now lost, yet much of outward paradise seems still to remain. Witness, ye shady groves and flowery meads! Ye verdant lawns and crystal streams! whose beauties have so often charmed the hearts of your beholders, and afforded a theme for the songs of the poets. Who can behold the spring, arrayed in all her youthful pride and gaiety, adorned with blooming blossoms, sprouting leaves, and an infinite variety of flowers, without admiration and delight?

As the face of heaven is tinctured with a gay azure, so that of the earth is spread with green, a colour which of all others is the most apt to revive the imagination, and excite alacrity in the soul. The surface of the earth is not all plain and flat, which would have taken away all variety of prospect, but agreeably diversified with hills and mountains, valleys and plains;

> – Sweet interchange
> Of Hill, and Valley, Rivers, Woods and Plains,
> Now Land, now Sea, and Shores with Forest crown'd.   Milton.

15

Mark Akenside, from
To David Fordyce, 18th June 1742

I should have answered your letter sooner, but that I was uncertain, till of late, whether to direct for you at Edinburgh or at Aberdeen. I durst not, however, reply in the language you wrote in; for though I could perhaps have filled two or three pages with Italian words ranged in grammatical order, yet, without assuming the natural air and spirit of the language, you would no more think I had wrote Italian than you would call that a musical composition which was only a number of concords put together without any regard to the rhythm or style of the whole. This reason was stronger in writing to you, who have attained so perfectly the wild elegance, the *vaghezza*, which the Italians are so fond of both in language and painting, and in which, I believe, they exceed all the moderns. What is good in the French authors is of a more sober, classical manner, and greater severity of design. The Spaniards, I imagine, approach much nearer to the Italian manners. Our English poetry has but little of it, and that chiefly among the older compositions of our countrymen – the juvenilia of Milton, and the fairy scenes of Spenser and Shakespeare. Our nervous and concise language does not willingly flow into this fanciful luxuriance; besides that the genius of our poetry delights in a vehemence of passion and philosophical sublimity of sentiments much above its reach.

Since we parted, I have been chiefly employed in reading the Greek philosophers, especially the Stoics. Upton's edition of Arrian was published just as I got hither; it is in two small quarto volumes, neat enough; the second consists principally of the editor's comments and notes variorum. He has got a great many remarks of Lord Shaftesbury, but they are entirely critical, and contain very ingenious conjectures on the reading of several passages.

I have had great pleasure from the writers of this sect; but, though I admire the strength and elevation of their moral, yet, in modern life especially, I am afraid it would lead to something splenetic and unconversable. Besides, it allows too little to domestic virtue and tenderness, it dwells too much on the awful and sublime of life; yet even its sublimity resembles that of a vast open prospect in winter, when the sun scarce can shine through the atmosphere, and looks on the rigour of the season with a kind of sullen majesty; to the generality of mankind, a much narrower landscape in the sunshine of a spring morning would be much more agreeable. I would therefore mix the Stoic with the Platonic philosophy; they would equally temper and adorn each other;

for, if mere stoicism be in hazard of growing surly and unsocial, it is no less certain that Platonic enthusiasm has always run to extravagance, but where it was kept steady by a severe judgment; besides that the constant pursuit of beauty and elegance is apt to fill the mind with high and florid desires, than which nothing is more dangerous to that internal freedom which is the basis of virtue. In short, the case seems much the same here as with the human sexes, either of which is liable to these very imperfections when apart, and therefore the perfection of human life is best found in their union. Were I a painter, and going to represent these two sects in an emblematic way, I would draw the genius of the Stoics like a man in his prime, or rather of a green and active old age, with a manly sternness and simplicity in his air and habit, seated on a rock overlooking the sea in a tempest of wind and lightning, and regarding the noise of the thunder and the rolling of the waves with a serene defiance. But the Platonic genius I would represent like another Muse – a virgin of a sweet and lively beauty, with wings to her head, and a loose robe of a bright azure colour. She should be seated in a garden, on the brink of a clear and smooth canal, while the sky were without a cloud, and the sun shining in the zenith. Our theological lady, conscious that her eyes could not endure the splendour of his immediate appearance, should be fixed in contemplating his milder image reflected from the water....

16

Mark Akenside,
from *The pleasures of imagination* (1744)

[Note]

The influence of the imagination on the conduct of life, is one of the most important points in moral philosophy. It were easy by an induction of facts to prove that the imagination directs almost all the passions, and mixes with almost every circumstance of action or pleasure. Let any man, even of the coldest head and soberest industry, analyse the idea of what he calls his interest; he will find that it consists chiefly of certain images of decency, beauty and order, variously combined into one system, the idol which he seeks to enjoy by labour, hazard, and self-denial. It is on this account of the last consequence to regulate these images by the standard of nature and the general good; otherwise the imagination, by heightening some objects beyond their real excellence and beauty, or by representing others in a more odious or terrible shape than they deserve, may of course engage us in pursuits utterly inconsistent with the laws of the moral order.

If it be objected, that this account of things supposes the passions to be merely accidental, whereas there appears in some a natural and hereditary disposition to certain passions prior to all circumstances of education or fortune; it may be answered that although no man is born *ambitious* or a *miser*, yet he may inherit from his parents a peculiar temper or complexion of mind, which shall render his imagination more liable to be struck with some particular objects, consequently dispose him to form opinions of good and ill, and entertain passions of a particular turn. Some men, for instance, by the original frame of their minds, are more delighted with the vast and magnificent, others on the contrary with the elegance and gentle aspects of nature. And it is very remarkable, that the disposition of the moral powers is always similar to this of the imagination; that those who are most inclined to admire prodigious and sublime objects in the physical world, are also most inclined to applaud examples of fortitude and heroic virtue in the moral. While those who are charmed rather with the *delicacy* and *sweetness* of colours, and forms, and sounds, never fail in like manner to yield the preference to the softer scenes of virtue and the sympathies of a domestic life. And this is sufficient to account for the objection.

17

John Baillie,
An essay on the sublime (1747)

Section I

We are now, Palemon, to treat of that kind of writing which of all others is
the truly excellent and great manner, and which is peculiar to a genius noble,
lofty, comprehensive. You will easily know I mean the Sublime, and perhaps
tell me the task is difficult; I acknowledge it, especially when I consider that
we have already a great author upon the subject, who has received the approbation of ages, and who, in the opinion of most, has exhausted it. – Yet I have
something to plead as my apology for my presumption, for such I believe it
may be reckoned, although not by you, yet by one, '*qui redit ad fastus, et
virtutem astimat annis.*'

Notwithstanding Longinus entitles his treatise, a *Treatise upon the Sublime*,
yet whoever considers the full extent of the work, will perceive the author
does not confine himself to the bare explanation of any one certain and particular manner in writing. Some part of his treatise regards the figurative style,
some the pathetic, and indeed some part regards what I think is properly
called the sublime. – However, the bulk of the performance relates more to
the perfection of writing in general, than to any particular kind or species.

As every different manner of writing has its peculiar character, it must
likewise have its different principles, and to treat of them separately must
undoubtedly be the clearer method. Besides, Longinus has entirely passed
over the inquiry of what the sublime is, as a thing perfectly well known, and
is principally intent upon giving rules to arrive at the elevated turn and manner. That the sublime no sooner presents itself than we are affected by it, I
readily acknowledge; but that we generally form accurate and distinct ideas
upon this subject, is by no means true; and although in itself perfectly distinct
from either the pathetic, or figurative manner, yet it is often confounded with
both. The genuine work therefore of criticism is to define the limits of each
kind of writing, and to prescribe their proper distinctions. Without this there
can be no legitimate performance, which is the just conformity to the laws or
rules of that manner of writing in which the piece is designed. But the manner
must be defined before the rules can be established; and we must know, for
example, what history is before we can know how it differs from novel and
romance, and before we can judge how it ought to be conducted.

Hence it seems, that rules for the sublime should most naturally result from an inquiry what the sublime is; and if this is an inquiry which Longinus has intirely passed over, there is still room for further speculation. But as the sublime in writing is no more than a description of the sublime in nature, and as it were painting to the imagination what nature herself offers to the senses, I shall begin with an inquiry into the sublime of natural objects, which I shall afterwards apply to writing.

Few are so insensible, as not to be struck even at first view with what is truly sublime; and every person upon seeing a grand object is affected with something which as it were extends his very being, and expands it to a kind of immensity. Thus in viewing the heavens, how is the soul elevated; and stretching itself to larger scenes and more extended prospects, in a noble enthusiasm of grandeur quits the narrow earth, darts from planet to planet, and takes in worlds at one view! Hence comes the name of sublime to every thing which thus raises the mind to fits of greatness, and disposes it to soar above her mother earth; hence arises that exultation and pride which the mind ever feels from the consciousness of its own vastness – that object can only be justly called the sublime, which in some degree disposes the mind to this enlargement of itself, and gives her a lofty conception of her own powers.

This exalted sensation, then, will always determine us to a right judgment; for wherever we feel the elevated disposition, there we are sure the sublime must be. But notwithstanding we acknowledge its presence, we are frequently ignorant what it is in objects which constitutes the grand, and gives them this power of expanding the mind. We often confess the sublime as we do the deity; it fills and dilates our soul without being able to penetrate into its nature, and define its essence. Yet however true this may be in many instances, a diligent inquiry may overcome the difficulty; and from an examination of particulars, as shall enable us universally to define the sublime of every natural object.

We know by experience, that nothing produces this elevation equal to large prospects, vast extended views, mountains, the heavens, and an immense ocean – but what in these objects affects us? for we can view, without being the least exalted, a little brook, although as smooth a surface, nay, clearer stream than the Nile or Danube; but can we behold these vast rivers, or rather, the vaster ocean, without feeling an elevated pleasure? A flowery vale, or the verdure of a hill, may charm; but to fill the soul, and raise it to the sublime sensations, the earth must rise into an Alp, or Pyrrhenean, and mountains piled upon mountains, reach to the very heavens – may not also the clearness of the sky, and its agreeable azure, be viewed through a crevice without the least admiration? But when a flood of light bursts in, and the vast heavens are on every side widely extended to the eye, it is then the soul enlarges, and would stretch herself out to the immense expanse. Is it not, therefore, the vastness of these objects which elevates us, and shall we not by looking a little narrowly into the mind be convinced that large objects only are fitted to raise this exaltedness?

The soul naturally supposes herself present to all the objects she perceives, and has lower or higher conceptions of her own excellency, as this extensiveness of her being is more or less limited. An universal presence is one of the sublime attributes of the deity; then how much greater an existence must the soul imagine herself, when contemplating the heavens she takes in the mighty orbs of the planets, and is present to a universe, than when shrunk into the narrow space of a room, and how much nearer advancing to the perfections of the universal presence? – This extending her being, raises in her a noble pride, and upon such occasions no wonder she conceives (as Longinus observes) something greater of herself. But as a consciousness of her own vastness is what pleases, so nothing can raise this consciousness but a vastness in the objects about which she is employed – for whatever the essence of the soul may be, it is the reflections arising from sensations only which makes her acquainted with herself, and know her faculties. Vast objects occasion vast sensations, and vast sensations give the mind a higher idea of her own powers – small scenes (except from association, which I shall hereafter consider) have never this effect; the beauty of them may please, and the variety be agreeable, but the soul is never filled by them.

Section II

Thus far, Palemon, we have proceeded in a kind of investigation; we have first inquired what disposition of mind was created by grand objects, the sublime of nature; this we found to be an effort of the soul to extend its being, and hence an exultation, from a consciousness of its own vastness: we then in particular and confessed instances examined what it was in objects raised this disposition, which we afterwards found to be their magnitude, and this likewise in a more universal manner from the very nature of our minds.

Yet notwithstanding we have demonstrated that the vastness of the object constitutes the sublime, to render the sublime perfect, two things are requisite; a certain degree of uniformity, and that by long custom the objects do not become familiar to the imagination.

From reason, as well as from experience, we may be convinced how requisite uniformity is; for when the object is uniform, by seeing part, the least glimpse gives a full and complete idea of the whole, and thus at once may be distinctly conveyed the vastest sensation. On the contrary, where this uniformity is wanting, the mind must run from object to object, and never get a full and complete prospect. Thus instead of having one large and grand idea, a thousand little ones are shuffled in. Here the magnitude of the scene is entirely broke, and consequently the noble pride and sublime sensation destroyed – for what a different conception must the soul have of herself, when with the greatest facility she can view the greatest objects, and when with pain she must hurry from part to part, and with difficulty acquire even an incomplete view? But as uniformity contributes much to the mind's receiving a grand idea of the object itself, so likewise does it greatly flatter that conscious pride I have already mentioned. Where an object is vast, and at the same time uniform, there is to the imagination no limits of its vastness, and the mind runs out into infinity, continually creating as it were from the pattern. Thus when the eye loses the vast ocean, the imagination having nothing to arrest it, catches up the scene and extends the prospect to immensity, which it could by no means do, were the uniform surface broke by innumerable little islands scattered up and down, and the mind thus led into the consideration of the various parts; for this adverting to dissimilar parts ever destroys the creative power of the imagination. However beautiful the hemisphere may be when curled over with little silver-tinged clouds, and the blue sky every where breaking through, yet the prospect is not near so grand as when in a vast and uniform heaven there is nothing to stop the eye, or limit the imagination. You will here, Palemon, object the evening heavens diversified by numberless stars, than which I grant nothing can be more sublime; but I believe your acuteness will no sooner start than resolve the difficulty. We who have considered the fixed stars as so many suns, the centres of systems, and know the planets, like our earth, move in vast orbits, how must our imagination, stretching to myriads of worlds, measure an immense space between each revolving planet? It will not be here improper to observe, that a solemn sedateness generally attends a sublime turn; for although the pathetic may be often joined with it, yet of itself the sublime rather composes, than agitates the mind; which being filled with one large, simple, and uniform idea, becomes (if I may use the expression) one simple, grand sensation.

Uncommonness, though it does not constitute the sublime of natural objects, very much heightens its effect upon the mind: for as great part of the elevation raised by vast and grand prospects, is owing to the mind's finding herself in the exercise of more enlarged powers, and hence judging higher of herself, custom makes this familiar, and she no longer admires her own perfection. It is here, as in all other things, variety is wanting; and indeed could there be a continual shifting of scenes, something of the admiration might be kept up, and even of that opinion the soul conceives of herself. But we are in a world too limited for such a change of prospects; a large mountain, the ocean, a rainbow, the heavens, and some few more of the like kind, yield all the variety we can here enjoy. The grandeur of the heavens seldoms affects us, it is our daily object, and two or three days at sea would sink all that elevated pleasure we feel upon viewing a vast ocean; yet, upon particular occasions, both the one and the other of these objects will raise the mind, how much soever accustomed to them – and this is when by any circumstance the imagination is set to work, and by its creative power the object is rendered new. – Thus in a clear evening heaven, each star awakens the imagination to new creation, and the whole firmament is extended out into systems of worlds; nay, perhaps, it is even true, that wherever the mind adverts to the vastness of the object, there she always feels the sublime sensation; but from long custom the object being made familiar, although before her, she does not advert to it – as kings themselves forget their dignity, till roused by the ensigns of power, they re-assume their grandeur. Admiration, a passion always attending the sublime, arises from uncommonness, and constantly decays as the object becomes more and more familiar.

An attempt to determine the greatness requisite to constitute the sublime of objects, would be vain and fruitless; upon the other hand, there is no affirming, that an object, although truly grand, will equally affect all minds; some are naturally fitted to consider things in the most enlarged views; others as naturally dissect great objects themselves, and by a diminutive genius render what is truly magnificent, little, and mean; for no object is so grand, but is attended with some trifling circumstance, upon which a little mind will surely fix; the universe has its cockle-shells, and its butterflies, the ardent pursuits of childish geniuses. Not that even great minds do not sometimes unbend, and amuse themselves with baubles; nay, they are not at all times equally fitted to receive sublime impressions; for when the soul flags and is depressed, the vastest object is incapable of raising her. But at other times, when the blood moves brisk, the pulse beats high, and the soul has lofty conceptions of herself, she sublimes every thing about her, or to speak more truly, snatches herself away from the minute of things, and throws herself into grand prospects, and the magnificence of nature.

From all this it is evident how different are the degrees of greatness, fitted to raise this passion: first, the Nile within his banks; then when he swelling overflows them, and widely extends himself over the whole country; but above all, when the eye loses itself in the immense ocean, or the imagination in infinite space and the unbounded system of things.

Section III

These, then, are the general principles, nor am I aware how many objections will be made against them. Is there not a sublime in painting, in music, in architecture, but above all, in virtue? – Yet are there large objects, or is there anything immense in Prodicus's Hercules, whose judgment or resolution is universally allowed noble and sublime? – Here we must own the difficult part of our task begins; yet if the principles we have laid down be applied even to such things as seemingly contradict them, it will be no small confirmation of their soundness and truth. We shall therefore consider the sublime of the passions, the sublime of science, and of the arts, such as architecture, music, and painting, and the sublime of such objects as arise merely from association.

In searching into the sublime of the passions, it is not my intent to re-examine the disposition we feel upon viewing the grand and magnificent; but to inquire into those affections, which when they appear in another, are ever deemed great, and affect the person who contemplates them with an elevated turn of mind. For the sublime of the passions must influence the mind in the same manner as the sublime of natural objects, and must produce the same exaltedness of disposition. – Were not their effect upon the mind, the same exaltedness of disposition; – they would with impropriety, bear the same name, and could by no means be the subject of this inquiry.

Although names are at first arbitrarily imposed, yet things of like nature ought ever to be classed under like appellations; and nothing brings greater confusion into knowledge than giving like names to things of unlike nature. Language abounds with too many inaccuracies of this kind, and hence arises the vast difficulty in adjusting and defining the proper limits to many things. Beauty attributed to ten thousand dissimilar objects has never yet, nor ever can be universally defined; for definition is the selecting of such common properties in objects as ever exist with the objects, and constitute their very nature, and thus regards a class, or arrangement of things similar, under the same head or appellation. Mathematicians, when they define a circle, disregarding the greatness or smallness, pitch upon a common property peculiar to the figure, by which they define and reduce all figures with this property under the same head. But if many things of different nature go by the same name, no one definition can be applicable to them. Beauty, indeed, when applied to figure and proportion, may be and has been defined, because here it regards a class. Thus when we call regular figures beautiful, and irregular ones deformed, we find the common property of uniformity amidst variety constitutes the beauty of the first, and the want of this uniformness, the ugliness or deformity of the latter.

But not to digress too far. It is equally incumbent upon the philosopher and critic to prevent names from being confounded, and to refer each thing to its proper class, if such there be; therefore when I treat of the sublime, I treat of a certain order of things, which from a similitude either in themselves, or their effects, are arranged under one head, and constitute a class, or species. And let the name of sublime be ever so frequently applied to a thing, yet if it bears no relation to this class, either in itself, or its effect, it is falsely so called, and is not the business of this present inquiry. I have been the more particular, Palemon, upon this point, because I know how often the word sublime is improperly used.

Such affections, then, or passions, as produce in the person who contemplates them an exalted and sublime disposition, can alone with propriety be called sublime: but affections which are only felt by him in whose breast they are, can never be the immediate object of another's knowledge; and when we contemplate passions out of ourselves, we know them only at a kind of second hand. But as no affection can subsist without its proper object, the cause or motive of the affections; we must argue from the cause to the effect, and judge and determine of the passion merely from a consideration of its object – what one person, in whose breast they are, knows immediately and by sensation, another can only know mediately and by induction; and therefore in considering the sublime of the passions, their objects only can be the proper subject for examination, the objects alone being really what affects the person who would contemplate the passions – and thus we judge of the courage of a person, by his steadiness in braving dangers; of his piety, by the just adoration he pays to the supreme being; and of his humanity, by his deportment to his fellow-creatures. He himself can only know the affection as it exists in his own breast.

Now, if the objects of such passions as are universally allowed sublime, be themselves vast and extended, the principles I have already laid down will be as equally applicable to the sublime of the passions, as to the sublime of inanimate objects; and we shall find that loftiness of mind, and elevated turn, which we feel upon contemplating any of these affections, to arise from the imagination being immediately thrown into large prospects, and extended scenes of action.

The affections unexceptionably sublime, as heroism, or desire of conquest, such as in an Alexander or a Cæsar; love of one's country; of mankind in general, or universal benevolence; a desire of fame and immortality: nor has the contempt of death, power, or of honour, a less title to be numbered amongst the sublime affections.

Heroism, or pursuit of conquest, generally arises either from a desire of power, or passion for fame; or from both. Power and fame, therefore, are objects of this affection, which let us separately consider.

It is not every power which is the ambition of a hero, nor every power which carries the idea of sublime. A Caligula commanding armies to fill their helmets with cockle-shells, is a power mean and contemptible, although ever so absolute; but suppose an Alexander laying level towns, depopulating countries, and ravaging the whole world, how does the sublime rise, nay although mankind be the sacrifice to his ambition! The same may be said of power when it regards strength; for the greatest strength, even that of the giants or terræ filii, if only employed in grinding the hardest adamant to powder, or in reducing the solidest gold to dust, has nothing sublime or grand – but consider them in their fabulous history rooting up mountains and piling Ossa upon Olympus, then is their strength attended with the sublime. Thus our idea of power is more or less sublime, as the power itself is more or less extended. The absolute authority of a master over his slaves, is a power nothing grand; yet the same authority in a prince is sublime. – But why? from his sway extending to multitudes, and from nations bowing to his commands. But it is in the almighty that this sublime is completed, who with a nod can shatter to pieces the foundation of a universe, as with a word he called it into being.

I cannot here pass over (although more properly belonging to the sublime of writing) the passage in Moses. – *"God said, let there be light, and there was light."* The sublime of this passage consists in the idea it gives us of the power of the almighty; but his power with regard to what? a vastly diffused being, unlimited as his own essence – and hence the idea becomes so exalted. *Let there be Earth, and there was Earth*, surely would come infinitely short of the other, as the object or power presents itself to us infinitely more limited. From all this, I think I may fairly conclude, that the sublime of power is from its object being vast and immense.

I need say little upon the head of fame. To be praised not only by the present generation, but through the revolving circle of ages down to latest posterity, is stretching our expectations and our ideas to an immensity; and from this the sublime of the passion itself arises; for although the approbation of a worthy man ought to bear more weight than the undistinguishing applause of thousands, yet the desire of such a single approbation, however virtuous, has nothing great or sublime in it. Thus, if it be true of any one passion, that the vastness of its object constitutes the sublime, it is most strictly so of this; and whatever is the motive of heroism, whether the desire of power, or of fame, or of both, the sublime of the affection is the greatness of its object.

As to the love of our country, or rather universal benevolence, which like the sun every where diffuses itself, who can have any idea of it, without taking into his view large societies, numberless nations, all mankind reaching from pole to pole, from the rising to the setting sun? and this is the sublime of benevolence, extending itself to the remotest of humankind. But how would the sublime sink, if in this large scene the imagination should fix upon a narrow object, a child, a parent, or a mistress! Indeed, love to any of the individuals, nay to all of them, when considered as individuals, and one by one, has nothing of exalted; it is when we love them collectively, when we love them in vast bodies stretching over large countries, that we feel the sublime rise.

The affection of a parent to a child, although more intense, perhaps, than any other, yet has nothing great in it; nay, I will venture to affirm, not even friendship itself, without it be accidental; as all the passions, by apt connection may exist with the sublime.

Thus when friendship prompts a man to sacrifice honours, wealth, and power, to despise the greatness of the world and brave death, it then becomes truly great; nor need I, Palemon, cloy you with the repeated reasons.

Hence the object of the passion only, not the intenseness of it, renders it great and noble; and hence a contempt of riches, of honours, power, and empire, may be justly reckoned amongst the grand affections. But perhaps it may be asked, how the contempt of that can be great, the desire of which I have already allowed so; or if it be true, that the contempt is great, how can I reconcile my former assertion to what Longinus affirms; to wit, – nothing is great – as riches, dignities, honours, and empire.

Section IV

Here, Palemon, I must observe that the sublime, and virtue, are quite different things; the decorum of actions, distinct from the exalted. Honours, dignities, and empire, in their own nature partake nothing of virtue; but that they do of the grand, I think I have plainly shown. Now in a moral sense it is certainly true, if in any circumstance the contempt of these things is great (by which Longinus can surely mean no more than becoming or virtuous,) in the same circumstance the desire of them can never be great; but if he understands the word great in its true and genuine sense, I cannot see why the desire, as well as the contempt of them may not be truly grand: for as the object is the same in both cases, and as it is the object which renders the affection sublime, in both cases there must be a sublime. And the passion of Cæsar to conquest and empire, is no less sublime, than the stoic apathy of the philosopher (if such there ever was, or ever shall be), who should reject them; although we might allow in the latter a more virtuous and laudable affection.

When virtue is at any time sublime, it is not that she is the same as the sublime, but that she associates with it, and from this association each acquires new charms: virtue becomes more commanding, the sublime more engaging. When Hercules rejecting the proffered luxury of palaces, and pomp of courts, prefers virtue, traverses the earth in pursuit of honour, and thinks the whole world scene little enough of action, how does the virtuous greatness of his soul charm and strike us with a sublime admiration! Had he only preferred an honest retirement to rosy garlands, banquet, song, and dance, the enticements of the alluring goddess, where would have been the sublime? Indeed his resolution would have been even then still virtuous.

A just order of affections, where no one desire, by a dissonance and jarring with the rest, breaks the harmony of the passions, is what constitutes the beauty and becomingness of character; and if virtue be the pursuit of our greatest happiness in the good of society, this becomingness is virtue herself: for proportioned affections render us most happy in ourselves, and most beneficial to mankind; and a virtuous passion or appetite is such as the satisfying of it neither necessarily produces disturbance in the affections, nor disorder in society. – I say, necessarily; – for often by accident the most virtuous affection is attended with bad consequences; but this is not equally true of the sublime passions – desire of fame, honours, or empire, often creates the greatest tumult in the affections, and the greatest mischief to mankind.

Thus most of the sublime passions, when virtuous, are so by association and accident; and although the indications of elevated souls, yet are not always virtuous. The hero who insults mankind, and ravages the earth merely for power and fame, is but an immense monster, and as such only ought to be gazed at; he may indeed, by a mild use of conquest, gild over the cruelty of his actions, but can never render them solidly good – yet such is the force of the sublime, that even these men, who in one light can be esteemed no other than the butchers of human race, yet when considered as braving dangers, conquering kingdoms, and spreading the terror of their name to the most distant nations, tower over the rest of mankind, and become almost the objects of worship. But there is a sublime which is always virtuous, and where the virtue as well as sublime increases with the object; I mean that of love; first to the particular community whereof we are members; then to our native country; to mankind in general; and last to the universal genius. When once the soul can be raised to this noble enthusiasm, and can make an infinitely great being the object of her love, and as it were take him into her affections, it is then she feels the greatest sublime possible, and conceives something infinitely grand of herself; honours, dignity, and empire are objects truly little and mean to a mind thus united with divinity.

Contempt of death is neither always virtuous, nor always sublime; the wretch who, intoxicated with liquor, braves death at a gallows, shows neither a virtuous nor a great soul; but a Cato, who will not barter the real dignity of character for all the false honours a cajoling Cæsar can heap upon him, and who in cool deliberation, rather than drag a life in the slavery of vile submission, and mean adulation, chooses to die with liberty and his country, evinces, in the action, the grandeur and virtue of a Roman soul. In these circumstances, the contempt of death is both laudable and sublime; the fear of it, mean and despicable. Cato, in giving up life, had in view immortality and everlasting liberty, the sublime enjoyment of the almighty; whilst the orator, who barely courted life in mean flatteries to a tyrant, had in prospect nothing but the contracted space of a few years spent in abject slavery: and yet this, perhaps, was more pardonable in the orator than it would have been in the patriot. For besides the beauty of virtue in general, there is likewise a decorum or becomingness belonging to character. – The easy manners of an Atticus can allow many things which would be deformed in the inflexible virtue of a Cato. The good-natured Atticus had the humaneness, not the dignity of character to support; roughness and cruelty would have defaced and deformed his character, not compliance and submission. But for the rigid Roman to have lived quietly under tyranny, would have been such a breach of character, such a depravity in his manners, that he must have preferred a thousand deaths before it. – For to see the stubborn oak bow to every blast, is unnatural, however agreeable it may be to see the yielding corn wave to the breeze.

I think now, Palemon, I have considered most, if not all the sublime passions, and have shewn that the greatness of the object makes the sublime of the affections. This we shall find true, should we yet in another manner render the passions the objects of our scenes. Allegory has already clothed most of them in human form, and should we attempt in the ancient way of fable to draw the sublime affections or their objects in emblematical portraitures, what a giant would heroism appear! Liberty, perhaps, like the deity, is too vast a being to be circumscribed by form; but fame has been already pictured to us, and pictured as a being of immense greatness: – *ingrediturq; solo, et caput inter nubila condit.* – Nor does power deserve a less size: but how would benevolence, spreading out her downy wings wide as the arched heavens, kindly brood over the world! In short, if we do these passions justice, we ought to paint them in all the grandeur and majesty Homer does his Neptune under whose vast strides, forests and mountains trembled.

Before I conclude this subject, I must observe, that all the passions of the human mind may exist each with the other, and hence it frequently happens that the sublime affections are blended with those of a quite contrary nature. There ever enters in the description of storms (as I have already observed) some small degree of dread, and this dread may be so heightened (when a person is actually in one) as entirely to destroy the sublime. By this means an object in itself grand may by association lose most if not all its effect. Yet, Palemon, it seems strange that a being so simple, so much one as the mind, should at the same time feel joy and grief, pleasure and pain, in short, be the subject of contradictions; or can it be true that the mind can feel pleasure and pain at the same instant? or rather, do not they succeed each other by such infinitely quick vicissitudes, as to appear instantaneous; as a lighted globe, moving in quick revolutions, seems one continued circle of fire? – But which ever way the mind perceives, it is certain to common observation, the most different passions and sensations possess the mind at the same time. The prick of a pin will give pain, while the most delicious food is flattering the palate, or the highest perfumes the smell. The sublime dilates and elevates the soul, fear sinks and contracts it; yet both are felt upon viewing what is great and awful. And we cannot conceive a deity armed with thunder without being struck with a sublime terror; but if we regard him as the infinite source of happiness, the benign dispenser of benefits, it is not then the dreadful, but the joyous sublime we feel. From these associations there arises different kinds of sublime, where yet the sublime is the predominant; and from these associations, likewise, results a greater beauty to it. – The fine blue of the heavens yields a more delightfully sublime prospect, than had they been of dusky obscure colour. These connections, however, often occasion not only a confusion of terms, but even of ideas; nor indeed is it always so easy to separate our sensations. The grand may be so blended with the pathetic and warm, in the description of battles, as difficultly to be divided, and consequently the complex sensation from thence as difficultly resolved. By this means the pathetic is often mistaken for the sublime; but whoever considers the different nature of the two, will upon all occasions easily distinguish them.

The sublime, when it exists simple and unmixed, by filling the mind with one vast and uniform idea, affects it with a solemn sedateness; by this means the soul itself becomes, as it were, one simple grand sensation. Thus the sublime not hurrying us from object to object, rather composes than agitates, whilst the very essence of the pathetic consists in an agitation of the passions, which is ever effected by crowding into the thoughts a thousand different objects, and hurrying the mind into various scenes.

Section V

Before I proceed to examine the sublime in arts and sciences, it will not perhaps be entirely useless to observe, that objects in general delight from two sources; either because naturally fitted to please, from a certain harmony and disposition of their parts, or because long associated with objects really agreeable; and thus, although in themselves there be nothing at first delightful, they at last become so. Perhaps of this kind of association the fondness which a lover conceives even to the imperfections of his mistress, may not be the worst instance; a cast of the eye, a lisp, or any other little blemish, shall by a fond lover quickly be deified into a beauty, and receive more adoration than the real beautiful and charming.

Hence we see the powerful force of connection. Nor does this only happen in the whimsical imagination of a fond lover; the gravest philosophers also owe great part of their pleasure to this stealing of beauty from one object to deck and adorn another: for by daily experience we know, when certain pleasures have been raised in the mind by certain objects, from an association of this kind, the very same pleasure shall be raised, although the objects themselves which first occasioned them are not so much as painted in the imagination; and it is from this source that the beauty and delight of metaphor flows. Who ever thought of the rosy blush of his mistress, without feeling something like that agreeable sensation which the rose itself excites, not only by its colour, but even by its fragrance?

But to return to our present purpose; we may hence perceive, that objects which in themselves are not great and immense, if long connected with such will often produce an exaltedness of mind; and this seems partly to be the case in architecture. The face of a fine building shall give a greater loftiness to the soul, than an object vastly more extended; neither indeed does the size of any building seem to rise to that largeness as constitutes the sublime: whence, therefore, is it, that it raises this passion? – One of the reasons certainly is, we have always found such buildings connected with great riches, power, and grandeur; and though the mind may not reflect on these connections, yet from what I before mentioned, the passion occasioned by these things may exist in the mind without the idea of the things themselves. Should the buildings be perfectly plain, without any manner of ornaments, though vastly large, as those in Edinburgh, they would not at all elevate the soul, for in these buildings we have found no necessary connection with power and grandeur. But besides this, with columns there is always connected the imagination of strength and durableness; and these working together, may very well give a sublimity to the mind. However, I am apt to think, we sometimes imagine a greater sublime in objects than what there really is. Thus in a fine building, the proportion of the parts, their aptitude, and a thousand other circumstances, which form the beauty of the structure, afford a refined delight, much different from the exalted disposition already mentioned; and may not two or three different pleasures existing in the mind at the same time by a kind of reverberating on each other, increase the intentness of each, as a parcel of diamonds, when artfully set, by a reciprocal reflection of their rays, strike the eye with redoubled lustre? What, indeed, is poetry, but the art of throwing a number of agreeable images together, whence each of them yields a greater delight than they possibly could separately. – There might be something likewise said from the variety of the parts, and yet so uniform as not to distract the imagination. – If a great crowd of ideas can be distinctly conveyed into a small portion of the mind, something of the pride of the sublime will be raised in her; for if she can take in so great a variety, and yet have room for so much more, she certainly must feel something exalted. That the uniformity does contribute to give this turn of mind, is plain by observing those buildings which abound in little and trifling ornaments, where every thing is broken into miniature – Here, though the bulk of the building be vastly large, no very great ideas are conveyed.

The sublime of painting consists mostly in finely representing the sublime of the passions, such as the Tablature of Hercules; and what a greatness of mind he shows in Hercules! – Behold what large scenes of action virtue points out to him in choosing them! The indolence of pleasure affords no such vast prospects – the whole world was a scene little enough for his enlarged soul. Landscape painting may likewise partake of the sublime; such as representing mountains, &c. which shows how little objects by an apt connection may affect us with this passion: for the space of a yard of canvas, by only representing the figure and colour of a mountain, shall fill the mind with nearly as great an idea as the mountain itself.

I know so little of music, that I will not pretend to determine the sublime of it. This I know; – all grave sounds, where the notes are long, exalt my mind much more than any other kind; and that wind instruments are the most fitted to elevate; such as the hautboy, the trumpet, and organ: – for, as Pope has it,

> In more lengthen'd Notes and flow,
> Deep, majestic, solemn Organs blow.

In all acute sounds, the vibrations are short and quick; on the contrary, in the grave. And may not long sounds be to the ear what extended prospects are to the eye? Here also connection takes great place; the most fantastic jig of a bagpipe shall elevate a highlander more than the most solemn music; for to such they have been ever accustomed even in their martial engagements.

Whatever outward appearance the sublime of the mind assumes, that appearance likewise acquires a name similar to that turn of soul, as lofty, majestic, &c. and indeed whatever conveys to us the imagination of such a disposition in another, affects us also with the like passion. For example; a grave and sedate gesture, especially in princes, we call majestic and noble; and it even gives a small degree of loftiness to the spectator himself: for, as I before hinted, the true sublime of the mind is grave and composed, which in gesture can only be expressed by a grave and composed gate. Should a prince frisk about in short and quick motions, it would take away very much from the imagination of his possessing a great and elevated soul. And this also may be something the case in music; it being inconsistent with a sedate mind to run through all the quick notes and short turns of a jig. Although after all, I believe the pathetic in music is frequently taken for the sublime; and not only here, but even in other cases. Nor, indeed, is it always so easy to separate our sensations: the grand may be so blended with the pathetic and warm, (*viz.* in the description of a battle) as difficultly to be divided, and consequently the complex sensation arising from thence as difficultly resolved. Hence not only comes a confusion of terms, but even of ideas. With a great storm, when the swelling waves rise in mountains to the skies, and the black clouds thicken from all quarters of the heavens, there is always joined the apprehension of danger, which puts the passions into a hurry: here the complex sensation is generally esteemed the sublime; but from what I have already said it will appear, that the vastness only of the objects produces it, by no means the agitation of the passions, which, if nicely considered, has rather fear than the sublime for its cause. After this manner the sublime may be connected with any one passion, and from such connections different kinds of sublime will arise; I mean in a lax way of speaking; and indeed, from the different ways of blending it in objects, our pleasure may be greatly encreased. Thus, the fine blue of the heavens makes the sublime itself yield a greater delight, and for the reason I before hinted.

Had I time, I would consider something of the sublime in sciences. But I shall only observe, that in mathematics it is the universal theorems, and the vast similarity in the properties of infinite curves. And in studying the sciences, it is the mark of a truly great mind not to dwell on the minutiæ of things, but rather to consider their universal relations: studies which seem dry, become exalted and agreeable, by such a management.

I shall end with this one remark, that the eyes and ears are the only inlets to the sublime. Taste, smell, nor touch convey nothing that is great and exalted; and this may be some farther confirmation that large objects only constitute the sublime.

18

David Hartley,
from *Observations on man* (1749)

Part First. Chapter IV. Of the six classes of intellectual pleasures and pains.
Section I
Of the Pleasures and Pains of Imagination

I begin with the pleasures and pains of imagination; and shall endeavour to derive each species of them by association, either from those of sensation, ambition, self-interest, sympathy, theopathy, and the moral sense, or from foreign ones of imagination. They may be distinguished into the seven kinds that follow.

First, the pleasures arising from the beauty of the natural world.
Secondly, those from the works of art.
Thirdly, from the liberal arts of music, painting, and poetry.
Fourthly, from the sciences.
Fifthly, from the beauty of the person.
Sixthly, from wit and humour.
Seventhly, the pains which arise from gross absurdity, inconsistency, or deformity.

Prop. 94.

To examine how the just-mentioned pleasures and pains of imagination are agreeable to the doctrine of association

Of the pleasures arising from the beauty of the natural world

The pleasures arising from the contemplation of the beauties of the natural world seem to admit of the following analysis.

The pleasant tastes, and smells, and the fine colours of fruits and flowers, the melody of birds, and the grateful warmth or coolness of the air, in the proper seasons, transfer miniatures of these pleasures upon rural scenes, which start up instantaneously so mixed with each other, and with such as will be immediately enumerated, as to be separately indiscernible.

If there be a precipice, a cataract, a mountain of snow, &c. in one part of the scene, the nascent ideas of fear and horror may magnify and enliven all the other ideas, and by degrees pass into pleasures, by suggesting the security from pain.

101

In like manner the grandeur of some scenes, and the novelty of others, by exciting surprise and wonder, i.e. by making a great difference in the preceding and subsequent states of mind, so as to border upon, or even enter the limits of pain, may greatly enhance the pleasure.

Uniformity and variety in conjunction are also principal sources of the pleasures of beauty, being made so partly by their association with the beauties of nature; partly by that with the works of art; and with the many conveniences which we receive from the uniformity and variety of the works of nature and art. They must therefore transfer part of the lustre borrowed from the works of art, and from the head of convenience, upon the works of nature.

Poetry and painting are much employed in setting forth the beauties of the natural world, at the same time that they afford us a high degree of pleasure from many other sources. Hence the beauties of nature delight poets and painters, and such as are addicted to the study of their works, more than others. Part of this effect is indeed owing to the greater attention of such persons to the other sources; but this comes to the same thing, as far as the general theory of the factitious, associated nature of these pleasures is concerned.

The many sports and pastimes, which are peculiar to the country, and whose ideas and pleasures are revived by the view of rural scenes, in an evanescent state, and so mixed together as to be separately indiscernible, do farther augment the pleasures suggested by the beauties of nature.

To these we may add, the opposition between the offensiveness, dangers, and corruption of populous cities, and the health, tranquillity, and innocence, which the actual view, or the mental contemplation, of rural scenes introduces; also the pleasures of sociality and mirth, which are often found in the greatest perfection in country retirements, the amorous pleasures, which have many connections with rural scenes, and those which the opinions and encomiums of others beget in us, in this, as in other cases, by means of the contagiousness observable in mental dispositions, as well as bodily ones.

Those persons who have already formed high ideas of the power, knowledge, and goodness, of the author of nature, with suitable affections, generally feel the exalted pleasures of devotion upon every view and contemplation of his works, either in an explicit and distinct manner, or in a more secret and implicit one. Hence, part of the general indeterminate pleasures, here considered, is deducible from the pleasures of theopathy.

We must not omit in this place to remind the reader of a remark made above; *viz.* that green, which is the middle colour of the seven primary ones, and consequently the most agreeable to the organ of sight, is also the general colour of the vegetable kingdom, *i.e.* of external nature.

These may be considered as some of the principal sources of the beauties of nature to mankind in general. Inquisitive and philosophical persons have some others, arising from their peculiar knowledge and study of natural history, astronomy, and philosophy, in general. For the profusion of beauties, uses, fitnesses, elegance in minute things, and magnificence in great ones, exceed all bounds of conception, surprise, and astonishment; new scenes, and those of unbounded extent, separately considered, ever presenting themselves to view, the more any one studies and contemplates the Works of God.

And, upon the whole, the reader may see, that there are sufficient sources for all those pleasures of imagination, which the beauties of nature excite in different persons; and that the differences which are found in different persons in this respect, are sufficiently analogous to the differences of their situations in life, and of the consequent associations formed in them.

An attentive person may also, in viewing or contemplating the beauties of nature, lay hold, as it were, of the remainders and miniatures of many of the particular pleasures here enumerated, while they recur in a separate state, and before they coalesce with the general indeterminate aggregate, and thus verify the history now proposed.

It is a confirmation of this history, that an attentive person may also observe great differences in the kind and degree of the relish which he has for the beauties of nature in different periods of his life; especially as the kind and degree may be found to agree in the main with this history.

To the same purpose we may remark, that these pleasures do not cloy very soon, but are of a lasting nature, if compared with the sensible ones; since this follows naturally from the great variety of their sources, and the evanescent nature of their constituent parts.

When a beautiful scene is first presented, there is generally great pleasure from surprise, from being struck with objects and circumstances which we did not expect. This presently declines; but is abundantly compensated afterwards by the gradual alternate exaltation of the several constituent parts of the complex pleasures, which also do probably enhance one another. And thus we may take several reviews of the same scene, before the pleasure, which it affords, comes to its *maximum*. After this the pleasure must decline, if we review it often: but if at considerable intervals, so as that many foreign states of mind intervene, also so as that new sources of the pleasures of this kind be broken up, the pleasure may recur for many successions of nearly the same magnitude.

The same observations hold in respect of the pleasures from the beauties of nature in general, and indeed from all the other sources, works of art, liberal arts, sciences, &c. These all strike and surprise the young mind at first, but require a considerable time before they come to their *maximum*; after which some or other will always be at its *maximum* for a considerable time. However, the pleasures of imagination in general, as well as each particular set and individual, must decline at last from the nature of our frame. In what manner they ought to decline, so as to be consistent with our *summum bonum*, by yielding, in due time, to more exalted and pure pleasures, whose composition they enter, I will endeavour to show hereafter.

These pleasures are a principal source of those which are annexed to the view of uniformity with variety, as above noted, *i.e.* of analogies of various orders; and consequently are a principal incitement to our tracing out real analogies, and forming artificial ones.

The novel, the grand, and the marvellous, are also most conspicuous in the works of nature; and the last strikes us particularly in many of the phænomena of nature, by seeming to exceed all bounds of credibility, at the same time that we are certified by irrefragable evidences of the truth of the facts. The satiety which every pleasure begets in us, after some continuance, makes us thirst perpetually after the grand and novel; and, as it were, grasp at infinity in number and extent; there being a kind of tacit expectation, that the pleasure will be in proportion to the magnitude and variety of the causes, in the same manner as we observe, in other cases, the effects to be in some degree proportional to their causes.

The pleasures of novelty decline not only in this class, but also in all the others sensible and intellectual, partly from our bodily frame, partly from the intermixture, and consequent association of neutral circumstances (such as afford neither pleasure nor pain) in their successive recurrences.

A disposition to a pleasurable state is a general attendant upon health, and the integrity of our bodily faculties; and that in such a degree, as that actual pleasure will spring up from moderate incitements, from the transient introduction of the associated circumstances of former pleasurable states. If the body be indisposed in some degree, it is, however, possible to force it into a state of pleasure by the vivid introduction of various and powerful circumstances; but this unnatural state cannot last long; and, if the indisposition to pleasure be great, it cannot be introduced at all. On the contrary, where the disposition to pleasure is preternaturally prevalent, as after wine and opium, and in certain morbid cases, the least hint will excite profuse joy, leaning chiefly to the pleasures of imagination, ambition, sympathy, or devotion, according to the circumstances.

It is easy to see how the doctrine of vibrations, which appears to be the only one that admits of permanent states of motion, and disposition to motion, in the brain, suits these last remarks in a peculiar manner.

Of the Beauties of the Works of Art

The works of art, which afford us the pleasures of beauty, are chiefly buildings, public and private, religious, civil, and military, with their appendages and ornaments, and machines of the several kinds, from the great ones employed in war, commerce, and public affairs, such as ships, military engines, machines for manufacturing metals, &c. down to clocks, watches, and domestic furniture. The survey of these things, when perfect in their kinds, affords great pleasures to the curious; and these pleasures increase for a certain time, by being cultivated and gratified, till at last they come to their height, decline, and give way to others, as has been already observed of the pleasures arising from the beauties of nature.

The chief sources of the pleasures, which the forementioned works of art afford, appear to be the following: the beautiful illuminations from gay colours; the resemblance which the playthings, that pleased us when we were children, bear to them; the great regularity and variety observable in them; the grandeur and magnificence of some, and the neatness and elegance of others, and that especially if they be small; the fitness to answer useful ends; their answering a multiplicity of these by simple means, or by analogous complex ones, not exceeding certain limits in complexness; the knowledge conveyed in many cases; the strong associations with religion, death, war, justice, power, riches, titles, high-birth, entertainments, mirth, &c.; fashion, with the opinions and encomiums of persons supposed to be judges; the vain desire of having a taste, and of being thought connoisseurs and judges, &c. &c.

In architecture there are certain proportions of breadths, lengths, depths, and entire magnitudes, to each other, which are by some supposed to be naturally beautiful, just as the simple ratios of 1 to 2, 2 to 3, 3 to 4, &c. in music, yield sounds, which are naturally pleasant to the ear. But it rather seems to me, that economical convenience first determined the ratios of doors, windows, pillars, &c. in a gross way; and then that the convenience of the artists fixed this determination to some few exact ratios, as in the proportion between the lengths and breadths of the pillars of the several orders. Afterwards these proportions became associated so often with a variety of beauties in costly buildings, that they could not but be thought naturally beautiful at all. In merely ornamental parts the beauty of the proportions seems to arise entirely from fashion, or from a supposed resemblance to something already fixed as a beautiful proportion. It is easy from these principles to account for the prevalency of different proportions, and general tastes, in different ages and countries.

19

Robert Lowth,
from *Lectures on the sacred poetry of the Hebrews* (1753/1787)

Lecture XIV
Of the sublime in general and of sublimity of expression in particular

...The word sublimity I wish in this place to be understood in its most extensive sense: I speak not merely of that sublimity, which exhibits great objects with a magnificent display of imagery and diction; but that force of composition, whatever it be, which strikes and overpowers the mind, which excites the passions, and which expresses ideas at once with perspicuity and elevation; not solicitous whether the language be plain or ornamented; refined or familiar: in this use of the word I copy Longinus, the most accomplished author on this subject, whether we consider his precepts or his example.

The sublime consists either in language or sentiment, or more frequently in an union of both, since they reciprocally assist each other, and since there is a necessary and indissoluble connection between them: this,

> Whose own example strengthens all his laws,
> And is himself the great sublime he draws.   Pope.

however, will not prevent our considering them apart with convenience and advantage. The first object, therefore, which presents itself for our investigation, is, upon what grounds the poetic diction of the Hebrews, whether considered in itself, or in comparison with prose composition, is deserving of an appellation immediately expressive of sublimity.

The poetry of every language has a style and form of expression peculiar to itself; forcible, magnificent, and sonorous; the words pompous and energetic; the composition singular and artificial; the whole form and complexion different from what we meet with in common life, and frequently (as with a noble indignation) breaking down the boundaries by which the popular dialect is confined. The language of reason is cool, temperate, rather humble than elevated, well arranged and perspicuous, with an evident care and anxiety lest any thing should escape which might appear perplexed or obscure. The language of the passions is totally different: the conceptions burst out in a turbid stream, expressive in a manner of the internal conflict; the more vehement break out in hasty confusion; they catch (without search or study) whatever is impetuous, vivid, or energetic. In a word, reason speaks literally, the passions

106

poetically. The mind, with whatever passion it be agitated, remains fixed upon the object that excited it; and while it is earnest to display it, is not satisfied with a plain and exact description; but adopts one agreeable to its own sensations, splendid or gloomy, jocund or unpleasant. For the passions are naturally inclined to amplification; they wonderfully magnify and exaggerate whatever dwells upon the mind, and labour to express it in animated, bold, and magnificent terms. This they commonly effect by two different methods; partly by illustrating the subject with splendid imagery, and partly by employing new and extraordinary forms of expression, which are indeed possessed of great force and efficacy in this respect especially, that they in some degree imitate or represent the present habit and state of the soul....

Lecture XVI
Of sublimity of sentiment

If we consider the very intimate connection, which on all occasions subsists between sentiment and language, it will perhaps appear, that the peculiar quality, of which we have just been treating, under the title of sublimity of expression, might ultimately be referred to that of sentiment. In the strictest sense, however, sublimity of sentiment may be accounted a distinct quality, and may be said to proceed, either from a certain elevation of mind, and a happy boldness of conception; or from a strong impulse of the soul, when agitated by the more violent affections. The one is called by Longinus *grandeur of conception*, the other *vehemence* or *enthusiasm of passion*. To each of these we must have recourse in the present disquisition, and in applying them to the sacred poets, I shall endeavour to detract nothing from the dignity of that inspiration, which proceeds from higher causes, while I allow to the genius of each writer his own peculiar excellence and accomplishments. I am indeed of opinion, that the divine spirit by no means takes such an entire possession of the mind of the prophet, as to subdue or extinguish the character and genius of the man: the natural powers of the mind are in general elevated and refined, they are neither eradicated nor totally obscured; and though the writings of Moses, of David, and of Isaiah, always bear the marks of a divine and celestial impulse, we may nevertheless plainly discover in them the particular characters of their respective authors.

That species of the sublime, which proceeds from a boldness of spirit, and an elevation of the soul, whether inherent in the author, or derived from a divine impulse and inspiration, is displayed first in the greatness and sublimity of the subject itself; secondly, in the choice of the adjuncts or circumstances (by the importance and magnitude of which a degree of force and elevation is added to the description); and lastly, in the splendour and magnificence of the imagery, by which the whole is illustrated. In all these the Hebrew writers have obtained an unrivalled pre-eminence. As far as respects the dignity and importance of the subject, they not only surpass all other writers, but even exceed the confines of human genius and intellect. The greatness, the power, the justice, the immensity of God; the infinite wisdom of his works and of his dispensations, are the subjects in which the Hebrew poetry is always conversant, and always excels. If we only consider with a common degree of candour how greatly inferior the poetry of all other nations appears, whenever it presumes to treat of these subjects; and how unequal to the dignity of the matter the highest conceptions of the human genius are found to be; we shall, I think, not only acknowledge the sublimity, but the divinity of that of the Hebrews. Nor does this greatness and elevation consist altogether in the subjects and sentiments, which however expressed, would yet retain some part at least of their native force and dignity, but the manner in which these lofty ideas are arranged, and the embellishments of description with which they abound, claim our warmest admiration: and this, whether we regard the adjuncts or circumstances, which are selected with so much judgment as uniformly to contribute to the sublimity of the principal subject; or the amplitude of that imagery, which represents objects the most remote from human apprehension in such enchanting colours, that, although debased by human painting, they still retain their genuine sanctity and excellence....

Lecture XVII
Of the sublime of passion

We have agreed with Longinus, that a violent agitation of the mind, or impetuosity of passion, constitutes another source of the sublime: he calls it "the vehemence and enthusiasm of passion." It will be proper, therefore, in the next place, to consider the nature of this enthusiasm; the principles on which the power of exciting or of imitating the passions in poetry may be supposed to depend; and what affinity subsists between passion and sublimity.

The language of poetry I have more than once described as the effect of mental emotion. Poetry itself is indebted for its origin, character, complexion, emphasis, and application, to the effects which are produced upon the mind and body, upon the imagination, the senses, the voice, and respiration by the agitation of passion. Every affection of the human soul, while it rages with violence, is a momentary frenzy. When therefore a poet is able by the force of genius, or rather of imagination, to conceive any emotion of the mind so perfectly as to transfer to his own feelings the instinctive passion of another, and, agreeably to the nature of the subject, to express it in all its vigour, such a one, according to a common mode of speaking, may be said to possess the true poetic enthusiasm, or, as the ancients would have expressed it "to be inspired, full of the God:" not however implying, that their ardour of mind was imparted by the gods, but that this ecstatic impulse became the God of the moment.

This species of enthusiasm I should distinguish by the term natural, were it not that I should seem to connect things which are really different, and repugnant to each other: the true and genuine enthusiasm, that which alone is deserving of the name, that I mean with which the sublimer poetry of the Hebrews, and particularly the prophetic, is animated, is certainly widely different in its nature, and boasts a much higher origin.

As poetry, however, derives its very existence from the more vehement emotions of the mind, so its greatest energy is displayed in the expression of them; and by exciting the passions it more effectually attains its end.

Poetry is said to consist in imitation: whatever the human mind is able to conceive, it is the province of poetry to imitate; things, places, appearances natural and artificial, actions, passions, manners and customs: and since the human intellect is naturally delighted with every species of imitation, that species in particular, which exhibits its own image, which displays and depicts those impulses, inflections, perturbations, and secret emotions, which it perceives and knows in itself, can scarcely fail to astonish and to delight above every other. The delicacy and difficulty of this kind of imitation are among its principal commendations; for to effect that which appears almost impossible naturally excites our admiration. The understanding slowly perceives the accuracy of the description in all other subjects, and their agreement to their archetypes, as being obliged to compare them by the aid and through the uncertain medium, as it were, of the memory: but when a passion is expressed, the object is clear and distinct at once; the mind is immediately conscious of itself and its own emotions; it feels and suffers in itself a sensation, either the same or similar to that which is described. Hence that sublimity, which arises from the vehement agitation of the passions, and the imitation of them, possesses a superior influence over the human mind; whatever is exhibited to it from without, may well be supposed to move and agitate it less than what it internally perceives, of the magnitude and force of which it is previously conscious.

And as the imitation or delineation of the passions is the most perfect production of poetry, so by exciting them it most completely effects its purpose. The intent of poetry is to profit while it entertains us; and the agitation of the passions, by the force of imagination, is in the highest degree both useful and pleasant.

This method of exciting the passions is in the first place useful, when properly and lawfully exercised; that is, when these passions are directed to their proper end, and rendered subservient to the dictates of nature and truth; when an aversion to evil, and a love of goodness is excited; and if the poet deviate on any occasion from this great end and aim, he is guilty of a most scandalous abuse and perversion of his art. For the passions and affections are the elements and principles of human action; they are all in themselves good, useful, and virtuous; and, when fairly and naturally employed, not only lead to useful ends and purposes, but actually prompt and stimulate to virtue. It is the office of poetry to incite, to direct, to temper the passions, and not to extinguish them. It professes to exercise, to amend, to discipline the affections:

it is this which is strictly meant by Aristotle, when he speaks of the *pruning of the passions*, though certain commentators have strangely perverted his meaning.

But this operation on the passions is also more immediately useful, because it is productive of pleasure. Every emotion of the mind, (not excepting even those which in themselves are allied to pain) when excited through the agency of the imitative arts, is ever accompanied with an exquisite sensation of pleasure. This arises partly from the contemplation of the imitation itself; partly from the consciousness of our own felicity, when compared with the miseries of others; but principally from the moral sense. Nature has endued man with a certain social and generous spirit; and commands him not to confine his cares to himself alone, but to extend them to all his fellow-creatures; to look upon nothing which relates to mankind as foreign to himself. Thus, "to rejoice with them that do rejoice, and to weep with them that weep;" to love and to respect piety and benevolence; to cherish and retain an indignant hatred of cruelty and injustice; that is, to obey the dictates of nature; is right, is honest, is becoming, is pleasant.

The sublime and the pathetic are intrinsically very different; and yet have in some respects a kind of affinity or connection. The pathetic includes the passions which we feel, and those which we excite. Some passions may be expressed without any thing of the sublime; the sublime also may exist, where no passion is directly expressed: there is however no sublimity where no passion is excited. That sensation of sublimity, which arises from the greatness of the thoughts and imagery, has admiration for its basis, and that for the most part connected with joy, love, hatred, or fear; and this I think is evident from the instances which were so lately under our consideration.

How much the sacred poetry of the Hebrews excels in exciting the passions, and in directing them to their noblest end and aim; how it exercises them upon their proper objects; how it strikes and fires the admiration by the contemplation of the Divine Majesty; and, forcing the affections of love, hope, and joy, from unworthy and terrestrial objects, elevates them to the pursuit of the supreme good; how it also stimulates those of grief, hatred, and fear, which are usually employed upon the trifling miseries of this life to the abhorrence of the supreme evil, is a subject, which at present wants no illustration, and which, though not unconnected with sublimity in a general view, would be improperly introduced in this place. For we are not at present treating of the general effects of sublimity on the passions; but of that species of the sublime which proceeds from vehement emotions of the mind, and from the imitation or representation of passion....

20

Samuel Johnson, from *A dictionary of the English language* (1755)

SUBLIME. *adj.* [*sublimis*, Latin.]
1. High in place; exalted aloft.

> They fum'd their pens, and soaring th' air *sublime*
> With clang despis'd the ground.   Milton.

> *Sublime* on these a tow'r of steel is rear'd,
> And dire Tisiphone there keeps the ward.   Dryden.

2. High in excellence; exalted by nature.

> My earthly strained to the height
> In that celestial colloquy *sublime*.   Milton.

> Can it be, that souls *sublime*
> Return to visit our terrestrial clime;
> And that the gen'rous mind releas'd by death,
> Can cover lazy limbs?   Dryden.

3. High in stile or sentiment; lofty; grand.

> Easy in stile, thy work in sense *sublime*.   Prior.

4. Elevated by joy.

> All yet left of that revolted rout,
> Heav'n-fall'n, in station stood or just array,
> *Sublime* with expectation.   Milton.

> Their hearts were jocund and *sublime*,
> Drunk with idolatry, drunk with wine.   Milton.

5. Haughty; proud.

> He was *sublime*, and almost tumorous in his looks and gestures.   Wotton.

SUBLIME. *n.s.* The grand or lofty stile. *The sublime* is a Gallicism, but now naturalized.

> Longinus strengthens all his laws,
> And is himself the great *sublime* he draws.   Pope.

> The *sublime* rises from the nobleness of thoughts, the magnificence of the words, or the harmonious and lively turn of the phrase; the perfect *sublime* arises from all three together.   Addison

To SUBLIME. *v.a.* [*sublime*, Fr. from the adjective.]
1. To raise by a chemical fire.

> Study our manuscripts, those myriads
> Of letters, which have past 'twixt thee and me,
> Thence write our annals, and in them lessons be
> To all, whom love's *subliming* fire invades.   Donne.

111

2. To raise on high.

> Although thy trunk be neither large nor strong,
> Nor can thy head, not helpt, itself *sublime*,
> Yet, like a serpent, a tall tree can climb.   Denham.

3. To exalt; to heighten; to improve.

> Flow'rs, and the fruit,
> Man's nourishment, by gradual scale *sublim'd*
> To vital spirits aspire.   Milton.

The fancies of most are moved by the inward springs of the corporeal machine, which even in the most *sublime* intellectuals is dangerously influential.

Glanville.

Art being strengthened by the knowledge of things, may pass into nature by slow degrees, and so be *sublimed* into a pure genius which is capable of distinguishing betwixt the beauties of nature and that which is low in her.

Dryden's Dufresnoy.

> Meanly they seek the blessing to confine,
> And force that sun but on a part to shine;
> Which not alone the southern wit *sublimes*,
> But ripens spirits in cold northern climes.   Pope.

To SUBLIME. *v.n.* To rise in the chemical vessel by the force of fire.

The particles of sal ammoniack in sublimation carry up the particles of antimony, which will not *sublime* alone.   Newton's. Optics.

This salt is fixed in a gentle fire, and *sublimes* in a great one.

Arbuthnot on Aliments.

SUBLIMELY. *adv.* [from *sublime.*] Loftily; grandly.

> This fustian's so *sublimely* bad;
> It is not poetry, but prose run mad.   Pope.

SUBLIMITY. *n.s.* [from *sublime*; *sublimité*, Fr. *sublimitas*, Lat.]

1. Height of place; local elevation.
2. Height of nature; excellence.

As religion looketh upon him who in majesty and power is infinite, as we ought we account not of it, unless we esteem it even according to that very height of excellency which our hearts conceive, when divine *sublimity* itself is rightly considered.   Hooker.

In respect of God's incomprehensible *sublimity* and purity, this is also true, that God is neither a mind, nor a spirit like other spirits, nor a light such as can be discerned.   Raleigh.

3. Loftiness of style or sentiment.

Milton's distinguishing excellence lies in the *sublimity* of his thoughts, in the greatness of which he triumphs over all the poets, modern and ancient, Homer only excepted.   Addison.

21

Edward Young, from *Conjectures on original composition* (1759)

The mind of a man of genius is a fertile and pleasant field, pleasant as Elysium, and fertile as Tempe; it enjoys a perpetual spring. Of that spring, originals are the fairest flowers: imitations are of quicker growth, but fainter bloom. Imitations are of two kinds; one of nature, one of authors: the first we call originals, and confine the term imitation to the second. I shall not enter into the curious enquiry of what is, or is not, strictly speaking, original, content with what all must allow, that some compositions are more so than others; and the more they are so, I say, the better. Originals are, and ought to be, great favourites, for they are great benefactors; they extend the republic of letters, and add a new province to its dominion: imitators only give us a sort of duplicates of what we had, possibly much better, before; increasing the mere drug of books, while all that makes them valuable, knowledge and genius, are at a stand. The pen of an original writer, like Armida's wand, out of a barren waste calls a blooming spring: out of that blooming spring an imitator is a transplanter of laurels, which sometimes die on removal, always languish in a foreign soil.

But suppose an imitator to be most excellent (and such there are), yet still he but nobly builds on another's foundation; his debt is, at least, equal to his glory; which therefore, on the balance, cannot be very great. On the contrary an original, although but indifferent (its originality being set aside), yet has something to boast; it is something to say with him in Horace,

> Meo *sum Pauper in ære*;

and to share ambition with no less than Cæsar, who declared he had rather be the first in a village, than the second at Rome.

Still farther: an imitator shares his crown, if he has one, with the chosen object of his imitation; an original enjoys an undivided applause. An original may be said to be of a vegetable nature; it rises spontaneously from the vital root of genius; it grows, it is not made: imitations are often a sort of manufacture wrought up by those mechanics, art, and labour, out of pre-existent materials not their own.

Again: we read imitation with somewhat of his languor, who listens to a twice-told tale: our spirits rouse at an original; that is a perfect stranger, and

113

all throng to learn what news from a foreign land: and although it comes, like an Indian prince, adorned with feathers only, having little of weight; yet of our attention it will rob the more solid, if not equally new: thus every telescope is lifted at a new-discovered star; it makes a hundred astronomers in a moment, and denies equal notice to the sun. But if an original, by being as excellent, as new, adds admiration to surprise, then are we at the writer's mercy; on the strong wing of his imagination, we are snatched from Britain to Italy, from climate to climate, from pleasure to pleasure; we have no home, no thought, of our own; till the magician drops his pen: and then falling down into ourselves, we awake to flat realities, lamenting the change, like the beggar who dreamt himself a prince.

It is with thoughts, as it is with words; and with both, as with men; they may grow old, and die. Words tarnished, by passing through the mouths of the vulgar, are laid aside as inelegant, and obsolete. So thoughts, when become too common, should lose their currency; and we should send new metal to the mint, that is, new meaning to the press. The division of tongues at Babel did not more effectually debar men from making themselves a name (as the scripture speaks), than the too great concurrence, or union of tongues will do for ever. We may as well grow good by another's virtue, or fat by another's food, as famous by another's thought. The world will pay its debt of praise but once; and instead of applauding, explode a second demand, as a cheat....

...Genius is a master-workman, learning is but an instrument; and an instrument, although most valuable, yet not always indispensable. Heaven will not admit of a partner in the accomplishment of some favourite spirits; but rejecting all human means, assumes the whole glory to itself. Have not some, although not famed for erudition, so written, as almost to persuade us, that they shone brighter, and soared higher, for escaping the boasted aid of that proud ally?

Nor is it strange; for what, for the most part, mean we by genius, but the power of accomplishing great things without the means generally reputed necessary to that end? A genius differs from a good understanding, as a magician from a good architect; that raises his structure by means invisible; this by the skilful use of common tools. Hence genius has ever been supposed to partake of something divine. *Nemo unquam vir magnus fuit, sine aliquo afflatus Divino.*

Learning, destitute of this superior aid, is fond, and proud, of what has cost it much pains; is a great lover of rules, and boaster of famed examples: as beauties less perfect, who owe half their charms to cautious art, she inveighs against natural unstudied graces, and small harmless indecorums, and sets rigid bounds to that liberty, to which genius often owes its supreme glory; but the no-genius its frequent ruin. For unprescribed beauties, and unexampled excellence, which are characteristics of genius, lie without the pale of learning's authorities, and laws; which pale, genius must leap to come at them: but by that leap, if genius is wanting, we break our necks; we lose that little credit, which possibly we might have enjoyed before. For rules, like crutches, are a needful aid to the lame, although an impediment to the strong. A Homer casts them away; and, like his Achilles,

> Jura negat sibi nata, nihil non arrogat,

by native force of mind. There is something in poetry beyond prose-reason; there are mysteries in it not to be explained, but admired; which render mere prose-men infidels to their divinity. And here pardon a second paradox; *viz.* "genius often then deserves most to be praised, when it is most sure to be condemned; that is, when its excellence, from mounting high, to weak eyes is quite out of sight."

If I might speak farther of learning, and genius, I would compare genius to virtue, and learning to riches. As riches are most wanted when there is least virtue; so learning where there is least genius. As virtue without much riches can give happiness, so genius without much learning can give renown. As it is said in Terence, *Pecuniam negligere interdum maximum est lucrum*; so to neglect of learning, genius sometimes owes its greater glory. Genius, therefore, leaves but the second place, among men of letters, to the learned. It is their merit, and ambition, to fling light on the works of genius, and point out its charms. We most justly reverence their informing radius for that favour; but we must much more admire the radiant stars pointed out by them.

A star of the first magnitude among the moderns was Shakespeare; among the ancients, Pindar; who, (as Vossius tells us) boasted of his no-learning, calling himself the eagle, for his flight above it. And such genii as these may, indeed, have much reliance on their own native powers. For genius may be compared to the body's natural strength; learning to the superinduced accoutrements of arms: if the first is equal to the proposed exploit, the latter rather encumbers, than assists; rather retards, than promotes, the victory. *Sacer nobis inest Deus*, says Seneca. With regard to the moral world, conscience, with regard to the intellectual, genius, is that God within. Genius can set us right in composition, without the rules of the learned; as conscience sets us right in life, without the laws of the land: this, singly, can make us good, as men; that, singly, as writers, can, sometimes, make us great.

22

James Burgh,
from *The art of speaking* (1761)

A correct speaker does not make a movement of limb, or feature, for which he has not a reason. If he addresses heaven, he looks upward. If he speaks to his fellow-creatures, he looks round upon them. The spirit of what he says, or is said to him, appears in his look. If he expresses amazement, or would excite it, he lifts up his hands and eyes. If he invites to virtue and happiness, he spreads his arms, and looks benevolence. If he threatens the vengeance of heaven against vice, he bends his eyebrow into wrath, and menaces with his arm and countenance. He does not needlessly saw the air with his arm, nor stab himself with his finger. He does not clap his right hand upon his breast, unless he has occasion to speak of himself, or to introduce conscience, or somewhat sentimental. He does not start back, unless he wants to express horror or aversion. He does not come forward, but when he has occasion to solicit. He does not raise his voice, but to express somewhat peculiarly emphatical. He does not lower it, but to contrast the raising of it. His eyes, by turns, according the humour of the matter he has to express, sparkle fury; brighten into joy; glance disdain; melt into grief; frown disgust and hatred; languish into love; or glare distraction.

But to apply properly and in a masterly manner, the almost endlessly various external expressions of the different passions and emotions of the mind, for which nature has so curiously fitted the human frame – *hic labor* – here is the difficulty. Accordingly a consummate public speaker is truly a phoenix. But much less than all this, is, generally speaking, sufficient for most occasions.

There is an error, which is too inconsiderately received by many judicious persons, *viz.* that a public speaker's showing himself to be in earnest, will alone secure him of duly affecting his audience. Were this true, the enthusiastic rant of the fanatic, who is often very much in earnest, ought to please the judicious; in whom, on the contrary, we know, it excites, only laughter, or pity. It is granted, that nature is the rule, by which we are to speak, and to judge of propriety in speaking. And every public speaker, who faithfully, and in a masterly manner, follows that universal guide, commands attention and approbation. But a speaker may, either through incurable natural deficiency, or by deviating into some incorrigible absurdity of manner, express the real and the warm sentiments of his heart, in such an awkward way, as shall effectually defeat his whole design upon those who hear him, and render himself the object of their ridicule....

There is a true sublime in delivery, as in the other imitative arts; in the manner as well as in the matter, of what an orator delivers. As in poetry, painting, sculpture, music, and the other elegancies, the true sublime consists in a set of masterly, large, and noble strokes of art, superior to florid littleness; so it is in delivery. The accents are to be clear and articulate; every syllable standing off from that which is next to it, so that they might be numbered as they proceed. The inflections of the voice are to be so distinctly suited to the matter, that the humour or passion might be known by the sound of the voice only, where there could not be one word heard. And the variations are to be, like the full swelling folds of the drapery in a fine picture, or statue, bold, and free, and forcible.

True eloquence does not wait for cool approbation. Like irresistible beauty, it transports, it ravishes, it commands the admiration of all, who are within its reach. If it allows us time to criticise, it is not genuine. It ought to hurry us out of ourselves, to engage and swallow up our whole attention; to drive every thing out of our minds, besides the subject it would hold forth, and the point, it wants to carry. The hearer finds himself as unable to resist it, as to blow out a conflagration with the breath of his mouth, or to stop the stream of a river with his hand. His passions are no longer his own. The orator has taken possession of them; and with superior power, works them to whatever he pleases.

There is no earthly object of making such various, and such forcible impressions upon the human mind, as a consummate speaker. In viewing the artificial creations, which flow from the pencil of a Raphael, the critical eye is indeed delighted to a high pitch, and the delight is rational, because it flows from sources, unknown to beings below the rational sphere. But the ear remains wholly un-engaged, and un-entertained.

In listening to the raptures of Corelli, Geminiani, and Handel, the flood of pleasure which pours upon the ear, is almost too much for human nature. And music applied to express the sublimities of poetry, as in the oratorio of Samson, and the *Allegro* and *Pensoroso*, yields a pleasure so truly rational, that a Plato, or a Socrates, need not be abandoned to declare their sensibility of it. But here again, the eye has not its gratification. For the opera (in which action is joined with music, in order to entertain the eye at the same time with the ear) I must beg leave, with all due submission to the taste of the great, to consider as a forced conjunction of two things, which nature does not allow to go together. For it never will be other than unnatural, to see heroes fighting, commanding, threatening, lamenting, and making love in the warblings of an Italian song.

It is only the elegant speaker, who can at once regale the eye with the view of its most amiable object, the human form in all its glory; the ear with the original of all music, the understanding with its proper and natural food, the knowledge of important truth; and the imagination with all that, in nature, or in art, is beautiful, sublime, or wonderful. For the orator's field is the universe, and his subjects are all that is known of God, and his works; of superior natures, good and evil, and their works; and of terrestrials, and theirs.

In a consummate speaker, whatever there is of corporeal dignity, or beauty, the majesty of the human face divine, the grace of action, the piercing glance, or gentle languish, or fiery flash of the eye; whatever of lively passion, or striking emotion of mind, whatever of fine imagination, of wise reflection, or irresistible reasoning; whatever of excellent in human nature, all that the hand of the Creator has impressed, of his own image upon the noblest creature we are acquainted with, all this appears in the consummate speaker to the highest advantage. And whoever is proof against such a display of all that is noble in human nature, must have neither eye, nor ear, nor passion, nor imagination, nor taste, nor understanding.

23

Joseph Priestley, from *A course of lectures on oratory and criticism* (1777)

Lecture XX. Of the sublime

Great objects please us for the same reason that *new* objects do, *viz.* by the exercise they give to our faculties. The mind, as was observed before, conforming and adapting itself to the objects to which its attention is engaged, must, as it were, enlarge itself, to conceive a great object. This requires a considerable *effort of the imagination*, which is also attended with a pleasing, though perhaps not a distinct and explicit consciousness of the strength and extent of our own powers.

As the ideas of *great* and *little* are confessedly relative, and have no existence but what they derive from a comparison with other ideas; hence, in all sublime conceptions, there is a kind of secret retrospect to preceding ideas and states of mind. The sublime, therefore, of all the species of excellence in composition, requires the most to be intermixed with ideas of an intermediate nature; as these contribute not a little, by their contrast, to raise and aggrandise ideas which are of a rank superior to themselves. Whenever any object, how great soever, becomes familiar to the mind, and its relations to other objects is no longer attended to, the sublime vanishes. Milton's battle of the angels, after the prelude to the engagement, would have been read with no greater emotions than are excited by the history of a common battle, had not the poet perpetually reinforced his sublime, as it were, by introducing frequent comparisons of those superior beings, and their actions, with human combatants and human efforts....

Objects of the first rank in point of magnitude, and which chiefly constitute the sublime of description, are large rivers, high mountains, and extensive plains; the ocean, the clouds, the heavens, and infinite space; also storms, thunder, lightning, volcanos, and earthquakes, in nature; and palaces, temples, pyramids, cities, &c. in the works of men. See a fine enumeration of those scenes of nature, which contribute the most to the sublime, in Akenside upon this subject:

> – Who but rather turns
> To heaven's broad fire his unconstrained view,
> Than to the glimmering of a waxen flame?
> Who that, from Alpine heights, his lab'ring eye
> Shoots round the wide horizon, to survey

The Nile or Ganges roll his wasteful tide,
Thro' mountains, plains, thro' empires black with shade,
And continents of sand, will turn his gaze
To mark the windings of a scanty rill
That murmurs at his feet? &c.   Pleasures of the Imagination, Lib.I.

But the account here given of the sublime, by no means confines it to the ideas of objects which have sensible and *corporeal* magnitude. *Sentiments* and *passions* are equally capable of it, if they relate to great objects, suppose extensive views of things, require a great effort of the mind to conceive them, and produce great effects. Fortitude, magnanimity, generosity, patriotism, and universal benevolence, strike the mind with the idea of the sublime. We are conscious that it requires a great effort to exert them; and in all cases when the mind is conscious of a similar exertion of its faculties, it refers its sensations to the same class. If the virtues above mentioned were more common, the idea of them would not be so sublime.

Who that considers the sentiments of Diomedes, when he prays to Jupiter to *give him day, and then destroy him*; the answer of Alexander to Parmenio (who had told him that he would accept the offers of Darius, if he were Alexander) *And so would I, if I were Parmenio*; and much more the prayer of our Saviour upon the cross, in behalf of his persecutors, *Father, forgive them, for they know not what they do*: who, I say, that attends to these sentiments, can entertain a doubt that they produce feelings similar to those which we receive from the view of grand and elevated objects? Or a person need only to read the following passage from Dr Akenside, to be convinced that there is a true sublime in sentiment:

Say why was man so eminently raised
Above the vast creation? Why advanced
Thro' life and death to dart his piercing eye,
With thoughts beyond the limits of his frame;
But that th'Omnipotent might send him forth,
In sight of mortal and immortal powers,
As on a boundless theatre, to run
The great career of justice, to exalt
His gen'rous aim to all diviner deeds? &c.

There is no surer method of discovering those sensations and ideas, which are apprehended to be analogous by mankind in general, than by observing the analogies of *words* in various languages; for the one will correspond to the other. As mankind, when the bulk of any language was invented, were not in a situation to invent superfluous terms, we may naturally conclude they would content themselves with the same term when there was a great resemblance in the ideas they represented; but in no other case, if they could avoid so great an inconvenience. If this clue be allowed to be of any use to us, in classing our ideas and sensations, there will remain no doubt but that there are a variety of things, not material, which raise sensations similar to those which are excited by objects which have corporeal magnitude and elevation.

How else came a man of distinguished abilities to be called *a great man*? Why do we say that a benevolent man is of an *open* as well as generous temper? and that a covetous man hath a *narrow* soul? How came the epithets *proud*, *haughty*, and *lofty*, to be synonymous? and how came the terms *superior taste*, *advancement in honour*, *head of the table*, *high note* in music, *ascending series* in numbers, and *high* and *low*, *near* or *distant*, with respect to *time*, to prevail so generally, and to become so familiar, that the figure is perfectly evanescent? Moreover, how came robes of state to be made large and full, and thrones to be lofty, &c.? Whence comes it that largeness of size contributes to make a person look majestic? And how came the Scythian ambassadors to be surprised to find Alexander the Great to be a *little man*?

I might mention a great many more terms borrowed from corporeal magnitude, extension and elevation, applied to things which have none of those qualities; but these are sufficient to show that the perception of the sentiments, dispositions, and circumstances, to which they are applied, are attended with a consciousness of a feeling, similar to that which is excited by the view of objects which have the qualities of corporeal magnitude, extension, and elevation; that is, with the sublime.

The sublime of science consists in general and comprehensive theorems, which, by means of very great and extensive consequences, present the idea of *vastness* to the mind. A person of true taste may perceive many instances of genuine sublime in geometry, and even in algebra; and the sciences of natural philosophy and astronomy, exhibit the noblest fields of the sublime that the mind of man was ever introduced to. Theorems may also be sublime by their relating to great objects.

For many things which, considered in themselves, and abstracted from every thing that is foreign to them, are incapable of the sublime, inspire that sentiment by their association with others that are capable of it. From this source it is that the ideas of wealth, honour, and power, borrow their sublime. It is the *causes*, the *adjuncts*, or the *effects* of these things, that are contemplated, when they fill and charm the soul. *Wealth* carries with it the idea of a large estate, and abundance of every thing that can contribute to the enjoyment of life. From *honour* we never separate the idea of the strength of body, the capacity of the mind, or the great achievements by which it was procured. With these also we join the number of people among whom a person is renowned, the extent of country through which his fame spreads, and the length of time to which it extends. To the idea of *power* we join ideas of the good or evil it may produce, and of the multitudes which are subject to its control. In the idea of a *conqueror*, we may clearly distinguish the idea of a great extent of country subdued; and in the idea of *nobility*, that of a long train of illustrious ancestors. A similar analysis would show us the sublime of *friendship*, *patriotism*, and many other abstract ideas.

The grandeur of a *palace*, besides what it derives from its exceeding other houses in bulk, is derived from the ideas of the labour, expense, length of time, and number of persons necessary to the erection of it; and from ideas of the wealth, honour, and power of him who inhabits it. Celebrated buildings and cities *in ruins*, along with these ideas, present that of the length of time that hath elapsed since they flourished; and the whole sensation is greatly magnified by a comparison of their former magnificence with their present desolation. The grandeur and peculiar awfulness with which we are struck upon the view of a *temple* is, in a great measure, derived from the ideas we have annexed to it of the power of the Deity to whom it is sacred; as all that is sublime in the idea of a *senate-house*, or other public building, arises from the idea of the *use* to which it is appropriated.

The *contempt* of power, wealth, and grandeur, is more sublime than the *possession* of them; because, after a view of those great objects, it presents us with the view of a *mind* above them. So that it is not true, that "nothing is great the contempt of which is great."

Though, in some cases of this species of *transferred sublimity*, the analysis of a complex idea should present no one idea which, singly taken, could be called sublime; yet, so long as those ideas continue separately indistinguishable, the mind perceives not a number of small objects, but one great one; as in the case before explained of the sublime of numbers.

As most of our emotions are of a complex nature, we are in great danger, unless we be extremely attentive, of making mistakes in the distribution and analysis of them. Hence emotions of *terror* have been often classed with the sublime. But terror is a mixed sensation, composed of the very different sensations of *fear* and *grandeur*, to the latter of which it owes all its sublimity. For, when we are in a situation in which we have nothing to fear, the sight of a monstrous beast, of a giant, or of the sea in a storm, &c. presents little more than the pure sublime, heightened by the secret pleasure we take in the idea of our own security. The pure sublime partakes nothing of fear, or of any other painful emotion.

Moreover, the pure sublime, by strongly engaging, tends to fix the attention, and to keep the mind in a kind of *awful stillness*; whereas it is of the nature of every species of the pathetic to throw it into an *agitation*. Hence the sensations we feel from *darkness* and *profound silence*, resembling the stillness the mind is thrown into when the attention is strongly fixed by a sublime object, partake of the nature of the sublime;...

Hence also deep and slow notes in music bear a nearer relation to the sublime than shrill and quick sounds.

It may be observed, that the account here given of the sublime confines it to the *sentiment*. However, as the term (which hath been used in a more vague sense than almost any other term in criticism) is frequently applied to *language*, I shall briefly explain how the sublime is affected by language.

Ideas in themselves sublime may entirely lose that quality by being expressed in terms which have connections with trivial and mean objects, or in metaphors borrowed from such objects. In this case the *secondary associations* which accompany those words are transferred upon the object described by them, and destroy the sublime they would otherwise have. Though, therefore, in general, the *plainest terms* are the most favourable to the sublime, as they exhibit the most just and the strongest idea of the object; yet every term, however plain and intelligible, that hath ever had the least connection with *mean subjects*, or even which hath been chiefly used by persons of a low and illiberal class of life, should be carefully avoided....

Proper names of great objects are often preferable to general terms, as they realise the ideas, and fix the attention to them. Thus, to mention the Alps, the Andes, or Teneriffe, presents a greater idea than saying, *very high mountains*; and to say, the Nile, the Ganges, or the La Plata, is to speak more magnificently than to say, *great rivers* only. Thus, the simple and sublime Ossian affects the imagination of his reader much more strongly by the hill of Cromla, *the waves of* Inistore, the reeds of the *lake of* Lægo, than he could have done by the use of any more general and abstract terms. This effect would be more sensible, if we were acquainted with the objects introduced in this manner.

Next to the *pathetic*, of all the excellencies of good composition, the *sublime* promises the most lasting reputation to an author. Compositions which are calculated only to *please* and to *divert*, are beings of a day. Few of them, even by the favour of a very extraordinary coincidence of circumstances, reach posterity, in comparison of those which *shake* and which *elevate* our souls. Let us only look into our own breasts, and we shall find that we are very differently affected to the writer who pleases the imagination, and to the poet or orator who either raises and enlarges our conceptions, or who thoroughly interests our passions. The former we may *admire*, but we may also soon *forget*. Our esteem for the latter rises to *reverence*; and when the pathetic and the sublime are joined (as they are capable of the most intimate union, and are perhaps never found in a very high degree entirely separate) they produce the strongest and the most lasting attachment.

A genius formed for the sublime is a mind which is naturally disposed to take the most extensive views of things, whose attention is turned to view every thing in the grandest and noblest point of light; whereas other minds are more inclined to attend to what is *little* and *beautiful* in the objects they view. And as every thing we are conversant with hath various, and very different properties, every mind hath an opportunity of indulging its own taste, by contemplating those forms of things which afford it the most pleasing gratification.

I cannot conclude this article without observing that instances of the true sublime abound nowhere more than in the Scriptures. Never were grander ideas presented to the human mind than we find in the representations of the Divine Being in Isaiah, particularly in chapter XL, in the book of Job, in several places in the Psalms, and in the writings of Moses....

24

Frances Reynolds,
from *An enquiry concerning the principles of taste* (1785)

Chapter I.
A Sketch of the Mental System respecting our Perceptions of Taste, &c.

The mind of man, introspecting itself, seems, as it were, (in conjunction with the inscrutable principles of nature), placed in the central point of the creation: from whence, impelled by her energetic powers and illumined by her light, the intellectual faculties, like rays, shoot forth in direct tendency to their ultimate point of perfection; and, as they advance, each individual mind imperceptibly imbibes the influence and light of each, and is by this imbibition alone enabled to approach it.

But, though the light of nature and of reason direct the human mind to perfection, or true good, yet, being in its progress perpetually impeded by adventitious causes, casual occurrences, &c. &c. which induce false opinions of good and evil, its progressive powers generally stop at a middle point between mere uncultivated nature and perfection, a medium which constitutes what we call common sense, and which, in degree, seems as distant from the perfection of the mental faculties as common form is from the perfection of form, beauty.

On meditating on this subject, and marking the progressive stages or degrees of human excellence, the great leading general truths, or mental rests, as I may call them, *the common, the beautiful, the graceful, and the sublime*, I have been naturally led to form a kind of diagrammatic representation of their respective distances, &c. &c. which I present to my reader on the opposite page, requesting him to refer to it now and then as he goes on, in order to facilitate his comprehension of my meaning.

And here it may be necessary to premise, that, however whimsical and absurd this delineation may appear to my reader, something analogous to the thought may be found in the works of many eminent philosophers, particularly in those of Bacon* and of Locke:† the latter suggesting that the whole system of morality might be reduced to mathematical demonstration; and the former, in his treatise on the Advancement of Learning, gives a description

---

* Advancement of Learning, Book 2d.
† Essay on human Understanding, Chap. 3d, Book the 4th, and Chap. 12th, same Book, Sect. 8th.

124

of the stages of science very much resembling my delineation of the stages of intellectual perfection, or taste.

It could have been no dishonour to me to have been led by such conductors! Yet, as the truth cannot dishonour me neither, I must aver, that my little system was projected, and brought to the exact state it now is in, without my having the least apprehension that any thing similar had been suggested before by any person whatever; nor have I, in consequence of the discovery I have lately made of the opinions of these respectable authors, added or omitted a single thought in my treatise. But to return from my digression.

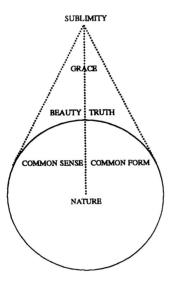

In the exact centre of my circle of humanity, I have placed nature, or the springs of the intellectual powers, which tend, in a straight line, to its boundary; and, on its boundary, I have placed demonstrable beauty and truth, and the utmost power of rules; and, midway, I have placed common sense and common form, half deriving their existence from pure nature, and half from its highest cultivation, as far as art or rules can teach. A conjunction which would itself be the perfection of humanity, but that it is mixed with all that is not nature, and all that is not art, and thereby made mediocrity, i.e. *common sense*.

The intellectual powers, arriving at the limit of my common circle, i.e. at the limit of the basis of my pyramidical system, where I have placed the fixed proportions of beauty and of truth, (if they progress), mount up as a flame, with undulating* motion, refining as they advance, and terminate in the pinnacle, or ultimate point, *sublimity*; forming in the imagination the figure of a pyramid, or cone, from the limit of whose base, (on which, as I have before observed, I have placed demonstrable truth and beauty, the utmost power of

---

* I use that expression, because it is the peculiar motion of grace as well as of a flame.

rules, &c.) from that limit up to the ultimate point of sublimity, I call the region of intellectual pleasure, genius, or taste; and in its centre I place grace, whose influence pervades, cheers, and nourishes, every part of it, an object which, in this ideal region, is similar in its situation and degree to that of common sense in the common or fundamental region. Grace seems to partake of the perception both of beauty and of sublimity, as common sense partakes of nature and of art. Grace is the characteristic object or general form of the ideal region, and its perception is the general limit of the powers of imagination or taste. Few, very few, attain to the point of sublimity; the *ne plus ultra* of human conception! the alpha and omega. The sentiment of sublimity sinks into the source of nature, and that of the source of nature mounts to the sentiment of sublimity, each point seeming to each the cause and the effect; the origin and the end!

Having thus drawn the outline of my pyramidical mental system, I propose to expatiate a little on each point or stage throughout the great characteristic line of intellectual power.

The first point. The exact centre, *nature*, or the origin of our intellectual faculties, admits of no investigation, its idea, as I have observed before, loses itself in the sentiment of sublimity, and we see nothing; and therefore I pass on to an object which is perceptible, *the common general character of humanity, exterior and interior.* I have placed them on a line, because their ideas are so analogous, that they unite in one.

Section 4. Sublimity

Where pure grace ends, the awe of the sublime begins, composed of the influence of pain, of pleasure, of grace, and deformity, playing into each other, that the mind is unable to determine which to call it, pain, pleasure, or terror. Without a conjunction of these powers there could be no sublimity.

Those only who have passed through the degrees, *common sense, truth,* and *grace,* i.e. the sentiment of grace, can have a sentiment of sublimity. It is the mild admiration of grace raised to *wonder* and *astonishment*; to a sentiment of *power* out of *our power* to produce or control. Grace must have been as familiar to the intellect, in order to discover sublimity, as common sense in the common region must have been to the discovery of truth and beauty. In fine, genius, or taste, which is the sentiment of grace, and which I have called the common sense of the ideal region, can alone discover the true sublime.

It is a pinnacle of beatitude, bordering upon horror, deformity, madness! an eminence from whence the mind, that dares to look farther, is lost! It seems to stand, or rather to waver, between certainty and uncertainty, between security and destruction. It is the point of terror, of undetermined fear, of undetermined power!

The idea of the supreme Being is, I imagine, in every breast, from the clown to the greatest philosopher, his point of sublimity!

Part III
Irish perspectives

One of the most intransigent problems in the conceptual mapping of the sublime is the relationship between the object taken to arouse heightened response and the affective quality of intense self-presence which results from such response. This problem is never satisfactorily resolved in the eighteenth-century tradition and indeed the 'contentless content' of the sublime continues to present difficulties in the post-Kantian tradition. Burke attempts to resolve the question through his assimilation of the self to the object, 'the mind so entirely filled with its object', thereby making self and the object taken to arouse the sublime sensation mutually containing. In this sense the sublime can be understood as a *pulsation* (which is why it is associated with the pulsation of consciousness in the post-Freudian tradition) in which first the conscious mind relinquishes its power over the world it perceives and in which it has experiential encounters in order to open itself to the object, to become suffused with the world. Then, in a secondary pulsation, this experience of opening up or of being overcome leads to an intensification of self-presence and a corresponding re-assertion of the power of the subject over the object [Burke]. This alternating location of the energy of the sublime, first all object then all subject, could be said to be an early precursor of more recent theories of the unconscious.[1]

While this Burkean dynamic has certainly prevailed in the transmission of the sublime tradition it was not without its detractors and dissenters. In this third part we find, for example, Usher making precisely the opposing point in his assertion that the object of the sublime is vacant [Usher]. This idea, the 'contentless content' of the sublime also has a contemporary outworking in Julia Kristeva's contention that the sublime has no object.

Burke is close to this point himself since in the final analysis the ultimate source or cause of the sublime is divine power [Burke]. The process of reasoning in Burke's text begins by noting that power, initially located and described in natural forms, is the ultimate cause or ground of sublime affect. Unfortunately at this point the analysis wavers since Burke maintains that it is 'some modification' of power which can be understood as the final cause, and this begins to beg a number of questions, such as: how much of a modification, modified by what, by whom? Burke's lapse back into a slightly mystified explanation in which Godhead is to be taken as the ultimate power does not help here since all we are left with is the sense of wonder we experience in the face of the almighty.

Negative impulses are far more successfully identified and analysed in the Burkean text, such as the annihilation of self in the sublime moment, a logical extension of a theory of sublimity based upon power [Burke]. This annihilation is required by the Burkean model since if it were possible for man to

---

[1] This has been the drift of contemporary work on the eighteenth-century sublime informed by psychoanalytic theory. See, for example, *New Literary History*, 16 (1984-5), an issue devoted to the topic of the sublime; Suzanne Guerlac, *The impersonal sublime* (Stanford: Stanford University Press, 1990); Frances Ferguson, *Solitude and the sublime* (London: Routledge, 1992).

harness, direct and control the ultimate power he would, in effect, be usurping the place of God. In the later outworking of this proposal self-annihilation becomes a part of the dynamics of self-consciousness and consciousness of self.

The rhetorical tradition had constantly invoked the ways in which specific forms of language were more or less efficient at raising sublime affect (see parts I and II). This form of analysis also prevails in the Burkean text in which we learn that language is better able to create or reflect sublime experiences than any other representational form [Burke]. This line of enquiry becomes particularly interesting to contemporary discussions of the sublime in which the question of presentability takes centre stage.[2] Burke's point is that words can convey things that we can only 'see' in the imaginative orbit of linguistic representation. Which is to say that language can image things to us which cannot be literally seen. This notion of the power of language to conceive concepts which are not a part of any present conceptual system is fundamental for a progressive development of concept formation; in this sense the eighteenth-century analysis of the sublime can be taken as a model for theoretical enquiry.

While such issues of grounding or foundational concept building permeate these mid-century discussions there are also more thoroughly recognisable augustan preoccupations jostling for attention. Ascertaining standards for judgment, for example, was almost an obsession of the age. In aesthetic speculation Hume's 'Of the standard of taste' is the most explicit and thorough investigation of the notion of a 'standard' in relation to aesthetic judgment, but these concerns are clearly active in Goldsmith as well. This minor obsession with rules governing judgment is a symptom of the neoclassical desire to control the public sphere, and in part motivates the observation made of Burke's *Enquiry* that it sets out to establish standards in the ascription of aesthetic categories.

For similar reasons the concern over terror as a major cause of the sublime, a position advanced by Burke, indicates the proximity of aesthetic and ethical judgments. It was argued in the light of Burke's analysis that anything operating analogously to terror may also give rise to sublimity. This is an extremely important moment in the tradition since it marks the move away from 'literal' causes of heightened response, such as qualities inhering in natural objects, towards the possibility that sublime affect may be generated through figuration. In this way the figurative work of analogy will enable the structure of the concept itself to be more minutely examined and explored; in the final analysis it will identify that structure with figuration itself. It is this which provides the impulse towards the 'contentless content', driving the object out of the trajectory of the analysis of the sublime.

This developing preoccupation with figuration rather than rhetoricity is an indicator of a deepening sophistication in the eighteenth-century discussion.

---

[2] See J.F. Lyotard, 'Presenting the unpresentable: the sublime', tr. L. Liebman, *Artforum* (February, 1981), 56-64.

Self-imitation in nature [Lawson], for example, is taken as a *naturally* occurring example of figuration and therefore underwrites the complex theory of tropes outlined in Lawson's *Lectures*. Without this aspect of the investigation the period would have been unable to begin the work of understanding the transformational character of the discourse of the sublime.

Furthermore, the figurative division of speech into a natural and artificial form [Lawson] echoes the division of naturally occurring qualities which arouse the sublime from representations of such forms. It would be difficult to envisage much progress in the analytic of the sublime while this distinction predominates, consequently it is of the utmost significance that this very division between the natural (literal language) and the artificial (rhetorical figures) is itself understood as a *figuration*.

Such a potentially totalising model of linguistic production is avoided when these theorists confront the sublime in terms of their own experience. In this case figuration loses its potential grip on the world as the subject experiences the breakdown of speech [Lawson]. This broken speech in the face of sublime transport is, for the period, an inevitable result of astonishment. This will be developed in the later tradition into a pathology of the blinking of consciousness in nineteenth-century models of the psyche.

Similarly the passions are another aspect of enlightenment anatomies of consciousness which attest to the breakdown in an all-embracing power of figuration [Lawson]. Such animated responses to heightened experience were to be contrasted to less vigorous modes. The sense of astonishment might, for example, lead to absorption [Ussher], a sensation occurring in a number of experiential realms. Prime among these is the reading scene in which the mind of the reader becomes completely absorbed within the process of the reading activity, but such absorptive states also result from the activity of looking.[3]

The pulsation of consciousness remarked above in the Burkean analysis could also be described as a suspension [Ussher] of the sublime moment, precisely the point at which experience of the outer world stops, producing a gap into which the sense of self rushes. The sublime, in fact, is constantly understood via reference to the arrestation of movement, sometimes figured quite literally in the progress over a mountain top, or more figuratively as in the notion that the eye 'moves' through a landscape and is suddenly arrested in its movement by a specific 'eye-catcher'. This notion of suspension, of hanging in mid air, will be well developed in the romantic tradition, most especially in Wordsworth's poetry.

A significant feature of the analytic of the sublime is its procedure of moving from effects to causes [Ussher]. The sublime always involves this retracing from the experiential (the sublime feeling) back to the cause and is, therefore, in its very founding moment preoccupied with transitional forms. This is, once again, a very clear indicator of the drive towards a discourse which is itself transformational.

---

[3] See Michael Fried, *Absorption and theatricality: painting and beholder in the age of Diderot* (Berkeley: University of California Press, 1980).

25

Edmund Burke,
from *A philosophical enquiry into the origin of our ideas of the sublime and beautiful* (1759)

Part One. Section VII
Of the sublime

Whatever is fitted in any sort to excite the ideas of pain, and danger, that is to say, whatever is in any sort terrible, or is conversant about terrible objects, or operates in a manner analogous to terror, is a source of the *sublime*; that is, it is productive of the strongest emotion which the mind is capable of feeling. I say the strongest emotion, because I am satisfied the ideas of pain are much more powerful than those which enter on the part of pleasure. Without all doubt, the torments which we may be made to suffer, are much greater in their effect on the body and mind, than any pleasures which the most learned voluptuary could suggest, or than the liveliest imagination, and the most sound and exquisitely sensible body could enjoy. Nay I am in great doubt, whether any man could be found who would earn a life of the most perfect satisfaction, at the price of ending it in the torments, which justice inflicted in a few hours on the late unfortunate regicide in France. But as pain is stronger in its operation than pleasure, so death is in general a much more affecting idea than pain; because there are very few pains, however exquisite, which are not preferred to death; nay, what generally makes pain itself, if I may say so, more painful, is, that it is considered as an emissary of this king of terrors. When danger or pain press too nearly, they are incapable of giving any delight, and are simply terrible; but at certain distances, and with certain modifications, they may be, and they are delightful, as we every day experience. The cause of this I shall endeavour to investigate hereafter.

Section XVIII
The recapitulation

To draw the whole of what has been said into a few distinct points. The passions which belong to self-preservation, turn on pain and danger; they are simply painful when their causes immediately affect us; they are delightful when we have an idea of pain and danger, without being actually in such

131

circumstances; this delight I have not called pleasure, because it turns on pain, and because it is different enough from any idea of positive pleasure. Whatever excites this delight, I call *sublime*. The passions belonging to self-preservation are the strongest of all the passions.

The second head to which the passions are referred with relation to their final cause, is society. There are two sorts of societies. The first is, the society of sex. The passion belonging to this is called love, and it contains a mixture of lust; its object is the beauty of women. The other is the great society with man and all other animals. The passion subservient to this is called likewise love, but it has no mixture of lust, and its object is beauty; which is a name I shall apply to all such qualities in things as induce in us a sense of affection and tenderness, or some other passion the most nearly resembling these. The passion of love has its rise in positive pleasure; it is, like all things which grow out of pleasure, capable of being mixed with a mode of uneasiness, that is, when an idea of its object is excited in the mind with an idea at the same time of having irretrievably lost it. This mixed sense of pleasure I have not called *pain*, because it turns upon actual pleasure, and because it is both in its cause and in most of its effects of a nature altogether different.

Next to the general passion we have for society, to a choice in which we are directed by the pleasure we have in the object, the particular passion under this head called sympathy has the greatest extent. The nature of this passion is to put us in the place of another in whatever circumstances he is in, and to affect us in a like manner; so that this passion may, as the occasion requires, turn either on pain or pleasure; but with the modifications mentioned in some cases in section II. As to imitation and preference nothing more need be said.

Part Two. Section I
Of the passion caused by the sublime

The passion caused by the great and sublime in nature, when those causes operate most powerfully, is. Astonishment; and astonishment is that state of the soul, in which all its motions are suspended, with some degree of horror. In this case the mind is so entirely filled with its object, that it cannot entertain any other, nor by consequence reason on that object which employs it. Hence arises the great power of the sublime, that far from being produced by them, it anticipates our reasonings, and hurries us on by an irresistible force. Astonishment, as I have said, is the effect of the sublime in its highest degree; the inferior effects are admiration, reverence and respect.

Section II
Terror

No passion so effectually robs the mind of all its powers of acting and reasoning as fear. For fear being an apprehension of pain or death, it operates in a manner that resembles actual pain. Whatever therefore is terrible, with regard to sight, is sublime too, whether this cause of terror, be endued with greatness of dimensions or not; for it is impossible to look on any thing as trifling, or contemptible, that may be dangerous. There are many animals, who though far from being large, are yet capable of raising ideas of the sublime, because they are considered as objects of terror. As serpents and poisonous animals of almost all kinds. And to things of great dimensions, if we annex an adventitious idea of terror, they become without comparison greater. A level plain of a vast extent on land, is certainly no mean idea; the prospect of such a plain may be as extensive as a prospect of the ocean; but can it ever fill the mind with any thing so great as the ocean itself? This is owing to several causes, but it is owing to none more than this, that the ocean is an object of no small terror. Indeed terror is in all cases whatsoever, either more openly or latently the ruling principle of the sublime. Several languages bear a strong testimony to the affinity of these ideas. They frequently use the same word, to signify indifferently the modes of astonishment or admiration and those of terror. 'ἄμβος is in Greek, either fear or wonder; δεινός is terrible or respectable; αἰδέω, to reverence or to fear. *Vereor* in Latin, is what αἰδέω is in Greek. The Romans used the verb *stupeo*, a term which strongly marks the state of an astonished mind, to express the effect either of simple fear, or of astonishment; the word *attonitus*, (thunderstruck) is equally expressive of the alliance of these ideas; and do not the French *etonnement*, and the English *astonishment* and *amazement*, point out as clearly the kindred emotions which attend fear and wonder? They who have a more general knowledge of languages, could produce, I make no doubt, many other and equally striking examples.

Section III
Obscurity

To make any thing very terrible, obscurity seems in general to be necessary. When we know the full extent of any danger, when we can accustom our eyes to it, a great deal of the apprehension vanishes. Every one will be sensible of this, who considers how greatly night adds to our dread, in all cases of danger, and how much the notions of ghosts and goblins, of which none can form clear ideas, affect minds, which give credit to the popular tales concerning such sorts of beings. Those despotic governments, which are founded on the passions of men, and principally upon the passion of fear, keep their chief as much as may be from the public eye. The policy has been the same in many cases of religion. Almost all the heathen temples were dark. Even in the barbarous temples of the Americans at this day, they keep their idol in a dark part of the hut, which is consecrated to his worship. For this purpose too the druids performed all their ceremonies in the bosom of the darkest woods, and in the shade of the oldest and most spreading oaks. No person seems better to have understood the secret of heightening, or of setting terrible things, if I may use the expression, in their strongest light by the force of a judicious obscurity, than Milton. His description of Death in the second book is admirably studied; it is astonishing with what a gloomy pomp, with what a significant and expressive uncertainty of strokes and colouring he has finished the portrait of the king of terrors.

> The other shape,
> If shape it might be called that shape had none
> Distinguishable, in member, joint, or limb;
> Or substance might be called that shadow seemed,
> For each seemed either; black he stood as night;
> Fierce as ten furies; terrible as hell;
> And shook a deadly dart. What seemed his head
> The likeness of a kingly crown had on.

In this description all is dark, uncertain, confused, terrible, and sublime to the last degree.

Section IV
Of the difference between Clearness and Obscurity with regard to the passions

It is one thing to make an idea clear, and another to make it *affecting* to the imagination. If I make a drawing of a palace, or a temple, or a landscape, I present a very clear idea of those objects; but then (allowing for the effect of imitation which is something) my picture can at most affect only as the palace, temple, or landscape would have affected in the reality. On the other hand, the most lively and spirited verbal description I can give, raises a very obscure and imperfect *idea* of such objects; but then it is in my power to raise a stronger *emotion* by the description than I could do by the best painting. This experience constantly evinces. The proper manner of conveying the *affections* of the mind from one to another, is by words; there is a great insufficiency in all other methods of communication; and so far is a clearness of imagery from being absolutely necessary to an influence upon the passions, that they may be considerably operated upon without presenting any image at all, by certain sounds adapted to that purpose; of which we have a sufficient proof in the acknowledged and powerful effects of instrumental music. In reality a great clearness helps but little towards affecting the passions, as it is in some sort an enemy to all enthusiasms whatsoever.

Section [IV]
The same subject continued

There are two verses in Horace's art of poetry that seem to contradict this opinion, for which reason I shall take a little more pains in clearing it up. The verses are,

> Segnius inritant animos demissa per aurem
> Quam quæ sunt oculis subjecta fidelibus.

On this the abbé du Bos founds a criticism, wherein he gives painting the prefer-ence to poetry in the article of moving the passions; principally on account of the greater *clearness* of the ideas it represents. I believe this excellent judge was led into this mistake (if it be a mistake) by his system, to which he found it more conformable than I imagine it will be found to experience. I know several who admire and love painting, and yet who regard the objects of their admiration in that art, with coolness enough, in comparison of that warmth with which they are animated by affecting pieces of poetry or rhetoric. Among the common sort of people, I never could perceive that painting had much influence on their passions. It is true that the best sorts of painting, as well as the best sorts of poetry, are not much understood in that sphere. But it is most certain, that their passions are very strongly roused by a fanatic preacher, or by the ballads of Chevy-Chase, or the children in the wood, and by other little popular poems and tales that are current in that rank of life. I do not know of any paintings, bad or good, that produce the same effect. So that poetry with all its obscurity, has a more general as well as a more powerful dominion over the passions than the other art. And I think there are reasons in nature why the obscure idea, when properly conveyed, should be more affecting than the clear. It is our ignorance of things that causes all our admiration, and chiefly excites our passions. Knowledge and acquaintance make the most striking causes affect but little. It is thus with the vulgar, and all men are as the vulgar in what they do not understand. The ideas of eternity, and infinity, are among the most affecting we have, and yet perhaps there is nothing of which we really understand so little, as of infinity and eternity. We do not anywhere meet a more sublime description than this justly celebrated one of Milton, wherein he gives the portrait of Satan with a dignity so suitable to the subject.

> He above the rest
> In shape and gesture proudly eminent
> Stood like a tower; his form had yet not lost
> All her original brightness, nor appeared
> Less than archangel ruin'd, and th' excess
> Of glory obscured: as when the sun new ris'n
> Looks through the horizontal misty air
> Shorn of his beams; or from behind the moon
> In dim eclipse disastrous twilight sheds
> On half the nations; and with fear of change
> Perplexes monarchs.

Here is a very noble picture; and in what does this poetical picture consist? in images of a tower, an archangel, the sun rising through mists, or in an eclipse, the ruin of monarchs, and the revolutions of kingdoms. The mind is hurried out of itself, by a crowd of great and confused images; which affect because they are crowded and confused. For separate them, and you lose much of the greatness, and join them, and you infallibly lose the clearness. The images raised by poetry are always of this obscure kind; though in general the effects of poetry, are by no means to be attributed to the images it raises; which point we shall examine more at large hereafter. But painting, when we have allowed for the pleasure of imitation, can only affect simply by the images it presents; and even in painting a judicious obscurity in some things contributes to the effect of the picture; because the images in painting are exactly similar to those in nature; and in nature dark, confused, uncertain images have a greater power on the fancy to form the grander passions than those have which are more clear and determinate. But where and when this observation may be applied to practice, and how far it shall be extended, will be better deduced from the nature of the subject, and from the occasion, than from any rules that can be given.

I am sensible that this idea has met with opposition, and is likely still to be rejected by several. But let it be considered that hardly any thing can strike the mind with its greatness, which does not make some sort of approach towards infinity; which nothing can do whilst we are able to perceive its bounds; but to see an object distinctly, and to perceive its bounds, is one and the same thing. A clear idea is therefore another name for a little idea. There is a passage in the book of Job amazingly sublime, and this sublimity is principally due to the terrible uncertainty of the thing described. *In thoughts from the visions of the night, when deep sleep falleth upon men, fear came upon me and trembling, which made all my bones shake. Then a spirit passed before my face. The hair of my flesh stood up. It stood still,* but I could not discern the form thereof; *an image was before mine eyes; there was silence; and I heard a voice, – Shall mortal man be more just than God?* We are first prepared with the utmost solemnity for the vision; we are first terrified, before we are let even into the obscure cause of our emotion; but when this grand cause of terror makes its appearance, what is it? is it not, wrapt up in the shades of its own incomprehensible darkness, more awful, more striking, more terrible, than the liveliest description, than the clearest painting could possibly represent it? When painters have attempted to give us clear representations of these very fanciful and terrible ideas, they have I think almost always failed; insomuch that I have been at a loss, in all the pictures I have seen of hell, whether the painter did not intend something ludicrous. Several painters have handled a subject of this kind, with a view of assembling as many horrid phantoms as their imagination could suggest; but all the designs I have chanced to meet of the temptations of St Anthony, were rather a sort of odd wild grotesques, than any thing capable of producing a serious passion. In all these subjects poetry is very happy. Its apparitions, its chimeras, its harpies, its allegorical figures, are grand and affecting; and though Virgil's Fame, and Homer's Discord, are obscure, they are magnificent figures. These figures in painting would be clear enough, but I fear they might become ridiculous.

Section V
Power

Besides these things which *directly* suggest the idea of danger, and those which produce a similar effect from a mechanical cause, I know of nothing sublime which is not some modification of power. And this branch rises as naturally as the other two branches, from terror, the common stock of every thing that is sublime. The idea of power at first view, seems of the class of these indifferent ones, which may equally belong to pain or to pleasure. But in reality, the affection arising from the idea of vast power, is extremely remote from that neutral character. For first, we must remember, that the idea of pain, in its highest degree, is much stronger than the highest degree of pleasure; and that it preserves the same superiority through all the subordinate gradations. From hence it is, that where the chances for equal degrees of suffering or enjoyment are in any sort equal, the idea of the suffering or enjoyment must always be prevalent. And indeed the ideas of pain, and above all of death, are so very affecting, that whilst we remain in the presence of whatever is supposed to have the power of inflicting either, it is impossible to be perfectly free from terror. Again, we know by experience, that for the enjoyment of pleasure, no great efforts of power are at all necessary; nay we know, that such efforts would go a great way towards destroying our satisfaction: for pleasure must be stolen, and not forced upon us; pleasure follows the will; and therefore we are generally affected with it by many things of a force greatly inferior to our own. But pain is always inflicted by a power in some way superior, because we never submit to pain willingly. So that strength, violence, pain and terror, are ideas that rush in upon the mind together. Look at a man, or any other animal of prodigious strength, and what is your idea before reflection? Is it that this strength will be subservient to you, to your ease, to your pleasure, to your interest in any sense? No; the emotion you feel is, lest this enormous strength should be employed to the purposes of rapine and destruction. That power derives all its sublimity from the terror with which it is generally accompanied, will appear evidently from its effect in the very few cases, in which it may be possible to strip a considerable degree of strength of its ability to hurt. When you do this, you spoil it of every thing sublime, and it immediately becomes contemptible. An ox is a creature of vast strength; but he is an innocent creature, extremely serviceable, and not at all dangerous; for which reason the idea of an ox is by no means grand. A bull is strong too; but his strength is of another kind; often very destructive, seldom (at least amongst us) of any use in our business; the idea of a bull is therefore great, and it has frequently a place in sublime descriptions, and elevating comparisons. Let us look at another strong animal in the two distinct lights in which we may consider him. The horse in the light of an useful beast, fit for the plough, the road, the draft, in every social useful light the horse has nothing of the sublime; but is it thus that we are affected with him, *whose neck is clothed with thunder, the glory of whose nostrils is terrible, who swalloweth the ground with fierceness and rage, neither believeth that it is the sound of the trumpet?* In this description the useful character of the horse entirely disappears, and the terrible and sublime blaze out together. We have continually about us animals of a strength that is considerable, but not pernicious. Amongst these we never look for the sublime: it comes upon us in the gloomy forest, and in the howling wilderness, in the form of the lion, the tiger, the panther, or rhinoceros. Whenever strength is only useful, and employed for our benefit or our pleasure, then it is never sublime; for nothing can act agreeably to us, that does not act in conformity to our will; but to act agreeably to our will, it must be subject to us; and therefore can never be the cause of a grand and commanding conception. The description of the wild ass, in Job, is worked up into no small sublimity, merely by insisting on his freedom, and his setting mankind at defiance; otherwise the description of such an animal could have had nothing noble in it. *Who hath loosed* (says he) *the bands of the wild ass? whose house I have made the wilderness, and the barren land his dwellings. He scorneth the multitude of the city, neither regardeth he the voice of the driver. The range of the mountains is his pasture.* The magnificent description of the unicorn and of leviathan in the same book, is full of the same heightening circumstances. *Will the unicorn be willing to serve thee? canst thou bind the unicorn with his band in the furrow? wilt thou trust him because his strength is great? – Canst thou draw out leviathan with an hook? will he make a covenant with thee? wilt thou take him for a servant for ever? shall not one be cast down even at the sight of him?* In short, wheresoever we find strength, and in what light soever we look upon power, we shall all along observe the sublime the concomitant of terror, and contempt the attendant on a strength that is subservient and innoxious. The race of dogs in many of their kinds, have generally a competent degree of strength and swiftness; and they exert these, and other valuable qualities which they possess, greatly to our convenience and pleasure. Dogs are indeed the most social, affectionate, and amiable animals of the whole brute creation; but love approaches much nearer to contempt than is commonly imagined; and accordingly, though we caress dogs, we borrow from them an appellation of the most despicable kind, when we employ terms of reproach; and this appellation is the common mark of the last vileness and contempt in every language. Wolves have not more strength than several species of dogs; but on account of their unmanageable fierceness, the idea of a wolf is not despicable; it is not excluded from grand descriptions and similitudes. Thus we are affected by strength, which is *natural* power. The power which arises from institution in kings and commanders, has the same connection with terror. Sovereigns are frequently addressed with the title of *dread majesty*. And it may be observed, that young persons little acquainted with the world, and who have not been used to approach men in power, are commonly struck with an awe which takes away the free use of their faculties. *When I prepared my seat in the street* (says Job) *the young men saw me, and hid themselves.* Indeed so natural is this timidity with regard to power, and so strongly does it inhere in our constitution, that very few are able to conquer it, but by mixing much in the business of the great world, or by using no small violence to their natural dispositions. I know some people are of opinion, that no awe, no degree of terror, accompanies the idea of power, and have hazarded to affirm, that we can contemplate the idea of God himself without any such emotion. I purposely avoided when I first considered this subject, to introduce the idea of that great and tremendous being, as an example in an argument so light as this; though it frequently occurred to me, not as an objection to, but as a strong confirmation of my notions in this matter. I hope, in what I am going to say, I shall avoid presumption, where it is almost impossible for any mortal to speak with strict propriety. I say then, that whilst we consider the Godhead merely as he is an object of the understanding, which forms a complex idea of power, wisdom, justice, goodness, all stretched to a degree far exceeding the bounds of our comprehension, whilst we consider the divinity in this refined and abstracted light, the imagination and passions are little or nothing affected. But because we are bound by the condition of our nature to ascend to these pure and intellectual ideas, through the medium of sensible images, and to judge of these divine qualities by their evident acts and exertions, it becomes extremely hard to disentangle our idea of the cause from the effect by which we are led to know it. Thus when we contemplate the Deity, his attributes and their operation coming united on the mind, form a sort of sensible image, and as such are capable of affecting the imagination. Now, though in a just idea of the Deity, perhaps none of his attributes are predominant, yet to our imagination, his power is by far the most striking. Some reflection, some comparing is necessary to satisfy us of his wisdom, his justice, and his goodness; to be struck with his power, it is only necessary that we should open our eyes. But whilst we contemplate so vast an object, under the arm, as it were, of almighty power, and invested upon every side with omnipresence, we shrink into the minuteness of our own nature, and are, in a manner, annihilated before him. And though a consideration of his other attributes may relieve in some measure our apprehensions; yet no conviction of the justice with which it is exercised, nor the mercy with which it is tempered, can wholly remove the terror that naturally arises from a force which nothing can withstand. If we rejoice, we rejoice with trembling; and even whilst we are receiving benefits, we cannot but shudder at a power which can confer benefits of such mighty importance....

Thus we have traced power through its several gradations unto the highest of all, where our imagination is finally lost; and we find terror quite throughout the progress, its inseparable companion, and growing along with it, as far as we can possibly trace them. Now as power is undoubtedly a capital source of the sublime, this will point out evidently from whence its energy is derived, and to what class of ideas we ought to unite it.

Part Three. Section XXVII
The Sublime and Beautiful compared

On closing this general view of beauty, it naturally occurs, that we should compare it with the sublime; and in this comparison there appears a remarkable contrast. For sublime objects are vast in their dimensions, beautiful ones comparatively small; beauty should be smooth, and polished; the great, rugged and negligent; beauty should shun the right line, yet deviate from it insensibly; the great in many cases loves the right line, and when it deviates, it often makes a strong deviation; beauty should not be obscure; the great ought to be dark and gloomy; beauty should be light and delicate; the great ought to be solid, and even massive. They are indeed ideas of a very different nature, one being founded on pain, the other on pleasure; and however they may vary afterwards from the direct nature of their causes, yet these causes keep up an eternal distinction between them, a distinction never to be forgotten by any whose business it is to affect the passions. In the infinite variety of natural combinations we must expect to find the qualities of things the most remote imaginable from each other united in the same object. We must expect also to find combinations of the same kind in the works of art. But when we consider the power of an object upon our passions, we must know that when any thing is intended to affect the mind by the force of some predominant property, the affection produced is like to be the more uniform and perfect, if all the other properties or qualities of the object be of the same nature, and tending to the same design as the principal;

> If black, and white blend, soften, and unite,
> A thousand ways, are there no black and white?

If the qualities of the sublime and beautiful are sometimes found united, does this prove, that they are the same, does it prove, that they are any way allied, does it prove even that they are not opposite and contradictory? Black and white may soften, may blend, but they are not therefore the same. Nor when they are so softened and blended with each other, or with different colours, is the power of black as black, or of white as white, so strong as when each stands uniform and distinguished.

Part Five. Section VII
How words influence the passions

Now, as words affect, not by any original power, but by representation, it might be supposed, that their influence over the passions should be but light; yet it is quite otherwise; for we find by experience that eloquence and poetry are as capable, nay indeed much more capable of making deep and lively impressions than any other arts, and even than nature itself in very many cases. And this arises chiefly from these three causes. First, that we take an extraordinary part in the passions of others, and that we are easily affected and brought into sympathy by any tokens which are shown of them; and there are no tokens which can express all the circumstances of most passions so fully as words; so that if a person speaks upon any subject, he can not only convey the subject to you, but likewise the manner in which he is himself affected by it. Certain it is, that the influence of most things on our passions is not so much from the things themselves, as from our opinions concerning them; and these again depend very much on the opinions of other men, conveyable for the most part by words only. Secondly; there are many things of a very affecting nature, which can seldom occur in the reality, but the words which represent them often do; and thus they have an opportunity of making a deep impression and taking root in the mind, whilst the idea of the reality was transient; and to some perhaps never really occurred in any shape, to whom it is notwithstanding very affecting, as war, death, famine, &c. Besides, many ideas have never been at all presented to the sense of any men but by words, as God, angels, devils, heaven and hell, all of which have however a great influence over the passions. Thirdly; by words we have it in our power to make such *combinations* as we cannot possibly do otherwise. By this power of combining we are able, by the addition of well-chosen circumstances, to give a new life and force to the simple object. In painting we may represent any fine figure we please; but we never can give it those enlivening touches which it may receive from words. To represent an angel in a picture, you can only draw a beautiful young man winged; but what painting can furnish out any thing so grand as the addition of one word, "the angel of the *Lord?*" It is true, I have here no clear idea, but these words affect the mind more than the sensible image did, which is all I contend for. A picture of Priam dragged to the altar's foot, and there murdered, if it were well executed would undoubtedly be very moving; but there are very aggravating circumstances which it could never represent.

> Sanguine fœdantem *quos ipse sacraverat* ignes.

As a further instance, let us consider those lines of Milton, where he describes the travels of the fallen angels through their dismal habitation,

> – O'er many a dark and dreary vale
> They pass'd, and many a region dolorous;
> O'er many a frozen, many a fiery Alp;

Rock, caves, lakes, fens, bogs, dens and shades of death,
A universe of death.

Here is displayed the force of union in

Rocks, caves, lakes, dens, bogs, fens and shades;

which yet would lose the greatest part of their effect, if they were not the

– Rocks, caves, lakes, dens, bogs, fens and shades
of Death. –

This idea or this affection caused by a word, which nothing but a word could annex to the others, raises a very great degree of the sublime; and this sublime is raised yet higher by what follows, a *"universe of death."* Here are again two ideas not presentable but by language; and an union of them great and amazing beyond conception; if they may properly be called ideas which present no distinct image to the mind; – but still it will be difficult to conceive how words can move the passions which belong to real objects, without representing these objects clearly. This is difficult to us, because we do not sufficiently distinguish, in our observations upon language, between a clear expression, and a strong expression. These are frequently confounded with each other, though they are in reality extremely different. The former regards the understanding; the latter belongs to the passions. The one describes a thing as it is; the other describes it as it is felt. Now, as there is a moving tone of voice, an impassioned countenance, an agitated gesture, which affect independently of the things about which they are exerted, so there are words, and certain dispositions of words, which being peculiarly devoted to passionate subjects, and always used by those who are under the influence of any passion; they touch and move us more than those which far more clearly and distinctly express the subject matter. We yield to sympathy, what we refuse to description. The truth is, all verbal description, merely as naked description, though never so exact, conveys so poor and insufficient an idea of the thing described, that it could scarcely have the smallest effect, if the speaker did not call in to his aid those modes of speech that mark a strong and lively feeling in himself. Then, by the contagion of our passions, we catch a fire already kindled in another, which probably might never have been struck out by the object described. Words, by strongly conveying the passions, by those means which we have already mentioned, fully compensate for their weakness in other respects. It may be observed that very polished languages, and such as are praised for their superior clearness and perspicuity, are generally deficient in strength. The French language has that perfection, and that defect. Whereas the oriental tongues, and in general the languages of most unpolished people, have a great force and energy of expression; and this is but natural. Uncultivated people are but ordinary observers of things, and not critical in distinguishing them; but, for that reason, they admire more, and are more affected with what they see, and therefore express themselves in a warmer and more passionate manner. If the affection be well conveyed, it will work its effect without any clear idea; often without any idea at all of the thing which has originally given rise to it.

It might be expected from the fertility of the subject, that I should consider poetry as it regards the sublime and beautiful more at large; but it must be observed that in this light it has been often and well handled already. It was not my design to enter into the criticism of the sublime and beautiful in any art, but to attempt to lay down such principles as may tend to ascertain, to distinguish, and to form a sort of standard for them; which purposes I thought might best be effected by an enquiry into the properties of such things in nature as raise love and astonishment in us; and by showing in what manner they operated to produce these passions. Words were only so far to be considered, as to show upon what principle they were capable of being the representatives of these natural things, and by what powers they were able to affect us often as strongly as the things they represent, and sometimes much more strongly.

26

John Lawson,
from *Lectures concerning oratory* (1758)

Lecture the Fifteenth.
Of figures, or tropes

Clearness, propriety, and harmony, are not sufficient to answer the ends of oratory, which require beside these, that discourse should be lively and animated: to this purpose the use of figures is necessary; concerning which I now proceed to make some observations.

It is a question which hath received various answers, and occasioned no small debate, whence it cometh to pass, that figures render discourse more pleasing: what is there in the mind of man, which disposeth it to entertain with more delight, notions conveyed to it in this disguise, than in their own natural form?

The variety of opinions concerning this point seemeth to have sprung from hence, that different men fixing upon different causes, have persisted in reducing the effect, each to the cause assigned by himself, excluding all others; to the production of which effect several, perhaps many do concur. I will explain myself.

First. It hath been observed long ago, indeed instances occur every day in proof of it, that the mind is pleased with things uncommon and new: now figurative speech hath this charm of novelty to recommend it, for leaving the usual track, it takes you through paths untrodden and unexpected: you see a certain point laid down to be proved; you have a general notion of the arguments likely to be made use of to this purpose; but instead of having these placed before you in the common form, you find them in one very different, and the knowledge you sought for communicated in expressions altogether foreign, yet these conducted by such happy skill, that they lead you as rightly and shortly to the end in view, as the plainest and most literal: thus you are entertained in your journey without being retarded.

Another cause that recommendeth figures, those especially distinguished by the name of *tropes*, to our liking, is the pleasure which the mind naturally feels in *comparison*. When a word which in its original sense conveys a certain idea to the mind, is used in such manner, as together with this to convey another, connected to the first by a natural resemblance; yet so that this latter accessory idea becomes now the principal; here the mind hath the pleasure of contemplating at once two images, yet without confusion: nay with this advantage, that by means of such comparison the principal image becomes more bright and striking: as in these examples,

"[a] Now laugh the fields." –
"[b] Admires new leaves and apples not it's own."
"[c] With floods and whirlwinds of tempestuous fire."

The pleasure received from the imitative arts hath its ground in this love of comparison. Thus we are delighted with the likeness between the forms and colours of nature, and those taken from her by the pencil: nay we are often pleased with seeing nature imitate as it were herself, reflecting to our sight the landskips of wood, and hills, and skies, portrayed on the glassy surface of untroubled water: something whereof I think there certainly is in the present case, in the use of *metaphors* or *translations*.

To which you should add, that these comparisons are frequently drawn from objects in themselves beautiful, which being of course pleasing, diffuse new charms as well as light over a whole discourse.

Other causes of less influence might be assigned, but I hasten to the chief and most universal.

The truest representations of nature please most: and it is for this reason, that figures are agreeable, being the voice of nature; when rightly used, the way wherein she expresseth herself on all such occasions. "Yet how may this be? Are not figures artificial speech, and considered as such? In what sense then do I style them the voice and language of nature?" This will need some explanation.

Determine first, what are the occasions, upon which figures are properly employed. Are they not chiefly those, in which the mind is seized, warmed, transported by a sudden or strong passion, as admiration, astonishment, love, rage? Now consult the great book of nature, the original and model of all true art: – how do all, young and old, learned and illiterate, men and women, express themselves in such conjunctures? Is their discourse clear, direct, and flowing? Or rather is it not disturbed, broken, disjointed? The mind overcharged by passion, labouring yet unable to pour it all forth, makes every effort, struggles in vain for words answerable to its ideas, starts from hint to hint, heaps images upon images, and paints its own disorder in the irregularity and confusion of its language. What doth indignation? Invoke heaven and earth, and seek to interest all nature in its quarrel....

From these considerations it appears, that figurative speech is so far from being as it has been oftentimes represented, merely artificial, and a departure from nature, that it is a faithful image of nature. Inward emotion displayeth itself as readily in the language as in the features; and he, who from the circumstances he describes, or subject of which he treats, ought to be, or appear to be possessed with a strong passion, yet speaks in a calm, untroubled easiness

[a] Nunc rident agri.   Virg.
[b] Miraturque novas frondes et non sua poma.   Virg.
[c] Milton's *Paradise Lost*. Book 1.

of style, acts as much against nature, as does the man who would express great inward agitation of mind by a smooth unaltered serenity of countenance.

Figures are the language of passion; universal experience demonstrates this to be the case, as all of every rank and capacity who are under the influence of such passion, speak figuratively: now it is acknowledged, that the orator in almost all causes of moment finds it requisite to excite some passion in his hearer, which he cannot otherwise accomplish than by feeling, or seeming himself to feel the same: and how shall he assume this appearance? How? But by making use of the language, which nature has rendered inseparable from the passions. If you are enflamed with anger or softened with pity, speak to me as men are wont to do, while they are under the power of such emotions: otherwise you talk in vain; I shall either not regard you at all, or shall turn away from you as an impostor. Nature hath rendered passions wheresoever strongly marked, catching; but where these marks are wanting, how shall they catch?

What I have been saying is however to be understood with some degree of caution. Ye have doubtless heard it observed, that figurative speech is not friendly to the pathetic, as carrying the air of much study and artifice, the work therefore of a mind vacant and at ease.

Which observation, how contradictory so ever it may appear, yet a little attention will reconcile, to what hath been advanced above. To this purpose, you should distinguish figures into two kinds: one sort consists in words, as *repetitions*, *likeness of sounds*, and *cadence*, and *oppositions*; to which we may add as being useful in embellishing style, certain kinds of *metaphors*, *transpositions*, *reduplications*. Now these being calculated to please the ear or imagination, being conducive to prettiness and elegance only, are enemies to the pathetic; are too insignificant and idle for occasions of such importance, and from all such ought to be excluded.

But there are figures of a second kind, whose power affects the sense principally, which bestow force and spirit; such as the rhetoricians name *apostrophes, hyperboles, feigning of persons*; to these it is, that what has been said is applicable; these are so far from hurting the pathetic or being inconsistent with it, that they are the natural language of passion. Agitated by passion, the peasant breaks out into such, no less than the orator; the only difference is, that in the latter, the rudeness of uninstructed nature is polished, its extravagances corrected, the air and resemblance are preserved, but softened and adorned. We may pronounce of eloquence in this respect, as the poet doth of comedy, it is not the less just representation of life for rising sometimes into a higher style:...

27

James Usher,
from *Clio; or a discourse on taste* (1769)

VIII. Thoughts on writing

...The first and noblest source of delight in works of genius, without com-
petition, arises from the sublime. The sublime, by an authority which the soul
is utterly unable to resist, takes possession of our attention, and of all our
faculties, and absorbs them in astonishment. The passion it inspires us with is
evidently a mixture of terror, curiosity, and exultation: but they are stamped
with a majesty that bestows on them a different air and character from those
passions on any other occasion. In the sublime we feel ourselves alarmed, our
motions are suspended, and we remain for some time until the emotion wears
off, wrapped in silence and inquisitive horror.

The combination of passions in the sublime, renders the idea of it obscure.
No doubt the sensation of fear is very distinct in it; but it is equally obvious,
that there is something in the sublime more than this abject passion. In all
other terrors the soul loses its dignity, and as it were shrinks below its usual
size: but at the presence of the sublime, although it be always awful, the soul
of man seems to be raised out of a trance; it assumes an unknown grandeur;
it is seized with a new appetite, that in a moment effaces its former little prospects and desires; it is rapt out of the sight and consideration of this diminutive world, into a kind of gigantic creation, where it finds room to dilate itself
to a size agreeable to its present nature and grandeur: it overlooks the
Appenines, and the clouds upon them, and sees nothing in view around it but
immense objects. In the poet's language it flies, it soars, it pursues a beauty in
the madness of rapture, that words or description cannot contain; and if these
expressions be extravagant and improper in the ordinary commerce of life,
they yet exactly describe the intellectual and real state of the mind at the presence of the sublime.

The sublime enters into the principles of taste with such distinction, and
rules the human spirit with such absolute sovereignty, that I would fain discover the origin and nature of its power; but fate seems to have covered it over
with mystery, the greatest writers have either stopped short, or failed in the
attempt, and I am safe enough although I turn aside, and leave it in the sacred
obscurity in which it has so long been veiled: however, I may, by an hypothesis, attempt to give you an intelligible idea of the manner in which it affects
us; I have a licence from custom for doing so; for I must inform you, that

modern philosophers often take the liberty of forming systems merely for the sake of illustration, and to resolve difficulties, without thinking themselves obliged to give a demonstration of the truth of their system. If it tends to make that conceivable which was before inconceivable; the inventors suppose that they have done some service to science.

The system I am going to lay before you, is that of a friend of mine, who was a true lover of knowledge. He found little satisfaction in the philosophy of colleges and schools, particularly in those enquiries he thought of most importance: he had withdrawn himself from the trifling bustle of the little world, to converse with his own heart, and end a stormy life in obscure quiet. One day after dinner, we walked out to indulge on our favourite topics. Our excursion terminated at a rock, whose base is washed by the Western Ocean. It was one of those fine days in August, when the cool of the evening brought on a refreshing sweetness. We sat down to rest, and enjoy the prospect of the sea, that stretched before us beyond the limits of the eye. The sun was just setting, and his last softened beams flying to the shore, seemed to dip in a thousand waves, and leave in the waters the blaze they lost. We had been reading Homer on our way to the sea-side. When we sat down, our conversation turned on the strange power of the sublime. It is easy, says the thoughtful philosopher, to describe the impressions the sublime makes on the mind, and this is all the writers on this subject have hitherto done with any success; but is it impossible, from a due attention to the symptoms, to unravel its meaning, and discover the spring of the silent and inquisitive astonishment it impresses on the spirit of man? I am sensible a just explication of the sublime must account for all its effects, as well for the noble elevation and the charming rapture, as for the terror it bestows. If I can produce a cause that accounts sufficiently for all the symptoms, and no other can be given, then mine ought by all the rules of good reasoning to be admitted for the true one, however novel it appears.

In order to proceed to the discovery we desire to make, let us turn our views to objects remarkably sublime, and from them obtain what intelligence we can. Observe this mountain that rises so high on the left, if we had been farther removed from it, you might see behind it other mountains rising in strange confusion, the farthest off almost lost in the distance, yet great in the obscurity, your imagination labours to travel over them, and the inhabitants seem to reside in a superior world. But here you have a different prospect, the next mountain covers all the rest from your view, and by its nearer approach, presents distinctly to your eye objects of new admiration. The rocks on its sides meet the clouds in vast irregularity; the pensive eye traces the rugged precipice down to the bottom, and surveys there the mighty ruins that time has mouldered and tumbled below. It is easy in this instance to discover that we are terrified and silenced into awe, at the *vestiges* we see of immense power; and the more manifest are the appearances of disorder, and the neglect of contrivance, the more plainly we feel the boundless might these rude monuments are owing to. But beside this silent fear, we feel our curiosity roused from its deepest springs in the soul; and while we tremble, we are seized with an exquisite delight, that attends on sublime objects only. The same mixed sensation weighs upon us, when we see an ocean disturbed and agitated in storms; or a forest roaring, and bending under the force of the tempest. We are struck by it with more calmness, but equal grandeur, in the starry heavens: the silence, the unmeasured distance, and the unknown power united in that prospect, render it very awful in the deepest serenity. Thunder, with broken bursts of lightning through black clouds; the view of a cataract, whose billows fling themselves down with eternal rage; or the unceasing sound of the falling waters by night; the howling of animals in the dark: all these produce the sublime, by the association of the idea of invisible immense power.

The soul of man naturally pays homage to unseen power. He feels obscure hopes, and obscure fears, which become a religious passion, and distinguish him more than any other difference between him and other inhabitants of the earth. The religious passion, attended with less tumult, but more constancy than the other passions, calls upon his heart in the majesty of darkness and silence, and is the source of the sublime sensation we are treating of. I see several objections crowding to your mind against my hypothesis; but hear me out, for I intend to obviate them all.

The object of the religious passion is no idea, it is unknown; therefore the passion itself is obscure, and wants a name; but its effects are very remarkable, for they form the peculiar character of human nature. Curiosity and hope carry with them the plainest symptoms of a passion that wanders, and is astray for its object. In their anxious search, they unite themselves with every great prospect in life, whose completion lies in the dark: but when we arrive at the point we proposed, we are fully sensible that curiosity and hope have been deceived, the enjoyment in our power whatever it be, falls infinitely below our expectations, yet the alacrity of the mind feels no decay by disappointment; we set out immediately with renewed vigour in pursuit of something farther, and nothing but death puts an end to the anxiety. These passions are exceedingly alarmed, at the appearances of the excessive power that gives us the idea of the sublime. In the disorder and confusion of seas in storms, or when lofty woods struggle with high winds, we are struck with an humiliating awe, surprise, and suspense: the mind views the effects of boundless power with still amazement: it recoils upon itself in a passion made up of terror, joy, and rapture, and feels in sentiment these questions: *who is the author of this? What is he to me? Is he the object of my eternal curiosity, of my mighty fears, and hopes?* I appeal to the feelings of every man, if his passions in these circumstances be not exactly applicable to this confused interested state of mind, whether he disentangles or reflects on his own ideas or no.

There is nothing more disputed than the origin of the idea of divinity. All nations, however barbarous, have it; and our latest discoveries prove that the relations of atheist nations are all fabulous, and that the savages of every quarter of the globe look up to a supernatural power. From the universality of the idea, men who did not sufficiently examine its origin suspected, and actually taught, that we had an innate idea of God. The grossness and want of precision with which they advanced this doctrine, afforded Mr Locke the happiest opportunity imaginable of triumphing over them, and of deducing religion and the idea of the deity from sensible ideas, and from the mere agency of reason, agreeable to his general system. It is true, we have not an innate idea of God; but we a thousand times feel the intruded influence of a mighty unknown power, that must, by the unavoidable transition the mind makes from the effect to the cause, give rise to the idea of divine power. Sensible ideas, indeed, and the passing show of this external world, divert the attention of the mind from its religious feelings; but as sensible ideas recede from the imagination, and leave us to a solitary intellectual state of mind, we find an awful and obscure presence surround us, that bestows on the soul an elevation and enthusiasm that do not attend on external ideas.

All mankind, whose common sense is not diverted by system, will agree, that darkness, solitude, and silence, naturally oppress the mind by a tremendous and sublime sensation. It is further evident, that they produce not this effect by any active power of theirs, but merely by stripping the imagination of its sensible ideas, of the noise, the mirth, and light that diverted its attention, and leaving it to its naked state and feelings; consequently, that the great influence that then rises upon the soul, and dwells upon it in terrors, is the effect of a power that has been always present to it, although it has not been always observed, on account of the interposition of the transitory ideas of sense. In short, it appears from a great variety of observations and reflected lights, that the human soul is always oppressed by a mighty presence, whose obscurity and stillness only keep it out of our attention when the mind is employed on exterior objects. To avoid this awful presence it is, that we for ever seek amusement and company, and that any diversion, however insipid and trifling in itself, becomes to us a pleasing relief, merely by taking up our attention. Reason smiles at the puerility of our amusements. The very slaves of pleasure hold them in contempt, and acknowledge they will not bear examination: yet the wise and the vain find solitude alike insupportable, and alike desire the company and diversion they despise.

Because the philosophers of our days can assign no form, nor size, nor colour, to the object of their sublime awe, they conclude it to be vain and superstitious: they take upon them to decide positively, that nature in the formation of the human mind has acted an unmeaning part; and where she appears remarkably solemn and regular, in her noblest production, has been absurd and puerile. Her vast sagacity, and the design that always appears in her works of a lower order, ought surely to procure her a degree of confidence, and give some suspicions that she did not act wholly at random in the plan of the human mind. The truth is, the impression of this obscure presence, however it be felt, is beyond the verge of the philosophy of the ideas of sense. The disciples of this philosophy cannot upon their principles admit that an object which neither the memory can treasure up, nor the imagination form, has been present to the mind. They are not able to conceive that an object has been there which was not represented by a sensible idea, and which makes itself felt only by its influence. But let it be considered, however the consequences may clash with this or that system, that awe is a relative idea, and bears as necessary a relation to something either ideal or intellectual that impresses terror, as vision does to something seen. Let it be further attended to, that the awe which surrounds us in solitude, in deep silence, and in darkness, is not acquired by habit, by association, religious tenets, or prejudices; seeing that it is not confined to particular nations or ages, but that it is inseparable from the human race at all eras of time, be their religion what it will; and that those men who have most effectually cast off the weaknesses of the human kind, have discovered the plainest symptoms of the awe I speak of: but we must carefully distinguish between common accidental fear, and this noble sensation that elevates whilst it overawes. Men often bear silence, solitude, and night, without distinct or ideal fear, such as is occasioned by tales of ghosts or goblins: but the still important attention, and solemn swell of mind, that is a concomitant of obscurity, of loneliness, and of deep silence, appears by the writings and sentiments of the greatest of mankind, to be an involuntary and universal impression on the intellect. It is not, as Mr Locke says, that the tales of nurses have made night the scene of terrors, but that the solemnity and real awfulness of the night, has made it the natural scene of frightful tales and apparitions in all nations. It is to meet the sublime impression undisturbed, the poet retires to the solitary walks of the country; that he seeks for vales hid from human eye, where silence seems to take up her dwelling; and loves to frequent the woods covered with darkness and shade: there he feels, with all the certainty of intuition, the presence of the universal genius, whose immediate influence tunes his voice to music, and fires the imagination to rapture. All the ideas that arrive to the mind by the ordinary avenues of sense, are the objects of common apprehension and discourse; but in the presence of the universal genius, those ideas grow brighter than the gilding of the sun can make them, and put on a strange beauty that belongs not to them. It is the beauty of a being, indistinct, and hid as it were in light, which the imagination in vain seeks to lay hold of: whence you may conceive the distress, that obliges the poet to fly from image to image, to express what he feels. No idea, however grand, answers his purpose; yet as he feels strongly, he still hopes, and rushes to snatch into view another grand prospect. The variety of his efforts shows the object the mind labours with to be different from any thing we know; to be beyond the power of utterance; and yet the very labour and confusion of images, and the despair he betrays, paint sufficiently the poet's perception; and we are sensible of what he cannot express, because we all feel it in our own bosoms.

The sublime influence of groves and lonely vales is not fantastic, or a work of the imagination: it is a most constant uniform effect in the same circumstances; and the change it makes in our ideas, or rather the creation of new beauty it bestows on them, which was never had from sense; and the mighty powers it bestows on us, are evidently supernatural. To say that the inspiration of poetry and enthusiasm, which are the most surprising and violent effects we know of, are produced by a *non-entity*, or by the native force of the imagination, is utterly unphilosophic and absurd. It is further manifest, upon reflection, that the supernatural presence is not confined to wood or dale; not to these long mountains beside us; nor to the winding shores, and hollow seas: it always meets the pensive meditating mind; in the remotest parts of the earth we are at no distance from it, and in the darkness of night it possesses us. Say, ye stars of heaven, almost lost in immense distance, does not the Father of Being sustain and cherish worlds around you, who receive life and rapture from his presence?

If the universal spirit had not always dwelt in the soul, enthusiasm would not be infectious, nor could fanatic preachers communicate it at all times to their audience. The enthusiastic orator expresses his own feelings, and his discourse is infectious; not by the production of any new and foreign passion, but by fixing the attention to the great sensations of the soul. If they were not there before, the preacher could no more raise them, than he could give a man born blind the idea of colours. Persons of a religious and solitary cast of thought often experience these inspirations, when prayer or meditation have led the soul to retirement, and taken external ideas out of its attention: and the religious fanatic experiences the same divine favour that the poet does in his gloomy forest or beside his consecrated stream. The sagacious ancients were so sensible of the identity of the spirit that inspired both, that they gave the same appellation to the prophet and poet, as I said before.

When we have carried our views thus far, it is easy to discover the springs of polytheism. The imagination found the divine idea rising before it in a variety of circumstances, and worshipped it under the several distinctions in which it appeared. The Greeks, the fathers of thought and sublime knowledge, always nicely observed the difference between the native powers of the mind over its stock of sensible ideas, and the sublime influence to which it was passive. They traced the latter through its various appearances, and never failed to attribute it to divine power; sometimes to the Muses, sometimes to Apollo, to the Furies, to Pan, to the Sylvan deities, and to the genius of the place; they never mistook the supernatural presence, but only divided it out, according as the imagination happened to be struck, and to the concomitant external ideas.

It was not fear made the gods, but God made his presence known by an awe that does not attend on sensible objects. If man falls down to worship in the groves; it is because the sacred impression he feels in solitude and obscurity makes him sensible of the presence of invisible power. From what I have just said, it is easy to conceive the reason why men educated in the country, and those especially whose employments are in the fields, are in general more religious than the inhabitants of towns and cities.

Terror is the first impression that meets us in the solitary presence; and the bulk of mankind have only feeling enough when they are alone to create uneasiness, and a confused gloom that drives them to seek for company and amusement; but men of more delicate sensations find admiration and extasy along with fear. Delight and fear are passions of almost opposite natures; yet they are united in this unknown object, in an immeasurable degree. By all the known rules of reasoning from mechanic principles, the fear of unknown power ought to be much more faint and dull than the fear of known power; and in men educated in doubt or disbelief of a future state, this fear of unknown power should be hardly perceptible, or active; and thus it would certainly be, if it were the issue of sensible ideas, or of reason: but in fact, all men who have leisure to observe their own internal sensations, find the terror of unknown power far beyond all limits, and beyond all degrees of known evil. When we see the limits of evil, we immediately see that it loses a great deal in our imagination. Men easily bear imprisonment, poverty, sickness, and even great degrees of pain; but the obscure despair, whose object we know not, is blacker than the grave, and more terrible than death, and to plunge from it men commit suicide. Every calamity of this life is supportable, and we suffer them by choice rather than death, until they bring us to a pensive solitary state of mind, in which we feel the pressure of unknown power; and then men often make the cruel choice, and seek death as a welcome release from the gloomy terrors that sink them. Fanatic preachers make admirable use of this state of mind; for experience shows, that when melancholy has continued some time, and the soul seems to itself utterly lost, secret fits of joy and transport beam in upon it through the gloom. Dealers in the spirit therefore take special care to raise enthusiastic terrors first in their followers, and to bring despair and reprobation full in the soul's view; under which some of them actually kill themselves; but as the mind cannot long remain in this state, and the intense possession of religious melancholy naturally turns to extasy and rapture, enthusiasts, from a state of despair, pass suddenly to a state of joy and transport, which is easily mistaken for election and the kind voice of the divinity. It is lucky for fanatic preachers of all ages, that the bulk of mankind are ignorant, and incapable of observing, that the divine presence they boast of has been common to every religion; that religion only unites an universal passion to this or that set of doctrines and ideas; and that there is a systematic method of acquiring the predestination and divine impulse they feel with great certainty.

The rapture of enthusiasm is as contradictory to all rules of reasoning from the received principles, as its fears. If it were the issue of our sensible ideas, and reflections made on them, it would never rise to the force of sensible beauty; and all the warmest imagination could do, is to make approaches to the charms of colours, and of form, and to the beauties of smell and taste. But the obscure unknown good that mortals seek with such anxiety is more than every joy and every good besides. It is the love-sick wish that brightens hope, the search of which makes us pass resolutely through all the evils of life. Shall I call it supreme beauty? This is but a figurative name, of that beauty of which we have no conception. But does not the want of conception make it indifferent to us? No; an intelligence clearer than sense, and stronger than reason, characterises it with rapture, and with inexpressible joy; and let us conceive of it as we will in theory, it is the loadstone to which the soul for ever tends with anxiety, in every unknown good and obscure prospect.

I observed before, that the remarkable curiosity and hope of our kind, are the symptoms of a wandering passion for a fugitive object necessary to our happiness that is for ever near us, and for ever hides from us; hence proceed the perpetual discontent and care that harbour in the human breast: for it is evident, that be our possessions what they will, we cannot be content while we desire or hope for any thing more than we possess; and that while this object of desire is unknown, the symptoms must be exactly what they are, and man's pursuits must be wild, inconsistent, and unsatisfied. This fond unknown object, on account of the vastness of the passion with which it is fought for, was by the ancients called the *summum bonum*, or chief felicity. Whether there be such an enjoyment in reality or no, the phantom, or visionary expectation of it, is pursued by mortals with endless and unwearied care. It was a noble effort of human reason, bewildered in ignorance, to enquire for the object of its sublime hopes. One who has a clear idea of the meaning of the ancients in this great enquiry, can hardly refrain from smiling at Mr Locke's ludicrous explication of it. If the question had been what is the most delicious fare; or whether the best relish were to be found in apples, plums, or nuts; the preference undoubtedly ought to be given by every one to that which pleases him best; for there is no disputing tastes: but the question here is, what is the vast object of content and bliss, for which all mankind have one common passion, and which every one who is not employed to procure the necessaries of life, sets out in search of with crowded sails. The orphan mind, in its fond expectations, imagines it sees a confused view of it in the first ideas of every thing that is beautiful, until possession convinces us of our mistake; but no disappointments cure the passion itself; we are actuated by a sense more present to us than demonstration, that the object of it is always near us.

Man is ennobled and distinguished from the other inhabitants of this earth by the universal passion I speak of. If he were bereft of it, he would fall to the condition of a sagacious brute. He would, in such case, as soon as he had eaten and drunk to satisfy nature, lie down on the next sunny bank, and repose in thoughtless content. We should have no heroes, no misers, and no mighty projects. Human love, that now refines and ennobles the soul, would never rise beyond the brutal appetite. Happiness would be cheaply attained, and we should never be uneasy, but when in actual distress. But then our happiness would be poor and tasteless; and indeed the mere glimmering hope of the obscure enthusiastic delight which we never enjoy, with all its endless cares and disappointments, is infinitely more noble and ravishing, than the unbroken supine content of sensible enjoyment. What makes content sound so fine in the human ear, is the satiation of the mighty unknown want, which we are obliged to unite in our idea of content, because without it we can never enjoy undisturbed unwishing tranquillity. But this heart-easing, this gilded content, is not the content of brutes; for as they have no desires but to allay the present appetite, their ease is stupid indifference. The annihilation of that bright-beaming human hope, that travels on before us during life, would be attended with a want of curiosity; nothing would be new to us, nor nothing old: we should run into few errors, and few cares; we should be wise, content, and worthless. Thus are our misery, our folly, and our grandeur, connected and inseparable.

I have given you, madam, this enthusiastic gentleman's rhapsody on the sublime, which I leave to your reflection, with this caution only, that before you judge, you consult the feelings of your own mind, in the same retired and calm state he did. I now proceed to a separate source of the sublime, which we discover in our own breasts, and observe with particular pleasure, because it is an undoubted evidence of the grandeur of human nature. I took some notice of it before, when I spoke of elegance.

We find in ourselves a sense of the base and of the noble; to the one are annexed by nature shame and blushes; to the other, pride and exultation. We may indeed be cheated by appearances; base actions may be disguised, or wholly covered from view, and lost in the concomitant circumstances; but the sense itself is constantly true to appearances; we are for ever prejudiced against the mean and base, and we always exult in a noble and disinterest part. That this direction of the sentiment was not formed by the precepts of philosophers, as sensual writers pretend, is evident from hence, that it is not in the power of art or management to alter or warp it. We can no more be brought to approve what appears to us base, or to condemn noble and benevolent actions, while they appear so, than we can be managed to like the screaming of the owl, or the jarring of iron bars.

It is this sentimental light without reflection which discovers to us, that it is great and exalted to condemn sensual pleasures, riches, and mundane interests; and makes severe, self-denying, suffering virtue appear an object of admiration. Generosity, even when ill-placed, is still noble, because it demonstrates a contempt for riches; and the love of truth is so, because it shows a settled firm habit of virtue; for falsehood is the disguise which shame bestows on vice.

The soul, actuated and determined by its own haughty and elevated sentiments of virtue and dignity, asserts fates and prospects superior to the low interests of this world. We are therefore charmed in the nobility of sentiment, by this clear and manifest majesty of the soul, just as beauty is delighted with the flattering view of itself in a mirror. The elevation every man feels in himself at a noble sentiment, is a plain intuition of the sublimity of his own spirit, and on that account it strikes him with rapture and exultation. If all ages have acknowledged the grandeur of Alexander's answer to Parmenio, it is because men in general feel in themselves a loftier passion than that which can be satisfied with kingdoms and sceptres. If we should imagine that it was a mere passion for empire stimulated that great conqueror to his enterprises, he himself informs us, with discontent, when he had no more to conquer, that he was not satisfied with empires and kingdoms. A passion to enjoy the sovereignty of the whole world had nothing admirable in it; but the noble dissatisfaction he expressed at the limits he found to his ambition, furnished an idea to poets, to painters, and statuaries, to form a grand picture of the hero....

Part IV
The Aberdonian enlightenment

Gerard's formation within the Aberdonian context of the Scottish enlightenment is clearly signalled in his interest in the category of 'genius', a popular
topic for discussion in the Aberdonian Philosophical Society. But Gerard can
also be read in the wider context of the British tradition in which analogues
for the sublime are constantly sought. The gestures towards the Alps and the
Nile, for example, can be found in the extract from Dennis in part I. The
investigation of presence [Gerard] is also a topic for discussion in the Scottish
school, finding its most sophisticated analysis in Kames's notion of 'ideal
presence'. Gerard mobilises a number of sub categories and qualifications of
the sublime, such as the sublime of science or that of heroism, most of which
are common topoi. Burke, for example, investigates the sublimity in heroism
in his early work on aesthetics which later, at the time of the French Revolution, causes considerable difficulties in reconciling heroic acts with ethically
sanctionable ones.

There is also a connection between ethics and power [Gerard] that is common to this discursive tradition, which is given an historical gloss in Gerard's
invocation of the weight of history. The grandeur of architecture [Gerard] is
also a common point of debate within the associational theory of architectural form which is itself derived from classical discussions of architecture.
Vitruvius, for example, described the classical orders in terms of their rela-
tionships to particular female types – Corinthian, for example, taking its
form from virgins. This associational aspect to architectural style was worked
up into a complete theory of character in relation to buildings. Perhaps the
earliest examples of this theory can be found in Shaftesbury, Addison and
Dennis, but it is not until mid-century that there is a recognisably systematic
account of the character of buildings.[1] Thomas Whately was to extend this
analysis of character in buildings to the landscape garden and produced the
first comprehensive theory of character applied both to landscape and
architectural design in his *Observations on modern gardening* (London,
1770).[2]

The sublime of music [Gerard] is here treated rather differently from Baillie's associational account which singles out music as the only art form that
contains an affective impulse divorced from association.[3] In contrast Gerard
maintains an imitative model for music thereby bringing the aural into close
proximity with the visual arts. This model can be found at the end of the
century in Archibald Alison's contention that 'the sublimity of ... sounds is to
be ascribed not to the mere quality of the Sound, but to those associated

[1] See John Shebbeare, *Letters on the English nation* (London, 1755); Henry Home,
Lord Kames, *Elements of criticism*, 3rd edn, 2 vols. (Edinburgh, 1765); Thomas
Wright, *Universal architecture* (London, 1755); William Chambers, *A treatise on civil
architecture* (London, 1759).
[2] This was complemented by William Newton's preface to his translation of Vitruvius
published in 1771 and by Thomas Sandby's six lectures on architecture given at the
Royal Academy beginning in 1770. See John Archer, 'Character in English architectural design', *Eighteenth-Century Studies*, 12: 3.
[3] See *An essay on the sublime* (London, 1747), pp. 38-9; and the fifth chapter following.

qualities of which it is significant', *Essays on the nature and principles of taste* (Edinburgh, 1790), p. 115, but it was not hegemonic in the period; James Ussher, for example, grapples with the qualities of indistinctness peculiar to the experience of listening to music. In a passage that has considerable interest he writes: 'The most elevated sensation of music arises from a confused perception of ideal or visionary beauty and rapture, which is sufficiently perceivable to fire the imagination, but not clear enough to become an object of knowledge. This shadowy beauty the mind attempts, with a languishing curiosity, to collect into a distinct object of view and comprehension; but it sinks and escapes, like the dissolving ideas of a delightful dream, that are neither within the reach of memory, nor yet totally fled. The charms of music then, though real and affecting, seem yet too confused and fluid to be collected into a distinct idea.' *Clio, or a discourse on taste* (London, 1767), pp. 52-4.[4]

The concept of original genius [Duff] was most thoroughly outlined by Edward Young in his *Conjectures on original composition* (London, 1759) in which we learn that 'imitation must be the lot... of most writers' [44] a sentiment which commanded general assent until the valorisation of the imagination began to redefine the creative aspects to composition.

It is this new ordering which leads to the discovery of 'unknown truth' and which will become in both Duff and Gerard the primary indicator of genius.

The reliance upon invention [Duff] is founded upon an earlier Scottish teacher's thoughts on this subject; George Turnbull who described the act of invention nearly twenty years earlier as 'nothing... but the habit acquired by practices of assembling ideas or truths, with facility and readiness, in various positions and arrangement, in order to have new views of them'.[5] Duff also breaks down invention into four distinct aspects, a structural assembly which should be read in relation to the five sources of the sublime in Longinus and the six marks of passion in Dennis.

History painting [Duff], the depiction of scenes from classical mythology or christian iconography were taken to present generalisable representations of the passions and intellect, and was understood to be the noblest form for painting. Its connection to the sublime is, therefore, hardly surprising. Sir Joshua Reynolds treats this subject in his fourth *Discourse* where we learn

[4] For a discussion of music in the period see: J.W. Draper, 'Poetry and music in eighteenth-century English aesthetics', *Englische Studien*, 67 (1932-3), pp. 70-85; Warren D. Allen, *Philosophies of music history: a study of general histories of music, 1600-1960*, 2nd edn, rev. (New York: American Book Co, 1939); H.M. Schueller, 'Correspondences between music and the sister arts, according to eighteenth-century aesthetic theory', *JAAC*, 11 (1953), 334-59; David Johnson, *Music and society in lowland Scotland in the eighteenth century* (London: Oxford University Press, 1972); James Malek, *The arts compared: an aspect of eighteenth century British aesthetics* (Detroit: Wayne State University Press, 1974); Peter Le Huray and James Day, eds. *Music and aesthetics in the eighteenth and early-nineteenth centuries* (Cambridge: Cambridge University Press, 1981); Kevin Barry, *Language, music and the sign* (Cambridge: Cambridge University Press, 1987).

[5] George Turnbull, *Principles of moral philosophy*, 2 vols. (London, 1740), I, 60.

that the greatest paintings elevate the spectator 'at a single blow'; it is this which is the effect of the sublime.

The figure of the bard flows through mid eighteenth-century thought in which the fantasy construction began to act as a cypher for a number of nationalist ideological arguments. He is often associated with particular geographical regions (Wales or the far north of Scotland) and with fantasies about ancient English society most commonly aroused through the invocation of the Druids. The rise in interest in gothic architecture can also be linked to this collective fantasy.[6]

The creative imagination [Duff] is one of the competing pathologies of the imagination essayed throughout the period. Akenside is probably the source for much of this debate, although his descriptions can, in turn, be traced back to Hobbes and Locke. It would be correct to understand Coleridge as marking the culmination point of this tradition. Throughout these debates the imagination is most commonly understood in active terms; it 'creates', 'blends', 'enlarges' and so forth.[7]

Such violence is also counterbalanced by the desire for security [Beattie], a departure from the Burkean analysis in which danger and the threat of insecurity and of pain or terror all instil a feeling of delight. In the Burkean framework whatever arouses this delight is sublime. In Beattie, however, security can be understood as a form of domestication of the sublime which was also evident in the development of landscape aesthetics. According to Richard Payne Knight, for example, William Chambers had attempted to 'introduce those charming delights of danger, pain, terror and astonishment into the art of landscape gardening'.[8]

Perhaps the most significant departure in this section, however, is the continuous stress on the participatory aspects of the subject's insertion into the sublime experience [Beattie]. Here natural objects are no longer the principal analogues and prompts for the sublime since the perceiving mind is increasingly understood as in and of itself capable of conferring qualities to experience of the outer world. Hence *relative* qualities of immensity, grandeur, vastness and so forth are as likely to arouse sublime affects as absolute qualities. The absolute, as in the case of Godhead, still has its place as primus inter pares, an aspect of the tradition we have found in Burke as well as in the Longinian debate, and here once again reformulated in the Aberdonian context [Beattie].

The transport of the oratorical performance is occasionally explicitly inflected in terms of violence [Reid] in which the pleasing rape upon the

6 The most well-known example of the figure of the Bard for the period is Ossian; see James Macpherson, *The works of Ossian*, 2 vols. (London, 1765); Thomas Gray, 'The Bard' and 'The Progress of Poetry' (London, 1757); and James Beattie, *The Minstrel, or the progress of genius* (London, 1771).

7 See James Engell, *The creative imagination* (Cambridge, Mass: Harvard University Press, 1981).

8 Richard Payne Knight, *An analytical inquiry into the principles of taste*, 4th edn (London, 1808), p. 384.

reader found in the Longinian tradition is turned towards the rather more aggressive and invasive non-consensual transport. Violence is a foundational feature of the sublime but open recognition of this fact only slowly emerges through the tradition. When the eighteenth-century tradition is taken up into nineteenth-century discussions the violent aspect of the sublime will become attached more clearly to the sexual politics of castration fantasies.[9] The uneasy alliance between the ethical and the aesthetic is also brought under some pressure in the Scottish tradition [Beattie] which can be taken as part of a continuous project to break or make the alliance. In the German tradition this will, of course, culminate in Kant's famous theses concerning the disinterestedness of the aesthetic. For the eighteenth-century British tradition the game is still all to play for since the full implications of the negative thesis – that morally unsanctionable actions may be equally aesthetically pleasing as sanctionable ones – were only to be brought home with overwhelming force in the post-1789 world. It is nevertheless the case that the political implications of this tension between the negative and positive theses regarding the ethical approbation of aesthetic experience lie at the heart of the sublime tradition.

We should locate Beattie, however, within the more speculative tradition of the Aberdonian school, deriving perhaps from Turnbull, in which these supposed 'Truths' are to be taken as *in the first instance* representational: they are only ways of expressing, embellishing or enforcing what we take to be absolutes known to us already in the mind and without form.

In order to sort this kind of problem out it was necessary to ground aesthetic experience in the 'reality' of the affect rather than in the mimetic simulacrum of representation. Arguments concerning the relative merits of 'the real' against pictures of reality [Beattie] are marshalled in the service of the investigation of the autonomy of the aesthetic. In terms of visual theory we can understand neoclassical art theory as mounting a rear-guard action on behalf of the representation in its insistence that the image ought not only please or delight in the aesthetic realm but must also morally instruct. Representations, according to this school, are at best *ideal* forms and cannot be substituted for the real which gives us evidence for the truth of empiricism. This idealising motif infiltrates neighbouring discourses, such as that on landscape, so that we can find it used as the basis for a distinction between real landscapes and painted ones in Whately's influential *Observations on modern gardening* when he states that gardening 'is as superior to landskip painting, as a reality to a representation'.[10] It is also at this point in the development of the tradition that the notion of the imaginary begins to exert a subversive power. Within the mainstream of eighteenth-century speculation on the powers of the imagination 'imaginary' objects in the modern sense of fantastic or solely the product of an overly stimulated imagination were thought to be unlicensed.

[9] See Neil Hertz, *The end of the line* (New York: Columbia University Press, 1985), pp. 161-215.
[10] Thomas Whately, *Observations on modern gardening* (London, 1770), p. 1.

The imagination, as in the doctrine of sympathy outlined by Adam Smith among others, was that peculiar power òf the mind which enabled an individual to think him or herself into an experience undergone by another person. Its products were always fully within the domain of the possible, within the 'real' realm of lived experience, it was merely that lacking the experience ourselves we have recourse to the imagination to, as it were, step into the shoes of another's experience. This sense of the imagination began to be augmented by a far more disturbing notion that the imagination might produce objects that were not based in the 'fact' of real experience, even if that experience were not one's own, but alternatively were the pure products of imaginative activity: they were, precisely, imaginary, which is to say not real. The tension between these diverging senses will become most acute in romantic theories of the creative faculties but the legacy of this tradition does not end there. If the sublime, as Beattie claims, is imaginary then its modes and structures of excess bring it into such proximity with what we have come to call the unconscious that the Freudian and post-Freudian analyses of our constitutive and constituting subjectivities must also be included within the scope of this tradition. In this sense the imaginary, in its contemporary usage, sits within the sublime tradition as a gloriously yet-to-be exploited source, as the pure potential of the discourse of the sublime.

28

Thomas Blackwell,
from *An enquiry into the life and writings of Homer* (1735)

Section II

...In the second or third age of this period was Homer born; that is, at a time when he might, as he grew up, be a spectator of all the various situations of the human race; might observe them in great calamities, and in high felicity; but more generally they were increasing in wealth and discipline. For, my lord, I cannot help observing, that from these hard beginnings, and jarring interests, the Greeks became early masters of the military art, and, by degrees, of all others that tend to enrich or adorn a city, and raise a commonwealth: shipping and commerce, domestic order, and foreign influence, with every subservient art of policy and government, were invented, or improved; and some of them brought to a very great degree of perfection.

And truly it could not be otherwise, while each city was independent, rivalling its neighbour, and trying its genius in peace, and its strength in war. Upon good or bad success, the citizens, all concerned in the administration, made a careful enquiry into the cause of it. What fault in their conduct had procured the one, or what excellency in their constitution the other? This liberty produced hardiness and discipline; which at length arose to that height, that ten thousand Greeks were an overmatch for the Persian monarch, with all the power of the Asiatic plains.

This, my lord, happened long after; but the struggle was fresh in Homer's days: arms were in repute, and force decided possession. He saw towns taken and plundered, the men put to the sword, and the women made slaves: he beheld their despairing faces, and suppliant postures; heard their moanings over their murdered husbands, and prayers for their infants to the victor. On the other hand, he might view cities blessed with peace, spirited by liberty, flourishing in trade, and increasing in wealth. He was not engaged in affairs himself, to draw off his attention; but he wandered through the various scenes, and observed them at leisure. Nor was it the least instructive sight, to see a colony led out, a city founded, the foundations of order and policy laid, with all the provisions for the security of the people: such scenes afford extended views, and natural ones too, as they are the immediate effect of the great parent of invention, necessity, in its young and untaught essays.

The importance of this good fortune will best appear, if your lordship

163

reflects on the pleasure which we receive from a representation of *natural* and *simple manners*: it is irresistible and enchanting; they best show human wants and feelings; they give us back the emotions of an artless mind, and the plain methods we fall upon to indulge them: goodness and honesty have their share in the delight; for we begin to like the men, and would rather have to do with them, than with more refined but double characters. Thus the various works necessary for building a house, or a ship; for planting a field, or forging a weapon, if described with an eye to the sentiments and attention of the man so employed, give us great pleasure, *because we feel the same*. Innocence, we say, is beautiful; and the sketches of it, wherever they are truly hit off, never fail to charm: witness the few strokes of that nature in Mr. Dryden's *Conquest of Mexico*, and the *Inchanted Island*.

Accordingly, my lord, we find Homer describing very minutely the houses, tables, and way of living of the ancients; and we read these descriptions with pleasure. But on the contrary, when we consider our own customs, we find that our first business, when we sit down to poetize in the higher strains, is to unlearn our daily way of life; to forget our manner of sleeping, eating and diversions: we are obliged to adopt a set of *more natural* manners, which however are foreign to us; and must be like plants raised up in hot-beds or green-houses, in comparison of those which grow in soils fitted by nature for such productions. Nay, so far are we from enriching poetry with *new* images drawn from nature, that we find it difficult to understand the *old*. We live within doors, covered, as it were, from nature's face; and passing our days supinely ignorant of her beauties, we are apt to think the similies taken from her *low*, and the ancient manners *mean*, or absurd. But let us be ingenuous, my lord, and confess, that while the moderns admire nothing but pomp, and can think nothing great or beautiful, but what is the produce of wealth, they exclude themselves from the pleasantest and most natural images that adorned the old poetry. State and form disguise man; and wealth and luxury disguise nature. Their effects in writing are answerable: a Lord-Mayor's show, or grand procession of any kind, is not very delicious reading, if described minutely, and at length; and great ceremony is at least equally tiresome in a poem, as in ordinary conversation.

It has been an old complaint, that we love to disguise everything, and most ourselves. All our titles and distinctions have been represented as coverings, and additions of grandeur to what nature gave us: happy indeed for the best of ends, I mean the public tranquillity and good order; but incapable of giving delight in fiction or poetry.

By this time your lordship sees I am in the case of a noble historian, who having related the constant superiority his Greeks had over the inhabitants of the Assyrian vales, concludes "That it has not been given by the Gods, to one and the same country, to produce rich crops and warlike men": neither indeed does it seem to be given to one and the same kingdom, to be thoroughly civilised, and afford proper subjects for poetry. The *marvellous* and *wonderful* is the nerve of the epic strain: but what marvellous things happen in a well-ordered state? We can hardly be surprised; we know the springs and method of acting; everything happens in order, and according to custom or law. But in a wide country, not under a regular government, or split into many, whose inhabitants live scattered, and ignorant of laws and discipline; in such a country, the manners are simple, and accidents will happen every day: exposition and loss of infants, encounters, escapes, rescues, and every other thing that can inflame the human passions while acting, or awake them when described, and recalled by imitation.

These are not to tbe found in a well-governed state, except it be in a civil war; which, with all the disorder and misery that attends it, is a fitter subject for an epic poem, than the most glorious campaign that ever was made in Flanders. Even the things that give the greatest lustre in a regular government; the greatest honours and highest trusts, will scarcely bear poetry: the Muse refuses to bestow her embellishments on a Duke's patent, or a General's commission. They can neither raise our wonder, nor gain our heart: for peace, harmony and good order, which make the happiness of a people, are the bane of a poem that subsists by wonder and surprise.

To be convinced of this, we need only suppose that the Greeks, at the time of the Trojan war, had been a nation eminent for loyalty and discipline: that commissions in due form had been issued out, regiments raised, arms and horses bought up, and a complete army set on foot. Let us suppose that all success had attended them in their expedition; that every officer had vied with another in bravery against the foe, and in submission to his general. That in consequence of these preparations, and of this good order, they had at first onset routed the Trojans, and driven them into the town: suppose this, and think, what will become of the glorious *Iliad*? The wrath of Achilles, the wisdom of Nestor, the bravery of Diomedes, and the craft of Ulysses will vanish in a moment. But matters are managed quite otherwise;

> *Seditione, Dolis, Scelere atque Libidine & Irâ,*
> *Iliacos intra Muros peccatur, & extrà.*

It is thus that a peoples felicity clips the wings of their verse: it affords few materials for admiration or pity; and although the pleasure arising from a taste of the sublimer kinds of writing, may make your lordship regret the silence of the Muses, yet I am persuaded you will join in with, *That we may never be a proper subject of an heroic poem....*

29

David Fordyce,
from *Theodorus: a dialogue concerning the art of preaching* (1752)

I am conscious to myself of no prejudices against our modern preachers, said Agoretes, and am very willing to allow them all the merit that you or their warmest advocates can plead for. I allow them generally a noble superiority to popular errors, great freedom and beauty of sentiment, clear reasoning and coherence of thought, deep critical skill, elegance of style, a just arrangement of periods, propriety of pronunciation, and much modesty in their action and manner. But after all, I have so unhappy a taste, or so unfashionable way of thinking, as not to be thoroughly satisfied even with all these combined excellencies. I want, my dear friend, to have my mind exalted above the world, and above itself, with the sacredness of divine things: I want to feel, warmly to feel, no less than to be coolly convinced of, the transcendant beauty, and excellence of virtue: I want to be suspended, and awed, as with the presence of God, to sink into deep prostration before Him, to be struck with the majesty of his perfections, and transported with the wonders of his love; I want to conceive an infinite horror at sin, to glow with an ardent passion for doing good, to pant after perfection and immortality, and to ripen apace for both: In short, I want to have my understanding enlightened, my heart inflamed, every affection thrilled, and my whole life reformed. But are these important ends likely to be gained by a well-reasoned harangue on some speculative point of orthodoxy, by a clear confutation of some infidel or heretic, by a dry, critical discussion of some dark or dubious text, by a cold elaborate dissertation on some moral subject, or a curious dissection of some passion of the mind, or a vague declamation on some virtue or vice, and their effects on society and individuals? Yet *such* I find the general taste of preaching now to be....

It is only by imitating, said Theodorus, the great artist of life and nature, who at once charms our sense by the wonderful apparatus and decorations of his works; astonishes our imagination by the immense variety, infinite complication, and yet marvellous regularity of his machinery; informs our reason by the simplicity, and coherence of design, which runs through the whole; and lastly, who interests and agitates every affection by the amazing subserviency of every single wheel and movement of the vast machine, to strike and delight us. – In like manner, ought the preacher, who means to produce the same

166

effects, to address himself to the reason, or understanding, to the conscience, to the imagination, to the ears, and to the eyes of his audience. If *any* of these inlets to perception and persuasion are neglected by him, the force of his address will, as I said, be proportionably diminished: but if he apply to them *all* at once, with the proper arts adapted to each, he will break in upon the mind, with such light and power, as will, with the help of the Almighty, bear down all opposition, and give him an absolute empire over the human heart....

The next grand principle, said Theodorus, to which the preacher ought to address himself with a peculiar energy, I take to be *Conscience*, or that moral faculty of perception, by which we distinguish between virtue and vice, are conscious of good or bad order within, and approve or condemn accordingly....

A faculty immediately subordinate to this, and which must be employed as a main instrument to work upon it is the *Imagination*, that active and wonderful power, which presents to us the various images of things, and invests them with the mighty force they have to charm or frighten, to attract our admiration, or excite our aversion. It must therefore be no mean part of the preacher's business to apply himself to this noble faculty, by laying proper materials before it, combining strong images, selecting those circumstances, which are most adapted to impress the mind, and to show things as it were *present* to its very sense, exhibiting natural and moving pictures of life and manners, employing bold sentiments and glowing figures, animating the whole with such strength and spirit, and adorning it with such elegance and grace, both in his diction and manner, as are fittest to allure, to seize, and to transport the hearers....

...Besides, a pulpit is a place of extraordinary eminence, in which heads not duly poised, must naturally turn giddy. There a preacher, like a statue placed in the centre of several vistas, stands exposed in a full light: every eye meets in *him*: the attention of the whole audience is fixed on *him*: he is the director, perhaps, the mouth of all; and on *him* hangs the entertainment and satisfaction of all: their passions are in *his* hand, which he may control at pleasure, and he may lead the listening, and generally the sequacious crowd, whithersoever he chooses.

30

Alexander Gerard,
from *An essay on taste* (1759)

Part I. Taste resolved into its simple principles
Section II. Of the sense or taste of grandeur and sublimity

Grandeur or sublimity gives us a still higher and nobler pleasure, by means of a sense appropriated to the perception of it; while meanness renders any object, to which it adheres, disagreeable and distasteful. Objects are sublime, which possess *quantity* or amplitude, and *simplicity* in conjunction.

Considerable *magnitude* or largeness of extension, in objects capable of it, is necessary to produce sublimity. It is not on a small rivulet, however transparent and beautifully winding; it is not on a narrow valley, though variegated with flowers of a thousand pleasing hues; it is not on a little hill, though clothed with the most delightful verdure, that we bestow the epithet *sublime*: but on the Alps, the Nile, the ocean, the wide expanse of heaven, or the immensity of space uniformly extended, without limit or termination.

We always contemplate objects and ideas with a disposition similar to their nature. When a large object is presented, the mind expands itself to the extent of that object, and is filled with one grand sensation, which totally possessing it, composes it into a solemn sedateness, and strikes it with deep silent wonder and admiration: it finds such a difficulty in spreading itself to the dimensions of its object, as enlivens and invigorates its frame: and having overcome the opposition which this occasions, it sometimes imagines itself present in every part of the scene, which it contemplates; and, from the sense of this immensity, feels a noble pride, and entertains a lofty conception of its own capacity.

Large objects can scarce indeed produce their full effect, unless they are also *simple*, or made up of parts, in a great measure similar. Innumerable little islands scattered in the ocean, and breaking the prospect, greatly diminish the grandeur of the scene. A variety of clouds, diversifying the face of the heavens, may add to their beauty, but must detract from their grandeur.

Objects cannot possess that largeness, which is necessary for inspiring a sensation of the sublime, without simplicity. Where this is wanting, the mind contemplates, not one large, but many small objects: it is pained with the labour requisite to creep from one to another; and is disgusted with the imperfection of the idea, with which, even after all this toil, it must remain contented. But we take in, with ease, one entire conception of a simple object, however large: in consequence of this facility, we naturally account it one: the view of any single part suggests the whole, and enables fancy to extend and enlarge it to infinity, that it may fill the capacity of the mind.

Many things are indeed denominated sublime, which, being destitute of extension, seem incapable of amplitude, the first and fundamental requisite of the sublime. But such objects will be found, on examination, to possess qualities, which have the same power to exalt the disposition of the observer. Length of duration; prodigious numbers of things similar united, or so related, as to constitute a whole, partake of the nature of *quantity*, and, as well as extension, enlarge and elevate the mind, which contemplates them. Eternity is an object, which fills the whole capacity of the soul, nay exceeds its comprehension; and strikes it with astonishment and admiration. We cannot survey a vast army or navy, without being sensible of their grandeur; which arises, not so much from the largeness of the space they occupy, as from the numbers of men or ships, which are in them united under one direction, and co-operate to a common end; the union and similitude of the parts adding *simplicity* to the *vastness* of their number. Hence too is derived the sublime of science, which lies in universal principles and general theorems, from which, as from an inexhaustible source, flow multitudes of corollaries and subordinate truths.

But do not we attribute grandeur and sublimity to some things, which are destitute of *quantity* of every kind? What can be more remote from quantity, than the passions and affections of the soul? Yet the most imperfect and uncultivated taste is sensible of a sublimity in heroism, in magnanimity, in a contempt of honours, of riches, of power, in a noble superiority to things external, in patriotism, in universal benevolence. To account for this, we must observe, that, as no passion can subsist without its causes, its objects, and its effects, so, in forming the idea of any passion, we do not satisfy ourselves with conceiving it as a simple emotion in the mind, but we run over, in thought, the objects about which it is employed, the things by which it is produced, and the effects by which it discovers itself. And as these always enter into our conception of the passion, and are often connected with quantity, they naturally render the passion sublime. What wonder that we esteem heroism grand, when, in order to imagine it, we suppose a mighty conqueror, in opposition to the most formidable dangers, acquiring power over *multitudes* of nations, subjecting to his dominion wide *extended* countries, and purchasing renown, which reaches to the extremities of the world, and shall continue through *all the ages* of futurity? What can be more truly great than the object of that benevolence, which, unconfined by the narrow limits of vicinity or relation, comprehends *multitudes*, grasps whole *large* societies, and even extends from pole to pole?

It must also be remarked, that whatever excites in the mind a sensation or emotion similar to what is excited by vast objects is on this account denominated sublime; it being natural to reduce to the same species, to express by the same name, and even frequently to confound together whole objects, which we contemplate with the same or a like disposition. Hence the raging of the sea in a storm, and the loud roaring thunder, which inspire an awful sedateness, are termed sublime. Objects exciting terror are, for this reason in general sublime; for terror always implies astonishment, occupies the whole soul, and suspends all its motions.

In like manner, we admire as sublime superior excellence of many kinds; such eminence in strength, or power, or genius, as is uncommon, and overcomes difficulties, which are insurmountable by lower degrees of ability; such vigour of mind, as indicates the absence of low and grovelling passions, and enables a person to despise honours, riches, power, pain, death; setting him above those enjoyments, on which men generally put an high value, and those sufferings, which they think intolerable. Such degrees of excellence excite wonder and astonishment, the same emotion which is produced by amplitude. A great degree of *quality* has here the same effect upon the mind, as vastness of *quantity*, and that by the same principles, by stretching and elevating the mind in the conception of it.

We shall but just observe that the sublime passions, habitually prevailing in the temper, and uniformly displaying themselves in suitable expressions and effects, constitute dignity and sublimity of character.

But in order to comprehend the whole extent of the sublime, it is proper to take notice that objects, which do not themselves possess that quality, may nevertheless acquire it, by *association* with such as do. It is the nature of association to unite different ideas so closely, that they become in a manner one. In that situation, the qualities of one part are naturally attributed to the whole, or to the other part. At least association renders the transition of the mind from one idea to another so quick and easy, that we contemplate both with the same disposition, and are therefore similarly affected by both. Whenever, then, any object uniformly and constantly introduces into the mind the idea of another that is grand, it will, by its connection with the latter, be itself rendered grand. Hence words and phrases are denominated lofty and majestic. Sublimity of style arises, not so much from the sound of the words, though that doubtless may have some influence, as from the nature of the ideas, which we are accustomed to annex to them, and the character of the persons, among whom they are in most common use. This too is the origin of the grandeur we ascribe to objects high and elevated in place; of the veneration, with which we regard things in any direction distant; and of the superior admiration excited by things remote in time; especially in antiquity or past duration.*

* The author of *a Treatise of Human Nature* has very ingeniously reduced these phænomena into the principle of association. B. ii. P. 3, S. 8. The sum of his reasoning, so far as it is necessary to take notice of it here, is as follows: "Because we are accustomed every moment to observe the difficulty with which things are raised in opposition to the impulse of gravity; the idea of ascending always implies the notion of force exerted in overcoming this difficulty; the conception of which invigorates and elevates the thought, after the same manner as a vast object, and thus gives a distance above us much more an appearance of greatness, than the same space could have in any other direction. The sensation of amplitude, which by this means comes to attend the interposed distance, is transferred to, and considered as excited by the object that is eminent and above us; and that object, by this transference, acquires grandeur and sublimity. And here we may observe in passing, that this natural tendency to associate

But the fine arts present the most numerous examples of grandeur produced by association. In all of them, the sublime is attained, chiefly by the artist's exciting *ideas* of sublime objects; and in such as are mimical, this quality is chiefly owing to our being led by the exactness of the imitation to form ideas and conceive images of sublime originals. Thought is a less intense energy than sense: yet *ideas* especially when lively, never fail to be contemplated with some degree of the same emotion, which attends their original *sensation*; and often yield almost equal pleasure to the reflex senses, when impressed upon the mind by a skilful imitation.

Grandeur in works of architecture may, in some instances, arise from their largeness: for we generally estimate the magnitude of things, by comparison with those of the same species: and though no edifice is equal in quantity to many works of nature by no means accounted great; yet lofty palaces and pyramids, far exceeding the bulk of other buildings, have a *comparative* magnitude, which has the same influence upon the mind, as if they had been *absolutely* large. But still the principal source of grandeur in architecture is *association*, by which the columns suggest ideas of strength and durability, and the whole structure introduces the sublime ideas of the riches and magnificence of the owner.

In painting, sublimity is sometimes introduced by an artful kind of disproportion, which assigns to some well chosen member a greater degree of *quantity* than it commonly has: but chiefly those performances are grand, which either by the artful disposition of colours, light, and shade, represent sublime natural objects, and suggest ideas of them;* or, by the expressiveness of the features and attitudes of the figures, lead us to conceive sublime passions operating in the originals. And so complete is the power of association, that a skilful painter can express any degree of sublimity in the smallest, as well as in the largest compass. It appears in the miniatures of Julio Clovio, as really as in the paintings of Titian or Michelangelo.

The sublime of those arts, in which the instrument of imitation is language, must evidently arise from association; as it is the only principle, from which

ideas of grandeur with things above us is the reason, why the term *sublime* is metaphorically applied to excellence of any kind, especially to that species of it, which elates the mind with noble pride in the conception. To our transferring, in like manner, the interposed space, and its attendant sensation, to the distant object, is owing the veneration, with which we regard, and the value we set upon things remote in place. And because we find greater difficulty, and must employ superior energy, in running over the parts of duration, than those of space; and in ascending through past duration, than in descending through what is future; therefore we value higher, and contemplate with greater veneration things distant in time than things remote in space, and the persons and objects of antiquity, than those which we figure to ourselves in the age of futurity."

* It may be here observed that, though the figures, in painting, can seldom have so great quantity, as is sufficient of itself to produce sublimity; yet the comparative *magnitude*, and also the *simplicity* of the figures, parts, and members, are among the principal means by which a work suggests sublime ideas, and thus becomes itself sublime. The preservation of magnitude and simplicity is therefore recommended as fundamental to sublimity, in the art of painting....

words derive their force and meaning. And in these arts, sublimity precisely considered, will be found resolvable into a very few general qualities....

...Subjects thus grand in themselves must bestow sublimity on a composition, whenever they are described in such a manner, as conveys entire, or augments, the feeling, which they naturally excite.

If an author's main subject is destitute of innate grandeur, it may be rendered grand, by comparing or someway associating it with objects naturally such. By the same means the real greatness of a subject is increased. Hence metaphor, comparison, and imagery are often productive of sublimity. Cicero raises Cæsar's idea of clemency, by representing it as godlike. Seneca gives a sublime idea of Cicero's genius, by comparing it with the majesty and extent of the Roman empire....

...The power of imparting sublimity to objects which naturally have it not, by giving them a relation to others, is an advantage peculiar to the arts, which imitate by language; for the rest can attain the sublime, only by copying such objects as are themselves possessed of that quality.

The principles we have laid down explain also the sublime of music; which seems to be derived in part from the length and the gravity of the notes; the former constituting a kind of amplitude to the ear; the latter contributing to that composure and sedate expansion of the mind, which attends the perception of sublimity; and is then completed, when the artist, by skilfully imitating the sublime passions or their objects, inspires them into his hearers, and renders them conscious of their operation.

It is farther proper to observe, that things may be destitute of grandeur, and yet not be accounted low or mean; but may, on the contrary, possess other qualities, which gratify us highly in a different way. It is only when grandeur is requisite and expected, that the mere absence of it produces meanness. Thus a remarkable defect in quantity, in comparison with things of the same kind; a resemblance in individuals of a superior species to the orders below them; or the defect of sublimity in compositions of art or genius, which propose to imitate originals or treat subjects confessedly noble, gives us distaste and inspires contempt. Meanness arises often likewise from association, when low and grovelling ideas are suggested; as when images and similes, taken from mean objects, are applied to an important subject. Thus also, words and phrases become mean, when they excite mean ideas, either by their proper signfication, or by their being ordinarily used only by those of inferior rank.

31

William Duff,
from *An essay on original genius* (1767)

Book II. Section III. Of original genius in poetry

... What we would be understood to maintain is this; that original genius will dictate the most proper sentiments on every subject, and in every species of Poetry, *indiscriminately*; but that it will dictate the sentiments most proper to that particular species to which it is *adapted*, and to which it applies its inventive powers. If, for instance, we suppose this quality adapted to Epic Poetry, it will discover itself in the invention both of sublime and pathetic sentiments, which will at once excite astonishment, and penetrate the heart. To a person who possesses a talent for this highest species of Poetry, such sentiments are as it were congenial; they arise naturally and spontaneously to his imagination. The sublime, in particular, is the proper walk of a great Genius, in which it delights to range, and in which alone it can display its powers to advantage, or put forth its strength. As such a Genius always attempts to grasp the most stupendous objects, it is much more delighted with surveying the rude magnificence of nature, than the elegant decorations of art; since the latter produce only an agreeable sensation of pleasure; but the former throws the soul into a divine transport of admiration and amazement, which occupies and fills the mind, and at the same time inspires that solemn dread, that religious awe, which naturally results from the contemplation of the vast and wonderful. By dwelling on such subjects, the soul is elevated to a sense of its own dignity and greatness.

We observed likewise, that an author possessed of that kind and degree of original Genius which is adapted to Epic Poetry, will admirably succeed in the invention of *pathetic* as well as *sublime* sentiments; if an author can be said to invent sentiments which rise to the Imagination, in a manner by a simple volition, without any labour, and almost without any effort. Such a person being endued with a vivacity and vigour of Imagination, as well as an exquisite sensibility of every emotion, whether pleasant or painful, which can affect the human heart, has nothing else to do, in order to move the passions of others, but to represent his own feelings in a strong and lively manner; and to exhibit the object, event or action he proposes to describe, in that particular attitude or view, which has most powerfully interested his own affections, for that will most certainly interest ours: we shall feel the same concern, and share in the same distress. Having by this means gained an ascendant over our hearts,

173

he will at pleasure melt them into tenderness and pity, or fire them with indignation and rage: every passion will be obedient to his impulse, as well as subject to his control; like the Poet described by Horace, he will raise in our souls every emotion of which they are susceptible:

> Irritat, mulcet, falsis terroribus implet
> Ut magus, et modo me Thebis, modo penit Athenis.

> 'Tis he who gives my breast a thousand pains,
> Can make me feel each passion that he feigns;
> Enrage, compose with more than magic art;
> With pity and with terror tear my heart;
> And snatch me o'er the earth, or thro' the air,
> To Thebes, to Athens, when he will, and where.   Pope.

The sentiments of an author of this kind are the natural dictates of the heart, not fictitious or copied, but original; and it is impossible they should fail in producing their proper effect upon the mind of the reader....

To the particular and essential ingredients of original Genius above enumerated, we shall subjoin three others of a more general nature; which however are as characteristical of this uncommon endowment, and as much distinguish its productions, as any of the particular properties above specified. These are an *irregular greatness, wildness,* and *enthusiasm* of Imagination. The qualities we have just now mentioned are distinct from each other; but as they are nearly allied, and are commonly found together, we include them in one class, considering them as unitedly forming one general indication of elevated and original Genius; though, for the sake of precision, we shall treat of them separately.

First we observed, that *irregular greatness* of imagination was characteristical of *original genius.* This expression is a little equivocal in its signification, and therefore it will be necessary to ascertain the sense in which we consider it.

An *irregular greatness* of Imagination is sometimes supposed to imply a mixture of great beauties and blemishes, blended together in any work of Genius; and thus we frequently apply it to the writings of Shakespeare, whose excellencies are as transcendent, as his faults are conspicuous. Without rejecting this sense altogether, or denying that an original author will be distinguished by his imperfections as well as by his excellencies, we may observe, that the expression above-mentioned is capable of a juster and more determinate meaning than that just specified. It may, we think, be more properly understood to signify that native grandeur of sentiment which disclaims all restraint, is subject to no certain rule, and is therefore various and unequal. In this sense principally we consider the expression, and are under no difficulty in declaring, that an irregular greatness of Imagination, as thus explained, is one remarkable criterion of exalted and original Genius. A person who is possessed of this quality, naturally turns his thoughts to the contemplation of the grand and wonderful, in nature or in human life, in the visible creation, or in that of his own fancy. Revolving these awful and magnificent scenes in his musing mind, he labours to express in his compositions the ideas which dilate and swell his Imagination; but is often unsuccessful in his efforts. In attempting to represent these, he feels himself embarrassed; words are too weak to convey the ardour of his sentiments, and he frequently sinks under the immensity of his own conceptions. Sometimes indeed he will be happy enough to paint his very thought, and to excite in others the very sentiments which he himself feels: he will not always however succeed so well, but, on the contrary, will often labour in a fruitless attempt; whence it should seem, that his composition will upon certain occasions be distinguished by an irregular and unequal greatness.

Whether this quality is to be ascribed to the cause above-mentioned in particular; or whether it is the effect of that fiery impetuosity of Imagination, which, breaking through the legal restraints of criticism, or overleaping the bounds of authority and custom, sometimes loses sight of the just and natural, while it is in pursuit of the new and wonderful, and, by attempting to rise above the sphere of humanity, tumbles from its towering height; or lastly, whether it is to be ultimately derived from the unavoidable imperfection of the human faculties, which admit not of perpetual extension, and are apt to flag in a long, though rapid flight; whichsoever of these may be the cause of the phenomenon above-mentioned, or whether all of them may contribute to produce it, certain it is, that an irregular greatness of Imagination, implying unequal and disproportioned grandeur, is always discernible in the compositions of an original Genius, however elevated, and is therefore an universal characteristic of such a Genius.

It deserves however to be observed, that the imperfection here suggested, is a natural effect and a certain proof of an exuberant Imagination. Ordinary minds seldom rise above the dull uniform tenor of common sentiments, like those animals that are condemned to creep on the ground all the days of their life; but the most lawless excursions of an original Genius, like the flight of an eagle, are towering, though devious; its path, as the course of a comet, is blazing, though irregular; and its errors and excellencies are equally inimitable.

We observed that original Genius is likewise distinguished by a *wildness* of Imagination. This quality, so closely allied to the former, seems also to proceed from the same causes; and is at the same time an infallible proof of a fertile and and luxuriant fancy. *Wildness* of imagery, scenery and sentiment, is the *pastime* of a playful and sportive imagination; it is the effect of its exuberance. This character is formed by an arbitrary assemblage of the most extravagant, uncommon, and romantic ideas, united in the most fanciful combinations; and is displayed in grotesque figures, in surprising sentiments, in picturesque and enchanting description. The quality of which we are treating, wherever it is discovered, will afford such a delicious entertainment to the mind, that it can scarce be ever satisfied with a banquet so exquisitely prepared, satiety being prevented by a succession of dainties, ever various and ever new.

The last quality by which we affirmed original Genius to be characterised, was an *enthusiasm* of Imagination. It frequently happens, that the original meaning of a word is lost or become obsolete, and another very different one, through accident, custom or caprice, is ordinarily substituted in its place. Sometimes expressions, which have been anciently taken in a good sense, are, by a strange perversion of language, used in a bad one; and by this means they become obnoxious upon account of the ideas, which, in their common acceptation they excite. This is the case with the word *enthusiasm*, which is almost universally taken in a bad sense; and, being conceived to proceed from an overheated and distempered Imagination, is supposed to imply weakness, superstition, and madness. *Enthusiasm*, in this modern sense, is in no respect a qualification of a Poet; in the ancient sense, which implied a kind of divine *inspiration*, or an ardour of fancy wrought up to transport, we not only admit, but deem it an essential one.

A glowing ardour of Imagination is indeed (if we may be permitted the expression) the very soul of Poetry. It is the principal source of *inspiration*, and the poet who is possessed of it, like the Delphian Priestess, is animated with a kind of *divine fury*. The intenseness and vigour of his sensations produce that *enthusiasm* of Imagination, which as it were hurries the mind out of itself; and which is vented in warm and vehement description, exciting in every susceptible breath the same emotions that were felt by the author himself. It is this *enthusiasm* which gives life and strength to poetical representations, renders them striking imitations of nature, and thereby produces that enchanting delight which genuine Poetry is calculated to inspire. Without this animating principle, all poetical and rhetorical compositions are spiritless and languid, like those bodies that are drained of their vital juices: they are therefore read with indifference or insipidity; the harmony of the numbers, if harmonious, may tickle the ear, but being destitute of nerves, that is of passion and sentiment, they can never affect the heart.

We observed likewise, that *original genius* will naturally discover itself in *visions*. This is a species of fiction, to succeed in which with applause, requires as much poetic inspiration as any other species of composition whatever. That enthusiasm of Imagination, which we considered as an essential characteristic of original Genius, is indispensibly necessary to the enraptured bard, who would make his readers feel those impetuous transports of passion which occupy and actuate his own mind. He must himself be wrought up to a high pitch of exstasy, if he expects to throw us into it. Indeed it is the peculiar felicity of an original author to feel in the most exquisite degree every emotion, and to see every scene he describes. By the vigorous effort of a creative Imagination, he calls shadowy substances and unreal objects into existence. They are present to his view, and glide, like spectres, in silent, sullen majesty, before his astonished and entranced sight. In reading the description of such apparitions, we partake of the author's emotion; the blood runs chill in our veins, and our hair stiffens with horror....

Upon the whole, we need not hesitate to affirm, that original Genius will probably discover itself either in *allegories, visions,* or in the creation of ideal figures of one kind or another. The probability that it will do so, is derived from that innate tendency to *fiction* which distinguishes such a Genius, and from the natural bias of *fiction* to run in this particular channel: for the Imagination of a poet, whose Genius is truly original, finding no objects in the visible creation sufficiently marvellous and new, or which can give full scope to the exercise of its powers, naturally bursts into the ideal world, in quest of more surprising and wonderful scenes, which it explores with insatiable curiosity, as well as with exquisite pleasure; and depending in its excursion wholly on its own strength, its success in this province of *fiction* will be proportionable to the plastic power of which it is possessed....

32

Thomas Reid,
from *Essays on the intellectual powers of man* (1785)

Essay VIII. Of taste
Chapter III. Of grandeur

...In the contemplation of uncommon excellence, the mind feels a noble enthusiasm, which disposes it to the imitation of what it admires.

When we contemplate the character of Cato, his greatness of soul, his superiority to pleasure, to toil, and to danger, his ardent zeal for the liberty of his country; when we see him standing unmoved in misfortunes, the last pillar of the liberty of Rome, and falling nobly in his country's ruin, who would not wish to be Cato rather than Cæsar in all his triumph?

Such a spectacle of a great soul struggling with misfortune, Seneca thought not unworthy of the attention of Jupiter himself, "Ecce spectaculum Deo dignum, ad quod respiciat Jupiter suo operi intentus vir fortis cum mala fortuna compositus."

As the Deity is of all objects of thought the most grand, the descriptions given in holy writ of his attributes and works, even when clothed in simple expression, are acknowledged to be sublime. The expression of Moses, "And God said, let there be light, and there was light," has not escaped the notice of Longinus, a heathen critic, as an example of the sublime.

What we call sublime in description, or in speech of any kind, is a proper expression of the admiration and enthusiasm which the subject produces in the mind of the speaker. If this admiration and enthusiasm appears to be just, it carries the hearer along with it involuntarily, and by a kind of violence rather than by cool conviction: for no passions are so infectious as those which hold of enthusiasm.

But, on the other hand, if the passion of the speaker appears to be in no degree justified by the subject or the occasion, it produces in the judicious hearer no other emotion but ridicule and contempt.

The true sublime cannot be produced solely by art in the composition; it must take its rise from grandeur in the subject, and a corresponding emotion raised in the mind of the speaker. A proper exhibition of these, though it should be artless, is irresistible, like fire thrown into the midst of combustible matter.

When we contemplate the earth, the sea, the planetary system, the universe, these are vast objects; it requires a stretch of imagination to grasp them in our minds. But they appear truly grand, and merit the highest admiration, when we consider them as the work of God, who, in the simple style of Scripture stretched out the heavens, and laid the foundation of the earth; or, in the poetical language of Milton,

> In his hand
> He took the golden compasses, prepar'd,
> In God's eternal store, to circumscribe
> This universe, and all created things.
> One foot he enter'd, and the other turn'd
> Round thro' the vast profundity obscure;
> And said, thus far extend, thus far thy bounds;
> This be thy just circumference, O world.

When we contemplate the world of Epicurus, and conceive the universe to be a fortuitous jumble of atoms, there is nothing grand in this idea. The clashing of atoms by blind chance has nothing in it fit to raise our conceptions, or to elevate the mind. But the regular structure of a vast system of beings produced by creating power, and governed by the best laws which perfect wisdom and goodness could contrive, is a spectacle which elevates the understanding, and fills the soul with devout admiration.

A great work is a work of great power, great wisdom, and great goodness, well contrived for some important end. But power, wisdom, and goodness, are properly the attributes of mind only: they are ascribed to the work figuratively, but are really inherent in the author: and, by the same figure, the grandeur is ascribed to the work, but is properly inherent in the mind that made it.

Some figures of speech are so natural and so common in all languages, that we are led to think them literal and proper expressions. Thus an action is called brave, virtuous, generous; but it is evident, that valour, virtue, generosity, are the attributes of persons only, and not of actions. In the action considered abstractly, there is neither valour, nor virtue, nor generosity. The same action done from a different motive may deserve none of these epithets. The change in this case is not in the action, but in the agent; yet, in all languages, generosity and other moral qualities are ascribed to actions. By a figure, we assign to the effect a quality which is inherent only in the cause.

By the same figure, we ascribe to a work that grandeur which properly is inherent in the mind of the author.

When we consider the *Iliad* as the work of the poet, its sublimity was really in the mind of Homer. He conceived great characters, great actions, and great events in a manner suitable to their nature, and with those emotions which they are naturally fitted to produce; and he conveys his conceptions and his emotions by the most proper signs. The grandeur of his thoughts is reflected to our eye by his work, and therefore it is justly called a grand work....

33

James Beattie,
from *Dissertations moral and critical* (1783)

Illustrations on sublimity

Longinus, the Secretary of Zenobia queen of Palmyra, who was conquered by
the emperor Aurelian about the middle of the third century, composed many
books of philosophy and criticism, and among others a discourse on Sublimity, which is the only part of his writings that has been preserved to our time.
He is an author, not more remarkable for accuracy of judgment, than for the
energy of his style, and a peculiar boldness and elevation of thought. And men
of learning have vied with each other, in celebrating and expounding that
work; which is indeed one of the best specimens that remain of ancient criticism, and well deserves the attention of every scholar.

But he has used the word *hupsos* in a more general sense, than is commonly
annexed to the term *sublimity*; not always distinguishing what is sublime
from what is elegant or beautiful. The distinction, however, ought to be
made. Both indeed give delight; but the gratification we derive from the one
is different from that which accompanies the other. It is pleasing to behold a
fine face, or an apartment elegantly furnished and of exact proportion; it is
also pleasing to contemplate a craggy mountain, a vast cathedral, or a magnificent palace: but surely, the one sort of pleasure differs as much from the
other, as complacency differs from admiration, or the soft melody of a flute
from the overpowering tones of a full organ.

Grammarians are not agreed about the etymology of the word *sublime*.
The most probable opinion is, that it may be derived from *supra* and *limus*;
and so denotes literally the circumstance of being raised *above* the *slime*, the
mud, or the *mould*, of this world. Be that as it may, it uniformly signifies in
the Latin, whence we have taken it, *elevation*, or *loftiness*. And, because
whatever is much elevated, as a high building, or a high mountain, infuses
into the beholder a sort of pleasing astonishment; hence those things in art or
nature, which have the same effect on the mind, are, with a view to that effect,
called by the same name. Great depth, being the correlative of great height,
and being indeed implied in it, (for whatever is high from below is deep from
above) and because it astonishes and pleases the imagination, is also to be
considered as sublime. For, if we be ourselves secure, every one must have
observed, that it is agreeable to look down, from a mountain, upon the plain,
or from the top of a high building, upon the various objects below....

It is pleasant to behold the sea in a storm, on account of its astonishing greatness and impetuosity; and it is pleasant to look down from an elevated situation, because here too there is greatness and delightful astonishment. But to see others in danger, or unhappy in their ignorance, must always give pain to a considerate mind, however conscious it may be of its own security, and wisdom.... Every generous mind *feels* the falsehood of this doctrine. It was, however, a favourite topic of Swift; as appears from those verses on his own death, in which he comments upon a silly and ambiguous maxim of Roche-foucault.* According to this theory, the most desirable of all human conditions would be that of the superintendent of an hospital, the keeper of Bedlam, or the commander of galley-slaves: who would every moment be rejoicing in the thought, that he was free from the miseries which he beheld around him.

What we admire, or consider as great, we are apt to speak of in such terms, as if we conceived it to be high in place: and what we look upon as less important we express in words that properly denote low situation. We go *up* to London; and thence *down* into the country. The Jews spoke in the same manner of their metropolis, which was to them the object of religious veneration. *"Jerusalem, says the psalmist, is a city, to which the tribes go up:"* and the parable of the good Samaritan begins thus, *"a certain man went down from Jerusalem to Jericho."* Conformably to the same idiom, heaven is supposed to be above, and hell to be beneath; and we say, that generous minds endeavour to reach the *summit* of excellence, and think it *beneath* them to do, or design, any thing that is base. The terms *base, grovelling, low*, &c. and those of opposite import, *elevated, aspiring, lofty*, as applied in a figurative sense to the energies of mind, do all take their rise from the same modes of thinking. The Latins expressed admiration by a verb which properly signifies *to look up (suspicere)*; and contempt by another *(despicere)* whose original meaning is *to look down*. A high seat is erected for a king, or a chief magistrate, and a lofty pedestal for the statue of a hero; partly, no doubt, that they may be seen at the greater distance, and partly also, out of respect to their dignity.

But mere local elevation is not the only source of sublimity. Things that surpass in magnitude; as a spacious building, a great city, a large river, a vast mountain, a wide prospect, the ocean, the expanse of heaven, fill the mind of the beholder with the same agreeable astonishment. And observe, that it is rather the relative magnitude of things, as compared with others of the same kind, that raises this emotion, than their absolute quantity of matter. That may be a sublime edifice, which in real magnitude falls far short of a small hill that is not sublime: and a river two furlongs in breadth is a majestic appearance, though in extent of water it is as nothing when compared with the ocean.

---

* The maxim is, *Dans l'adversité de nos meilleurs amis nous trouvons toujours quelque chose, qui ne nous deplaist pas*: in the adversity of our best friends we find always something that does not displease us....

Of the sublimities of art and nature the human soul would be a very incompetent judge, if it were so mean, so contemptible, and so hateful a thing, as some writers would have us believe. Our taste for the sublime is considered by two great authors (who will be quoted in the sequel) as a proof of the dignity of our nature.

Great number, too, when it gives rise to admiration, may be referred to the same class of things. Hence an army, or navy, a long succession of years, eternity, and the like, are sublime, because they at once please and astonish. In contemplating such ideas or objects, we are conscious of something like an expansion of our faculties, as if we were exerting our whole capacity to comprehend the vastness of that which commands our attention. This energy of the mind is pleasing, as all mental energies are when unaccompanied with pain: and the pleasure is heightened by our admiration of the object itself; for admiration is always agreeable.

In many cases, great number is connected with other grand ideas, which add to its own grandeur. A fleet, or army, makes us think of power, and courage, and danger, and presents a variety of brilliant images. A long succession of years brings to view the vicissitude of human things, and the uncertainty of life, which sooner or later must yield to death, the irresistible destroyer. And eternity reminds us of that awful consideration, our own immortality; and is connected with an idea still more sublime, and indeed the most sublime of all, namely, with the idea of HIM, who fills immensity with his presence; creates, preserves, and governs all things; and is from everlasting to everlasting.

In general, whatever awakens in us this pleasurable astonishment is accounted sublime, whether it be connected with quantity and number, or not. The harmony of a loud and full organ conveys, no doubt, an idea of expansion and of power; but, independently on this, it overpowers with so sweet a violence, as charms and astonishes at the same time: and we are generally conscious of an elevation of mind when we hear it, even though the ear be not sensible of any melody. Thunder and tempest are still more elevating, when one hears them without fear; because the sound is still more stupendous; and because they fill the imagination with the magnificent idea of the expanse of heaven and earth, through which they direct their terrible career, and of that Almighty Being, whose will controls all nature. The roar of cannon, in like manner, when considered as harmless, gives a dreadful delight; partly by the overwhelming sensation wherewith it affects the ear, and partly by the ideas of power and danger, triumph and fortitude, which it conveys to the fancy.

Those passions of the soul yield a pleasing astonishment, which discover a high degree of moral excellence, or are in any way connected with great number, or great quantity. Benevolence and piety are sublime affections; for the object of the one is the Deity himself, the greatest, and the best; and that of the other is the whole human race, or the whole system of percipient beings. Fortitude and generosity are sublime emotions: because they discover a degree of virtue, which is not everywhere to be met with; and exert themselves in actions, that are at once difficult, and beneficial to mankind. – Great intellectual abilities, as the genius of Homer, or of Newton, we cannot contemplate without wonder and delight, and must therefore refer to that class of things whereof I now speak. – Nay great bodily strength is a sublime object; for we are agreeably astonished, when we see it exerted, or hear of its effects. – There is even a sublime beauty, which both astonishes and charms: but this will be found in those persons only, or chiefly, who unite fine features with a majestic form; such as we may suppose an ancient statuary would have represented Juno, or Minerva, Achilles, or Apollo.

When great qualities prevail in any person, they form what is called a sublime character. Every good man is a personage of this order: but a character may be sublime, which is not completely good, nay, which is upon the whole very bad. For the test of sublimity is not moral approbation, but that pleasurable astonishment wherewith certain things strike the beholder. Sarpedon, in the *Iliad*, is a sublime character, and at the same time a good one: to the valour of the hero he joins the benignity of a gracious prince, and the moderation of a wise man. Achilles, though in many respects not virtuous, is yet a most sublime character. We hate his cruelty, passionate temper, and love of vengeance: but we admire him for his valour, strength, swiftness, generosity, beauty, and intellectual accomplishments, for the warmth of his friendship, and for his filial tenderness. In a word, notwithstanding his violent nature, there is in his general conduct a mixture of goodness and of greatness, with which we are both pleased and astonished. Julius Cæsar was never considered a man of of strict virtue. But, in reading his *Memoirs*, it is impossible not to be struck with the sublimity of his character: that strength of mind, which nothing can bear down; that self-command, which is never discomposed; that intrepidity in danger; that address in negotiation; that coolness and recollection in the midst of perplexity; and that unwearied activity, which crowds together in every one of his campaigns as many great actions as would make a hero. Nay even in Satan, as Milton has represented him in *Paradise Lost*, though there are no qualities that can be called good in a moral view; nay, though every purpose of that wicked spirit is bent to evil, and to that only; yet there is the grandeur of a ruined archangel: there is force able to contend with the most boisterous elements; and there is boldness, which no power, but what is Almighty, can intimidate. These qualities are astonishing: and, though we always detest his malignity, we are often compelled to admire that very greatness by which we are confounded and terrified.

And be not surprised, that we sometimes admire what we cannot approve. These two emotions may, and frequently do, coincide: Sarpedon and Hector, Epaminondas and Aristides, David and Jonathan, we both approve and admire. But they do not necessarily coincide: for goodness calls forth the one, and greatness the other; and that which is great is not always good, and that may be good which is not great. Troy in flames, Palmyra in ruins, the ocean in a storm, and Etna in thunder and conflagration, are magnificent appearances, but do not immediately impress our minds with the idea of good: and a clear fountain is not a grand object, though in many parts of the world it would be valued above all treasures. So in the qualities of the mind and body: we admire the strong, the brave, the eloquent, the beautiful, the ingenious, the learned; but the virtuous only we approve. There have been authors indeed, one at least there has been, who, by confounding admiration with

184 Part IV: The Aberdonian enlightenment

approbation, laboured to confound intellectual accomplishments with moral virtues; but it is a shameful inaccuracy, and vile sophistry: one might as well endeavour to confound crimes with misfortunes, and strength of body with purity of mind; and say, that to be a knave and to lose a leg are equally worthy of punishment, and that one man deserves as much praise for being born with a healthy constitution, as another does for leading a good life.

But if sublime ideas are known by their power of inspiring agreeable astonishment, and if Satan in *Paradise Lost* is a sublime idea, does it not follow, that we must be both astonished at his character, and pleased with it? And is it possible to take pleasure in a being, who is the author of evil, and the adversary of God and man?

I answer; that, though we know there is an evil spirit of this name, we know also, that Milton's Satan is partly imaginary; and we believe, that those qualities as so in particular, which we admire in him as great: for we have no reason to think, that he has really that boldness, irresistible strength, or dignity of form, which the poet ascribes to him. So far, therefore, as we admire him for sublimity of character, we consider him, not as the great enemy of our souls, but as a fictitious being, and a mere poetical hero. Now the human imagination can easily combine ideas in an assemblage, which are not combined in nature; and make the same person the object of admiration in one respect, who in another is detestable: and such inventions are in poetry the more probable, because such persons are to be met with in real life. Achilles and Alexander, for example, we admire for their magnanimity, but abhor for their cruelty. And the poet, whose aim is to please, finds it necessary to give some good qualities to his bad characters; for, if he did not, the reader would not be interested in their fortune, nor, consequently, pleased with the story of it.

In the *picture* of a burning city, we may admire the splendour of the colours, the undulation of the flames, the arrangements of light and shade, and the other proofs of the painter's skill; and nothing gives a more exquisite delight of the melancholy kind, than Virgil's account of the burning of Troy. But this does not imply, that we should, like Nero, take any pleasure in such an event, if it were real and present. Indeed, few appearances are more beautiful, or more sublime, than a mass of flame, rolling in the wind, and blazing to heaven: whence illuminations, bonfires, and fireworks make part of a modern triumph. Yet destruction by fire is of all earthly things the most terrible.

An object more astonishing, both to the eye, and to the ear, there is hardly in nature, than (what is sometimes to be seen in the West Indies) a plantation of sugar-canes on fire, flaming to a vast height, sweeping the whole country, and every moment sending forth a thousand explosions, like those of artillery. A good description of such a scene we should admire as sublime; for a description can neither burn nor destroy. But the planter, who sees it desolating his fields, and ruining all his hopes, can feel no other emotions than horror and sorrow. – In a word, the sublime, in order to give pleasing astonishment, must be either imaginary, or not immediately pernicious.

There is a kind of horror, which may be infused into the mind both by natural appearances, and by verbal description; and which, though it make the blood seem to run cold, and produce a momentary fear, is not unpleasing, but may be even agreeable: and therefore, the objects that produce it are justly denominated sublime. Of natural appearances that affect the mind in this manner, are vast caverns, deep and dark woods, overhanging precipices, the agitation of the sea in a storm: and some of the sounds above-mentioned have the same effect, as those of cannon and thunder. Verbal descriptions infusing sublime horror are such as convey lively ideas, of the objects of superstition, as ghosts and enchantments; or of the thoughts that haunt the imaginations of the guilty; or of those external things, which are pleasingly terrible, as storms, conflagrations, and the like.

It may seem strange, that horror of any kind should give pleasure. But the fact is certain. Why do people run to see battles, executions, and shipwrecks? Is it, as an Epicurean would say, to compare themselves with others, and exult in their own security while they see the distress of those who suffer? No, surely: good minds are swayed by different motives. Is it, that they may be at hand, to give every assistance in their power to their unhappy brethren? This would draw the benevolent, and even the tender-hearted, to a ship-wreck; but to a battle, or to an execution, could not bring spectators, because there the humanity of individuals is of no use. – It must be, because a sort of gloomy satisfaction, or terrific pleasure, accompanies the gratification of that curiosity which events of this nature are apt to raise in minds of a certain frame.

No parts of Tasso are read with greater relish, than where he describes the darkness, silence, and other horrors, of the enchanted forest: and the poet himself is so sensible of the captivating influence of such ideas over the human imagination, that he makes the catastrophe of the poem in some measure depend upon them. Milton is not less enamoured "of forests and enchant-ments drear;" as appears from the use to which he applies them in *Comus*: the scenery whereof charms us the more, because it affects our minds, as it did the bewildered lady, and causes "a thousand fantasies" –

> – to throng into the memory,
> Of calling shapes, and beckoning shadows dire,
> And aery tongues, that syllable mens names
> On sands, and shores, and desert wildernesses.

Forests in every age must have had attractive horrors: otherwise so many nations would not have resorted thither, to celebrate the rites of superstition. And the inventors of what is called the Gothic, but perhaps should rather be called the Saracen, architecture, must have been enraptured with the same imagery, when, in forming and arranging the pillars and aisles of their churches, they were so careful to imitate the rows of lofty trees in a deep grove.

Observe a few children assembled about a fire, and listening to tales of apparitions and witchcraft. You may see them grow pale, and crowd closer and closer through fear: while he who is snug in the chimney corner, and at the greatest distance from the door, considers himself as peculiarly fortunate; because he thinks that, if the ghost should enter, he has a better chance to escape, than if he were in a more exposed situation. And yet, notwithstanding their present, and their apprehension of future, fears, you could not perhaps propose any amusement that would at this time be more acceptable. The same love of such horrors as are not attended with sensible inconvenience continues with us through life: and Aristotle has affirmed, that the end of tragedy is to purify the soul by the operations of pity and terror.

The mind and body of man are so constituted, that, without action, neither can the one be healthy, nor the other happy. And as bodily exercises, though attended with fatigue, as dancing, or with some degree of danger, as hunting, are not on that account the less agreeable; so those things give delight, which rouse the soul, even when they bring along with them horror, anxiety, or sorrow, provided these passions be transient, and their causes rather imaginary than real.

The most perfect models of sublimity are seen in the works of nature. Pyramids, palaces, fireworks, temples, artificial lakes and canals, ships of war, fortifications, hills levelled and caves hollowed by human industry, are mighty efforts, no doubt, and awaken in every beholder a pleasing admiration; but appear as nothing, when we compare them, in respect of magnificence, with mountains, volcanoes, rivers, cataracts, oceans, the expanse of heaven, clouds and storms, thunder and lightning, the sun, moon, and stars. So that, without the study of nature, a true taste in the sublime is absolutely unattainable. And we need not wonder at what is related of Thomson, the author of *the Seasons*; who, on hearing that a certain learned gentleman of London was writing an epic poem exclaimed, "*He write an epic poem! it is impossible: he never saw a mountain in his life.*" This at least is certain, that if we were to strike out of Homer, Virgil, and Milton, those descriptions and sentiments that allude to the grand phenomena of nature, we should deprive these poets of the best part of their sublimity.

And yet, the true sublime may be attained by human art. Music is sublime, when it inspires devotion, courage, or other elevated affections: or when by its mellow and sonorous harmonies it overwhelms the mind with sweet astonishment: or when it infuses that pleasing horror above mentioned; which, when joined to words descriptive of terrible ideas, it sometimes does very effectually.

Architecture is sublime, when it is large and durable, and withal so simple and well-proportioned as that the eye can take in all its greatness at once. For when an edifice is loaded with ornaments, our attention to them prevents our attending to the whole; and the mind, though it may be amused with the beauty or the variety of the little parts, is not struck with that sudden astonishment, which accompanies the contemplation of sublimity. Hence the Gothic style of building, where it abounds in minute decorations, and where greater pains are employed on the parts, than in adjusting the general harmony of the fabric, is less sublime than the Grecian, in which proportion, simplicity, and usefulness, are more studied than ornament. It is true, that Gothic buildings may be very sublime: witness the old cathedral churches. But this is owing, rather to their vast magnitude, to the stamp of antiquity that is impressed on them, and to their having been so long appropriated to religious service, than to those peculiarities that distinguish their architecture from the Grecian.

The Chinese mode of building has no pretensions to sublimity; its decorations being still more trivial than the Gothic; and because it derives no dignity from associated ideas, and has no vastness of magnitude to raise admiration. Yet is it not without its charms. There is an air of neatness in it, and of novelty, which to many is pleasing, and which of late it has been much the fashion to imitate.

Painting is sublime, when it displays men invested with great qualities, as bodily strength, or actuated by sublime passions, as courage, devotion, benevolence. That picture by Guido Reni, which represents Michael triumphing over the evil spirit, I have always admired for its sublimity, though some critics are not pleased with it. The attitude of the angel, who holds a sword in his right hand in a threatening posture, conveys to me the idea of dignity and grace, as well as of irresistible strength. Nor is the majestic beauty of his person less admirable: and his countenance, though in a slight degree expressive of contempt or indignation, retains that sweet composure, which we think essential to the angelic character.... Painting is also sublime, when it imitates grand natural appearances, as mountains, precipices, storms, huge heaps of rocks and ruins, and the like.

At the time when Raphael began to distinguish himself, two styles of painting were cultivated in Italy. His master Pietro Perugino copied nature with an exactness bordering upon servility: so that his figures had less dignity and grace than their originals. Michael Angelo ran into the opposite extreme; and, with an imagination fraught with great ideas, and continually aspiring to sublimity, so enlarged the proportions of nature, as to raise his men to giants, and stretch out every form into an extension that might almost be called monstrous. To the penetration of Raphael both styles seemed to be faulty, and both in an equal degree. The one appeared insipid in its accuracy, and the other almost ridiculous in its extravagance. He therefore pursued a middle course; tempering the fire of Angelo with the caution of Perugino: and thus exhibited the true sublime of painting; wherein the graces of nature are heightened, but nothing is gigantic, disproportioned, or improbable. While we study his cartoons, we seem to be conversing with a species of men, like ourselves indeed, but of heroic dignity and size.

This great artist is in painting, what Homer is in poetry. Homer magnifies in like manner; and transforms men into heroes and demigods; and, to give the more grandeur to his narrative, sets it off with marvellous events, which, in his time, though not improbable, were however astonishing. But Ariosto, and the authors of the Old Romance, resemble Michael Angelo in exalting their champions, not into heroes, but into giants and monsters. Achilles, though superior to all men in valour, would not venture to battle without his arms: but a warrior of romance, whether armed or not, could fell a troop of horse to the earth at one blow, tear up trees by the root, and now and then throw a piece of a mountain at the enemy. The true sublime is always natural and credible: but unbounded exaggerations, that surpass all proportion and all belief, are more apt to provoke laughter than astonishment.

Poetry becomes sublime in many ways: and as this is the only fine art, which can at present supply us with examples, I shall from it select a specimen or two of the different sorts of sublimity.

1. Poetry is sublime, when it elevates the mind. This indeed is a general character of greatness. But I speak here of sentiments so happily conceived and expressed, as to raise our affections above the low pursuits of sensuality and avarice, and animate us with the love of virtue and of honour. As a specimen, let me recommend the account, which Virgil gives in his eighth book, of the person, family, and kingdom of Evander; an Arcadian prince, who, after being trained up in all the discipline of Greece, established himself and his people in that part of Italy, where a few centuries after was built the great metropolis of the Roman empire. In the midst of poverty, that good old man retains a philosophical and a royal dignity. *"This habitation (says he, to Aeneas, who had made him a visit) has been honoured with the presence of Hercules himself. Dare, my guest, to despise riches; and do thou also fashion thyself into a likeness of God:"* or, as some render it, *"do thou also make thyself worthy of immortality."*

> Aude, hospes, contemnere opes; et te quoque dignum
> Finge Deo. –

There is strength in the expression, whereof our language is not capable. *"I despise the world (says Dryden) when I read it, and myself when I attempt to translate it."*

2. Poetry is sublime, when it conveys a lively idea of any grand appearance in art or nature. A nobler description of this sort I do not at present remember, than that which Virgil gives, in the first book of the *Georgics*, of a dark night, with wind, rain, and lightning: where Jupiter appears, encompassed with clouds and storms, darting his thunderbolts, and overturning the mountains, while the ocean is roaring, the earth trembling, the wild beasts fled away, the rain pouring down in torrents, the woods resounding to the tempest, and all mankind overwhelmed with consternation....

As examples of the same sort of sublimity, namely of great images with a mixture of horror, I might call the reader's attention to the storm in the beginning of the *Aeneid*, the death of Cacus in the eighth book, to the account of Tartarus in the sixth, and that of the burning of Troy in the second. But in the style of dreadful magnficence, nothing is superior, and scarce any thing equal, to Milton's representation of hell and chaos, in the first and second books of *Paradise Lost*.

In the concluding paragraph of the same work, there is brought together, with uncommon strength of fancy, and rapidity of narrative, a number of circumstances, wonderfully adapted to the purpose of filling the mind with ideas of terrific grandeur: the descent of the cherubim; the flaming sword; the archangel leading in haste our first parents down from the heights of paradise, and then disappearing; and, above all, the scene that presents itself on their looking behind them.

> They, looking back, all th' eastern cliff beheld
> Of Paradise, so late their happy seat,
> Waved over by that flaming brand; the gate
> With dreadful faces throng'd and fiery arms.

To which the last verses form the most striking contrast that can be imagined.

> Some natural tears they drop'd, but wiped them soon.
> The world was all before them, where to chuse
> Their place of rest, and Providence their guide.
> They, hand in hand, with wandering steps, and slow,
> Through Eden took their solitary way.

The final couplet renews our sorrow; by exhibiting, with picturesque accuracy, the most mournful scene in nature; which yet is so prepared, as to raise comfort, and dispose to resignation. And thus, while we are at once melting in tenderness, elevated with pious hope, and overwhelmed with the grandeur of description, the divine poem concludes. What luxury of mental gratification is here! Who would exchange this frame of mind (if nature could support it) for any other! How exquisitely does the faith of a Christian accord with the noblest feelings of humanity!

3. Poetry is sublime, when, without any great pomp of images or of words, it infuses horror by a happy choice of circumstances. When Macbeth (in Shakespeare) goes to consult the witches, he finds them performing rites in a cave; and, upon asking what they were employed about, receives no other answer than this short one, *"A deed without a name."* One's blood runs cold at the thought, that their work was of so accursed a nature, that they themselves had no name to express it by, or were afraid to speak of it by any name. Here is no solemnity of style, nor any accumulation of great ideas; yet here is the true sublime; because here is something that astonishes the mind, and fills it, without producing any real inconvenience....

Horror has long been a powerful, and a favourite, engine in the hands of the tragic poet. Aeschylus employed it more than any other ancient artist. In his play called *the Furies*, he introduced Orestes haunted by a company of those frightful beings; intending thereby an allegorical representation of the torment which that hero suffered in his mind, in consequence of having slain his mother Clytemnestra, for the part she had taken in the murder of his father. But to raise the greater horror in the spectators, the poet was at pains to describe, with amazing force of expression, the appearance of the Furies; and he brought upon the stage no fewer than fifty of them; whose infernal looks, hideous gestures, and horrible screams, had such effects on the women and children, that, in the subsequent exhibitions of the play, the number of furies was by an express law limited, first to fifteen, and afterwards to twelve. There are, no doubt, sublime strokes in the poet's account of these furies; and there is something very great in the idea of a person haunted by his own thoughts, in the form of such terrific beings. Yet horror of this kind I would hardly call sublime, because it is addressed rather to the eyes, than to the mind; and because it is easier to disfigure a man so, as to make him have the appearance of an ugly woman, than, by a brief description, or well-chosen sentiment, to alarm and astonish the fancy....

4. Poetry is sublime, when it awakens in the mind any great and good affection, as piety, or patriotism. This is one of the noblest effects of the art. The Psalms are remarkable, beyond all other writings, for their power of inspiring devout emotions. But it is not in this respect only that they are sublime. Of the divine nature they contain the most magnificent descriptions that the soul of man can comprehend. The hundred and fourth psalm, in particular, displays the power and goodness of providence, in creating and preserving the world, and the various tribes of animals in it, with such majestic brevity and beauty, as it is vain to look for in any human composition. The morning song of Adam and Eve, and many other parts of *Paradise Lost*, are noble effusions of piety, breathed in the most captivating strains: and Thomson's Hymn on the Seasons, if we overlook an unguarded word or two, is not inferior.

Of that sublimity which results from the strong expression of patriotic sentiments, many examples might be quoted from the Latin poets, particularly Virgil, Horace, and Lucan...

5. Poetry is also sublime, when it describes in a lively manner the visible effects of any of those passions that give elevation to the character. Such is that passage, in the conclusion of the same twelfth book of the *Iliad*, which paints the impetuosity and terrible appearance of Hector, storming the entrenchments, and pursuing the enemy to their ships. Extraordinary efforts of magnanimity, valour, or any other virtue, and extraordinary exertions of strength or power, are grand objects, and give sublimity to those pictures or poems, in which they are well represented. All the great poets abound in examples.

Yet in great strength, for example, there may be unwieldiness, or awkwardness, or some other contemptible quality, whereby the sublime is destroyed. Polyphemus is a match for five hundred Greeks; but he is not a grand object. We hate his barbarity, and despise his folly, too much, to allow him a single grain of admiration. Ulysses, who in the hands of Polyphemus was nothing, is incomparably more sublime, when, in walking to his palace, disguised like a beggar, he is insulted, and even kicked, by one of his own slaves, who was in the service of those rebels that were tempting his queen, plundering his household, and alienating the affections of his people. Homer tells us, that the hero stood firm, without being moved from his place by the stroke; that he deliberated for a moment, whether he should at one blow fell the traitor to the earth; but that patience and prudential thoughts restrained him. The brutal force of the Cyclops is not near so striking as this picture; which displays bodily strength and magnanimity united. For what we despise we never admire; and therefore despicable greatness cannot be sublime....

In describing what is great, poets often employ sonorous language. This is suitable to the nature of human speech: for while we give utterance to that which elevates our imagination, we are apt to speak louder, and with greater solemnity, than at other times. It must not however be thought, that high-sounding words are essential to the sublime. Without a correspondent dignity of thought, or grandeur of images, a sonorous style is ridiculous; and puts one in mind of those persons, who raise great expectation, and assume a look of vast importance, when they have either nothing at all to say, or nothing that is worth notice. That style is sublime, which makes us conceive a great object, or a great effort, in a lively manner; and this may be done, when the words are very plain and simple. Nay, the plainest and simplest words have sometimes a happy effect in setting off what is intrinsically great; as an act of vast bodily strength is the more astonishing, when performed by a slight effort. This sort of sublimity we have in perfection in many of those passages of Holy Writ, that describe the operation of Omnipotence: as, "*God said, Let there be light, and there was light: – He spoke, and it was done; he commanded, and it stood fast: – Thou openest thy hand, they are filled with good; thou hidest thy face, and they are troubled.*"...

It may now be remarked in general, that the sublime is often heightened, when, by means of figurative language, the qualities of a superior nature are judiciously applied to what is inferior. Hence we see in poetry, and in more familiar language, the passions and feelings of rationality ascribed to that which is without reason, and without life, or even to abstract ideas. – On Adam's eating the forbidden fruit,

> Earth trembled from her entrails, as again
> In pangs, and Nature gave a second groan;
> Sky lower'd, and, muttering thunder, some sad drops
> Wept, at compleating of the mortal sin
> Original.

Who is not sensible of the greatness of the thought conveyed in these words; which represent the earth and heaven affected with horror at the sin then committed, and nature, or the universe, uttering in low thunder a groan of anguish? Had the poet simply said, that there was an earthquake, that the sky grew dark, and that some drops of rain fell, the account would no doubt have been sublime, as he would have given it. But is it not much more so, when we are informed, that this convulsion of nature was the effect of a sort of sensation diffused at that instant through the whole inanimate world? How dreadful must be the enormity of that guilt, which could produce an event so great, and withal so preternatural! Here are two sources of the sublime: the prodigy strikes with horror; the vastness of the idea overwhelms with astonishment.

In this place an unskilful poet would probably have brought on such a storm of thunder and lightning, and so violent an earthquake, as must have overturned the mountains, and set the woods on fire. But Milton, with better judgment, makes the alarm of that deep and awful kind, which cannot express itself in any other way, than by an inward and universal trembling: a sensation more affecting to the fancy, than those passions are, which vent themselves in outrageous behaviour; even as that sorrow is the most pathetic, which deprives one of the power of lamentation, and discovers itself only by fainting and groans. Besides, if this convulsion of the universe had been more violent, the unhappy offenders must have been confounded and terrified; which would not have suited the poet's purpose. For he tells us, and indeed the circumstances that follow in the narrative (which, by the by, are exquisitely contrived) do all suppose, that our first parents were so intent on gratifying their impious appetite, that they took no notice of the prodigies, which accompanied the transgression....

Yet he, who aims at the sublime, must not trust so implicitly to the grandeur of his thoughts, as to be careless about his expression. Well chosen words, and an elegant arrangement of them, are justly reckoned by Longinus among the sources of sublimity. Even when the thought is both good and great, the greatness, or the elegance, may be lost or lessened by an unskilful writer: and that in several ways.

First, by too minute description, and too many words. For, when we are engrossed by admiration or astonishment, it is not natural for us to speak much, or attend to the more diminutive qualities of that which we contemplate....

In sublime description, though the circumstances that are specified be few, yet, if they be well chosen and great, the reader's fancy will complete the picture: and often, as already hinted, the image will not be less astonishing, if in its general appearance there be something indefinite. When Hector forces the Greek entrenchments, the poet describes him by several grand allusions, and by this in particular,

> Now rushing in the furious chief appears,
> *Gloomy as night*, and shakes two shining spears.

In what respect he resembled night, Homer leaves to be determined by the reader's fancy. This conveys no positive idea; but we are hence led to imagine, that there must have been something peculiarly dark and dreadful in his look, as it appeared to the enemy: and thus we make the picture stronger perhaps than it would have been, if the author had drawn it more minutely.* A genius

---

* That poetical description ought to be distinct and lively, and such as might both assist the fancy, and direct the hand of the painter, is an acknowledged truth in criticism. The best poets are the most picturesque. Homer is in this respect so admirable, that he has been justly called the prince of painters, as well as of poets. And one cause of the insipidity of the Henriade, is, that its scenery and images are described in too general terms, and want those distinguishing peculiarities that captivate the fancy, and interest the passions.

like Cowley would have interrupted the narrative, in order to enumerate all those particulars in which Hector resembled night; comparing his shield to the full moon; his eyes to stars; the flashing of his armour to comets and meteor; the dust that flew about him, to clouds and darkness; the clangour of his weapons to the scream of the owl; the terror he struck into the enemy, to the fear occasioned by apparitions; with perhaps a great deal more to the same purpose: which would have taken off our attention from the hero, and set us a-wondering at the singularity of the author's wit. It ought to be considered, that the rapidity of Hector's motion requires a correspondent rapidity in the narrative, and leaves no time for long description; and it may be supposed, that the persons who saw him would not stand gazing, and making similes, but would fly before him if they were Greeks, or rush on along with him if they were his own people.

When an author, in exhibiting what he thinks great, says every thing that can be said, he confounds his readers with the multitude of circumstances; and, instead of rousing their imagination leaves it in a state of indolence, by giving it nothing to do; making them at the same time suspect, that, as he has but few great ideas to offer, he is determined to make the most of what he has. Besides, long details encumber the narrative, and lengthen the poem without necessity. Brief description, therefore, and concise expression, may be considered as essential to the sublime....

Secondly: though an author's ideas be great, they may yet fall short of sublimity by excessive amplification. Hyperbolical phrases, for reasons assigned in another place, are often natural, and may therefore promote the

But should every thing in poetry be picturesque? No. To the right imitation of nature shade is necessary, as well as light. We may be powerfully affected by that which is not visible at all; and of visible things some cannot be, and many ought not to be, painted: and the mind is often better pleased with images of its own forming, or finishing, than with those that are set before it complete in all their colours and proportions. From the passage referred to in the text, and from many others that might be quoted, it appears that in description Homer himself is not always definite; and that he knows how to affect his readers by leaving occasionally a part of his picture to be supplied by their imagination. Of Helen's person he gives no minute account: but, when he tells us, that her loveliness was such as to extort the admiration of the *oldest* Trojan senators, who had, and who owned they had, so good reason to dislike her, he gives a higher idea of the power of her charms, than could have been conveyed by any description of her eyes, mouth, shape, and other distinguishing beauties.

Algarotti is of opinion, that the poetry of the northern nations is, in general, less picturesque than that of Italy....

Of this criticism I would observe, that the censure here passed on the poetry of the north, as compared with that of the *modern* Italians at least, will hardly be admitted by those who understand and have read our great poets, Chaucer, Spenser, Shakespeare, and Thomson; from whom instances without number might be brought of imagery as vivid and particular, as it is in the power of language to convey. Milton, where his subject requires that he should be *exactly descriptive*, as in his fourth, seventh, ninth, and eleventh books, is in this respect not inferior to Homer himself. Indeed, when his scene of action lies *beyond the visible diurnal sphere*; when, with a view to raise astonishment or horror, he paints what was never seen by mortal eye, it is impossible for him to be strictly picturesque. Figures so deeply shaded cannot present a definite outline: forms of such terrific grandeur must be to a certain degree invested with darkness....

sublime; but if they are not used with discretion and a due regard to the pro-portions of nature, they become ridiculous....

Thirdly: mean words and mean circumstances, introduced in the descrip-tion of what is great or elegant, will destroy the sublimity, and debase the beauty....

I shall only add, that our taste for the sublime, cherished into a habit, and directed to proper objects, may, by preserving us from vice, which is the vilest of all things, and by recommending virtue for its intrinsic dignity, be useful in promoting our moral improvement. The same taste will also lead to the study of nature, which everywhere displays the sublimest appearances. And no study has a better effect upon the heart. For it keeps men at a distance from criminal pursuits, yields a variety of inoffensive and profitable amusement, and gives full demonstration of the infinite goodness and greatness of the adorable creator.

Part V
Edinburgh and Glasgow

Preoccupation with distance is a hallmark of eighteenth-century visual aesthetics, and can be found in writings on art as well as landscape. Within the analytic of the sublime distance is related to size [Hume] so that far-off objects appear to be less threatening or terrifying. Hume, however, makes the opposite case in his invocation of esteem and admiration, thereby giving a greater value to distant objects. Hume also considers temporal as well as spatial parameters and makes an important and early case for the historical imagination.

The movement from low to high [Hume] is also a pretty constant feature of the sublime tradition, unsurprisingly given the tendency to think of mountains when contemplating the sublime. Similarly the elevation of the soul is associated with the gradual ascent from the human towards the divine and furnishes the discursive analytic with another well-worn figuration. It is for this reason that, by association, virtue, riches and power [Hume] become cyphers for the sublime. This will present problems at both the ethical and political levels since some forms of power and wealth cannot be ethically sanctioned within the mainstream of civic humanism. The Scottish enlightenment attempts to square this circle, most obviously in the work of Smith, but the moral goodness of wealth and power nevertheless remain problematic.

In this movement from low to high it sometimes happens that difficulty is encountered [Hume]; given this the concept of difficulty itself comes under scrutiny and is gradually associated in and of itself with the sublime effect.

Theories of sublimity often draw upon the wider concerns and intellectual debates animating the Scottish enlightenment, such as early social theory and anthropology. Theories of the origin and progress of society [Blair], for example, were much debated in the context of the Scottish enlightenment. Many of these theories, in common with those of Jean-Jacques Rousseau, attempted to work out a description of culture with reference to differences in climate, a theory first articulated by Jean Bodin in his *Method* of 1566 and later embraced by both Voltaire and Montesquieu. According to this scheme of things both language and the development of culture were geographically and therefore climate specific.[1]

Perhaps the most important context remains, however, moral-sense theory, clearly signalled by Blair's discussion of the sublimity of moral sentiments [Blair]. The ethical which had been a feature of early eighteenth-century speculation returns here in a conjoining of these two vigorous strains of Scottish enlightenment thought. Such a conjunction is not necessarily self-evident by the time Blair writes since the sentimental, in and of itself, has no claim to the sublime. It is only in the special case of the ethical dimension to the

---

[1] See Ira O. Wade, *Intellectual origins of the French enlightenment* (Princeton: Princeton University Press, 1970); Christopher J. Berry, '"Climate" in the eighteenth century: James Dunbar and the Scottish case', *Texas Studies in Language and Literature* 16:2 (Summer, 1974), 281-92; and on Rousseau see Jean Starobinski, *Jean-Jacques Rousseau: transparency and obstruction*, tr. A. Goldhammer (Chicago: University of Chicago Press, 1988), esp. pp. 304-22.

sentiment, precisely in the notion of the moral sentiments, that the ethical and aesthetic can be brought together.

Given this embracing of sentimentalism the physical aspect to sublime affect becomes a legitimate, even pressing concern. Consequently we find a pretty continuous attention being paid to the bodily, as in Smith's comments concerning the 'natural symptoms' of aesthetic experience. The physical manifestation of the effect of wonder [Smith], for example, is closely linked to the physicalisation of oratorical performance. Rolling the eyes, staring, suspension of breath are all used for both positive and negative effect in the delivery of speech. Here Smith approves of the outward manifestation of an inward sensation; teachers of oratory, however, are not so convinced by such physical demonstration, especially when there is a chance that the outward show may not correspond at all to an inward emotion.[2]

Smith is well known for his theory of the theatricality of moral sentiments, a feature of this sentimental physicalisation which tends towards spectacle. In terms of the sublime tradition the outward demonstration of inward emotion is deeply problematic since the means by which inner experience might be translated into outward show are unclear. Furthermore, the possibility that outward appearances may be false is constantly invoked.[3]

In the *Theory of moral sentiments* Smith proposed the most elaborate account of how aesthetic affect is conjoined to benevolence, a general project of the Scottish school [Smith]. While this theory does not attempt to claim that all aesthetic experiences are necessarily ethically good it does nevertheless propose ways in which we might understand how to restrain selfish affections in favour of benevolent ones.[4]

In the more specialised realm of literary aesthetics the Scottish school also developed the means by which internal feelings could be dissociated from outward demonstrations of emotion. In Kames's thought, for example, the distance between inner feelings and outward expression is to some extent modified by the imagination and it is his original contribution to this area of discussion to insert the concept of 'ideal presence' as an objectification of imaginative activity [Kames]. There are a number of ways in which the imagination is seen to operate in this difficult matter but Kames's solution to the problem of 'imaginary' objects resulting from the activity of the imagination is perhaps the most elegant.[5]

[2] See on this Thomas Sheridan, *A course of lectures on elocution* (London, 1762), pp. 131-3; Henry Lemoine, *The art of speaking,* (London, 1797), pp. 57-8; and John Wesley, *Directions concerning pronunciation and gesture* (Bristol, 1770).
[3] For a good discussion of theatricality in Smith's work see David Marshall, 'Adam Smith and the theatricality of moral sentiments', *Critical Inquiry,* 10 (1984), 592-613; and D.D. Raphael, 'The impartial spectator', in *Essays on Adam Smith,* ed. Andrew S. Skinner and Thomas Wilson (Oxford: Clarendon Press, 1975), pp. 83-99.
[4] On affect see Wallace Jackson, 'Affective values in later eighteenth-century aesthetics', *JAAC,* 24:2 (Winter, 1965); and 'Affective values in early eighteenth-century aesthetics', *JAAC,* 27:1 (Fall, 1968), 87-92.
[5] On the imagination see Donald F. Bond, 'The distrust of the imagination in English neoclassicism', *Philological Quarterly,* 14 (January, 1935), 54-69, and 'The neo-

Matters of social class or rank [Kames] are rarely explicitly discussed within the context of the sublime, but they nevertheless underpin much of the tradition. If one's education were very rudimentary how could one be able to appreciate aesthetic forms? The period in question had a particularly acute sense of social rank but this had to be tempered by a continuous erosion of the boundaries between social divisions. There are countless examples of how this acute sense worked in the realm of the appreciation of art, the most telling, perhaps, being Johnson's preface to the 1762 catalogue for the Spring Garden Exhibition of paintings which explained why the admission price of one shilling needed to be charged: in order to keep out the lower ranks of society who had in previous years crowded out the exhibition.[6]

The most significant development in this section is the fracturing of a once harmonious co-existence enjoyed by the analytic of the sublime with rhetoric and imitation. This fracturing leads to a number of new and complex inter-relations between a wide range of discourses. Thus, the belief in the complex interrelatedness of the 'commercial arts', the 'elegant arts', civil society and ethics begins to produce an equally complex vocabulary of sublimity. The idea of 'repose', for example, becomes central to sublimity. For Smith 'repose' is elaborated in terms of a type of secondary sublimity which interposes itself after the imagination has been affected by wonder, and has therefore, gained a freedom to operate distinctly from the objects of perception [Smith].

For Ferguson, however, 'repose' is a movement away from sublimity and, therefore, understood as a form of imprisonment [Ferguson]. Another key feature of this newly articulated complexity of inter-discursive relations is the growing awareness that unforeseen positions arise as a direct result of the confrontation of moral paradoxes. Ferguson is the most vigorous and robust writer in relation to this but it is nevertheless highly characteristic of all the writers in this section. Both Smith and Kames, for example, consider the moral paradoxes of the transporting sublimities of conquering heroes such as Caesar and Alexander which are irreconcilable with notions of virtue and justice [Smith, Kames].

classical psychology of imagination', *ELH*, 4:4 (December, 1937), 245-64; Alfred Owen Aldridge, 'Akenside and imagination', *Studies in Philology*, 42:4 (October, 1945), pp. 769-92; Ernest Lee Tuveson, *The imagination as a means of grace*, (Berkeley: University of California Press, 1960); Alexander Manson Kinghorn, 'Literary aesthetics and the sympathetic emotions – a main trend in eighteenth-century Scottish criticism', *Studies in Scottish Literature*, I:1 (July, 1963), 35-47; and Eric Rothstein, '"Ideal presence" and the "non finito" in eighteenth-century aesthetics', *Eighteenth Century Studies*, 11:3 (Spring, 1976), 307-32.

6 On this and other early exhibitions see Edward Edwards, *Anecdotes of painters* (London, 1808); and for a more recent discussion David Solkin, *Painting for money* (New Haven: Yale University Press, 1993).

34

David Hume,
from *A treatise of human nature* (1739-40)

Book II. Of the passions
Part III. Of the will and direct passions
Section VIII. Of contiguity and distance in space and time continued.

Thus we have accounted for three phænomena, which seem pretty remarkable. Why distance weakens the conception and passion: why distance in time has a greater effect than that in space: and why distance in past time has still a greater effect than that in future. We must now consider three phænomena, which seem to be, in a manner, the reverse of these: why a very great distance increases our esteem and admiration for an object: why such a distance in time increases it more than that in space: and a distance in past time more than that in future. The curiousness of the subject will, I hope, excuse my dwelling on it for some time.

To begin with the first phænomenon, why a great distance increases our esteem and admiration for an object; it is evident that the mere view and contemplation of any greatness, whether successive or extended, enlarges the soul, and [gives] it a sensible delight and pleasure. A wide plain, the ocean, eternity, a succession of several ages; all these are entertaining objects, and excel every thing, however beautiful, which accompanies not its beauty with a suitable greatness. Now when any very distant object is presented to the imagination, we naturally reflect on the interposed distance, and by that means, conceiving something great and magnificent, receive the usual satisfaction. But as the fancy passes easily from one idea to another related to it, and transports to the second all the passions excited by the first, the admiration, which is directed to the distance, naturally diffuses itself over the distant object. Accordingly we find, that it is not necessary the object should be actually distant from us, in order to cause our admiration; but that it is sufficient, if, by the natural association of ideas, it conveys our view to any considerable distance. A great traveller, although in the same chamber, will pass for a very extraordinary person; as a Greek medal, even in our cabinet, is always esteemed a valuable curiosity. Here the object, by a natural transition, conveys our view to the distance; and the admiration, which arises from that distance, by another natural transition, returns back to the object.

But although every great distance produces an admiration for the distant object, a distance in time has a more considerable effect than that in space.

199

Ancient busts and inscriptions are more valued than Japan tables: and not to mention the Greeks and Romans, it is certain we regard with more veneration the old Chaldeans and Egyptians, than the modern Chinese and Persians, and bestow more fruitless pains to clear up the history and chronology of the former, than it would cost us to make a voyage, and be certainly informed of the character, learning and government of the latter. I shall be obliged to make a digression in order to explain this phænomenon.

It is a quality very observable in human nature, that any opposition, which does not entirely discourage and intimidate us, has rather a contrary effect, and inspires us with a more than ordinary grandeur and magnanimity. In collecting our force to overcome the opposition, we invigorate the soul, and give it an elevation with which otherwise it would never have been acquainted. Compliance, by rendering our strength useless, makes us insensible of it; but opposition awakens and employs it.

This is also true in the inverse. Opposition not only enlarges the soul; but the soul, when full of courage and magnanimity, in a manner seeks opposition.

> Spumantemque dari pecora inter inertia votis
> Optat aprum, aut fulvum descendere monte leonem.

Whatever supports and fills the passions is agreeable to us; as on the contrary, what weakens and enfeebles them is uneasy. As opposition has the first effect, and facility the second, no wonder the mind, in certain dispositions, desires the former, and is averse to the latter.

These principles have an effect on the imagination as well as on the passions. To be convinced of this we need only consider the influence of *heights* and *depths* on that faculty. Any great elevation of place communicates a kind of pride or sublimity of imagination and gives a fancied superiority over those that lie below; and *vice versa*, a sublime and strong imagination conveys the idea of ascent and elevation. Hence it proceeds, that we associate, in a manner, the idea of whatever is good with that of height, and evil with lowness. Heaven is supposed to be above, and hell below. A noble genius is called an elevate and sublime one. *Atque udam spernit humum fugiente penna.* On the contrary, a vulgar and trivial conception is styled indifferently low or mean. Prosperity is denominated ascent, and adversity descent. Kings and princes are supposed to be placed at the top of human affairs; as peasants and day-labourers are said to be in the lowest stations. These methods of thinking, and of expressing ourselves, are not of so little consequence as they may appear at first sight.

It is evident to common sense, as well as philosophy, that there is no natural nor essential difference betwixt high and low, and that this distinction arises only from the gravitation of matter, which produces a motion from the one to the other. The very same direction, which in this part of the globe is called *ascent*, is denominated *descent* in our antipodes; which can proceed from nothing but the contrary tendency of bodies. Now it is certain, that the tendency of bodies continually operating upon our senses, must produce, from custom, a like tendency in the fancy, and that when we consider any object situated in an ascent, the idea of its weight gives us a propensity to transport it from the place, in which it is situated, to the place immediately below it, and so on, till we come to the ground, which equally stops the body and our imagination. For a like reason we feel a difficulty in mounting, and pass not without a kind of reluctance from the inferior to that which is situated above it; as if our ideas acquired a kind of gravity from their objects. As a proof of this, do we not find, that the facility, which is so much studied in music and poetry, is called the fall or cadency of the harmony or period; the idea of facility communicating to us that of descent, in the same manner as descent produces a facility?

Since the imagination, therefore, in running from low to high, finds an opposition in its internal qualities and principles, and since the soul, when elevated with joy and courage, in a manner seeks opposition, and throws itself with alacrity into any scene of thought or action, where its courage meets with matter to nourish and employ it; it follows, that every thing, which invigorates and enlivens the soul, whether by touching the passions or imagination, naturally conveys to the fancy this inclination for ascent, and determines it to run against the natural stream of its thoughts and conceptions. This aspiring progress of the imagination suits the present disposition of the mind; and the difficulty, instead of extinguishing its vigour and alacrity, has the contrary effect, of sustaining and increasing it. Virtue, genius, power, and riches are for this reason associated with height and sublimity; as poverty, slavery, and folly are conjoined with descent and lowness. Were the case the same with us as Milton represents it to be with the angels, to whom *descent is adverse*, and who *cannot sink without labour and compulsion*, this order of things would be entirely inverted; as appears hence, that the very nature of ascent and descent is derived from the difficulty and propensity, and consequently every one of their effects proceeds from that origin.

All this is easily applied to the present question, why a considerable distance in time produces a great veneration for the distant objects than a like removal in space. The imagination moves with more difficulty in passing from one portion of time to another, than in a transition through the parts of space; and that because space or extension appears united to our senses, while time or succession is always broken and divided. This difficulty, when joined with a small distance, interrupts and weakens the fancy: but has a contrary effect in a great removal. The mind, elevated by the vastness of its object, is still farther elevated by the difficulty of the conception; and being obliged every moment to renew its efforts in the transition from one part of time to another, feels a more vigorous and sublime disposition, than in a transition through the parts of space, where the ideas flow along with easiness and facility. In this disposition, the imagination, passing, as is usual, from the consideration of the distance to the view of the distant objects, gives us a proportionable veneration for it; and this is the reason why all the relicts of antiquity are so precious in our eyes, and appear more valuable than what is brought even from the remotest parts of the world.

The third phænomenon I have remarked will be a full confirmation of this.

It is not every removal in time, which has the effect of producing veneration and esteem. We are not apt to imagine our posterity will excel us, or equal our ancestors. This phænomenon is the more remarkable, because any distance in futurity weakens not our ideas so much as an equal removal in the past. Although a removal in the past, when very great, increases our passions beyond a like removal in the future, yet a small removal has a greater influence in diminishing them.

In our common way of thinking we are placed in a kind of middle station betwixt the past and future; and as our imagination finds a kind of difficulty in running along the former, and a facility in following the course of the latter, the difficulty conveys the notion of ascent, and the facility of the contrary. Hence we imagine our ancestors to be, in a manner, mounted above us, and our posterity to lie below us. Our fancy arrives not at the one without effort, but easily reaches the other: which effort weakens the conception, where the distance is small; but enlarges and elevates the imagination, when attended with a suitable object. As on the other hand, the facility assists the fancy in a small removal, but takes off from its force when it contemplates any considerable distance.

It may not be improper, before we leave this subject of the will, to resume, in a few words, all that has been said concerning it, in order to set the whole more distinctly before the eyes of the reader. What we commonly understand by *passion* is a violent and sensible emotion of mind, when any good or evil is presented, or any object, which, by the original formation of our faculties, is fitted to excite an appetite. By *reason* we mean affections of the very same kind with the former; but such as operate more calmly, and cause no disorder in the temper: which tranquillity leads us into a mistake concerning them, and causes us to regard them as conclusions only of our intellectual faculties. Both the *causes* and *effects* of these violent and calm passions are pretty variable, and depend, in a great measure, on the peculiar temper and disposition of every individual. Generally speaking, the violent passions have a more powerful influence on the will; although it is often found, that the calm ones, when corroborated by reflection, and seconded by resolution, are able to control them in their most furious movements. What makes this whole affair more uncertain, is, that a calm passion may easily be changed into a violent one, either by a change of temper, or of the circumstances and situation of the object, as by the borrowing of force from any attendant passion, by custom, or by exciting the imagination. Upon the whole, this struggle of passion and of reason, as it is called, diversifies human life, and makes men so different not only from each other, but also from themselves in different times. Philosophy can only account for a few of the greater and more sensible events of this war; but must leave all the smaller and more delicate revolutions, as dependant on principles too fine and minute for her comprehension.

Book III. Of morals
Part III. Of the other virtues and vices
Section II. Of greatness of mind

...I believe no one, who has any practice of the world, and can penetrate into the inward sentiments of men, will assert, that the humility, which good-breeding and decency require of us, goes beyond the outside, or that a thorough sincerity in this particular is esteemed a real part of our duty. On the contrary, we may observe, that a genuine and hearty pride, or self-esteem, if well concealed and well founded, is essential to the character of a man of honour, and that there is no quality of the mind, which is more indispensibly requisite to procure the esteem and approbation of mankind. There are certain deferences and mutual submissions, which custom requires of the different ranks of men towards each other; and whoever exceeds in this particular, if through interest, is accused of meanness; if through ignorance, of simplicity. It is necessary, therefore, to know our rank and station in the world, whether it be fixed by our birth, fortune, employments, talents or reputation. It is necessary to feel the sentiment and passion of pride in conformity to it, and to regulate our actions accordingly. And should it be said, that prudence may suffice to regulate our actions in this particular, without any real pride, I would observe, that here the object of prudence is to conform our actions to the general usage and custom; and that it is impossible those tacit airs of superiority should ever have been established and authorized by custom, unless men were generally proud, and unless that passion were generally approved, when well-grounded.

If we pass from common life and conversation to history, this reasoning acquires new force, when we observe, that all those great actions and sentiments, which have become the admiration of mankind, are founded on nothing but pride and self-esteem. 'Go', says Alexander the Great to his soldiers, when they refused to follow him to the Indies, 'go tell your countrymen, that you left Alexander completing the conquest of the world.' This passage was always particularly admired by the prince of *Conde*, as we learn from *St. Evremond*. 'Alexander' said that prince, 'abandoned by his soldiers, among barbarians, not yet fully subdued, felt in himself such a dignity and right of empire, that he could not believe it possible any one could refuse to obey him. Whether in Europe or in Asia, among Greeks or Persians, all was indifferent to him: Wherever he found men, he fancied he had found subjects.'

In general we may observe, that whatever we call *heroic virtue*, and admire under the character of greatness and elevation of mind, is either nothing but a steady and well-established pride and self-esteem, or partakes largely of that passion. Courage, intrepidity, ambition, love of glory, magnanimity, and all the other shining virtues of that kind, have plainly a strong mixture of self-esteem in them, and derive a great part of their merit from that origin. Accordingly we find, that many religious declaimers decry those virtues as purely pagan and natural, and represent to us the excellency of the Christian religion, which places humility in the rank of virtues, and corrects the judgment of the world, and even of philosophers, who so generally admire all the efforts of pride and ambition. Whether this virtue of humility has been rightly understood, I shall not pretend to determine. I am content with the concession, that the world naturally esteems a well-regulated pride, which secretly animates our conduct, without breaking out into such indecent expressions of vanity, as may offend the vanity of others.

The merit of pride or self-esteem is derived from two circumstances, *viz.* its utility and its agreeableness to ourselves; by which it capacitates us for business, and, at the same time, gives us an immediate satisfaction. When it goes beyond its just bounds, it loses the first advantage, and even becomes prejudicial; which is the reason why we condemn an extravagant pride and ambition, however regulated by the decorums of good-breeding and politeness. But as such a passion is still agreeable, and conveys an elevated and sublime sensation to the person, who is actuated by it, the sympathy with that satisfaction diminishes considerably the blame, which naturally attends its dangerous influence on his conduct and behaviour. Accordingly we may observe, that an excessive courage and magnanimity, especially when it displays itself under the frowns of fortune, contributes, in a great measure, to the character of a hero, and will render a person the admiration of posterity; at the same time, that it ruins his affairs, and leads him into dangers and difficulties, with which otherwise he would never have been acquainted.

Heroism, or military glory, is much admired by the generality of mankind. They consider it as the most sublime kind of merit. Men of cool reflection are not so sanguine in their praises of it. The infinite confusions and disorder, which it has caused in the world, diminish much of its merit in their eyes. When they would oppose the popular notions on this head, they always paint out the evils, which this supposed virtue has produced in human society; the subversion of empires, the devastation of provinces, the sack of cities. As long as these are present to us, we are more inclined to hate than admire the ambition of heroes. But when we fix our view on the person himself, who is the author of all this mischief, there is something so dazzling in his character, the mere contemplation of it so elevates the mind, that we cannot refuse it our admiration. The pain, which we receive from its tendency to the prejudice of society, is over-powered by a stronger and more immediate sympathy....

Section IV. Of natural abilities

No distinction is more usual in all systems of ethics, than that between *natural abilities* and *moral virtues*; where the former are placed on the same footing with bodily endowments, and are supposed to have no merit or moral worth annexed to them. Whoever considers the matter accurately, will find, that a dispute upon this head would be merely a dispute of words and that although these qualities are not altogether of the same kind, yet they agree in in the most material circumstances. They are both of them equally mental qualities: and both of them equally produce pleasure; and have of course an equal tendency to procure the love and esteem of mankind. There are few, who are not as jealous of their character, with regard to sense and knowledge, as to honour and courage; and much more than with regard to temperance and sobriety. Men are even afraid of passing for good-natured; lest *that* should be taken for want of understanding: and often boast of more debauches than they have been really engaged in, to give themselves airs of fire and spirit. In short, the figure a man makes in the world, the reception he meets with in company, the esteem paid him by his acquaintance; all these advantages depend almost as much upon his good sense and judgment, as upon any other part of his character. Let a man have the best intentions in the world, and be the farthest from all injustice and violence, he will never be able to make himself be much regarded, without a moderate share, at least, of parts and understanding. Since then natural abilities, although, perhaps, inferior, yet are on the same footing, both as to their causes and effects, with those qualities which we call moral virtues, why should we make any distinction between them?

Although we refuse to natural abilities the title of virtues, we must allow, that they procure the love and esteem of mankind; that they give a new lustre to the other virtues; and that a man possessed of them is much more entitled to our good-will and services, than one entirely void of them. It may, indeed, be pretended, that the sentiment of approbation, which those qualities produce, besides its being *inferior*, is also somewhat *different* from that, which attends the other virtues. But this, in my opinion, is not a sufficient reason for excluding them from the catalogue of virtues. Each of the virtues, even benevolence, justice, gratitude, integrity, excites a different sentiment or feeling in the spectator. The characters of Cæsar and Cato, as drawn by Sallust, are both of them virtuous, in the strictest sense of the word; but in a different way: Nor are the sentiments entirely the same, which arise from them. The one produces love; the other esteem: The one is amiable; the other awful: We could wish to meet with the one character in a friend; the other character we would be ambitious of in ourselves. In like manner, the approbation, which attends natural abilities, may be somewhat different to the feeling from that, which arises from the other virtues, without making them entirely of a different species. And indeed we may observe, that the natural abilities, no more than the other virtues, produce not, all of them, the same kind of approbation. Good sense and genius beget esteem: wit and humour excite love.*

Those, who represent the distinction between natural abilities and moral virtues as very material, may say, that the former are entirely involuntary,

---

* Love and esteem are at the bottom the same passions, and arise from like causes. The qualities, that produce both, are agreeable, and give pleasure. But where this pleasure is severe and serious; or where its object is great, and makes a strong impression; or where it produces any degree of humility and awe: In all these cases, the passion, which arises from the pleasure, is more properly denominated esteem than love. Benevolence attends both: but is connected with love in a more eminent degree.

and have therefore no merit attending them, as having no dependance on liberty and free-will. But to this I answer, *first*, that many of those qualities, which all moralists, especially the ancients, comprehend under the title of moral virtues, are equally involuntary and necessary, with the qualities of the judgment and imagination. Of this nature are constancy, fortitude, magnanimity; and, in short, all the qualities which form the *great* man. I might say the same, in some degree, of the others; it being almost impossible for the mind to change its character in any considerable article, or cure itself of a passionate or splenetic temper, when they are natural to it. The greater degree there is of these blameable qualities, the more vicious they become, and yet they are the less voluntary. *Secondly*, I would have any one give me a reason, why virtue and vice may not be involuntary, as well as beauty and deformity. These moral distinctions arise from the natural distinctions of pain and pleasure; and when we receive those feelings from the general consideration of any quality or character, we denominate it vicious or virtuous. Now I believe no one will assert, that a quality can never produce pleasure or pain to the person who considers it, unless it be perfectly voluntary in the person who possesses it. *Thirdly*, as to free-will, we have shown that it has no place with regard to the actions, no more than the qualities of men. It is not a just consequence, that what is voluntary is free. Our actions are more voluntary than our judgments; but we have not more liberty in the one than in the other....

35

Hugh Blair,
from *A critical dissertation on the poems of Ossian* (1763)

Among the monuments remaining of the ancient state of nations, few are more valuable than their poems or songs. History, when it treats of remote and dark ages, is seldom very instructive. The beginnings of society, in every country, are involved in fabulous confusion; and though they were not, they would furnish few events worth recording. But, in every period of society, human manners are a curious spectacle; and the most natural pictures of ancient manners are exhibited in the ancient poems of nations. These present to us, what is much more valuable than the history of such transactions as a rude age can afford, the history of human imagination and passion. They make us acquainted with the notions and feelings of our fellow-creatures in the most artless ages; discovering what objects they admired, and what pleasures they pursued, before those refinements of society had taken place, which enlarge indeed, and diversify the transactions, but disguise the manners of mankind.

Besides this merit, which ancient poems have with philosophical observers of human nature, they have another with persons of taste. They promise some of the highest beauties of poetical writing. Irregular and unpolished we may expect the productions of uncultivated ages to be; but abounding, at the same time, with that enthusiasm, that vehemence and fire, which are the soul of poetry. For many circumstances of those times which we call barbarous, are favourable to the poetical spirit. That state, in which human nature shoots wild and free, though unfit for other improvements, certainly encourages the high exertions of fancy and passion.

In the infancy of societies, men live scattered and dispersed, in the midst of solitary rural scenes, where the beauties of nature are their chief entertainment. They meet with many objects, to them new and strange; their wonder and surprise are frequently excited; and by the sudden changes of fortune occurring in their unsettled state of life, their passions are raised to the utmost. Their passions have nothing to restrain them: their imagination has nothing to check it. They display themselves to one another without disguise: and converse and act in the uncovered simplicity of nature. As their feelings are strong, so their language, of itself, assumes a poetical turn. Prone to exaggerate, they describe every thing in the strongest colours; which of course renders their speech picturesque and figurative. Figurative language owes its rise chiefly to two causes; to the want of proper names for objects, and to the influence of imagination and passion over the form of expression. Both these causes concur in the infancy of society. Figures are commonly considered as artificial modes of speech, devised by orators and poets, after the world had advanced to a refined state. The contrary of this is the truth. Men never have used so many figures of style, as in those rude ages, when, besides the power of a warm imagination to suggest lively images, the want of proper and precise terms for the ideas they would express, obliged them to have recourse to circumlocution, metaphor, comparison, and all those substituted forms of expression, which give a poetical air to language. An American chief, at this day, harangues at the head of his tribe, in a more bold metaphorical style, than a modern European would adventure to use in an epic poem.

In the progress of society, the genius and manners of men undergo a change more favourable to accuracy than to sprightliness and sublimity. As the world advances, the understanding gains ground upon the imagination; the understanding is more exercised; the imagination less. Fewer objects occur that are new or surprising. Men apply themselves to trace the causes of things; they correct and refine one another; they subdue or disguise their passions; they form their exterior manners upon one uniform standard of politeness and civility. Human nature is pruned according to method and rule. Language advances from sterility to copiousness, and at the same time, from fervour to enthusiasm, to correctness and precision. Style becomes more chaste; but less animated. The progress of the world in this respect resembles the progress of age in man. The powers of imagination are most vigorous and predominant in youth; those of the understanding ripen more slowly, and often attain not their maturity, till the imagination begin to flag. Hence, poetry, which is the child of imagination, is frequently most glowing and animated in the first stages of society. As the ideas of our youth are remembered with a peculiar pleasure on account of their liveliness and vivacity; so the most ancient poems have often proved the greatest favourites of nations.

Poetry has been said to be more ancient than prose: and however paradoxical such an assertion may seem, yet, in a qualified sense it is true. Men certainly never conversed with one another in regular numbers; but even their ordinary language would, in ancient times, for the reasons before assigned, approach to a poetical style; and the first compositions transmitted to posterity, beyond doubt, were, in a literal sense, poems; that is, compositions in which imagination had the chief hand, formed into some kind of numbers, and pronounced with a musical modulation or tone. Music or song has been found coæval with society among the most barbarous nations. The only subjects which could prompt men, in their first rude state, to utter their thoughts in compositions of any length, were such as naturally assumed the tone of poetry; praises of their gods, or of their ancestors; commemorations of their own warlike exploits; or lamentations over their misfortunes. And before writing was invented, no other compositions, except songs or poems, could take such hold on the imagination and memory, as to be preserved by oral tradition, and handed down from one race to another....

Assuming it then, as we well may, for certain, that the poems now under consideration, are genuine venerable monuments of very remote antiquity; I proceed to make some remarks upon their general spirit and strain. The two great characteristics of Ossian's poetry are, tenderness and sublimity. It breathes nothing of the gay and cheerful kind; an air of solemnity and serious-ness is diffused over the whole. Ossian is perhaps the only poet who never relaxes, or lets himself down into the light and amusing strain; which I readily admit to be no small disadvantage, to him, with the bulk of readers. He moves perpetually in the high region of the grand and the pathetic. One key note is struck at the beginning and supported to the end; nor is any ornament intro-duced but what is perfectly concordant with the general tone or melody. The events recorded, are all serious and grave; the scenery throughout, wild and romantic. The extended heath by the sea shore; the mountain shaded with mist; the torrent rushing through a solitary valley; the scattered oaks, and the tombs of warriors overgrown with moss; all produce a solemn attention in the mind, and prepare it for great and extraordinary events. We find not in Ossian, an imagination that sports itself, and dresses out gay trifles to please the fancy. His poetry, more perhaps than that of any other writer, deserves to be styled, *the poetry of the heart*. It is a heart penetrated with noble senti-ments, and with sublime and tender passions; a heart that glows, and kindles the fancy; a heart that is full, and pours itself forth. Ossian did not write, like modern poets, to please readers and critics. He sung from the love of poetry and song. His delight was to think of the heroes among whom he had flourished; to recall the affecting incidents of his life; to dwell upon his past wars and loves and friendships; until, as he expresses it himself, "there comes a voice to Ossian and awakes his soul. It is the voice of years that are gone; they roll before me with all their deeds;" and under this true poetic inspiration, giving vent to his genius, no wonder we should so often hear, and acknowledge in his strains, the powerful and ever-pleasing voice of nature.

— Arte, natura potentior omni. –
Est Deus in nobis, agitante calescimus illo.

It is necessary here to observe, that the beauties of Ossian's writings cannot be felt by those who have given them only a single or a hasty perusal. His man-ner is so different from that of the poets, to whom we are most accustomed; his style is so concise, and so much crowded with imagery; the mind is kept at such a stretch in accompanying the author; that an ordinary reader is at first apt to be dazzled and fatigued, rather than pleased. His poems require to be taken up at intervals, and to be frequently reviewed; and then it is impossi-ble but his beauties must open to every reader who is capable of sensibility. Those who have the highest degree of it, will relish them the most....

...Both poets are eminently sublime; but a difference may be remarked in the species of their sublimity. Homer's sublimity is accompanied with more impetuosity and fire; Ossian's with more of a solemn and awful grandeur. Homer hurries you along; Ossian elevates, and fixes you in astonishment. Homer is most sublime in actions and battles; Ossian, in description and sentiment. In the pathetic, Homer, when he chooses to exert it, has great power; but Ossian exerts that power much oftener, and has the character of tenderness far more deeply imprinted on his works. No poet knew better how to seize and melt the heart. With regard to dignity of sentiment, the pre-eminence must clearly be given to Ossian. This is indeed a surprising circumstance, that in point of humanity, magnanimity, virtuous feelings of every kind, our rude Celtic bard should be distinguished to such a degree, that not only the heroes of Homer, but even those of the polite and refined Virgil, are left far behind by those of Ossian....

But it is not enough that sentiments be natural and proper. In order to acquire any high degree of poetical merit, they must also be sublime and pathetic.

The sublime is not confined to sentiment alone. It belongs to description also; and whether in description or in sentiment, imports such ideas presented to the mind, as raise it to an uncommon degree of elevation, and fill it with admiration and astonishment. This is the highest effect either of eloquence or poetry: and to produce this effect, requires a genius glowing with the strongest and warmest conception of some object awful, great, or magnificent. That this character of genius belongs to Ossian, may, I think, sufficiently appear from many of the passages I have already had occasion to quote. To produce more instances, were superfluous. If the engagement of Fingal with the spirit of Loda, in Carric-thura; if the encounters of the armies, in Fingal; if the address to the sun, in Carthon; if the similes founded upon ghosts and spirits of the night, all formerly mentioned, be not admitted as examples, and illustrious ones too, of the true poetical sublime, I confess myself entirely ignorant of this quality in writing.

All the circumstances, indeed, of Ossian's composition, are favourable to the sublime, more perhaps than to any other species of beauty. Accuracy and correctness; artfully connected narration; exact method and proportion of parts, we may look for in polished times. The gay and the beautiful, will appear to more advantage in the midst of smiling scenery and pleasurable themes. But amidst the rude scenes of nature, amidst rocks and torrents, and whirlwinds and battles, dwells the sublime. It is the thunder and lightning of genius. It is the offspring of nature, not of art. It is negligent of all the lesser graces, and perfectly consistent with a certain noble disorder. It associates naturally with that grave and solemn spirit, which distinguishes our author. For the sublime, is an awful and serious emotion; and is heightened by all the images of Trouble, and Terror, and Darkness....

Simplicity and conciseness, are never-failing characteristics of the style of a sublime writer. He rests on the majesty of his sentiments, not on the pomp of his expressions. The main secret of being sublime, is to say great things in few, and in plain words: for every superfluous decoration degrades a sublime idea. The mind rises and swells, when a lofty description or sentiment is presented to it, in its native form. But no sooner does the poet attempt to spread out this sentiment or description, and to deck it round and round with glittering ornaments, than the mind begins to fall from its high elevation; the transport is over; the beautiful may remain, but the sublime is gone. Hence the concise and simple style of Ossian, gives great advantage to his sublime conceptions; and assists them in seizing the imagination with full power.

Sublimity as belonging to sentiment, coincides in a great measure with magnanimity, heroism, and generosity of sentiment. Whatever discovers human nature in its greatest elevation; whatever bespeaks a high effort of soul; or shows a mind superior to pleasures, to dangers, and to death, forms what may be called the moral or sentimental sublime. For this, Ossian is eminently distinguished. No poet maintains a higher tone of virtuous and noble sentiment, throughout all his works. Particularly in all the sentiments of Fingal, there is a grandeur and loftiness proper to swell the mind with the highest ideas of human perfection. Wherever he appears, we behold the hero. The objects which he pursues, are always truly great; to bend the proud; to protect the injured; to defend his friends; to overcome his enemies by generosity more than by force. A portion of the same spirit actuates all the other heroes. Valour reigns; but it is a generous valour, void of cruelty, animated by honour, not by hatred. We behold no debasing passions among Fingal's warriors; no spirit of avarice or of insult; but a perpetual contention for fame; a desire of being distinguished and remembered for gallant actions; a love of justice; and a zealous attachment to their friends and their country. Such is the strain of sentiment in the works of Ossian.

But the sublimity of moral sentiments, if they wanted the softening of the tender, would be in hazard of giving a hard and stiff air to poetry. It is not enough to admire. Admiration is a cold feeling, in comparison of that deep interest, which the heart takes in tender and pathetic scenes; where, by a mysterious attachment to the objects of compassion, we are pleased and delighted, even whilst we mourn. With scenes of this kind, Ossian abounds; and his high merit in these, is incontestable. He may be blamed for drawing tears too often from our eyes; but that he has the power of commanding them, I believe no man, who has the least sensibility, will question. The general character of his poetry, is the heroic, mixed with the elegiac strain; admiration tempered with pity. Ever fond of giving, as he expresses it, "the joy of grief," it is visible, that on all moving subjects, he delights to exert his genius; and accordingly, never were there finer pathetic situations, than what his works present. His great art in managing them lies in giving vent to the simple and natural emotions of the heart. We meet with no exaggerated declamation; no subtle refinements on sorrow; no substitution of description in place of passion. Ossian felt strongly himself; and the heart when uttering its native language never fails, by powerful sympathy, to affect the heart....

Upon the whole; if to feel strongly, and to describe naturally, be the two chief ingredients in poetical genius, Ossian must, after fair examination, be held to possess that genius in a high degree. The question is not, whether a few improprieties may be pointed out in his works; whether this, or that passage, might not have been worked up with more art and skill, by some writer of happier times? A thousand such cold and frivolous criticisms, are altogether indecisive as to his genuine merit. But, has he the spirit, the fire, the inspiration of a poet? Does he utter the voice of nature? Does he elevate his sentiments? Does he interest by his descriptions? Does he paint to the heart as well as to the fancy? Does he make his readers glow, and tremble, and weep? These are the great characteristics of true poetry. Where these are found, he must be a minute critic indeed, who can dwell upon slight defects. A few beauties of this high kind, transcend whole volumes of faultless mediocrity. Uncouth and abrupt, Ossian may sometimes appear by reason of his conciseness. But he is sublime, he is pathetic, in an eminent degree. If he has not the extensive knowledge, the regular dignity of narration, the fulness and accuracy of description, which we find in Homer and Virgil, yet in strength of imagination, in grandeur of sentiment, in native majesty of passion, he is fully their equal. If he flows not always like a clear stream, yet he breaks forth often like a torrent of fire. Of art too, he is far from being destitute; and his imagination is remarkable for delicacy as well as strength. Seldom or never is he either trifling or tedious; and if he be thought too melancholy, yet he is always moral. Though his merit were in other respects much less than it is, this alone ought to entitle him to high regard, that his writings are remarkably favourable to virtue. They awake the tenderest sympathies, and inspire the most generous emotions. No reader can rise from him, without being warmed with the sentiments of humanity, virtue and honour....

36

Hugh Blair,
from *Lectures on rhetoric and belles lettres* (1783)

Lecture III
Criticism. – Genius. – Pleasures of taste. –Sublimity in objects

...I shall begin with considering the pleasure which arises from sublimity or grandeur, of which I propose to treat at some length; both, as this has a character more precise and distinctly marked, than any other, of the Pleasures of the Imagination, and as it coincides more directly with our main subject. For the greater distinctness I shall, first, treat of the grandeur or sublimity of external objects themselves, which will employ the rest of this lecture; and, afterwards, of the description of such objects, or, of what is called the sublime in writing, which shall be the subject of a following lecture. I distinguish these two things from one another, the grandeur of the objects themselves when they are presented to the eye, and the description of that grandeur in discourse or writing; though most critics, inaccurately I think, blend them together; and I consider grandeur and sublimity as terms synonymous, or nearly so. If there be any distinction between them, it arises from sublimity's expressing grandeur in its highest degree.

It is not easy to describe, in words, the precise impression which great and sublime objects make upon us, when we behold them; but every one has a conception of it. It consists in a kind of admiration and expansion of the mind; it raises the mind much above its ordinary state; and fills it with a degree of wonder and astonishment, which it cannot well express. The emotion is certainly delightful; but it is altogether of the serious kind: a degree of awfulness and solemnity, even approaching to severity, commonly attends it when at its height; very distinguishable from the more gay and brisk emotion raised by beautiful objects.

The simplest form of external grandeur appears in the vast and boundless prospects presented to us by nature; such as wide extended plains, to which the eye can see no limits; the firmament of heaven; or the boundless expanse of the ocean. All vastness produces the impression of sublimity. It is to be remarked, however, that space, extended in length, makes not so strong an impression as height or depth. Though a boundless plain be a grand object, yet a high mountain, to which we look up, or an awful precipice or tower whence we look down on the objects which lie below, is still more so. The excessive grandeur of the firmament arises from its height, joined to its boundless extent; and that of the ocean, not from its extent alone, but from the perpetual motion and irresistible force of that mass of waters. Wherever space is concerned, it is clear, that amplitude or greatness of extent, in one dimension or other, is necessary to grandeur. Remove all bounds from any object, and you presently render it sublime. Hence infinite space, endless numbers, and eternal duration, fill the mind with great ideas.

From this some have imagined, that vastness, or amplitude of extent, is the foundation of all sublimity. But I cannot be of this opinion, because many objects appear sublime which have no relation to space at all. Such, for instance, is great loudness of sound. The burst of thunder or of cannon, the roaring of winds, the shouting of multitudes, the sound of vast cataracts of water, are all incontestibly grand objects. *"I heard the voice of a great multitude, as the sound of many waters, and of mighty thunderings, saying Allelujah."* In general we may observe, that great power and force exerted, always raise sublime ideas: and perhaps the most copious source of these is derived from this quarter. Hence the grandeur of earthquakes and burning mountains; of great conflagrations; of the stormy ocean, and overflowing waters; of tempests of wind; of thunder and lightning; and of all the uncommon violence of the elements. Nothing is more sublime than mighty power and strength. A stream that runs within its banks, is a beautiful object; but when it rushes down with the impetuosity and noise of a torrent, it presently becomes a sublime one. From lions, and other animals of strength, are drawn sublime comparisons in poets. A race horse is looked upon with pleasure; but it is the war horse, *"whose neck is clothed with thunder,"* that carries grandeur in its idea. The engagement of two great armies, as it is the highest exertion of human might, combines a variety of sources of the sublime; and has accordingly been always considered as one of the most striking and magnificent spectacles that can be either presented to the eye, or exhibited to the imagination in description.

For the farther illustration of this subject, it is proper to remark, that all ideas of the solemn and awful kind, and even bordering on the terrible, tend greatly to assist the sublime; such as darkness, solitude, and silence. What are the scenes of nature that elevate the mind in the highest degree, and produce the sublime sensation? Not the gay landscape, the flowery field, or the flourishing city; but the hoary mountain, and the solitary lake; the aged forest, and the torrent falling over the rock. Hence too, night-scenes are commonly the most sublime. The firmament when filled with stars, scattered in such vast numbers, and with such magnificent profusion, strikes the imagination with a more awful grandeur, than when we view it enlightened by all the splendour of the sun. The deep sound of a great bell, or the striking of a great clock, are at any time grand; but, when heard amid the silence and stillness of the night, they become doubly so. Darkness is very commonly applied for adding sublimity to all our ideas of the Deity....

Obscurity, we are farther to remark, is not unfavourable to the sublime. Though it render the object indistinct, the impression, however, may be great; for, as an ingenious author has well observed, it is one thing to make an idea clear, and another to make it affecting to the imagination; and the imagination may be strongly affected, and, in fact, often is so, by objects of which we have no clear conception. Thus we see, that almost all the descriptions given us of the appearances of supernatural beings, carry some sublimity, though the conceptions which they afford us be confused and indistinct. Their sublimity arises from the ideas, which they always convey, of superior power and might, joined with an awful obscurity.... In general, all objects that are greatly raised above us, or far removed from us, either in space or in time, are apt to strike us as great. Our viewing them, as through the mist of distance or antiquity, is favourable to the impressions of their sublimity.

As obscurity, so disorder too, is very compatible with grandeur; nay, frequently heightens it. Few things that are strictly regular, and methodical, appear sublime. We see the limits on every side; we feel ourselves confined; there is no room for the mind's exerting any great effort. Exact proportion of parts, though it enters often into the beautiful, is much disregarded in the sublime. A great mass of rocks, thrown together by the hand of nature with wildness and confusion, strike the mind with more grandeur, than if they had been adjusted to each other with the most accurate symmetry.

In the feeble attempts, which human art can make towards producing grand objects (feeble, I mean, in comparison with the powers of nature), greatness of dimensions always constitutes a principal part. No pile of building can convey any idea of sublimity, unless it be ample and lofty. There is, too, in architecture, what is called greatness of manner; which seems chiefly to arise, from presenting the object to us in one full point of view; so that it shall make its impression whole, entire, and undivided, upon the mind. A gothic cathedral raises ideas of grandeur in our minds, by its size, its height, its awful obscurity, its strength, its antiquity, and its durability.

There still remains to be mentioned one class of sublime objects; what may be called the moral, or sentimental sublime; arising from certain exertions of the human mind; from certain affections, and actions, of our fellow-creatures. These will be found to be all, or chiefly, of that class, which comes under the name of magnanimity or heroism; and they produce an effect extremely similar to what is produced by the view of grand objects in nature; filling the mind with admiration, and elevating it above itself....

Wherever, in some critical and high situation, we behold a man uncommonly intrepid, and resting upon himself; superior to passion and to fear; animated by some great principle to the contempt of popular opinion, of selfish interest, of dangers, or of death; there we are struck with a sense of the sublime.

High virtue is the most natural and fertile source of this moral sublimity. However, on some occasions, where virtue either has no place, or is but imperfectly displayed, yet if extraordinary vigour and force of mind be discovered, we are not insensible to a degree of grandeur in the character; and from the splendid conqueror, or the daring conspirator, whom we are far from approving, we cannot withhold our admiration.

I have now enumerated a variety of instances, both in inanimate objects and in human life, wherein the sublime appears. In all these instances, the emotion raised in us is of the same kind, although the objects that produce the emotion be of widely different kinds. A question next arises, whether we are able to discover some one fundamental quality in which all these different objects agree, and which is the cause of their producing an emotion of the same nature in our minds? Various hypotheses have been formed concerning this; but, as far as appears to me, hitherto unsatisfactory. Some have imagined that amplitude, or great extent, joined with simplicity, is either immediately, or remotely, the fundamental quality of whatever is sublime; but we have seen that amplitude is confined to one species of sublime objects; and cannot, without violent straining, be applied to them all. The author of "*A Philosophical Enquiry into the Origin of our Ideas of the Sublime and Beautiful,*" to whom we are indebted for several ingenious and original thoughts upon this subject, proposes a formal theory upon this foundation, that terror is the source of the sublime, and that no objects have this character, but such as produce impressions of pain and danger. It is indeed true, that many terrible objects are highly sublime; and that grandeur does not refuse an alliance with the idea of danger. But though this is very properly illustrated by the author (many of whose sentiments on that head I have adopted), yet he seems to stretch his theory too far, when he represents the sublime as consisting wholly in modes of danger, or of pain. For the proper sensation of sublimity, appears to be very distinguishable from the sensation of either of those; and, on several occasions, to be entirely separated from them. In many grand objects, there is no coincidence with terror at all; as in the magnificent prospect of wide extended plains, and of the starry firmament; or in the moral dispositions and sentiments, which we view with high admiration; and in many painful and terrible objects also, it is clear, there is no sort of grandeur. The amputation of a limb, or the bite of a snake, are exceedingly terrible; but are destitute of all claim whatever to sublimity. I am inclined to think, that mighty force or power, whether accompanied with terror or not, whether employed in protecting, or in alarming us, has a better title, than any thing that has yet been mentioned, to be the fundamental quality of the sublime; as, after the review which we have taken, there does not occur to me any sublime object, into the idea of which, power, strength, and force, either enter not directly, or are not, at least, intimately associated with the idea, by leading our thoughts to some astonishing power, as concerned in the production of the object. However, I do not insist upon this as sufficient to found a general theory: it is enough, now, to have given this view of the nature and different kinds of sublime objects; by which I hope to have laid a proper foundation for discussing, with greater accuracy, the sublime in writing and composition.

Lecture IV. The sublime in writing

Having treated of grandeur or sublimity in external objects, the way seems now to be cleared, for treating, with more advantage, of the description of such objects; or, of what is called the sublime in writing. Though it may appear early to enter on the consideration of this subject; yet, as the sublime is a species of writing which depends less than any other on the artificial embellishments of rhetoric, it may be examined with as much propriety here, as in any subsequent part of the lectures.

Many critical terms have unfortunately been employed, in a sense too loose and vague; none more so, than that of the sublime. Every one is acquainted with the character of Cæsar's *Commentaries*, and of the style in which they are written; a style remarkably pure, simple, and elegant; but the most remote from the sublime, of any of the classical authors. Yet this author has a German critic, Johannes Gulielmus Bergerus, who wrote no longer ago than the year 1720, pitched upon as the perfect model of the sublime, and has composed a quarto volume, entitled, *de naturali pulchritudine orationis*, the express intention of which, is to show, that Cæsar's *Commentaries* contain the most complete exemplification of all Longinus's rules relating to sublime writing. This I mention as a strong proof of the confused ideas which have prevailed, concerning this subject. The true sense of sublime writing, undoubtedly, is such a description of objects, or exhibition of sentiments, which are in themselves of a sublime nature, as shall give us strong impressions of them. But there is another very indefinite, and therefore very improper, sense, which has been too often put upon it; when it is applied to signify any remarkable and distinguishing excellency of composition; whether it raise in us the ideas of grandeur, or those of gentleness, elegance, or any other sort of beauty. In this sense, Cæsar's *Commentaries* may, indeed, be termed sublime, and so may many sonnets, pastorals, and love elegies, as well as Homer's *Iliad*. But this evidently confounds the use of words; and marks no one species, or character, of composition whatever.

I am sorry to be obliged to observe, that the sublime is too often used in this last and improper sense, by the celebrated critic Longinus, in his treatise on this subject. He sets out, indeed, with describing it in its just and proper meaning; as something that elevates the mind above itself, and fills it with high conceptions, and a noble pride. But from this view of it he frequently departs; and substitutes in the place of it, whatever, in any strain of composition, pleases highly. Thus, many of the passages which he produces as instances of the sublime, are merely elegant, without have the most distant relation to proper sublimity; witness Sappho's famous Ode, on which he descants at considerable length. He points out five sources of the sublime. The first is, boldness or grandeur in the thoughts; the second is, the pathetic; the third, the proper application of figures; the fourth, the use of tropes and beautiful expressions; the fifth, musical structure and arrangement of words. This is the plan of one who was writing a treatise of rhetoric, or of the beauties of writing in general; not of the sublime in particular. For of these five heads, only the two first have any peculiar relation to the sublime; boldness and grandeur in the thoughts, and, in some instances, the pathetic, or strong exertions of passion: the other three, tropes, figures, and musical arrangement, have no more relation to the sublime, than to other kinds of good writing; perhaps less to the sublime than to any other species whatever; because it requires less the assistance of ornament. From this it appears, that clear and precise ideas on this head are not to be expected from that writer. I would not, however, be understood, as if I meant, by this censure, to represent his treatise as of small value. I know no critic, ancient or modern, that discovers a more lively relish of the beauties of fine writing, than Longinus; and he has also the merit of being himself an excellent, and, in several passages, a truly sublime writer. But, as his work has been generally considered as a standard on this subject, it was incumbent on me to give my opinion concerning the benefit to be derived from it. It deserves to be consulted, not so much for distinct instruction concerning the sublime, as for excellent general ideas concerning beauty in writing.

I return now to the proper and natural idea of the sublime in composition. The foundation of it must always be laid in the nature of the object described. Unless it be such an object as, if presented to our eyes, is exhibited to us in reality, would raise ideas of that elevating, that awful, and magnificent kind, which we call sublime; the description, however finely drawn, is not entitled to come under this class. This excludes all objects that are merely beautiful, gay, or elegant. In the next place, the object must not only, in itself, be sublime, but it must be set before us in such a light as is most proper to give us a clear and full impression of it; it must be described with strength, with conciseness, and simplicity. This depends, principally, upon the lively impression which the poet, or orator has of the object which he exhibits; and upon his being deeply affected, and warmed, by the sublime idea which he would convey. If his own feeling be languid, he can never inspire us with any strong emotion. Instances, which are extremely necessary on this subject, will clearly show the importance of all those requisites which I have just now mentioned.

It is, generally speaking, among the most ancient authors, that we are to look for the most striking instances of the sublime. I am inclined to think, that the early ages of the world, and the rude unimproved state of society, are peculiarly favourable to the strong emotions of sublimity. The genius of men is then much turned to admiration and astonishment. Meeting with many objects, to them new and strange, their imagination is kept glowing, and their passions are often raised to the utmost. They think, and express themselves boldly, and without restraint. In the progress of society, the genius and manners of men undergo a change more favourable to accuracy, than to strength or sublimity.

Of all writings, ancient or modern, the Sacred Scriptures afford us the highest instances of the sublime. The descriptions of the Deity, in them, are wonderfully noble; both from the grandeur of the object, and the manner of representing it. What an assemblage, for instance, of awful and sublime ideas is presented to us, in that passage of the XVIIIth Psalm, where an appearance of the Almighty is described? *"In my distress I called upon the Lord; he heard my voice out of his temple, and my cry came before him. Then, the earth shook and trembled; the foundations also of the hills were moved; because he was wroth. He bowed the heavens, and came down, and darkness was under his feet; and he did ride upon a Cherub, and did fly; yea, he did fly upon the wings of the wind. He made darkness his secret place; his pavilion round about him were dark waters, and thick clouds of the sky."* Here, agreeably to the principles established in the last lecture, we see, with what propriety and success the circumstances of darkness and terror are applied for heightening the sublime....

Homer is a poet, who, in all ages, and by all critics, has been greatly admired for sublimity; and he owes much of his grandeur to that native and unaffected simplicity which characterises his manner. His descriptions of hosts engaging; the animation, the fire, and rapidity, which he throws into his battles, present to every reader of the *Iliad*, frequent instances of sublime writing. His introduction of the Gods, tends often to heighten, in a high degree, the majesty of his warlike scenes. Hence Longinus bestows such high and just commendations on that passage, in the XVth book of the *Iliad*, where Neptune, when preparing to issue forth into the engagement, is described as shaking the mountains with his steps, and driving his chariot along the ocean. Minerva, arming herself to fight in the Vth book; and Apollo, in the XVth, leading on the Trojans, and flashing terror with his Ægis on the face of the Greeks, are similar instances of great sublimity added to the description of battles, by the appearances of those celestial beings. In the XXth book, where all the Gods take part in the engagement, according as they severally favour either the Grecians, or the Trojans, the poet seems to put forth one of his highest efforts, and the description rises into the most awful magnificence. All nature is represented as in commotion. Jupiter thunders in the heavens; Neptune strikes the earth with his trident; the ships, the city, and the mountains shake; the earth trembles to its centre; Pluto starts from his throne, in dread lest the secrets of the infernal region should be laid open to the view of mortals....

The works of Ossian (as I have elsewhere shewn) abound with examples of the sublime. The subjects of that author, and the manner in which he writes, are particularly favourable to it. He possesses all the plain and venerable manner of the ancient times. He deals in no superfluous or gaudy ornaments; but throws forth his images with a rapid conciseness, which enable them to strike the mind with the greatest force. Among poets of more polished times, we are to look for the graces of correct writing, for just proportion of parts, and skilfully conducted narration. In the midst of smiling scenery and pleasurable themes, the gay and the beautiful will appear, undoubtedly, to more advantage. But amidst the rude scenes of nature and of society, such as Ossian describes; amidst rocks, and torrents, and whirlwinds, and battles, dwells the sublime; and naturally associates itself with that grave and solemn spirit which distinguishes the author of Fingal....

...Simplicity, I place in opposition to studied and profuse ornament; and conciseness, to superfluous expression. The reason why a defect, either in conciseness or simplicity, is hurtful in a peculiar manner to the sublime, I shall endeavour to explain. The emotion occasioned in the mind by some great or noble object, raises it considerably above its ordinary pitch. A sort of enthusiasm is produced, extremely agreeable while it lasts; but from which the mind is tending every moment to fall down into its ordinary situation. Now, when an author has brought us, or is attempting to bring us, into this state; if he multiplies words unnecessarily, if he decks the sublime object which he presents to us, round and round, with glittering ornaments; nay, if he throws in any one decoration that sinks in the least below the capital image, that moment he alters the key; he relaxes the tension of the mind; the strength of the feeling is emasculated; the beautiful may remain, but the sublime is gone. – When Julius Cæsar said to the pilot who was afraid to put to sea with him in a storm, "*quid times? Cæsarem vehis;*" we are struck with the daring magnanimity of one relying with such confidence on his cause and his fortune. These few words convey every thing necessary to give us the impression full....

On account of the great importance of simplicity and conciseness, I conceive rhyme, in English verse, to be, if not inconsistent with the sublime, at least very unfavourable to it. The constrained elegance of this kind of verse, and studied smoothness of the sounds, answering regularly to each other at the end of the line, though they be quite consistent with gentle emotions, yet weaken the native force of sublimity; besides, that the superfluous words which the poet is often obliged to introduce, in order to fill up the rhyme, tend farther to enfeeble it. Homer's description of the nod of Jupiter, as shaking the heavens, has been admired, in all ages, as highly sublime. Literally translated, it runs thus: "*he spoke, and bending his sable brows, gave the awful nod; while he shook the celestial locks of his immortal head, all Olympus was shaken.*" Mr Pope translates it thus:

> He spoke; and awful bends his sable brows,
> Shakes his ambrosial curls, and gives the nod,
> The stamp of fate, and sanction of a God.
> High Heaven with trembling the dread signal took,
> And all Olympus to its centre shook.

The image is spread out, and attempted to be beautified; but it is, in truth, weakened. The third line – "*The stamp of fate, and sanction of a God,*" is merely expletive; and introduced for no other reason but to fill up the rhyme; for it interrupts the description, and clogs the image. For the same reason, out of mere compliance with the rhyme, Jupiter is represented as shaking his locks before he gives the nod; – "*Shakes his ambrosial curls, and gives the nod,*" which is trifling, and without meaning. Whereas, in the original, the hair of his head shaken, is the effect of his nod, and makes a happy picturesque circumstance in the description.

The boldness, freedom, and variety of our blank verse, is infinitely more favourable than rhyme, to all kinds of sublime poetry. The fullest proof of this is afforded by Milton; an author, whose genius led him eminently to the sublime. The whole first and second books of *Paradise Lost*, are continued instances of it. Take only, for an example, the following noted description of Satan, after his fall, appearing at the head of the infernal hosts:

> – He, above the rest,
> In shape and gesture proudly eminent,
> Stood like a tower: his form had not yet lost
> All her original brightness, nor appeared
> Less than archangel ruined; and the excess
> Of glory obscured: As when the sun, new risen,
> Looks through the horizontal misty air,
> Shorn of his beams; or, from behind, the moon,
> In dim eclipse, disastrous twilight sheds
> On half the nations, and with fear of change
> Perplexes monarchs. Darken'd so, yet shone
> Above them all th' Archangel. –

Here concur a variety of sources of the sublime: the principal object eminently great; a high superior nature, fallen indeed, but erecting itself against distress; the grandeur of the principal object heightened, by associating it with so noble an idea as that of the sun suffering an eclipse; this picture shaded with all those images of change and trouble, of darkness and terror, which coincide so finely with the sublime emotion; and the whole expressed in a style and versification, easy, natural, and simple, but magnificent.

I have spoken of simplicity and conciseness, as essential to sublime writing. In my general description of it, I mentioned strength, as another necessary requisite. The strength of description arises, in a great measure, from a simple conciseness; but, it supposes also something more; namely, a proper choice of circumstances in the description, so as to exhibit the object in its full and most striking point of view. For every object has several faces, so to speak, by which it may be presented to us, according to the circumstances with which we surround it; and it will appear eminently sublime, or not, in proportion as all these circumstances are happily chosen, and of a sublime kind. Here lies the great art of the writer; and indeed, the great difficulty of sublime description. If the description be too general, and divested of circumstances, the object appears in a faint light; it makes a feeble impression, or no impression at all, on the reader. At the same time, if any trivial or improper circumstances are mingled, the whole is degraded.

A storm or tempest, for instance, is a sublime object in nature. But, to render it sublime in description, it is not enough, either to give us more general expressions concerning the violence of the tempest, or to describe its common, vulgar effects, in overthrowing trees and houses. It must be painted with such circumstances as fill the mind with great and awful ideas....

The high importance of the rule which I have been now giving, concerning the proper choice of circumstances, when description is meant to be sublime, seems to me not to have been sufficiently attended to. It has, however, such a foundation in nature, as renders the least deflection from it fatal. When a writer is aiming at the beautiful only, his descriptions may have improprieties in them, and yet be beautiful still. Some trivial, or misjudged circumstances, can be overlooked by the reader; they make only the difference of more or less; the gay, or pleasing emotion, which he has raised, subsists still. But the case is quite different with the sublime. There, one trifling circumstance, one mean idea, is sufficient to destroy the whole charm. This is owing to the nature of the emotion aimed at by sublime description, which admits of no mediocrity, and cannot subsist in a middle state; but must either highly transport us, or, if unsuccessful in the execution, leave us greatly disgusted, and displeased. We attempt to rise along with the writer; the imagination is awakened, and put upon the stretch; but it requires to be supported; and if, in the midst of its effort, you desert it unexpectedly, down it comes with a painful shock....

If it shall now be enquired, what are the proper sources of the sublime? My answer is, that they are to be looked for every where in nature. It is not by hunting after tropes, and figures, and rhetorical assistances, that we can expect to produce it. No: it stands clear, for the most part, of these laboured refinements of art. It must come unsought, if it come at all; and be the natural offspring of a strong imagination.

> Est Deus in nobis; agitante calescimus illo.

Wherever a great and awful object is presented in nature, or a very magnanimous and exalted affection of the human mind is displayed; thence, if you can catch the impression strongly, and exhibit it warm and glowing, you may draw the sublime. These are its only proper sources. In judging of any striking beauty in composition, whether it is, or is not, to be referred to this class, we must attend to the nature of the emotion which it raises; and only, if it be of that elevating, solemn, and awful kind, which distinguishes this feeling, we can pronounce it sublime.

From the account which I have given of the nature of the sublime, it clearly follows, that it is an emotion which can never be long protracted. The mind, by no force of genius, can be kept, for any considerable time, so far raised above its common tone; but will, of course, relax into its ordinary situation. Neither are the abilities of any human writer sufficient to supply a continued run of unmixed sublime conceptions. The utmost we can expect is, that this fire of imagination should sometimes flash upon us like lightning from heaven, and then disappear. In Homer and Milton, this effulgence of genius breaks forth more frequently, and with greater lustre than in most authors. Shakespeare also rises often into the true sublime. But no author whatever is sublime throughout. Some, indeed, there are, who, by a strength and dignity in their conceptions, and a current of high ideas that runs through their whole composition, preserve the reader's mind always in a tone nearly allied to the sublime; for which reason they may, in a limited sense, merit the name of continued sublime writers; and, in this class, we may justly place Demosthenes and Plato.

As for what is called the sublime style, it is, for the most part, a very bad one; and has no relation whatever to the real sublime. Persons are apt to imagine, that magnificent words, accumulated epithets, and a certain swelling kind of expression, by rising above what is usual or vulgar, contributes to, or even forms, the sublime. Nothing can be more false. In all the instances of sublime writing, which I have given, nothing of this kind appears. "*God said, let there be light, and there was light.*" This is striking and sublime. But put it into what is commonly called the sublime style: "*the Sovereign Arbiter of nature, by the potent energy of a single word, commanded the light to exist;*" and, as Boileau has well observed, the style indeed is raised, but the thought is fallen. In general, in all good writing, the sublime lies in the thought, not in the words; and when the thought is truly noble, it will, for the most part, clothe itself in a native dignity of language. The sublime, indeed, rejects mean, low, or trivial expressions; but it is equally an enemy to such as are turgid. The main secret of being sublime, is to say great things in few and plain words. It will be found to hold, without exception, that the most sublime authors are the simplest in their style; and wherever you find a writer, who affects a more than ordinary pomp and parade of words, and is always endeavouring to magnify his subject by epithets, there you may immediately suspect that, feeble in sentiment, he is studying to support himself by mere expression....

The faults opposite to the sublime are chiefly two; the frigid, and the bombast. The frigid consists, in degrading an object, or sentiment, which is sublime in itself, by our mean conception of it; or by our weak, low, and childish description of it. This betrays entire absence, or at least great poverty of genius.... The bombast lies, in forcing an ordinary or trivial object out of its rank, and endeavouring to raise it into the sublime; or, in attempting to exalt a sublime object beyond all natural and reasonable bounds. Into this error, which is but too common, writers of genius may sometimes fall, by unluckily losing sight of the true point of the sublime. This is also called fustian, or rant. Shakespeare, a great, but incorrect genius, is not unexceptionable here. Dryden and Lee, in their tragedies, abound with it....

37

Henry Home, Lord Kames,
from *Elements of criticism* (1765)

Chapter IV
Grandeur and sublimity

Nature hath not more remarkably distinguished us from the other animals by an erect posture, than by a capacious and aspiring mind, attaching us to things great and elevated. The ocean, the sky, seize the attention, and make a deep impression:* robes of state are made large and full to draw respect: we admire an elephant for its magnitude, notwithstanding its unwieldiness.

The elevation of an object affects us not less than its magnitude: a high place is chosen for the statue of a deity or hero: a tree growing on the brink of a precipice, looks charming when viewed from the plain below: a throne is erected for the chief magistrate; and a chair with a high seat for the president of a court.

In some objects, greatness and elevation concur to make a complicated impression: the Alps and the pike of Teneriffe are proper examples; with the following difference, that in the former greatness seems to prevail, elevation in the latter.

The emotions raised by great and by elevated objects, are clearly distinguishable, not only in the internal feeling, but even in their external expressions. A great object makes the spectator endeavour to enlarge his bulk; which is remarkable in plain people who give way to nature without reserve; in describing a great object, they naturally expand themselves by drawing in air with all their force. An elevated object produces a different expression: it makes the spectator stretch upward, and stand a-tiptoe.

Great and elevated objects considered with relation to the emotions produced by them, are termed *grand* and *sublime*. *Grandeur* and *sublimity* have a double signification: they generally signify the quality or circumstance in objects by which the emotions of grandeur and sublimity are produced; sometimes the emotions themselves.

In handling the present subject, it is essential to ascertain, with all possible accuracy, the impression that is made upon the mind by the magnitude of an object, abstracting from its other qualities. And because abstraction is a

* Longinus observes, that nature inclines us to admire, not a small rivulet, however clear and transparent, but the Nile, the Ister, the Rhine, or still more the ocean. The sight of a small fire produceth no emotion; but we are struck with the boiling furnaces of Etna, pouring out whole rivers of liquid flame. *Treatise of the Sublime*, chap. 29.

mental operation of some difficulty, the safest method for judging is, to choose a plain object that is neither beautiful nor deformed, if such a one can be found. The plainest that occurs, is a huge mass of rubbish, the ruins perhaps of some extensive building, or a large heap of stones, which are sometimes seen collected together as a memorial of a battle or other remarkable event. Such an object, which in miniature would be perfectly indifferent, makes an impression by its magnitude, and appears agreeable. And supposing it so large, as to fill the eye, and to prevent the attention from wandering upon other objects, the impression it makes will be so much the deeper.

But though a plain object of this kind be agreeable, it is not termed *grand*: it is not entitled to that character, unless, together with its size, it be possessed of other qualities that contribute to beauty, such as regularity, proportion, order, or colour: and according to the number of such qualities combined with magnitude, it is more or less grand. Thus St Peter's church at Rome, the great pyramid of Egypt, the Alps towering above the clouds, a great arm of the sea, and above all a clear and serene sky, are grand, because, beside their size, they are beautiful in an eminent degree. On the other hand, an over-grown whale, having a disagreeable appearance, is not grand. A large build-ing agreeable by its regularity and proportions, is grand, and yet a much larger building destitute of regularity, has not the least tincture of grandeur. A single regiment in battle-array, makes a grand appearance; which the sur-rounding crowd does not, though perhaps ten for one in number. Thus great-ness or magnitude is the circumstance that distinguishes grandeur from beauty. Agreeableness is the genus, of which beauty and grandeur are species.

Next as to the emotion of grandeur, which duly examined will be found an additional proof of the foregoing doctrine. That this emotion is pleasant in a high degree, requires no other evidence but once to have seen a grand object; and if an emotion of grandeur be pleasant, its cause or object, as observed above, must infallibly be agreeable in proportion.

The qualities of grandeur and beauty are not more distinct, than the emo-tions are which these qualities produce in a spectator. It is observed in the chapter immediately foregoing, that all the various emotions of beauty have one common character of sweetness and gaiety. The emotion of grandeur has a different character: a large object that is agreeable, occupies the whole attention, and swells the heart into a vivid emotion, which, though extremely pleasant, is rather serious than gay. And this affords a good reason, for distin-guishing in language these different emotions. The emotions raised by colour, by regularity, by proportion, and by order, have such a resemblance to each other, as readily to come under one general term, *viz. the emotion of beauty*; but the emotion of grandeur is so different from those mentioned, as to merit a peculiar name.

Though regularity, proportion, order, and colour, contribute to grandeur as well as to beauty, yet these qualities are not by far so essential to the former as to the latter. To make out this proposition some preliminaries are requisite. In the first place, the mind, not being totally occupied with a small object, can give its attention at the same time to every minute part; but in a great or extensive object, the mind being totally occupied with the capital and striking parts, has no attention left for those that are little or indifferent. In the next place, two similar objects appear not at all similar when viewed at different distances: the similar parts of a very large object, cannot be seen but at different distances; and for that reason, its regularity, and the proportion of its parts, are in some measure lost to the eye; neither are the irregularities of a very large object, so conspicuous as of one that is small. Hence it is, that a large object is not so agreeable by its regularity, as a small object; nor so disagreeable by its irregularities.

These considerations make it evident, that grandeur is satisfied with a less degree of regularity, and of the other qualities mentioned, than is requisite for beauty; which may be illustrated by the following experiment. Approaching to a small conical hill, we take an accurate survey of every part, and are sensible of the slightest deviation from regularity and proportion. Supposing this hill to be considerably enlarged, so as to make us less sensible of its regularity, it will upon that account appear less beautiful. It will not however appear less agreeable, because some slight emotion of grandeur comes in place of what is lost in beauty. And at last, when this hill is enlarged to a great mountain, the small degree of beauty that is left, is sunk in its grandeur. Hence it is, that a towering hill is delightful, if it have but the slightest resemblance to a cone; and a chain of mountains not less so, though deficient in the accuracy of order and proportion. We require a small surface to be smooth; but in an extensive plain, considerable inequalities are overlooked. In a word, regularity, proportion, order, and colour, contribute to grandeur as well as to beauty; but with a remarkable difference, that in passing from small to great, they are not required in the same degree of perfection. This remark serves to explain the extreme delight we have in viewing the face of nature, when sufficiently enriched and diversified with objects. The bulk of the objects in a natural landscape are beautiful, and some of them grand: a flowing river, a spreading oak, a round hill, an extended plain, are delightful; and even a rugged rock, or barren heath, though in themselves disagreeable, contribute by contrast to the beauty of the whole: joining to these the verdure of the fields, the mixture of light and shade, and the sublime canopy spread over all; it will not appear wonderful, that so extensive a group of splendid objects, should swell the heart to its utmost bounds, and raise the strongest emotion of grandeur. The spectator is conscious of an enthusiasm, which cannot bear confinement, nor the strictness of regularity and order: he loves to range at large; and is so enchanted with magnificent objects, as to overlook slight beauties or defects.

The same observation is applicable in some measure to works of art: in a small building, the slightest irregularity is disagreeable; but in a magnificent palace, or a large gothic church, irregularities are less regarded: in an epic poem we pardon many negligences, which would be intolerable in a sonnet or epigram. Notwithstanding such exceptions; it may be justly laid down for a rule, that in works of art, order and regularity ought to be governing principles:

and hence the observation of Longinus, *"In works of art we have regard to exact proportion; in those of nature, to grandeur and magnificence."*

The same reflections are in a good measure applicable to sublimity; particularly that, like grandeur, it is a species of agreeableness; that a beautiful object placed high, appearing more agreeable than formerly, produces in the spectator a new emotion, termed *the emotion of sublimity*; and that the perfection of order, regularity, and proportion, is less required in objects placed high, or at a distance, than at hand....

Though a grand object is agreeable, we must not conclude that a little object is disagreeable; this would be unhappy for man, considering that he is surrounded with so many objects of that kind. The same holds with respect to place: a body placed low, is not by that circumstance rendered disagreeable. Littleness, and lowness of place, are precisely similar in the following particular, that they neither give pleasure nor pain. And in this may visibly be discovered peculiar attention, in fitting the internal constitution of man to his external circumstances: were littleness, and lowness of place, agreeable, greatness and elevation could not be so: were littleness, and lowness of place, disagreeable, they would occasion uninterrupted uneasiness.

The difference between great and little with respect to agreeableness, is remarkably felt in a series when we pass gradually from the one extreme to the other. A mental progress from the capital to the kingdom, from that to Europe – to the whole earth – to the planetary system – to the universe, is extremely pleasant: the heart swells, and the mind is dilated, at every step. The returning in an opposite direction is not positively painful, though our pleasure lessens at every step, till it vanish into indifference: such a progress may sometimes produce a pleasure of a different sort, which arises from taking a narrower and narrower inspection. The same observation holds in a progress upward and downward. Ascent is pleasant because it elevates us: but descent is never painful; it is for the most part pleasant from a different cause, that it is according to the order of nature. The fall of a stone from any height, is extremely agreeable by its accelerated motion. I feel it pleasant to descend from a mountain, because the descent is natural and easy. Neither is looking downward painful; on the contrary, to look down upon objects, makes part of the pleasure of elevation: looking down becomes then only painful when the object is so far below as to create dizziness; and even when that is the case, we feel a sort of pleasure mixed with the pain, witness Shakespeare's description of Dover cliffs:

> – How fearful
> And dizzy 'tis, to cast one's eye so low!
> The crows and choughs, that wing the midway air,
> Shew scarce so gross as beetles. Half-way down
> Hangs one that gathers samphire; dreadful trade!
> Methinks he seems no bigger than his head.
> The fishermen that walk upon the beach,
> Appear like mice; and yon tall anchoring bark

Diminish'd to her cock; her cock, a buoy
Almost too small for sight. The murmuring surge,
That on th'unnumber'd idle pebbles chases,
Cannot be heard so high. I'll look no more,
Lest my brain turn, and the deficient sight
Topple down headlong.　　　　　　　　　*King Lear*, Act 4. Scene 6.

An observation is made above, that the emotions of grandeur and sublimity are nearly allied; for which reason, the one term is frequently put for the other: an increasing series of numbers, for example, producing an emotion similar to that of mounting upward, is commonly termed *an ascending series*: a series of numbers gradually decreasing, producing an emotion similar to that of going downward, is commonly termed *a descending series*: we talk familiarly of going *up* to the capital, and of going *down* to the country: from a lesser kingdom we talk of going *up* to a greater; whence the *anabasis* in the Greek language, when one travels from Greece to Persia. We discover the same way of speaking in the language even of Japan; and its universality proves it the offspring of a natural feeling.

The foregoing observation leads us to consider grandeur and sublimity in a figurative sense, and as applicable to the fine arts. Hitherto these terms have been taken in their proper sense, as applicable to objects of sight only: and it was of importance to bestow some pains upon that article; because, generally speaking, the figurative sense of a word is derived from its proper sense, which holds remarkably in the present subject. Beauty in its original signification, is confined to objects of sight; but as many other objects, intellectual as well as moral, raise emotions resembling that of beauty, the resemblance of the effects prompts us naturally to extend the term *beauty* to these objects. This equally accounts for the terms *grandeur* and *sublimity* taken in a figurative sense. Every emotion, from whatever cause proceeding, that resembles an emotion of grandeur or elevation, is called by the same name: thus generosity is said to be an *elevated* emotion, as well as great courage; and that firmness of soul which is superior to misfortunes, obtains the peculiar name of *magnanimity*. On the other hand, every emotion that contracts the mind, and fixeth it upon things trivial or of no importance, is termed *low*, by its resemblance to an emotion produced by a little or low object of sight: thus an appetite for trifling amusements, is called *a low taste*. The same terms are applied to characters and actions: we talk familiarly of an *elevated* genius, of a *great* man, and equally so of *littleness* of mind: some actions are great and elevated, others are *little* and *grovelling*. Sentiments, and even expressions, are characterised in the same manner: an expression or sentiment that raises the mind, is denominated *great* or *elevated*; and hence the sublime* in poetry. In such

---

*　Longinus gives a pretty good description of the sublime, though not entirely just in every circumstance, "*that the mind is elevated by it, and so sensibly affected as to swell in transport and inward pride, as if what is only heard or read, were its own invention.*" But he adheres not to this description: in his 6th chapter he justly observes, that many passions have nothing of the grand, such as grief, fear, pity, which depress the

figurative terms, we lose the distinction that is made between *great* and *elevated* in their proper sense; for the resemblance is not so entire, as to preserve these terms distinct in their figurative application. We carry this figure still farther. Elevation in its proper sense, imports superiority of place; and lowness, inferiority of place: and hence a man of *superior* talents, of *superior* rank, of *inferior* parts, of *inferior* taste, and such like. The veneration we have for our ancestors, and for the ancients in general, being similar to the emotion produced by an elevated object of sight, justifies the figurative expression, of the ancients being *raised* above us, or possessing a *superior* place....

In order to have a just conception of grandeur and sublimity, it is necessary to be observed, that within certain limits they produce their strongest effects, which lessen by excess as well as by defect. This is remarkable in grandeur and sublimity taken in their proper sense: the strongest emotion of grandeur, is raised by an object that can be taken in at one view; if so immense as not to be comprehended but in parts, it tends rather to distract than satisfy the mind: in like manner, the strongest emotion produced by elevation, is where the object is seen distinctly; a greater elevation lessens in appearance the object, till it vanish out of sight with its pleasant emotion. The same is equally remarkable in figurative grandeur and elevation, which shall be handled together, because, as observed above, they are scarce distinguishable. Sentiments may be so strained, as to become obscure, or to exceed the capacity of the human mind: against such licence of imagination, every good writer will be upon his guard. And therefore it is of greater importance to observe, that even the true sublime may be carried beyond that pitch which produces the highest entertainment: we are undoubtedly susceptible of a greater elevation than can be inspired by human actions, the most heroic and magnanimous; witness what we feel from Milton's description of superior beings: yet every man must be sensible of a more constant and sweet elevation, when the history of his own species is the subject; he enjoys an elevation equal to that of the greatest hero, of an Alexander, or a Cæsar, of a Brutus, or an Epaminondas; he accompanies these heroes in their sublimest sentiments and most hazardous exploits, with a magnanimity equal to theirs; and finds it no stretch, to preserve the same tone of mind for hours together, without sinking. The case is by no means the same, in describing the actions or qualities of superior beings: the reader's imagination cannot keep pace with that of the poet; the mind, unable to support itself in a strained elevation, falls as from a height; and the fall is immoderate like the elevation: where this effect is not felt, it must be prevented by some obscurity in the conception, which frequently attends the description of unknown objects....

Objects of sight that are not remarkably great nor high, scarce raise any

mind instead of raising it; and yet in chapter 8, he mentions Sappho's ode upon love as sublime: beautiful it is undoubtedly, but it cannot be sublime, because it really depresses the mind instead of raising it. His translator Boileau is not more successful in his instances: in his 10th reflection he cites a passage from Demosthenes and another from Herodotus as sublime, which are far from being so.

emotion of grandeur or of sublimity: and the same holds in other objects; for we often find the mind roused and animated, without being carried to that height. This difference may be discerned in many sorts of music, as well as in some musical instruments: a kettledrum rouses, and a hautboy is animating; but neither of them inspires an emotion of sublimity: revenge animates the mind in a considerable degree; but I think it never produceth an emotion that can be termed *grand* or *sublime*; and I shall have occasion afterward to observe that no disagreeable passion ever has that effect....

No desire is more universal than to be exalted and honoured; and upon that account chiefly, are we ambitious of power, riches, titles, fame, which would suddenly lose their relish, did they not raise us above others, and command submission and deference: and it may be thought, that our attachment to things grand and lofty, proceeds from their connection with our favourite passion. But the preference that is given to things grand and sublime, must have a deeper root in human nature. Many bestow their time upon low and trifling amusements, without having the least tincture of this favourite passion: yet these very persons talk the same language with the rest of mankind; and at least in their judgment, if not in their taste, prefer the more elevated pleasures: they acknowledge a more refined taste, and are ashamed of their own as low and grovelling. This sentiment, constant and universal, must be the work of nature; and it plainly indicates an original attachment in human nature, to every object that elevates the mind: some men may have a greater relish for an object not of the highest rank; but they are conscious of the preference given by mankind in general, to things grand and sublime; and they are sensible, that their peculiar taste, ought to yield to the general taste.

What is said above, suggests a capital rule for reaching the sublime, in such works of art as are susceptible of it; and that is, to present those parts or circumstances only, which make the greatest figure, keeping out of view every thing low or trivial: for the mind, from an elevation inspired by important objects, cannot, without reluctance, be forced down to bestow any share of its attention upon trifles. Such judicious selection of capital circumstances, is by an eminent critic styled *grandeur of manner*. In none of the fine arts is there so great scope for this rule as in poetry, which, by that means, enjoys a remarkable power, of bestowing upon objects and events an air of grandeur: when we are spectators, every minute object presents itself in its order; but in describing at second hand, these are laid aside, and the capital objects are brought close together. A judicious taste in thus selecting the most interesting incidents, to give them an united force, accounts for a fact that may appear surprising; which is, that we are more moved by a spirited narrative at second hand, than by being spectators of the event itself, in all its circumstances....

Another rule chiefly regards the sublime, though it is applicable to every sort of literary performance intended for amusement; and that is, to avoid as much as possible abstract and general terms. Such terms, similar to mathematical signs, are contrived to express our thoughts in a concise manner; but images, which are the life of poetry, cannot be raised in any perfection, other-

wise than by introducing particular objects. General terms that comprehend
a number of individuals, must be excepted from this rule: our kindred, our
clan, our country, and words of the like import, though they scarce raise any
image, have notwithstanding a wonderful power over our passions: the greatness of the complex object overbalances the obscurity of the image.

Grandeur being one of the strongest emotions that can occupy the human
mind, it is not easily produced in perfection but by reiterated impressions.
The effect of a single impression can be but momentary; and if one feel suddenly somewhat like a swelling or exaltation of mind, the emotion vanisheth
as soon as felt. Single thoughts or sentiments, I know, are often cited as examples of the sublime; but their effect is far inferior to that of a grand subject display'd in its capital parts....

...I shall produce but one instance, from Shakespeare, which sets a few
objects before the eye, without much pomp of language: it operates its effect,
by representing these objects in a climax, raising the mind higher and higher
till it feel the emotion of grandeur in perfection:

> The cloud-capt tow'rs, the gorgeous palaces,
> The solemn temples, the great globe itself,
> Yea all which it inherit, shall dissolve, &tc.

The cloud-capt tow'rs produce an elevating emotion, heightened by the
gorgeous palaces; and the mind is carried still higher and higher by the images
that follow. Successive images, making thus stronger and stronger impressions, must elevate more than any single image can do.

As, on the one hand, no means directly applied have more influence to raise
the mind than grandeur and sublimity; so, on the other, no means indirectly
applied have more influence to sink and depress it: for in a state of elevation,
the artful introduction of an humbling object, makes the fall great in proportion to the elevation. Of this observation Shakespeare gives a beautiful example, in a passage, part of which is cited above for another purpose:

> The cloud-capt tow'rs, the gorgeous palaces,
> The solemn temples, the great globe itself,
> Yea all which it inherit, shall dissolve,
> And like the baseless fabric of a vision
> Leave not a rack behind, –   *Tempest*, Act 4. Scene 4.

The elevation of the mind in the former part of this beautiful passage, makes
the fall great in proportion, when the most humbling of all images is introduced, that of an utter dissolution of the earth and its inhabitants. The mind,
when warmed, is more susceptible of impressions than in a cool state; and a
depressing or melancholy object makes the strongest impression, when it
reaches the mind in its highest state of elevation or cheerfulness.

But a humbling image is not always necessary to produce this effect; a remark
is made above, that in describing superior beings, the reader's imagination,

unable to support itself in a strained elevation, falls often as from a height, and sinks even below its ordinary tone. The following instance comes luckily in view; for a better cannot be given: "*God said, let there be light, and there was light.*" Longinus cites this passage from Moses as a shining example of the sublime; and it is scarce possible, in fewer words, to convey so clear an image of the infinite power of the Deity: but then it belongs to the present subject to remark, that the emotion of sublimity raised by this image is but momentary; and that the mind, unable to support itself in an elevation so much above nature, immediately sinks down into humility and veneration, for a being so far exalted above grovelling mortals....

This chapter shall be closed with the following observations: when the sublime is carried to its due height, and circumscribed within proper bounds, it enchants the mind, and raises the most delightful of all emotions: the reader, engrossed by a sublime object, feels himself raised as it were to a higher rank. When such is the effect, it is not wonderful that the history of conquerors and heroes, should be universally the favourite entertainment. And this fairly accounts for what I once erroneously suspected to be a wrong bias originally in human nature; which is, that the grossest acts of oppression and injustice, scarce blemish the character of a great conqueror: we, notwithstanding, warmly espouse his interest, accompany him in his exploits, and are anxious for his success: the splendour and enthusiasm of the hero transfused into the readers, elevate their minds far above the rules of justice, and render them in a great measure insensible of the wrongs that are committed....

The irregular influence of grandeur reaches also to other matters: however good, honest, or useful, a man may be, he is not so much respected, as is one of a more elevated character, though of less integrity; nor do the misfortunes of the former, affect us so much as those of the latter: and I add, because it cannot be disguised, that the remorse which attends breach of engagement, is in a great measure proportioned to the figure that the injured person makes; the vows and protestations of lovers are an illustrious example of this observation, for these commonly are little regarded when made to women of inferior rank.

38

Adam Smith, from *Essays on philosophical subjects* (wr. circa 1758; pub. 1795)

The principles which lead and direct philosophical enquiries; illustrated by the history of astronomy

Wonder, Surprise, and Admiration, are words which, though often confounded, denote, in our language, sentiments that are indeed allied, but that are in some respects different also, and distinct.from one another. What is new and singular, excites that sentiment which, in strict propriety, is called Wonder; what is unexpected, Surprise; and what is great or beautiful, Admiration.

We wonder at all extraordinary and uncommon objects, at all the rare phaenomena of nature, at meteors, comets, eclipses, at singular plants and animals, and at every thing, in short, with which we have before been either little or not at all acquainted; and we still wonder, though forewarned of what we are to see.

We are surprised at those things which we have seen often, but which we least of all expected to meet with in the place where we find them; we are surprised at the sudden appearance of a friend, whom we have seen a thousand times, but whom we did not imagine we were to see then.

We admire the beauty of a plain or the greatness of a mountain, though we have seen both often before, and though nothing appears to us in either, but what we had expected with certainty to see....

...All that I contend for is, that the sentiments excited by what is new, by what is unexpected, and by what is great and beautiful, are really different, however the words made use of to express them may sometimes be confounded. Even the admiration which is excited by beauty, is quite different (as will appear more fully hereafter) from that which is inspired by greatness, though we have but one word to denote them.

These sentiments, like all others when inspired by one and the same object, mutually support and enliven one another: an object with which we are quite familiar, and which we see every day, produces, though both great and beautiful, but a small effect upon us; because our admiration is not supported either by Wonder or by Surprise: and if we have heard a very accurate description of a monster, our Wonder will be the less when we see it; because our previous knowledge of it will in a great measure prevent our surprise.

It is the design of this Essay to consider particularly the nature and causes

233

of each of these sentiments, whose influence is of far wider extent than we should be apt upon a careless view to imagine. I shall begin with Surprise.

Section I
Of the Effects of Unexpectedness, or of Surprise

When an object of any kind, which has been for some time expected and fore-seen, presents itself, whatever be the emotion which it is by nature fitted to excite, the mind must have been prepared for it, and must even in some measure have conceived it beforehand; because the idea of the object having been so long present to it, must have beforehand excited some degree of the same emotion which the object itself would excite: the change, therefore, which its presence produces comes thus to be less considerable, and the emo-tion or passion which it excites glides gradually and easily into the heart, without violence, pain, or difficulty. *

But the contrary of all this happens when the object is unexpected; the pas-sion is then poured in all at once upon the heart, which is thrown, if it is a strong passion, into the most violent and convulsive emotions, such as some-times cause immediate death; sometimes, by the suddenness of the extacy, so entirely disjoint the whole frame of the imagination, that it never after returns to its former tone and composure, but falls either into a frenzy or habitual lunacy; and such as almost always occasion a momentary loss of reason, or of that attention to other things which our situation or our duty requires.

How much we dread the effects of the more violent passions, when they come suddenly upon the mind, appears from those preparations which all men think necessary when going to inform any one of what is capable of exciting them. Who would choose all at once to inform his friend of an extra-ordinary calamity that had befallen him, without taking care beforehand, by alarming him with an uncertain fear, to announce, if one may say so, his mis-fortune, and thereby prepare and dispose him for receiving the tidings?

Those panic terrors which sometimes seize armies in the field, or great cities, when an enemy is in the neighbourhood, and which deprive for a time the most determined of all deliberate judgments are never excited but by the sudden apprehension of unexpected danger. Such violent consternations, which at once confound whole multitudes, benumb their understandings, and agitate their hearts, with all the agony of extravagant fear, can never be produced by any foreseen danger, how great soever. Fear, though naturally a very strong passion, never rises to such excesses, unless exasperated both by Wonder, from the uncertain nature of the danger, and by Surprise, from the suddenness of the apprehension.

Surprise, therefore, is not to be regarded as an original emotion of a species distinct from all others. The violent and sudden change produced upon the

* Cf. Hume, *Treatise of Human Nature*, I.i.4 'Of the connection or association of ideas'.

mind, when an emotion of any kind is brought suddenly upon it, constitutes the whole nature of Surprise.

But when not only a passion and a great passion comes all at once upon the mind, but when it comes upon it while the mind is in the mood most unfit for conceiving it, the Surprise is then the greatest. Surprises of joy when the mind is sunk into grief, or of grief when it is elated with joy, are therefore the most unsupportable. The change is in this case the greatest possible. Not only a strong passion is conceived all at once, but a strong passion the direct opposite of that which was before in possession of the soul. When a load of sorrow comes down upon the heart that is expanded and elated with gaiety and joy, it seems not only to damp and oppress it, but almost to crush and bruise it, as a real weight would crush and bruise the body. On the contrary, when from an unexpected change of fortune, a tide of gladness seems, if I may say so, to spring up all at once within it, when depressed and contracted with grief and sorrow, it feels as if suddenly extended and heaved up with violent and irresistible force, and is torn with pangs of all others most exquisite, and which almost always occasion faintings, deliriums, and sometimes instant death. For it may be worth while to observe, that though grief be a more violent passion than joy, as indeed all uneasy sensations seem naturally more pungent than the opposite agreeable ones, yet of the two, Surprises of joy are still more insupportable than Surprises of grief. We are told that after the battle of Thrasimenus, while a Roman lady, who had been informed that her son was slain in the action, was sitting alone bemoaning her misfortunes, the young man who escaped came suddenly into the room to her, and that she cried out and expired instantly in a transport of joy. Let us suppose the contrary of this to have happened, and that in the midst of domestic festivity and mirth, he had suddenly fallen down dead at her feet, is it likely that the effects would have been equally violent? I imagine not. The heart springs to joy with a sort of natural elasticity, it abandons itself to so agreeable an emotion, as soon as the object is presented; it seems to pant and leap forward to meet it, and the passion in its full force takes at once entire and complete possession of the soul. But it is otherways with grief; the heart recoils from, and resists the first approaches of that disagreeable passion, and it requires some time before the melancholy object can produce its full effect. Grief comes on slowly and gradually, nor ever rises at once to that height of agony to which it is increased after a little time. But joy comes rushing upon us all at once like a torrent. The change produced therefore by a Surprise of joy is more sudden, and upon that account more violent and apt to have more fatal effects, than that which is occasioned by a surprise of grief; there seems too to be something in the nature of Surprise, which makes it unite more easily with the brisk and quick motion of joy, than with the slower and heavier movement of grief....

Section II
Of Wonder, or of the Effects of Novelty

It is evident that the mind takes pleasure in observing the resemblances that are discoverable betwixt different objects. It is by means of such observations that it endeavours to arrange and methodise all its ideas, and to reduce them into proper classes and assortments. Where it can observe but one single quality, that is common to a great variety of otherwise widely different objects, that single circumstance will be sufficient for it to connect them all together, to reduce them to one common class, and to call them by one general name. It is thus that all things endowed with a power of self-motion, beasts, birds, fishes, insects, are classed under the general name of Animal; and that these again, along with those which want that power, are arranged under the still more general word Substance: and this is the origin of those assortments of objects and ideas which in the schools called genera and species, and of those abstract and general names, which in all languages are made use of to express them.

The further we advance in knowledge and experience, the greater number of divisions and subdivisions of those genera and species we are both inclined and obliged to make. We observe a greater variety of particularities amongst those things which have a gross resemblance; and having made new divisions of them, according to those newly observed particularities, we are then no longer to be satisfied with being able to refer an object to a remote genus, or very general class of things, to many of which it has but a loose and imperfect resemblance. A person, indeed, unacquainted with botany may expect to satisfy your curiosity, by telling you, that such a vegetable is a weed, or, perhaps in still more general terms, that it is a plant. But a botanist will neither give nor accept such an answer. He has broken and divided that great class of objects into a number of inferior assortments, according to those varieties which his experience has discovered among them; and he wants to refer each individual plant to some tribe of vegetables, with all of which it may have a more exact resemblance, than with many things comprehended under the extensive genus of plants. A child imagines that it gives a satisfactory answer when it tells you, that an object whose name it knows not is a thing, and fancies that it informs you of something, when it thus ascertains to which of the two most obvious and comprehensive classes of objects a particular impression ought to be referred; to the class of realities or solid substances which it calls *things*, or to that of appearances which it calls *nothings*.

Whatever, in short, occurs to us we are fond of referring to some species or class of things, with all of which it has a nearly exact resemblance; and though we often know no more about them than about it, yet we are apt to fancy that by being able to do so, we show ourselves to be better acquainted with it, and to have a more thorough insight into its nature. But when something quite new and singular is presented, we feel ourselves incapable of doing this. The memory cannot, from all its stores, cast up any image that nearly resembles this strange appearance. If by some of its qualities it seems to resemble, and to be connected with a species which we have before been acquainted with, it is by others separated and detached from that, and from all the other assortments of things we have hitherto been able to make. It stands alone and by itself in the imagination, and refuses to be grouped or confounded with any set of objects whatever. The imagination and memory exert themselves to no purpose, and in vain look around all their classes of ideas in order to find one under which it may be arranged. They fluctuate to no purpose from thought to thought, and we remain still uncertain and undetermined where to place it, or what to think of it. It is this fluctuation and vain recollection, together with the emotion or movement of the spirits that they excite, which constitute the sentiment properly called *wonder*, and which occasion that staring, and sometimes that rolling of the eyes, that suspension of the breath, and that swelling of the heart, which we may all observe, both in ourselves and others, when wondering at some new object, and which are the natural symptoms of uncertain and undetermined thought. What sort of thing can that be? What is that like? are the questions which, upon such an occasion, we are all naturally disposed to ask. If we can recollect many such objects which exactly resemble this new appearance, and which present themselves to the imagination naturally, and as it were of their own accord, our Wonder is entirely at an end. If we can recollect but a few, and which it requires too some trouble to be able to call up, our Wonder is indeed diminished, but not quite destroyed. If we can recollect none, but are quite at a loss, it is the greatest possible.

With what curious attention does a naturalist examine a singular plant, or a singular fossil, that is presented to him? He is at no loss to refer it to the general genus of plants or fossils; but this does not satisfy him, and when he considers all the different tribes or species of either with which he has hitherto been acquainted, they all, he thinks, refuse to admit the new object among them. It stands alone in his imagination, and as it were detached from all the other species of that genus to which it belongs. He labours, however, to connect it with some one or other of them. Sometimes he thinks it may be placed in this, and sometimes in that other assortment; nor is he ever satisfied, till he has fallen upon one which, in most of its qualities, it resembles. When he cannot do this, rather than that it should stand quite by itself, he will enlarge the precincts, if I may say so, of some species, in order to make room for it; or he will create a new species on purpose to receive it, and call it a play of nature, or give it some other appellation, under which he arranges all the oddities that he knows not what else to do with. But to some class or other of known objects he must refer it, and betwixt it and them he must find out some resemblance or other, before he can get rid of that Wonder, that uncertainty and anxious curiosity excited by its singular appearance, and by its dissimilitude with all the objects he had hitherto observed.

As single and individual objects thus excite our Wonder when, by their uncommon qualities and singular appearance, they make us uncertain to what species of things we ought to refer them; so a succession of objects which follow one another in an uncommon train or order, will produce the same effect, though there be nothing particular in any one of them taken by itself.

When one accustomed object appears after another, which it does not usually follow, it first excites, by its unexpectedness, the sentiment properly called Surprise, and afterwards, by the singularity of the succession, or order of its appearance, the sentiment properly called Wonder. We start and are surprised at feeling it there, and then wonder how it came there. The motion of a small piece of iron along a plain table is in itself no extraordinary object, yet the person who first saw it begin, without any visible impulse, in consequence of the motion of a loadstone at some little distance from it, could not behold it without the most extreme Surprise; and when that momentary emotion was over, he would still wonder how it came to be conjoined to an event with which, according to the ordinary train of things, he could have so little suspected it to have any connection.

When two objects, however unlike, have often been observed to follow each other, and have constantly presented themselves to the sense in that order, they come to be so connected together in the fancy, that the idea of the one seems, of its own accord, to call up and introduce that of the other. If the objects are still observed to succeed each other as before, this connection, or, as it has been called, this association of their ideas, becomes stricter and stricter, and the habit of the imagination to pass from the conception of the one to that of the other, grows more and more rivetted and confirmed. As its ideas move more rapidly than external objects, it is continually running before them, and therefore anticipates, before it happens, every event which falls out according to this ordinary course of things. When objects succeed each other in the same train in which the ideas of the imagination have thus been accustomed to move, and in which, though not conducted by that chain of events presented to the senses, they have acquired a tendency to go on of their own accord, such objects appear all closely connected with one another, and the thought glides easily along them, without effort and without interruption. They fall in with the natural career of the imagination; and as the ideas which represented such a train of things would seem all mutually to introduce each other, every last thought to be called up by the foregoing, and to call up the succeeding; so when the objects themselves occur, every last event seems, in the same manner, to be introduced by the foregoing, and to introduce the succeeding. There is no break, no stop, no gap, no interval. The ideas excited by so coherent a chain of things seem, as it were, to float through the mind of their own accord, without obliging it to exert itself, or to make any effort in order to pass from one of them to another.

But if this customary connection be interrupted, if one or more objects appear in an order quite different from that to which the imagination has been accustomed, and for which it is prepared, the contrary of all this happens. We are at first surprised by the unexpectedness of the new appearance, and when that momentary emotion is over, we still wonder how it came to occur in that place. The imagination no longer feels the usual facility of passing from the event which goes before to that which comes after. It is an order or law of succession to which it has not been accustomed, and which it therefore finds some difficulty in following, or in attending to. The fancy is stopped and interrupted in that natural movement or career, according to which it was proceeding. Those two events seem to stand at a distance from each other; it endeavours to bring them together, but they refuse to unite; and it feels, or imagines it feels, something like a gap or interval betwixt them. It naturally hesitates, and, as it were, pauses upon the brink of this interval; it endeavours to find out something which may fill up the gap, which, like a bridge, may so far at least unite those seemingly distant objects, as to render the passage of the thought betwixt them smooth, and natural, and easy. The supposition of a chain of intermediate, though invisible, events, which succeed each other in a train similar to that in which the imagination has been accustomed to move, and which link together those two disjointed appearances, is the only means by which the imagination can fill up this interval, is the only bridge which, if one may say so, can smooth its passage from the one object to the other. Thus, when we observe the motion of the iron, in consequence of that of the load-stone, we gaze and hesitate, and feel a want of connection betwixt the two events which follow one another in so unusual a train. But when, with Descartes, we imagine certain invisible effluvia to circulate round one of them, and by their repeated impulses to impel the other, both to move towards it, and to follow its motion, we fill up the interval betwixt them, we join them together by a sort of bridge, and thus take off that hesitation and difficulty which the imagination felt in passing from the one to the other. That the iron should move after the loadstone seems, upon this hypothesis, in some measure according to the ordinary course of things. Motion after impulse is an order of succession with which of all things we are the most familiar. Two objects which are so connected seem no longer to be disjoined, and the imagination flows smoothly and easily along them.

Such is the nature of this second species of Wonder, which arises from an unusual succession of things. The stop which is thereby given to the career of the imagination, the difficulty which it finds in passing along such disjointed objects, and the feeling of something like a gap or interval betwixt them, constitute the whole essence of this emotion. Upon the clear discovery of a connecting chain of intermediate events, it vanishes altogether. What obstructed the movement of the imagination is then removed. Who wonders at the machinery of the opera-house who has once been admitted behind the scenes? In the Wonders of nature, however, it rarely happens that we can discover so clearly this connecting chain. With regard to a few even of them, indeed, we seem to have been really admitted behind the scenes, and our Wonder accordingly is entirely at an end. Thus the eclipses of the sun and moon, which once, more than all the other appearances in the heavens, excited the terror and amazement of mankind, seem now no longer to be wonderful, since the connecting chain has been found out which joins them to the ordinary course of things. Nay, in those cases in which we have been less successful, even the vague hypotheses of Descartes, and the yet more indetermined notions of Aristotle, have, with their followers, contributed to give some coherence to the appearances of nature, and might diminish, though they could not destroy, their Wonder. If they did not completely fill up the interval betwixt the two disjointed objects, they bestowed upon them, however, some sort of loose connection which they wanted before....

Philosophy is the science of the connecting principles of nature. Nature, after the largest experience that common observation can acquire, seems to abound with events which appear solitary and incoherent with all that go before them; which therefore disturb the easy movement of the imagination; which make its ideas succeed each other, if one may say so, by irregular starts and sallies; and which thus tend, in some measure, to introduce these confusions and distractions we formerly mentioned. Philosophy, by representing the invisible chains which bind together all these disjointed objects, endeavours to introduce order into this chaos of jarring and discordant appearance, to allay this tumult of the imagination, and to restore it, when it surveys the great revolutions of the universe, to that tone of tranquillity and composure, which is both most agreeable in itself, and most suitable to its nature. Philosophy, therefore, may be regarded as one of those arts which address themselves to the imagination; and whose theory and history, upon that account, fall properly within the circumference of our subject. Let us endeavour to trace it, from its first origin, up to that summit of perfection to which it is at present supposed to have arrived, and to which, indeed, it has equally been supposed to have arrived in almost all former times. It is the most sublime of all the agreeable arts, and its revolutions have been the greatest, the most frequent, and the most distinguished of all those that have happened in the literary world. Its history, therefore, must, upon all accounts, be the most entertaining and the most instructive. Let us examine, therefore, all the different systems of nature, which, in these western parts of the world, the only parts of whose history we know any thing, have successively been adopted by the learned and ingenious; and, without regarding their absurdity or probability, their agreement or inconsistency with truth and reality, let us consider them only in that particular point of view which belongs to our subject; and content ourselves with inquiring how far each of them was fitted to soothe the imagination, and to render the theatre of nature a more coherent, and therefore a more magnificent spectacle, than otherwise it would have appeared to be. According as they have failed or succeeded in this, they have constantly failed or succeeded in gaining reputation and renown to their authors; and this will be found to be the clue that is most capable of conducting us through all the labyrinths of philosophical history: for, in the mean time, it will serve to confirm what has gone before, and to throw light upon what is to come after, that we observe, in general, that no system, how well soever in other respects supported, has ever been able to gain any general credit in the world, whose connecting principles were not such as were familiar to all mankind....

In the same manner also, others have written parallels of painting and poetry, of poetry and music, of music and architecture, of beauty and virtue, of all the fine arts; systems which have universally owed their origin to the lucubrations of those who were acquainted with the one art, but ignorant of the other; who therefore explained to themselves the phaenomena, in that which was strange to them, by those in that which was familiar; and with whom, upon that account, the analogy, which in other writers gives occasion to a few ingenious similitudes, became the great hinge upon which every thing turned.

Section III
Of the origin of philosophy

Mankind, in the first ages of society, before the establishment of law, order, and security, have little curiosity to find out those hidden chains of events which bind together the seemingly disjointed appearances of nature. A savage, whose subsistence is precarious, whose life is every day exposed to the rudest dangers, has no inclination to amuse himself with searching out what, when discovered, seems to serve no other purpose than to render the theatre of nature a more connected spectacle to his imagination. Many of these smaller incoherences, which in the course of things perplex philosophers, entirely escape his attention. Those more magnificent irregularities, whose grandeur he cannot overlook, call forth his amazement. Comets, eclipses, thunder, lightning, and other meteors, by their greatness, naturally overawe him, and he views them with a reverence that approaches to fear. His inexperience and uncertainty with regard to every thing about them, how they came, how they are to go, what went before, what is to come after them, exasperate his sentiment into terror and consternation. But our passions, as Father Malbranche observes, all justify themselves; that is, suggest to us opinions which justify them. As those appearances terrify him, therefore, he is disposed to believe every thing about them which can render them still more the objects of his terror. That they proceed from some intelligent, though invisible causes, of whose vengeance and displeasure they are either the signs or the effects, is the notion of all others most capable of enhancing this passion, and is that, therefore, which he is most apt to entertain. To this too, that cowardice and pusillanimity, so natural to man in his uncivilised state, still more disposes him; unprotected by the laws of society, exposed, defenceless, he feels his weakness upon all occasions; his strength and security upon none.

But all the irregularities of nature are not of this awful or terrible kind. Some of them are perfectly beautiful and agreeable. These, therefore, from the same impotence of mind, would be beheld with love and complacency, and even with transports of gratitude; for whatever is the cause of pleasure naturally excites our gratitude. A child caresses the fruit that is agreeable to it, as it beats the stone that hurts it. The notions of a savage are not very different. The ancient Athenians, who solemnly punished the axe which had

accidentally been the cause of the death of a man, erected altars, and offered sacrifices to the rainbow. Sentiments not unlike these, may sometimes, upon such occasions, begin to be felt even in the breasts of the most civilised, but are presently checked by the reflection, that the things are not their proper objects. But a savage, whose notions are guided altogether by wild nature and passion, waits for no other proof that a thing is the proper object of any sentiment, than that it excites it. The reverence and gratitude, with which some of the appearances of nature inspire him, convince him that they are the proper objects of reverence and gratitude, and therefore proceed from some intelligent beings, who take pleasure in the expressions of those sentiments. With him, therefore, every object of nature, which by its beauty or greatness, its utility or hurtfulness, is considerable enough to attract his attention, and whose operations are not perfectly regular, is supposed to act by the direction of some invisible and designing power. The sea is spread out into a calm, or heaved into a storm, according to the good pleasure of Neptune. Does the earth pour forth an exuberant harvest? It is owing to the indulgence of Ceres. Does the vine yield a plentiful vintage? It flows from the bounty of Bacchus. Do either refuse their presents? It is ascribed to the displeasure of those offended deities. The tree, which now flourishes, and now decays, is inhabited by a Dryad, upon whose health or sickness its various appearances depend. The fountain, which sometimes flows in a copious, and sometimes in a scanty stream, which appears sometimes clear and limpid, and at other times muddy and disturbed, is affected in all its changes by the Naiad who dwells within it. Hence the origin of polytheism, and of that vulgar superstition which ascribes all the irregular events of nature to the favour or displeasure of intelligent, though invisible beings, to gods, daemons, witches, genii, fairies. For it may be observed, that in all polytheistic religions, among savages, as well as in the early ages of heathen antiquity, it is the irregular events of nature only that are ascribed to the agency and power of their gods. Fire burns, and water refreshes; heavy bodies descend, and lighter substances fly upwards, by the necessity of their own nature; nor was the invisible hand of Jupiter ever apprehended to be employed in those matters. But thunder and lightning, storms and sunshine, those more irregular events, were ascribed to his favour, or his anger. Man, the only designing power with whom they were acquainted, never acts but either to stop, or to alter the course, which natural events would take, if left to themselves. Those other intelligent beings, whom they imagined, but knew not, were naturally supposed to act in the same manner; not to employ themselves in supporting the ordinary course of things, which went on of its own accord, but to stop, to thwart, and to disturb it. And thus, in the first ages of the world, the lowest and most pusillanimous superstition supplied the place of philosophy.

But when law has established order and security, and subsistence ceases to be precarious, the curiosity of mankind is increased, and their fears are diminished. The leisure which they then enjoy renders them more attentive to the appearances of nature, more observant of her smallest irregularities, and more desirous to know what is the chain which links them all together. That some such chain subsists betwixt all her seemingly jointed phaenomena, they are necessarily led to conceive; and that magnanimity, and cheerfulness, which all generous natures acquire who are bred in civilised societies, where they have so few occasions to feel their weakness, and so many to be conscious of their strength and security, renders them less disposed to employ, for this connecting chain, those invisible beings whom the fear and ignorance of their rude forefathers has engendered. Those of liberal fortunes, whose attention is not much occupied either with business or with pleasure, can fill up the void of their imagination, which is thus disengaged from the ordinary affairs of life, no other way than by attending to that train of events which passes around them. While the great objects of nature thus pass in review before them, many things occur in an order to which they have not been accustomed. Their imagination, which accompanies with ease and delight the regular progress of nature, is stopped and embarrassed by those seeming incoherences; they excite their wonder, and seem to require some chain of intermediate events, which, by connecting them with something that has gone before, may thus render the whole course of the universe consistent and of a piece. Wonder, therefore, and not any expectation of advantage from its discoveries, is the first principle which prompts mankind to the study of philosophy, of that science which pretends to lay open the concealed connections that unite the various appearances of nature; and they pursue this study for its own sake, as an original pleasure or good in itself, without regarding its tendency to procure them the means of many other pleasures.

39

Adam Smith,
from *The theory of moral sentiments*
(1759/1790)

Part I. Of the propriety of action
Section I. Of the sense of propriety
Chapter V. Of the amiable and respectable virtues

Upon these two different efforts, upon that of the spectator to enter into the
sentiments of the person principally concerned, and upon that of the person
principally concerned, to bring down his emotions to what the spectator can
go along with, are founded two different sets of virtues. The soft, the gentle,
the amiable virtues, the virtues of candid condescension and indulgent humanity, are founded upon the one: the great, the awful and respectable, the virtues
of self-denial, of self-government, of that command of the passions which
subjects all the movements of our nature to what our own dignity and honour,
the propriety of our own conduct require, take their origin from the other....

And hence it is, that to feel much for others and little for ourselves, that to
restrain our selfish, and to indulge our benevolent affections, constitutes the
perfection of human nature; and can alone produce among mankind that harmony of sentiments and passions in which consists their whole grace and
propriety. As to love our neighbour as we love ourselves is the great law of
Christianity, so it is the great precept of nature to love ourselves only as we
love our neighbour, or what comes to the same thing, as our neighbour is
capable of loving us.

As taste and good judgment, when they are considered as qualities which
deserve praise and admiration, are supposed to imply a delicacy of sentiment
and an acuteness of understanding not commonly to be met with; so the
virtues of sensibility and self-command are not apprehended to consist in the
ordinary, but in the uncommon degrees of those qualities. The amiable virtue
of humanity requires, surely, a sensibility, much beyond what is possessed by
the rude vulgar of mankind. The great and exalted virtue of magnanimity
undoubtedly demands much more than that degree of self-command, which
the weakest of mortals is capable of exerting. As in the common degree of the
intellectual qualities, there are no abilities; so in the common degree of the
moral, there is no virtue. Virtue is excellence, something uncommonly great
and beautiful, which rises far above what is vulgar and ordinary. The amiable
virtues consist in that degree of sensibility which surprises by its exquisite and

244

unexpected delicacy and tenderness. The awful and respectable, in that degree of self-command which astonishes by its amazing superiority over the most ungovernable passions of human nature....

Part II. Of merit and demerit; or, of the objects of reward and punishment. Section III. Of the influence of fortune upon the sentiments of mankind, with regard to the merit or demerit of actions. Chapter II. Of the extent of this influence of fortune.

...Even the merit of talents and abilities which some accident has hindered from producing their effects, seems in some measure imperfect, even to those who are fully convinced of their capacity to produce them. The general who has been hindered by the envy of ministers from gaining some great advantage over the enemies of his country, regrets the loss of the opportunity for ever after. Nor is it only upon account of the public that he regrets it. He laments that he was hindered from performing an action which would have added a new lustre to his character in his own eyes, as well as in those of every other person. It satisfies neither himself nor others to reflect that the plan or design was all that depended on him, that no greater capacity was required to execute it than what was necessary to concert it: that he was allowed to be every way capable of executing it, and that had he been permitted to go on, success was infallible. He still did not execute it; and though he might deserve all the approbation which is due to a magnanimous and great design, he still wanted the actual merit of having performed a great action. To take the management of any affair of public concern from the man who has almost brought it to a conclusion, is regarded as the most invidious injustice. As he had done so much, he should, we think, have been allowed to acquire the complete merit of putting an end to it. It was objected to Pompey, that he came in upon the victories of Lucullus, and gathered those laurels which were due to the fortune and valour of another. The glory of Lucullus, it seems, was less complete even in the opinion of his own friends, when he was not permitted to finish that conquest which his conduct and courage had put in the power of almost any man to finish.

It mortifies an architect when his plans are either not executed at all, or when they are so far altered as to spoil the effect of the building. The plan, however, is all that depends upon the architect. The whole of his genius is, to good judges, as completely discovered in that as in the actual execution. But a plan does not, even to the most intelligent, give the same pleasure as a noble and magnificent building. They may discover as much both of taste and genius in the one as in the other. But their effects are still vastly different, and the amusement derived from the first, never approaches to the wonder and admiration which are sometimes excited by the second. We may believe of many men, that their talents are superior to those of Caesar and Alexander; and that in the same situations they would perform still greater actions. In the mean time, however, we do not behold them with that astonishment and admiration with which those two heroes have been regarded in all ages and nations. The calm judgments of the mind may approve of them more, but they want the splendour of great actions to dazzle and transport it. The superiority of virtues and talents has not, even upon those who acknowledge that superiority, the same effect with the superiority of achievements....

Part III. Of the foundation of our judgments concerning our own sentiments and conduct, and of the sense of duty
Chapter III. Of the influence and authority of conscience.

...Our sensibility to the feelings of others, so far from being inconsistent with the manhood of self-command, is the very principle upon which that manhood is founded. The very same principle or instinct which, in the misfortune of our neighbour, prompts us to compassionate his sorrow; in our own misfortune, prompts us to restrain the abject and miserable lamentations of our own sorrow. The same principle or instinct which, in his prosperity and success, prompts us to congratulate his joy; in our own prosperity and success, prompts us to restrain the levity and intemperance of our own joy. In both cases, the propriety of our own sentiments and feelings seems to be exactly in proportion to the vivacity and force with which we enter into and conceive his sentiments and feelings.

The man of the most perfect virtue, the man whom we naturally love and revere the most, is he who joins, to the most perfect command of his own original and selfish feelings, the most exquisite sensibility both to the original and sympathetic feelings of others. The man who, to all the soft, the amiable, and the gentle virtues, joins all the great, the awful, and the respectable, must surely be the natural and proper object of our highest love and admiration.

The person best fitted by nature for acquiring the former of those two sets of virtues, is likewise best fitted for acquiring the latter. The man who feels the most for the joys and sorrows of others, is best fitted for acquiring the most complete control of his own joys and sorrows. The man of the most exquisite humanity, is naturally the most capable of acquiring the highest degree of self-command. He may not, however, always have acquired it; and it very frequently happens that he has not. He may have lived too much in ease and tranquillity. He may have never been exposed to the violence of faction, or to the hardships and hazards of war. He may have never experienced the insolence of his superiors, the jealous and malignant envy of his equals, or the pilfering injustice of his inferiors. When, in an advanced age, some accidental change of fortune exposes him to all these, they all make too great an impression upon him. He has the disposition which fits him for acquiring the most perfect self-command; but he has never had the opportunity of acquiring it. Exercise and practice have been wanting; and without these no habit can ever be tolerably established. Hardships, dangers, injuries, misfortunes, are the only masters under whom we can learn the exercise of this virtue. But these are all masters to whom nobody willingly puts himself to school.

The situations in which the gentle virtue of humanity can be most happily cultivated, are by no means the same with those which are best fitted for forming the austere virtue of self-command. The man who is himself at ease can best attend to the distress of others. The man who is himself exposed to hardships is most immediately called upon to attend to, and to control his own feelings. In the mild sunshine of undisturbed tranquillity, in the calm retirement of undissipated and philosophical leisure, the soft virtue of humanity flourishes the most, and is capable of the highest improvement. But, in such situations, the greatest and noblest exertions of self-command have little exercise. Under the boisterous and stormy sky of war and faction, of public tumult and confusion, the sturdy severity of self-command prospers the most, and can be the most successfully cultivated. But, in such situations, the strongest suggestions of humanity must frequently be stifled or neglected; and every such neglect necessarily tends to weaken the principle of humanity. As it may frequently be the duty of a soldier not to take, so it may sometimes be his duty not to give quarter; and the humanity of the man who has been several times under the necessity of submitting to this disagreeable duty, can scarce fail to suffer a considerable diminution. For his own case, he is too apt to learn to make light of the misfortunes which he is so often under the necessity of occasioning; and the situations which call forth the noblest exertions of self-command, by imposing the necessity of violating sometimes the property, and sometimes the life of our neighbour, always tend to diminish, and too often to extinguish altogether, that sacred regard to both, which is the foundation of justice and humanity. It is upon this account, that we so frequently find in the world men of great humanity who have little self-command, but who are indolent and irresolute, and easily disheartened, either by difficulty or danger, from the most honourable pursuits; and, on the contrary, men of the most perfect self-command, whom no difficulty can discourage, no danger appal, and who are at all times ready for the most daring and desperate enterprises, but who, at the same time, seem to be hardened against all sense either of justice or humanity....

Part IV. Of the effect of utility upon the sentiment of approbation
Chapter I. Of the beauty which the appearance of utility bestows upon all the productions of art, and of the extensive influence of this species of beauty

...Power and riches appear then to be, what they are, enormous and operose machines contrived to produce a few trifling conceniencies to the body, consisting of springs the most nice and delicate, which must be kept in order with the most anxious attention, and which in spite of all our care are ready every moment to burst into pieces, and to crush in their ruins their unfortunate possessor. They are immense fabrics, which it requires the labour of a life to raise, which threaten every moment to overwhelm the person that dwells in them, and which while they stand, though they may save him from some smaller inconveniencies, can protect him from none of the severer inclemencies of the season. They keep off the summer shower, not the winter storm, but leave him always as much, and sometimes more exposed than before, to anxiety, to fear, and to sorrow; to diseases, to danger, and to death.

But though this splenetic philosophy, which in time of sickness or low spirits is familiar to every man, thus entirely depreciates those great objects of human desire, when in better health and in better humour, we never fail to regard them under a more agreeable aspect. Our imagination, which in pain and sorrow seems to be confined and cooped up within our own persons, in times of ease and prosperity expands itself to every thing around us. We are then charmed with the beauty of that accommodation which reigns in the palaces and economy of the great; and admire how every thing is adapted to promote their ease, to prevent their wants, to gratify their wishes, and to amuse and entertain their most frivolous desires. If we consider the real satisfaction which all these things are capable of affording, by itself and separated from the beauty of that arrangement which is fitted to promote it, it will always appear in the highest degree contemptible and trifling. But we rarely view it in this abstract and philosophical light. We naturally confound it in our imagination with the order, the regular and harmonious movement of the system, the machine or economy by means of which it is produced. The pleasures of wealth and greatness, when considered in this complex view, strike the imagination as something grand and beautiful and noble, of which the attainment is well worth all the toil and anxiety which we are so apt to bestow upon it.

And it is well that nature imposes upon us in this manner. It is this deception which rouses and keeps in continual motion the industry of mankind. It is this which first prompted them to cultivate the ground, to build houses, to found cities and commonwealths, and to invent and improve all the sciences and arts, which ennoble and embellish human life; which have entirely changed the whole face of the globe, have turned the rude forests of nature into agreeable and fertile plains, and made the trackless and barren ocean a new fund of subsistence, and the great high road of communication to the different nations of the earth. The earth by these labours of mankind has been obliged to redouble her natural fertility, and to maintain a greater multitude of inhabitants. It is to no purpose, that the proud and unfeeling landlord views his extensive fields, and without a thought for the wants of his brethren, in imagination consumes himself the whole harvest that grows upon them. The homely and vulgar proverb, that the eye is larger than the belly, never was more fully verified than with regard to him. The capacity of his stomach bears no proportion to the immensity of his desires, and will receive no more than that of the meanest peasant. The rest he is obliged to distribute among those, who prepare, in the nicest manner, that little which he himself makes use of, among those who fit up the palace in which this little is to be consumed,

among those who provide and keep in order all the different baubles and trin-
kets, which are employed in the economy of greatness; all of whom thus
derive from his luxury and caprice, that share of the necessaries of life, which
they would in vain have expected from his humanity or his justice. The produce of the soil maintains at all times nearly that number of inhabitants which
it is capable of maintaining. The rich only select from the heap what is most
precious and agreeable. They consume little more than the poor, and in spite
of their natural selfishness and rapacity, though they mean only their own
conveniency, though the sole end which they propose from the labours of all
the thousands whom they employ, be the gratification of their own vain and
insatiable desires, they divide with the poor the produce of all their improvements. They are led by an invisible hand to make nearly the same distribution
of the necessaries of life, which would have been made, had the earth been
divided into equal portions among all its inhabitants, and thus without
intending it, without knowing it, advance the interest of the society, and
afford the means to the multiplication of the species. When Providence
divided the earth among a few lordly masters, it neither forgot nor abandoned
those who seemed to have been left out in the partition. These last too enjoy
their share of all that it produces. In what constitutes the real happiness of
human life, they are in no respect inferior to those who would seem so much
above them. In ease of body and peace of mind, all the different ranks of life
are nearly upon a level, and the beggar, who suns himself by the side of the
highway, possesses that security which kings are fighting for.

The same principle, the same love of system, the same regard to the beauty
of order, of art and contrivance, frequently serves to recommend those
institutions which tend to promote the public welfare. When a patriot exerts
himself for the improvement of any part of the public police, his conduct does
not always arise from pure sympathy with the happiness of those who are to
reap the benefit of it. It is not commonly from a fellow-feeling with carriers
and waggoners that a public-spirited man encourages the mending of high
roads. When the legislature establishes premiums and other encouragements
to advance the linen or woollen manufactures, its conduct seldom proceeds
from pure sympathy with the wearer of cheap or fine cloth, and much less
from that with the manufacturer or merchant. The perfection of police, the
extension of trade and manufactures, are noble and magnificent objects. The
contemplation of them pleases us, and we are interested in whatever can tend
to advance them. They make part of the great system of government, and the
wheels of the political machines seem to move with more harmony and ease
by means of them. We take pleasure in beholding the perfection of so beautiful and grand a system, and we are uneasy till we remove any obstruction that
can in the least disturb or encumber the regularity of its motions. All constitu-
tions of government, however, are valued only in proportion as they tend to
promote the happiness of those who live under them. This is their sole use and
end. From a certain spirit of system, however, from a certain love of art and
contrivance, we sometimes seem to value the means more than the end, and

to be eager to promote the happiness of our fellow-creatures, rather from a view to perfect and improve a certain beautiful and orderly system, than from any immediate sense or feeling of what they either suffer or enjoy. There have been men of the greatest public spirit, who have shown themselves in other respects not very sensible to the feelings of humanity. And on the contrary, there have been men of the greatest humanity, who seem to have been entirely devoid of public spirit. Every man may find in the circle of his acquaintance instances both of the one kind and the other....

Part VI. Of the character of virtue
Section III. Of self-command

...Great warlike exploit, though undertaken contrary to every principle of justice, and carried on without any regard to humanity, sometimes interests us, and commands even some degree of a certain sort of esteem for the very worthless characters which conduct it. We are interested even in the exploits of the Buccaneers; and read with some sort of esteem and admiration, the history of the most worthless men, who, in pursuit of the most criminal purposes, endured greater hardships, surmounted great difficulties, and encountered greater dangers, than, perhaps, any which the ordinary course of history gives an account of....

The esteem and admiration which every impartial spectator conceives for the real merit of those spirited, magnanimous, and high-minded persons, as it is a just and well-founded sentiment, so it is a steady and permanent one, and altogether independent of their good or bad fortune. It is otherwise with that admiration which he is apt to conceive for their excessive self-estimation and presumption. While they are successful, indeed, he is often perfectly conquered and overborne by them. Success covers from his eyes, not only the great imprudence, but frequently the great injustice of their enterprises; and, far from blaming this defective part of their character, he often views it with the most enthusiastic admiration. When they are unfortunate, however, things change their colours and their names. What was before heroic magnanimity, resumes its proper appellation of extravagant rashness and folly; and the blackness of that avidity and injustice, which was before hid under the splendour of prosperity, comes full into view, and blots the whole lustre of their enterprise. Had Caesar, instead of gaining, lost the battle of Pharsalia, his character would, at this hour, have ranked a little above that of Catiline, and the weakest man would have viewed his enterprise against the laws of his. country in blacker colours, than, perhaps, even Cato, with all the animosity of a party-man, ever viewed it at the time. His real merit, the justness of his taste, the simplicity and elegance of his writings, the propriety of his eloquence, his skill in war, his resources in distress, his cool and sedate judgment in danger, his faithful attachment to his friends, his unexampled generosity to his enemies, would all have been acknowledged at this day. But the insolence and injustice of his all-grasping ambition would have darkened and extinguished the glory of all that real merit. Fortune has in this, as well as in some other respects already mentioned, great influence over the moral sentiments of mankind, and, according as she is either favourable or adverse, can render the same character the object, either of general love and admiration, or of universal hatred and contempt. This great disorder in our moral sentiments is by no means, however, without its utility; and we may on this, as well as on many other occasions, admire the wisdom of God even in the weakness and folly of man. Our admiration of success is founded upon the same principle with our respect for wealth and greatness, and is equally necessary for establishing the distinction of ranks and the order of society. By this admiration of success we are taught to submit more easily to those superiors, whom the course of human affairs may assign to us; to regard with reverence, and sometimes even with a sort of respectful affection, that fortunate violence of such splendid characters as those of a Caesar or an Alexander, but often that of the most brutal and savage barbarians, of an Attila, a Genghis, or a Tamerlane. To all such mighty conquerors the great mob of mankind are naturally disposed to look up with a wondering, though, no doubt, with a very weak and foolish admiration. By this admiration, however, they are taught to acquiesce with less reluctance under that government which an irresistible force imposes upon them, and from which no reluctance could deliver them....

Part VII. Of systems of moral philosophy
Section II. Of the different accounts which have been given of the nature of virtue
Chapter IV. Of licentious systems

All those systems, which I have hitherto given an account of, suppose that there is a real and essential distinction between vice and virtue, whatever these qualities may consist in. There is a real and essential difference between the propriety and impropriety of any affection, between benevolence and any other principle of action, between real prudence and short-sighted folly or precipitate rashness. In the main too all of them contribute to encourage the praise-worthy, and to discourage the blamable disposition.

It may be true, perhaps, of some of them, that they tend, in some measure, to break the balance of the affections, and to give the mind a particular bias to some principles of action, beyond the proportion that is due to them. The ancient systems, which place virtue in propriety, seem chiefly to recommend the great, the awful, and the respectable virtues, the virtues of self-government and self-command; fortitude, magnanimity, independency upon fortune, the contempt of all outward accidents, of pain, poverty, exile, and death. It is in these great exertions that the noblest propriety of conduct is displayed. The soft, the amiable, the gentle virtues, all the virtues of indulgent humanity are, in comparison, but little insisted upon, and seem, on the contrary, by the Stoics in particular, to have been often regarded as mere weaknesses which it behoved a wise man not to harbour in his breast.

The benevolent system, on the other hand, while it fosters and encourages all those milder virtues in the highest degree, seems entirely to neglect the more awful and respectable qualities of the mind. It even denies them the appellation of virtues. It calls them moral abilities, and treats them as qualities which do not deserve the same sort of esteem and approbation, that is due to what is properly denominated virtue. All those principles of action which aim only at our own interest, it treats, if that be possible, still worse. So far from having any merit of their own, they diminish, it pretends, the merits of benevolence, when they co-operate with it: and prudence, it is asserted, when employed only in promoting private interest, can never even be imagined a virtue.

That system, again, which makes virtue consistent in prudence only, while it gives the highest encouragement to the habits of caution, vigilance, sobriety, and judicious moderation, seems to degrade equally both the amiable and respectable virtues, and to strip the former of all their beauty, and the latter of all their grandeur....

40

Adam Ferguson, from *An essay on the history of civil society* (1767)

Part First. Of the general characteristics of human nature
Section I. Of the questions relating to the state of nature

…We speak of art as distinguished from nature; but art itself is natural to man. He is in some measure the artificer of his own frame, as well as his fortune, and is destined, from the first age of his being, to invent and contrive. He applies the same talents to a variety of purposes, and acts nearly the same part in very different scenes. He would be always improving on his subject, and he carries this intention wherever he moves, through the streets of the populous city, or the wilds of the forest. While he appears equally fitted to every condition, he is upon this account unable to settle in any. At once obstinate and fickle, he complains of innovations, and is never sated with novelty. He is perpetually busied in reformations, and is continually wedded to his errors. If he dwell in a cave, he would improve it into a cottage; if he has already built, he would still build to a greater extent. But he does not propose to make rapid and hasty transitions; his steps are progressive and slow; and his force, like the power of a spring, silently presses on every resistance; and effect is sometimes produced before the cause is perceived; and with all his talent for projects, his work is often accomplished before the plan is devised. It appears, perhaps, equally difficult to retard or to quicken his pace; if the projector complain he is tardy, the moralist thinks him unstable; and whether his motions be rapid or slow, the scenes of human affairs perpetually change in his management: his emblem is a passing stream, not a stagnating pool. We may desire to direct his love of improvement to its proper object, we may wish for stability of conduct; but we mistake human nature, if we wish for a termination of labour, or a scene of repose.

The occupations of men, in every condition, bespeak their freedom of choice, their various opinions, and the multiplicity of wants by which they are urged: but they enjoy, or endure, with a sensibility, or a phlegm, which are nearly the same in every situation. They possess the shores of the Caspian, or the Atlantic, by a different tenure, but with equal ease. On the one they are fixed to the soil, and seem to be formed for settlement, and the accommodation of cities: the names they bestow on a nation, and on its territory, are the same. On the other they are mere animals of passage, prepared to roam on the face of the earth, and with their herds, in search of new pasture and favourable seasons, to follow the sun in his annual course.

253

Man finds his lodgment alike in the cave, the cottage, and the palace; and his subsistence equally in the woods, in the dairy, or the farm. He assumes the distinction of titles, equipage, and dress; he devises regular systems of government, and a complicated body of laws: or, naked in the woods, has no badge of superiority but the strength of his limbs and the sagacity of his mind; no rule of conduct but choice; no tie with his fellow-creatures but affection, the love of company, and the desire of safety. Capable of a great variety of arts, yet dependent on none in particular for the preservation of his being; to whatever length he has carried his artifice, there he seems to enjoy the conveniences that suit his nature, and to have found the condition to which he is destined. The tree which an American, on the banks of the Oroonoko, has chosen to climb for the retreat, and the lodgment of his family, is to him a convenient dwelling. The sofa, the vaulted dome, and the colonnade, do not more effectually content their native inhabitant.

If we are asked therefore, where the state of nature is to be found? we may answer, it is here; and it matters not whether we are understood to speak in the island of Great Britain, at the Cape of Good Hope, or the Straits of Magellan. While this active being is in the train of employing his talents, and of operating on the subjects around him, all situations are equally natural. If we are told, that vice, at least, is contrary to nature; we may answer, it is worse; it is folly and wretchedness. But if nature is only opposed to art, in what situation of the human race are the footsteps of art unknown? In the condition of the savage, as well as in that of the citizen, are many proofs of human invention; and in either is not any permanent station, but a mere stage through which this travelling being is destined to pass. If the palace be unnatural, the cottage is so no less; and the highest refinements of political and moral apprehension, are not more artificial in their kind, than the first operations of sentiment and reason.

If we admit that man is susceptible of improvement, and has in himself a principle of progression, and a desire of perfection, it appears improper to say, that he has quitted the state of his nature, when he has begun to proceed; or that he finds a station for which he was not intended, while, like other animals, he only follows the disposition, and employs the powers that nature has given.

The latest efforts of human invention are but a continuation of certain devices which were practised in the earliest ages of the world, and in the rudest state of mankind. What the savage projects, or observes, in the forest, are the steps which led nations, more advanced, from the architecture of the cottage to that of the palace, and conducted the human mind from the perceptions of sense, to the general conclusions of science....

Section V
Of intellectual powers

...When nations succeed one another in the career of discoveries and inquiries, the last is always the most knowing. Systems of science are gradually formed.

The globe itself is traversed by degrees, and the history of every age, when past, is an accession of knowledge to those who succeed. The Romans were more knowing than the Greeks; and every scholar of modern Europe is, in this sense, more learned than the most accomplished person that ever bore either of those celebrated names. But is he on that account their superior?

Men are to be estimated, not from what they know, but for what they are able to perform; from their skill in adapting materials to the several purposes of life; from their vigour and conduct in pursuing the objects of policy, and in finding the expedients of war and national defence. Even in literature, they are to be estimated from the works of their genius, not from the extent of their knowledge. The scene of mere observation was extremely limited in a Grecian republic; and the bustle of an active life appeared inconsistent with study: but there the human mind, notwithstanding, collected its greatest abilities, and received its best informations, in the midst of sweat and of dust.

It is peculiar to modern Europe, to rest so much of the human character on what may be learned in retirement, and from the information of books. A just admiration of ancient literature, an opinion that human sentiment, and human reason, without this aid, were to have vanished from the societies of men, have led us into the shade, where we endeavour, through the grammar of dead languages, and the channel of commentators, to arrive at the beauties of thought and elocution, which sprang from the animated spirit of society, and were taken from the living impressions of an active life. Our attainments are frequently limited to the elements of every science, and seldom reach to that enlargement of ability and power which useful knowledge should give. Like mathematicians, who study the *Elements* of Euclid, but never think of mensuration, we read of societies, but do not propose to act with men: we repeat the language of politics, but feel not the spirit of nations: we attend to the formalities of a military discipline, but know not how to employ numbers of men to obtain any purpose by stratagem or force.

But for what end, it may be said, point out a misfortune that cannot be remedied? If national affairs called for exertion, the genius of men would awake; but in the recess of better employment, the time which is bestowed on study, if even attended with no other advantage, serves to occupy with innocence the hours of leisure, and set bounds to the pursuit of ruinous and frivolous amusements. From no better reason than this, we employ so many of our early years, under the rod, to acquire what is not expected we should retain beyond the threshold of the school; and whilst we carry the same frivolous character in our studies that we do in our amusements, the human mind could not suffer more from a contempt of letters, than it does from the false importance which is given to literature, as a business for life, not as a help to our conduct, and the means of forming a character that may be happy in itself, and useful to mankind.

If that time which is passed in relaxing the powers of the mind, and in withholding every object but what tends to weaken and to corrupt, were employed in fortifying those powers, and in teaching the mind to recognise its objects, and its strength, we should not, at the years of maturity, be so much at a loss for occupation; nor, in attending the chances of a gaming-table, misemploy our talents, or waste the fire which remains in the breast. They, at least, who by their stations have a share in the government of their country, might believe themselves capable of business; and while the state had its armies and councils, might find objects enough to amuse, without throwing a personal fortune into hazard, merely to cure the yawnings of a listless and insignificant life. It is impossible for ever to maintain the tone of speculation; it is impossible not sometimes to feel that we live among men.

Part V. Of the decline of nations
Section iii. Of relaxations in the national spirit incident to political realities

...We may fancy to ourselves, that in ages of progress, the human race, like scouts gone abroad on the discovery of fertile lands, having the world open before them, are presented at every step with the appearance of novelty. They enter on every new ground with expectation and joy: they engage in every enterprise with the ardour of men, who believe they are going to arrive at national felicity, and permanent glory; and forget past disappointments amidst the hopes of future success. From mere ignorance, rude minds are intoxicated with every passion; and partial to their own condition, and to their own pursuits, they think that every scene is inferior to that in which they are placed. Roused alike by success, and by misfortune, they are sanguine, ardent, and precipitant; and leave to the more knowing ages which succeed them, monuments of imperfect skill, and of rude execution in every art; but they leave likewise the marks of a vigorous and ardent spirit, which their successors are not always qualified to sustain, or to imitate.

This may be admitted, perhaps, as a fair description of prosperous societies, at least during certain periods of their progress. The spirit with which they advance may be unequal, in different ages, and may have its paroxysms, and intermissions, arising from the inconstancy of human passions, and from the casual appearance or removal of occasions that excite them. But does this spirit, which for a time continues to carry on the project of civil and commercial arts, find a natural pause in the termination of its own pursuits? May the business of civil society be accomplished, and may the occasion of farther exertion be removed? Do continued disappointments reduce sanguine hopes, and familiarity with objects blunt the edge of novelty? Does experience itself cool the ardour of the mind? May the society be again compared to the individual? And may it be suspected, although the vigour of a nation, like that of a natural body, does not waste by a physical decay, that yet it may sicken for want of exercise, and die in the close of its own exertions? May societies, in the completion of all their designs, like men in years, who disregard the amusements, and are insensible to the passions, of youth, become cold and indifferent to objects that used to animate in a ruder age? And may a polished community be compared to a man, who having executed his plan, built his house, and made his settlement; who having, in short, exhausted the charms of every subject, and wasted all his ardour, sinks into languor and listless indifference? If so, we have found at least another simile to our purpose. But it is probable, that here too, the resemblance is imperfect; and the inference that would follow, like that of most arguments drawn from analogy, tends rather to amuse the fancy, than to give any real information on the subject to which it refers.

The materials of human art are never entirely exhausted, and the applications of industry are never at an end. The national ardour is not, at any particular time, proportioned to the occasion there is for activity; nor curiosity, to the extent of subject that remains to be studied.

The ignorant and the artless, to whom objects of science are new, and who are worst furnished with the conveniences of life, instead of being more active, and more curious, are commonly more quiescent, and less inquisitive, than the knowing and the polished. When we compare the particulars which occupy mankind in their rude and in their polished condition, they will be found greatly multiplied and enlarged in the last. The questions we have put, however, deserve to be answered; and if, in the advanced ages of society, we do not find the objects of human pursuit removed, or greatly diminished, we may find them at least changed; and in estimating the national spirit, we may find a negligence in one part, but ill compensated by the growing attention which is paid to another.

It is true, in general, that in all our pursuits, there is a termination of trouble, and a point of repose to which we aspire. We would remove this inconvenience, or gain that advantage, that our labours may cease. When I have conquered Italy and Sicily, says Pyrrhus, I shall then enjoy my repose. This termination is proposed in our national as well as in our personal exertions; and in spite of frequent experience to the contrary, is considered at a distance as the height of felicity. But nature has wisely, in most particulars, baffled our project; and placed nowhere within our reach this visionary blessing of absolute ease. The attainment of one end is but the beginning of a new pursuit; and the discovery of one art is but a prolongation of the thread by which we are conducted to further inquiries, and only hope to escape from the labyrinth.

Among the occupations that may be enumerated, as tending to exercise the invention, and to cultivate the talents of men, are the pursuits of accommodation and wealth, including all the different contrivances which serve to increase manufactures, and to perfect the mechanical arts. But it must be owned, that as the materials of commerce, may continue to be accumulated without any determinate limit, so the arts which are applied to improve them, may admit of perpetual refinements. No measure of fortune, or degree of skill, is found to diminish the supposed necessities of human life; refinement and plenty foster new desires, while they furnish the means, or practise the methods, to gratify them.

In the result of commercial arts, inequalities of fortune are greatly increased, and the majority of every people are obliged by necessity, or at least strongly incited by ambition and avarice, to employ every talent they possess. After a history of some thousand years employed in manufacture and commerce, the inhabitants of China are still the most laborious and industrious of any people on the surface of the earth.

Some part of this observation may be extended to the elegant and literary arts. They too have their materials, which cannot be exhausted, and proceed from desires which cannot be satiated. But the respect paid to literary merit is fluctuating, and matter of transient fashion. When learned productions accumulate, the acquisition of knowledge occupies the time that might be bestowed on invention. The object of mere learning is attained with moderate or inferior talents, and the growing list of pretenders diminishes the lustre of the few who are eminent. When we only mean to learn what others have taught, it is probable, that even our knowledge will be less than that of our masters. Great names continue to be repeated with admiration, after we have ceased to examine the foundations of our praise; and new pretenders are rejected, not because they do not excel them; or because, in reality, we have, without examination, taken for granted, the merit of the first, and cannot judge of either.

After libraries are furnished, and every path of ingenuity is occupied, we are, in proportion to our admiration of what is already done, prepossessed against farther attempts. We become students and admirers, instead of rivals; and substitute the knowledge of books, instead of the inquisitive or animated spirit in which they were written.

The commercial and lucrative arts may continue to prosper, but they gain an ascendant at the expense of other pursuits. The desire of profit stifles the love of perfection. Interest cools the imagination, and hardens the heart; and, recommending employments in proportion as they are lucrative, and certain in their gains, it drives ingenuity, and ambition itself, to the counter and the workshop.

But apart from these conditions, the separation of professions, while it seems to promise improvement of skill, and is actually the cause why the productions of every art becomes more perfect as commerce advances; yet in its termination, and ultimate effects, serves, in some measure, to break the bands of society, to substitute form in place of ingenuity, and to withdraw individuals from the common scene of occupation, on which the sentiments of the heart, and the mind, are most happily employed....

When we are involved in any of the divisions into which mankind are separated, under the denominations of a country, a tribe, or an order of men any way affected by common interests, and guided by communicating passions, the mind recognises its natural station; the sentiments of the heart, and the talents of the understanding, find their natural exercise. Wisdom, vigilance, fidelity, and fortitude, are the characters requisite in such a scene, and the qualities which it tends to improve.

In simple or barbarous ages, when nations are weak, and beset with enemies, the love of a country, of a party, or a faction, are the same. The public is a knot of friends, and its enemies are the rest of mankind. Death, or slavery, are the ordinary evils which they are concerned to ward off; victory and dominion, the objects to which they aspire. Under the sense of what they may suffer from foreign invasions, it is one object, in every prosperous society, to increase its force, and to extend its limits. In proportion as this object is gained, security increases. They who possess the interior districts, remote from the frontier, are unused to alarms from abroad. They who are placed on the extremities, remote from the seats of government, are unused to hear of political interests; and the public becomes an object perhaps too extensive, for the conceptions of either. They enjoy the protection of its laws, or of its armies; and they boast of its splendour, and its power; but the glowing sentiments of public affection, which, in small states, mingle with the tenderness of the parent and the lover, of the friend and the companion, merely by having their object enlarged, lose great part of their force.

The manners of rude nations require to be reformed. Their foreign quarrels, and domestic dissensions, are the operations of extreme and sanguinary passions. A state of greater tranquillity hath many happy effects. But if nations pursue the plan of enlargement and pacification, till their members can no longer apprehend the common ties of society, nor be engaged by affection in the cause of their country, they must err on the opposite side, and by leaving too little to agitate the spirits of men, bring on ages of languor, if not of decay.

The members of a community may, in this manner, like the inhabitants of a conquered province, be made to lose the sense of every connection, but that of kindred or neighbourhood; and have no common affairs to transact, but those of trade: connections, indeed, or transactions, in which probity and friendship may still take place; but in which the national spirit, whose ebbs and flows we are now considering, cannot be exerted....

Whatever be the national extent, civil order, and regular government, are advantages of the greatest importance; but it does not follow, that every arrangement made to obtain these ends, and which may, in the making, exercise and cultivate the best qualities of men, is therefore of a nature to produce permanent effects, and to secure the preservation of that national spirit from which it arose.

We have reason to dread the political refinements of ordinary men, when we consider, that repose, or inaction itself, is in a great measure their object; and that they would frequently model their governments, not merely to prevent injustice and error, but to prevent agitation and bustle; and by the barriers they raise against the evil actions of men, would prevent them from acting at all. Every dispute of a free people, in the opinion of such politicians, amounts to disorder, and a breach of the national peace. What heart-burnings? What delay to affairs? What want of secrecy and dispatch? What defect of police? Men of superior genius sometimes seem to imagine, that the vulgar have no title to act, or to think....

If the precautions which men thus take against each other be necessary to repress their crimes, and do not arise from a corrupt ambition, or from cruel jealousy in their rulers, the proceeding itself must be applauded, as the best remedy of which the vices of men will admit. The viper must be held at a distance, and the tiger chained. But if a rigorous policy, applied to enslave, not to restrain from crimes, has an actual tendency to corrupt the manners, and to extinguish the spirit of nations; if its severities be applied to terminate the agitations of a free people, not to remedy their corruptions; if forms be often applauded as salutary, because they tend merely to silence the voice of mankind, or be condemned as pernicious, because they allow this voice to be heard; we may expect that many of the boasted improvements of civil society, will be mere devices to lay the political spirit at rest, and will chain up the active virtues more than the restless disorders of men.

If to any people it be the avowed object of policy, in all its internal refinements, to secure the person and the property of the subject, without any regard to his political character, the constitution indeed may be free, but its members may likewise become unworthy of the freedom they possess, and unfit to preserve it. The effects of such a constitution may be to immerse all orders of men in their separate pursuits of pleasure, which they may now enjoy with little disturbance; or of gain, which they may preserve without any attention to the commonwealth.

If this be the end of political struggles, the design, when executed, in securing to the individual his estate, and the means of subsistence, may put an end to the exercise of those very virtues that were required in conducting its execution. A man who, in concert with his fellow-subjects, contends with usurpation in defence of his estate or his person, may find an exertion of great generosity, and of a vigorous spirit; but he who, under political establishments, supposed to be fully confirmed, betakes him, because he is safe, to the mere enjoyment of fortune, has in fact turned to a source of corruptions the very advantages which the virtues of the other procured. Individuals, in certain ages, derive their protection chiefly from the strength of the party to which they adhere; but in times of corruption, they flatter themselves, that they may continue to derive from the public that safety which, in former ages, they must have owed to their own vigilance and spirit, to the warm attachment of their friends, and to the exercise of every talent which could render them respected, feared, or beloved. In one period, therefore, mere circumstances serve to excite the spirit, and to preserve the manners of men; in another, great wisdom and zeal for the good of mankind on the part of their leaders, are required for the same purposes....

Section IV. The same subject continued

Men frequently, while they study to improve their fortunes, neglect themselves; and while they reason for their country, forget the considerations that most deserve their attention. Numbers, riches, and the other resources of war, are highly important: but nations consist of men; and a nation consisting of degenerate and cowardly men, is weak; a nation consisting of a vigorous, public-spirited, and resolute men, is strong. The resources of war, where other advantages are equal, may decide a contest; but the resources of war, in hands that cannot employ them, are of no avail.

Virtue is a necessary constituent of national strength: capacity, and a vigorous understanding, are no less necessary to sustain the fortune of states. Both are improved by discipline, and by the exercises in which men are engaged. We despise, or we pity, the lot of mankind, while they lived under uncertain establishments, and were obliged to sustain in the same person, the character of the senator, the statesman, and the soldier. Polished nations discover, that any one of these characters is sufficient in one person; and that the ends of each, when disjoined, are more easily accomplished. The first, however, were circumstances under which nations advanced and prospered; the second were those in which the spirit relaxed, and the nation went to decay.

We may, with good reason, congratulate our species on their having escaped from a state of barbarous disorder and violence, into a state of domestic peace and regular policy; when they have sheathed the dagger, and disarmed the animosities of civil contention; when the weapons with which they contend are the reasonings of the wife, and the tongue of the eloquent. But we cannot, meantime, help to regret, that they should ever proceed, in search of perfection, to place every branch of administration behind the counter, and come to employ, instead of the statesman and warrior, the mere clerk and accountant.

By carrying this system to its height, men are educated, who could copy for Cæsar his military instructions, or even execute a part of his plans; but none who could act in all the different scenes for which the leader himself must be qualified, in the state and in the field, in times of order or of tumult, in times of division or of unanimity; none who could animate the council when deliberating on ordinary occasions, or when alarmed by attacks from abroad....

The winding path [Chambers] is one of the most used schemes of garden design since it introduces time and delay, expectation and revelation into the circuit walk. This was exploited to the full in Kent's design of Rousham which not only incorporates the winding route into its large-scale design but also literally figures the serpentine form in the rill that serpentines through the upper part of the garden towards the area known as Venus' vale. The serpentine line was proclaimed by Hogarth to be 'the line of beauty'.[1]

Ruins were much admired for their being picturesque [Price]. The picturesque aesthetic developed by Gilpin and his followers had precise notions about the type and form of ruinated structures. Gilpin, for example, thought that Tintern Abbey, even though substantially a ruin when he visited it in 1770, was too uniform and recommended taking a mallet to the regular gables remaining in order to render them more picturesque. Fake ruins were also a part of landscape aesthetics; one of the earliest structures was designed by Sanderson Millar for Hagley Park in 1748.[2]

Objects in the landscape were often designed so as to present different 'fronts' depending on the direction from which they were seen lending to the experience of landscape a kind of theatricality – which was directly invoked by the term used to describe Brownian plantations of trees: screens. But the visual was not only structured rhythmically by a variety of objects and views, there was also a sense in which space itself was taken to be a feature of landscape aesthetics [Marshall]. Indeed, looking out towards the heavens, as in the study of astronomy, provided a very obvious analogue for sublime effect.[3]

The analytic of the sublime takes its most awkward turn in the writings of the later Burke, whose early *Enquiry* had, of course, created a major part of the sublime tradition. It is, therefore, noteworthy that Burke's attempts to

[1] See William Hogarth, *The analysis of beauty* (London, 1753), and for recent discussions of Hogarth's use of the serpentine see Ronald Paulson, 'Hogarth and the English garden: visual and verbal structures', in *Encounters: essays on literature and the visual arts*, ed. J.D. Hunt (London: Studio Vista, 1971); and for an account of the line in renaissance art see David Summers, 'Maniera and movement: the Figura Serpentinata', *Art Quarterly*, 35 (1972), 269-301.

[2] For Gilpin see *Observations on the River Wye, and several parts of South Wales* (London, 1782), also note Arthur Young, *A six months tour through the north of England*, 4 vols. (London, 1770) in which he suggests that ruins are best seen from a distance. Discussion of the eighteenth-century predilection for ruins can be found in Christopher Hussey, *The picturesque: studies in a point of view* (London: Cass & Co, 1927); Rose Macaulay, *Pleasure of ruins* (London: Thames and Hudson, 1953); Stuart Piggot, *Ruins in a landscape: essays in antiquarianism* (Edinburgh: Edinburgh University Press, 1976); Ian Ousby, *The Englishman's England* (Cambridge: Cambridge University Press, 1990); Anne Janowitz, *England's ruins: poetic purpose and the national landscape* (Oxford: Basil Blackwell, 1990).

[3] See the extract from Adam Smith's 'Essay on astronomy' in Part 5. De Quincey will later expand upon this in his essay on the astronomer Lord Rosse. See De Quincey, *Collected writings*, 14 vols. (Edinburgh, 1890), 8, pp. 15-16; and for a recent discussion see Robert Platzner, ' "Persecutions of the infinte": De Quincey's "System of the heavens as revealed by Lord Rosse's telescopes" as an inquiry into the sublime', in *Sensibility in transformation*, ed. Syndy McMillen Conger (London: Associated University Presses, 1990).

discredit the revolution continually run up against the problem of redefining categories which in his earlier treatise had been associated with the sublime, and therefore by extension morally sanctionable, but which now in the context of the revolution cannot remain so for political reasons. Self preservation [Burke], for example, is a source of the sublime; however, when it is marshalled on behalf of the corrupt state it becomes 'debauched' and degraded into 'cannibalism'. In this way the human, in the aftermath of the revolution, becomes bestial: perhaps the ultimate fall from the sublime. Burke's sense of discomfort in the face of a, to him, politically rebarbative event pervades almost all his later thinking on the sublime. The active striving powers which, for example, had been essential to sublime morality in Ferguson are now revised by Burke into the 'enterprising talents' of dissenters and French revolutionaries, both of whom are seen as evil. In the same way, terror, which had previously been the unique feature of sublimity is now distanced from the sublime. In its place the previously important but submerged notions of rank and class, together with distance and time, combine to produce a sublime of harmony, civil order and virtue. Consequently the political implications of the moral paradoxes inherent in the sublime lead to a re-ordering of sublime characteristics [Burke]. In effect this corruption of the sublime is already foreseen in the earlier analytic discourse. The power of oratory, for example, may not necessarily be marshalled in the service of ethically good principles.

Central to many dissenters such as Godwin and Wollstonecraft is a new category within the sublime: the sublime of knowledge. Just as the experience of landscape or literature produces moments of ravishment and transport which lead on to an enhanced sense of self and personal freedom, so too the experience of knowledge leads on to a similar enhanced sense of self and political freedom [Godwin]. Thus the political events of the 1790s effectively rupture the discourse of the sublime into a set of irreconcilable positions, with Burke and Godwin mapping out the extremes.

Lying somewhere in between these end-points are some of the most interesting reactions to the revolution, many of them by women. In particular two exemplary women visitors to France during the period wrote about their experiences: Mary Wollstonecraft and Helen Maria Williams. Essential to Wollstonecraft's sensibility and sensitiveness was a feeling imbued in her from early on that she was, in some way, set apart from 'the grand mass of mankind'. This sense of isolation doubtless contributed to the attraction of the desolate landscape of the north which she documented in her *Letters written during a short residence in Sweden, Norway and Denmark*. It is here, as in the frozen north, that she came to understand the full measure of how nature schools sensibility.[4] The hand of nature, in a metaphor that almost

---

[4]   There is a long history covering the instruction of sensibility by nature, and the topic became important in dissenting circles. See Thomas Percival, 'On the advantages of a taste for the general beauties of nature and art', in *Moral and literary dissertations* (Warrington, 1774); Mary Wollstonecraft, 'On poetry and our relish for the beauties of nature', in *Posthumous works*, ed. W. Godwin, 4 vols. (London, 1798), IV, 162-73.

emblematises the writing of this period, strokes and caresses the sensibility as the wind touches the aeolian harp.

In many cases the resulting sensation is one in which the sublime stands as the ultimate extension of human feeling; indeed this transforming experience leads one out of the human entirely towards the divine. Once again, in common with other writers of her age, Wollstonecraft reserved this ecstatic form of experience for particular kinds of individual, most notably for poets.

It is the intuitive genius of the poet which singles him out for a particularly sensitised mode of experience; indeed, the poet must at some level abandon reason which when actively applied tends to destroy the sublime. Such an aesthetic clearly has dangers for a politics of the sublime, precisely Burke's point and fear, but it also counters Kant's notion that rationality is the highest form of human experience, and is therefore sublime.

The two separate tributaries of the eighteenth-century tradition, the ethical and the religious, rejoin each other in Helen Maria Williams's account of revolutionary France in which the 'pomp' of religious ceremony is connected to the 'enthusiasm' of moral sentiment [Williams]. In this sense the tradition has come full circle as understanding and aesthetic affect conjoin in the spectator.

The direction in which analogy functions has also come full circle in that natural objects no longer function as the cause or analogical example of sublime affect, rather the direction has changed in which the analogy now moves from the sublime affect back to the external object. Thus we learn that Paris, on account of its 'narrow, dark, and dirty' streets is sublime whereas London, with its 'broad, airy, light, and elegant' streets is beautiful [Williams]. This is a form of transferred sublimity in which the qualities used for the description of the objects confer sublimity upon them.

By the time Williams is writing the imaginative and affective topography of the sublime was extremely well established. So it is that she imaginatively projected herself in to an experience of the Alps before she actually saw them [Williams]. This 'enthusiastic awe' is the logical conclusion to the analytic of the sublime which in effect produces from within itself sublime affect.

There is, nevertheless, a very strong impulse to witness the established topoi of the sublime tour, such as Shaffhausen [Williams], whether or not there was a threat of disappointment. Indeed, the threat only served to make the experience yet more sublime. As Williams recounts, however, she need not have been concerned since the experience of the falls fulfilled every expectation; indeed it led towards the ultimate sublime experience: the 'annihilation of self' [Williams].

It is curious that the temporal aspect to sublime experiences is relatively infrequently marked. Hume, we may recall, discusses the temporal in historical terms; his version of the time of the sublime invokes long duration. The opposite temporal register in sublime experience, the now of the instant, is rarely analysed. Williams, however, does attempt to comment upon this aspect in her contention that not only does the sublime experience annihilate the sense of self it also takes one out of clock time altogether [Williams].[5]

The culminating point of the political sublime is, of course, the triumph of the French Revolution [Williams] in which human ingenuity and social practice were taken to have reached the greatest heights. Without the analytic of the sublime already in place this kind of analysis and description of the Revolution would have been impossible, a fact uncomfortably known to and recognised by the greatest British critic of the Revolution, Edmund Burke. It is both fitting and ironic, then, that the tradition comes to a kind of resting point where one of the major theorists of sublime was forced to confront his theoretical progeny.

[5] See Barnet Newman, 'The sublime is now', *The Tiger's Eye*, 15 December 1948.

41

William Chambers,
from *A dissertation on oriental gardening* (1772)

The scenes which I have hitherto described, are chiefly of the pleasing kind: but the Chinese Gardeners have many sorts, which they employ as circumstances vary; all which they range in three separate classes; and distinguish them by the appellations of the pleasing, the terrible, and the surprising.

The first of these are composed of the gayest and most perfect productions of the vegetable world; intermixed with rivers, lakes, cascades, fountains, and water-works of all sorts: being combined and disposed in all the picturesque forms that art or nature can suggest. Buildings, sculptures, and paintings are added, to give splendour and variety to these compositions; and the rarest productions of the animal creation are collected; to enliven them: nothing is forgot that can either exhilarate the mind, gratify the senses, or give a spur to the imagination.

Their scenes of terror are composed of gloomy woods, deep valleys inaccessible to the sun, impending barren rocks, dark caverns, and impetuous cataracts rushing down the mountains from all parts. The trees are ill formed, forced out of their natural directions, and seemingly torn to pieces by the violence of tempests: some are thrown down, and intercept the course of the torrents; others look as if blasted and shattered by the power of lightning: the buildings are in ruins; or half consumed by fire, or swept away by the fury of the waters: nothing remaining entire but a few miserable huts dispersed in the mountains, which serve at once to indicate the existence and wretchedness of the inhabitants. Bats, owls, vultures, and every bird of prey flutter in the groves; wolves, tigers and jackals howl in the forests; half-famished animals wander upon the plains; gibbets, crosses, wheels, and the whole apparatus of torture, are seen from the roads; and in the most dismal recesses of the woods, where the ways are rugged and overgrown with weeds, and where every object bears the marks of depopulation, are temples dedicated to the king of vengeance, deep caverns in the rocks, and descents to subterraneous habitations, overgrown with brushwood and brambles; near which are placed pillars of stone, with pathetic descriptions of tragical events, and many horrid acts of cruelty, perpetrated there by outlaws and robbers of former times: and to add both to the horror and sublimity of these scenes, they sometimes conceal in cavities, on the summits of the highest mountains, foundries, lime kilns, and glassworks; which send forth large volumes of flame, and continued columns of thick smoke, that give to these mountains the appearance of volcanoes.

Their surprising, or supernatural scenes, are of the romantic kind, and abound in the marvellous; being calculated to excite in the minds of the spectators, quick successions of opposite and violent sensations. Sometimes the passenger is hurried by steep descending paths to subterranean vaults, divided into apartments, where lamps, which yield a faint glimmering light, discover the pale images of ancient kings and heroes, reclining on beds of state; their heads are crowned with garlands of stars, and in their hands are tablets of moral sentences: flutes, and soft harmonious organs, impelled by subterraneous waters, interrupt, at stated intervals, the silence of the place, and fill the air with solemn melody.

Sometimes the traveller, after having wandered in the dusk of the forest, finds himself on the edge of precipices, in the glare of daylight, with cataracts falling from the mountains around, and torrents raging in the depths beneath him; or at the foot of impending rocks, in gloomy valleys, overhung with woods, on the banks of dull moving rivers, whose shores are covered with sepulchral monuments, under the shade of willows, laurels, and other plants, sacred to Manchew, the genius of sorrow.

His way now lies through dark passages cut in the rocks, on the side of which are recesses, filled with colossal figures of dragons, infernal fiends, and other horrid forms, which hold in their monstrous talons, mysterious, cabalistical sentences, inscribed on tables of brass; with preparations that yield a constant flame; serving at once to guide and to astonish the passenger: from time to time he is surprised with repeated shocks of electrical impulse, with showers of artificial rain, or sudden violent gusts of wind, and instantaneous explosions of fire; the earth trembles under him, by the power of confined air; and his ears are successively struck with many different sounds, produced by the same means; some resembling the cries of men in torment; others the roaring of bulls, and howl of ferocious animals, with the yell of hounds, and the voices of hunters; others are like the mixed croaking of ravenous birds; and others imitate thunder, the raging of the sea, the explosion of cannon, the sound of trumpets, and all the noise of war.

His road then lies through lofty woods, where serpents and lizards of many beautiful sorts crawl upon the ground, and where innumerable monkeys, cats and parrots, clamber upon the trees, and intimidate him as he passes; or through flowery thickets, where he is delighted with the singing of birds, the harmony of flutes, and all kinds of soft instrumental music: sometimes, in this romantic excursion, the passenger finds himself in extensive recesses, surrounded with arbors of jessamine, vine and roses, where beauteous Tartarean damsels, in loose transparent robes, that flutter in the air, present him with rich wines, mangostans, ananas, and fruits of Quangsi; crown him with garlands of flowers, and invite him to taste the sweets of retirement, on Persian carpets, and beds of camusath skin down....

Their roads, walks and avenues, are either directed in a single straight line, twisted in a crooked one, or carried zigzag, by several straight lines, altering their course at certain points. They observe that there are few objects more strikingly great than a spacious road, planted on each side with lofty trees, and stretching in a direct line, beyond the reach of the eye; and that there are few things more variously entertaining, than a winding one, which opening gradually to the sight, discovers, at every step, a new arrangement; and although, in itself, it has not the power of raising violent emotions, yet, by bringing the passenger suddenly and unexpectedly to great or uncommon things, it occasions strong impressions of surprise and astonishment, which are more forcibly felt, as being more opposite to the tranquil pleasure enjoyed in the confined parts of the road: and, in small compositions, they find crooked directions exceedingly useful to the planter, who, by winding his walks, may give an idea of great extent, notwithstanding the narrowness of his limits.

They say that roads which are composed of repeated straight lines, altering their directions at certain points, have all the advantages both of crooked and straight ones, with other properties, peculiar to themselves. The variety and new arrangement of objects, say they, which present themselves at every change of direction, occupy the mind agreeably: their abrupt appearance occasions surprise; which, when the extent is vast, and the repetitions frequent, swells into astonishment and admiration: the incertitude of the mind where these repetitions will end, and its anxiety as the spectator approaches towards the periods, are likewise very strong impressions, preventing that state of languor into which the mind naturally sinks by dwelling long on the same objects.

42

Uvedale Price,
from *An Essay on the picturesque, as compared with the sublime and beautiful* (1794)

Chapter III

There are few words whose meaning has been less accurately determined than that of the word Picturesque..

In general, I believe, it is applied to every object, and every kind of scenery, which has been, or might be represented with good effect in painting, and that without any exclusion. But, considered as a separate character, it has never yet been accurately distinguished from the sublime and the beautiful; though as no one has ever pretended that they are synonymous, (for it is sometimes used in contradistinction to them) such a distinction must exist....

The principles of those two leading characters in nature, the sublime and the beautiful, have been fully illustrated and discriminated by a great master; but even when I first read that most original work, I felt that there were numberless objects which give great delight to the eye, and yet differ as widely from the beautiful as from the sublime. The reflections I have since been led to make have convinced me that these objects form a distinct class, and belong to what may properly be called the picturesque.

That term (as we may judge from its etymology) is applied only to objects of sight, and that indeed in so confined a manner as to be supposed merely to have a reference to the art from which it is named. I am well convinced, however, that the name and reference only are limited and uncertain, and that the qualities which make objects picturesque are not only as distinct as those which make them beautiful or sublime, but are equally extended to all our sensations, by whatever organs they are received; and that music (though it appears like a solecism) may be as truly picturesque, according to the general principles of picturesqueness, as it may be beautiful or sublime, according to those of beauty or sublimity....

In reality, the picturesque not only differs from the beautiful in those qualities Mr Burke has so justly ascribed to it, but arises from qualities the most diametrically opposite.

According to Mr Burke, one of the most essential qualities of beauty is smoothness; now, as the perfection of smoothness is absolute equality and

271

uniformity of surface, wherever that prevails there can be but little variety or intricacy; as, for instance, in smooth level banks, on a small, or in naked downs, on a large scale. Another essential quality of beauty is gradual variation; that is (to make use of Mr Burke's expression) where the lines do not vary in a sudden and broken manner, and where there is no sudden protuberance. It requires but little reflection to perceive, that the exclusion of all but flowing lines cannot promote variety; and that sudden protuberances, and lines that cross each other in a sudden and broken manner, are among the most fruitful causes of intricacy.

I am therefore persuaded, that the two opposite qualities of roughness, and of sudden variation, joined to that of irregularity, are the most efficient causes of the picturesque.

This, I think, will appear very clearly, if we take a view of those objects, both natural and artificial, that are allowed to be picturesque, and compare them with those which are as generally allowed to be beautiful.

A temple or palace of Grecian architecture in its perfect entire state, and its surface and colour smooth and even, either in painting or reality, is beautiful; in ruin it is picturesque....

Chapter IV

Picturesqueness, therefore, appears to hold a station between beauty and sublimity; and on that account, perhaps, is more frequently and more happily blended with them both than they are with each other. It is, however, perfectly distinct from either; and first, with respect to beauty, it is evident, from all that has been said, that they are founded on very opposite qualities; the one on smoothness,* the other on roughness; – the one on gradual, the other on sudden variation; – the one on ideas of youth and freshness, the other on that of age, and even of decay.

But as most of the qualities of visible beauty (excepting colour) are made known to us through the medium of another sense, the sight itself is hardly more to be attended to than the touch, in regard to all those sensations which are excited by beautiful forms; and the distinction between the beautiful and the picturesque will, perhaps, be most strongly pointed out by means of the latter sense....

These are the principal circumstances by which the picturesque is separated from the beautiful. It is equally distinct from the sublime; for though there are some qualities common to them both, yet they differ in many essential points, and proceed from very different causes. In the first place, greatness of dimension†

---

*   Baldness seems to be an exception, as there smoothness is picturesque, and not beautiful. It is, however, an exception, which, instead of weakening, confirms what I have said, and shows the constant opposition of the two characters, even where their causes appear to be confounded.

†   I would by no means lay too much stress on greatness of dimension; but what Mr Burke has observed with regard to buildings, is true of many natural objects, such as rocks, cascades, &c.; where the scale is too diminutive, no greatness of manner will give them grandeur.

is a powerful cause of the sublime; the picturesque has no connection with dimension of any kind (in which it differs from the beautiful also) and is as often found in the smallest as in the largest objects. – The sublime being founded on principles of awe and terror, never descends to any thing light or playful; the picturesque, whose characteristics are intricacy and variety, is equally adapted to the grandest and to the gayest scenery. – Infinity is one of the most efficient causes of the sublime; the boundless ocean, for that reason, inspires awful sensations: to give it picturesqueness you must destroy that cause of its sublimity; for it is on the shape and disposition of its boundaries that the picturesque in great measure must depend.

Uniformity (which is so great an enemy to the picturesque) is not only compatible with the sublime, but often the cause of it. That general equal gloom which is spread over all nature before a storm, with the stillness so nobly described by Shakespeare, is in the highest degree sublime. The picturesque requires greater variety, and does not show itself till the dreadful thunder has rent the region, has tossed the clouds into a thousand towering storms, and opened (as it were) the recesses of the sky. A blaze of light unmixed with shade, on the same principles, tends to the sublime only: Milton has placed light, in its most glorious brightness, as an inaccessible barrier round the throne of the Almighty:

> For God is light,
> And never but in unapproached light
> Dwelt from eternity.

And such is the power he has given even to its diminished splendour,

> That the brightest seraphim
> Approach not, but with both wings veil their eyes.

In one place, indeed, he has introduced very picturesque circumstances in his sublime representation of the deity; but it is of the deity in wrath, – it is when from the weakness and narrowness of our conceptions we give the names and the effects of our passions to the all-perfect Creator:

> And clouds began
> To darken all the hill, and smoke to roll
> In dusky wreaths reluctant flames, the sign
> Of wrath awak'd.

In general, however, where the glory, power, or majesty of God are represented, he has avoided that variety of form and of colouring which might take off from simple and uniform grandeur, and has encompassed the divine essence with unapproached light, or with the majesty of darkness.

Again, (if we descend to earth) a perpendicular rock of vast bulk and height, though bare and unbroken, – a deep chasm under the same circumstances, are objects that produce awful sensations; but without some variety and intricacy, either in themselves or their accompaniments, they will not be picturesque. – Lastly, a most essential difference between the two characters is, that the sublime by its solemnity takes off from the loveliness of beauty,* whereas the picturesque renders it more captivating.

According to Mr Burke, the passion caused by the great and sublime in *nature*, when those causes operate most powerfully, is astonishment; and astonishment is that state of the soul in which all its motions are suspended with some degree of horror: the sublime also, being founded on ideas of pain and terror, like them operates by stretching the fibres beyond their natural tone. The passion excited by beauty is love and complacency; it acts by relaxing the fibres somewhat below their natural tone,† and this is accompanied by an inward sense of melting and languor.

Whether this account of the effects of sublimity and beauty be strictly philosophical, has, I believe, been questioned, but whether the fibres, in such cases, are really stretched or relaxed, it presents a lively image of the sensations often produced by love and astonishment. To pursue the same train of ideas, I may add, that the effect of the picturesque is curiosity; an effect which, though less splendid and powerful, has a more general influence; it neither relaxes nor violently stretches the fibres, but by its active agency keeps them to their full tone, and thus, when mixed with either of the other characters, corrects the languor of beauty, or the horror of sublimity. But as the nature of every corrective must be to take off from the peculiar affect of what it is to correct, so does the picturesque when united to either of the others. It is the coquetry of nature; it makes beauty more amusing, more varied, more playful, but also, "Less winning soft, less amiably mild." Again, by its variety, its intricacy, its partial concealments, it excites that active curiosity which gives play to the mind, loosening those iron bonds with which astonishment chains up its faculties.

* Majesty and love, says the poet who had most studied the art of love, never can dwell together; and therefore Juno, whose beauty was united with majesty, had no captivating charms till she had put on the cestus; that is, till she had changed dignity for coquetry.

† I have heard this part of Mr Burke's book criticised, on a supposition that pleasure is more generally produced from the fibres being stimulated than from their being relaxed. To me it appears that Mr Burke is right with respect to that pleasure which is the effect of beauty, or whatever has an analogy to beauty, according to the principles he has laid down. No man (if we may judge from his confessions) ever felt more strongly than Rousseau both the stimulus of sensual pleasure and all the violent and rapturous emotions of passion; yet what he describes as the most exquisite enjoyment of love and beauty is clearly when the fibres are relaxed somewhat below their natural tone: *O jeunesse, si je regrette tes plaisirs, ce n'est pas pour l' heure de la jouissance, c'est pour celle qui la fuit.*

If we examine our feelings on a warm genial day, in a spot full of the softest beauties of nature, the fragrance of spring breathing around us, pleasure then seems to be our natural state; to be received, not sought after; it is the happiness of existing to sensations of delight only; we are unwilling to move, almost to think, and desire only to feel, to enjoy.

How different is that active pursuit of pleasure when the fibres are braced by a keen air in a wild romantic situation; when the activity of the body almost keeps pace with that of the mind, and eagerly scales every rocky promontory, explores every new recess. Such is the difference between the beautiful and the picturesque.

Where characters, however distinct in their nature, are perpetually mixed together in such various degrees and manners, it is not always easy to draw the exact line of separation: I think, however, we may conclude, that where an object, or a set of objects, is without smoothness or grandeur, but from its intricacy, its sudden and irregular deviations, its variety of forms, tints, and lights and shadows, is interesting to a cultivated eye, it is simply picturesque; such, for instance, are the rough banks that often enclose a byroad or a hollow lane: imagine the size of these banks and the space between them to be increased till the lane becomes a deep dell, – the coves large caverns, – the peeping stones hanging rocks, so that the whole may impress an idea of awe and grandeur; – the sublime will then be mixed with the picturesque, though the scale only, not the style of the scenery, would be changed. On the other hand, if parts of the banks were smooth and gently sloping, – or the middle space a soft close-bitten turf, – or if a gentle stream passed between them, whose clear unbroken surface reflected all their varieties, – the beautiful and the picturesque, by means of that *softness and smoothness, would then be united.

---

* Softness as well as smoothness is become by habit a visible quality, and from the same kind of sympathy is a principle of beauty in many visible objects. But as the hardest bodies are those which receive the highest polish, and consequently the highest degree of smoothness, there are a number of objects in which smoothness and softness are for that reason incompatible. The one however is not unfrequently mistaken for the other, and I have more than once heard pictures which were so smoothly finished that they looked like ivory commended for their softness.

The skin of a delicate woman is an example of softness and smoothness united; but if by art a higher polish is given to the skin, the softness and (in that case I may say) the beauty is destroyed....

43

William Marshall,
from *A review of The Landscape, a didactic poem* (1795)

Sublimity. This attribute of objects of sight seldom occurs on the face of nature, in its natural state, comparatively with most of those which have been enumerated. Mountain scenery, how grand or magnificent it may be, is not, on that account, the more sublime; an extent of water, though wide as the sea itself, will not admit of the epithet, while it remains in a calm, unagitated state; any more than will an extent of country covered with snow; unless the idea of unbounded space raise it in some degree: but how infinitely more is this idea capable of exciting it, in viewing space itself, – in beholding the universe, – in looking towards infinity!

The sublime seems to require that the higher degrees of astonishment should be roused, to demonstrate its presence: a degree of terror, if not of horror, is required to produce the more forcible emotions of the mind, which sublimity is capable of exciting.

A giant precipice, frowning over its base, whether we view it from beneath, or look downward from its brink, is capable of producing sublime emotions. A river tumbling headlong over such a precipice, especially if it be viewed with difficulty and a degree of danger, real or imaginary, still heightens those emotions. Lightning, thunder, and hurricanes may produce them.

But, of all natural scenery, the ocean, agitated by a violent storm, attended with thunder and lightning, is perhaps the most capable of filling the mind with sublime emotions, and most especially the mind of a spectator who is himself exposed on its frail surface; and who is not incapable, either from constant habit, or from an excess of apprehension, of contemplating the scenery which surrounds him.

On the whole, *sublimity* must rouse some extraordinary emotion in the mind; it cannot be dwelt on with indifference, by an eye unhabituated to its effects, and a mind possessing the least sensibility. *Magnificence, grandeur, or simple greatness*, may excite some degree of astonishment; but it must be unmixed with awe; the emotions they excite are of the more pleasurable kind. *Ugliness* disgusts; yet when *adorned*, it is capable of giving delight; as a contrast to the more rational gratifications of *ornamented beauty*. All that *simple beauty* has to bestow is pleasure, heightened, perhaps, by a degree of admiration. Even *simplicity*, in a state of polished neatness, is capable of giving a degree of pleasure; but, in a state of slovenliness and neglect, it disgusts, as ugliness, or *deformity*, which is simplicity, or beauty, disgustingly defaced.

44

William Godwin,
from *The history of the life of*
William Pitt, Earl of Chatham (1783)

But the eloquence of Lord Chatham was one of his most striking characteristics. *He far outstripped his competitors, and stood alone, the rival of antiquity.* When he took his place in parliament, it has been observed, by a celebrated writer, that there were half a dozen speakers, in both houses, who, in the judgment of the public, had reached nearly the same pitch of eloquence. Voltaire represents them, as rivalling, or surpassing the greatest orators of Greece and Rome. But the equality of their fame has justly been considered, as an unanswerable argument, against this supposition. In an art, which is either necessarily, or casually, in a state of mediocrity, twenty workmen will perform equally well; but, where true eminence has been reached, the comparative merit of the artists will be no longer doubtful. And indeed, how cold and jejune, in a poetical view, do the harangues of a Wyndham, or a Pulteney appear? But neither of these objections can be urged against Lord Chatham. He has tropes and sallies, that may justly vie, with the noblest flights of antiquity. And he certainly leaves his coadjutors, as far behind him, as ever did a Cicero, or a Demosthenes.

His eloquence was of every kind. No man excelled him, in close argument, and methodical deduction. But this was not the style, into which he naturally fell. His oratory was unlaboured and spontaneous. He rushed, at once, upon his subject; and usually illustrated it, rather by glowing language, and original conception, than by cool reasoning. His person was tall and dignified. His face was the face of an eagle. His piercing eye withered the nerves, and looked through the souls of his opponents. His countenance was stern, and the voice of thunder sat upon his lips. Anon however, he could descend to the easy and the playful. His voice seemed scarcely more adapted, to energy, and to terror; than it did, to the melodious, the insinuating, and the sportive. If however, in the enthusiasm of admiration, we can find room, for the frigidity of criticism; his action seemed the most open to objection. It was forcible, uniform, and ungraceful. In a word, the most celebrated orators of antiquity, were, in a great measure, the children of labour and cultivation. Lord Chatham was always natural and himself. And perhaps action, in order to be various and beautiful, is, of all the accomplishments of an orator, that, which most requires the support of art.

To the misfortune of the republic of letters, and of posterity, Lord Chatham never sought the press. How easy had it then been, to have refuted those elegant critics, who have thought proper, to tell us, that his language was incorrect, and his orations immethodical and superficial? How indisputably had he then taken his place, in the roll of immortality, with a Demosthenes, and a Cicero? But he voluntarily submitted, in a great measure, to that evanescent fame, as a speaker; which was the inevitable misfortune, of his excellent contemporary, Mr. Garrick, as an actor. Posterity will hardly be persuaded, that, in the meagreness of modern times, a Demosthenes should have existed, without his Æschines; and a Cicero, without an Hortensius and a Cæsar. Posterity will hardly be persuaded, that one man could have concentred the arduous characters of the greatest statesman, and the most accomplished rhetorician, that ever lived. In a word, posterity will, with difficulty, believe the felicity of Britain: that Lord Chatham was, among the orators, what Shakespear is, among the poets of every age. "The child of fancy, he warbled the irregular notes, that nature gave," with so sweet a grace; as turned the cheek of envy pale, and drove refinement, and trammelled science, into coward flight. Honeyed music dropped unbidden from his lips. Had he, like his great predecessor, addressed his effusions, to the troubled waves; the troubled waves had suspended themselves to listen. His lips were clothed, with inspiration and prophecy. Sublimity, upon his tongue, sat, so enveloped in beauty, that it seemed, unconscious of itself. It fell upon unexpected. it took us by surprise, and, like the fearful whirlpool, it drew every understanding, and every heart, into it's vortex....

45

William Godwin,
from *Enquiry concerning political justice* (1798)

Book IV. Of the operation of opinion in societies and individuals
Chapter V. Of the cultivation of truth

...In the discovery and knowledge of truth seems to be comprised, for the most part, all that an impartial and reflecting mind is accustomed to admire. No one is ignorant of the pleasures of knowledge. In human life there must be a distribution of time, and a variety of occupations. Now there is perhaps no occupation so much at our command, no pleasure of the means of which we are so little likely to be deprived, as that which is intellectual. Sublime and expansive ideas produce delicious emotions. The acquisition of truth, the perception of the regularity with which proposition flows out of proportion, and one step of science leads to another, has never failed to reward the man who engaged in this species of employment. Knowledge contributes two ways to our happiness: first by the new sources of enjoyment which it opens upon us, and next by furnishing us with a clue in the selection of all other pleasures. No well informed man can seriously doubt of the advantages with respect to happiness, of a capacious and improved intellect, over the limited conceptions of a brute. Virtuous sentiments are another source of personal pleasure, and that of a more exquisite kind than intellectual improvements. But virtue itself depends for its value upon the energies of intellect. If the beings we are capable of benefiting were susceptible of nothing more than brutes are, we should have little pleasure in benefiting them, or in contemplating their happiness. But man has so many enjoyments, is capable of so high a degree of perfection, of exhibiting, socially considered, so admirable a spectacle, and of himself so truly estimating and savouring the spectacle, that, when we are engaged in promoting his benefit, we are indeed engaged in a sublime and ravishing employment. This is the case, whether our exertions are directed to the advantage of the species, or the individual. We rejoice when we save an ordinary man from destruction, more than when we save a brute, because we recollect how much more he can feel, and how much more he can do. The same principle produces a still higher degree of congratulation, in proportion as the man we save is more highly accomplished in talents and virtues.

Secondly, truth conduces to our improvement in virtue. Virtue, in its purest and most liberal sense, supposes an extensive survey of causes and their consequences, that, having struck a just balance between the benefits and injuries that adhere to human affairs, we may adopt the proceeding which leads to the greatest practicable advantage. Virtue, like every other endowment of man, admits of degrees. He therefore must be confessed to be most virtuous, who chooses with the soundest judgment the greatest and most universal over-balance of pleasure. But, in order to choose the greatest and most excellent pleasures, he must be intimately acquainted with the nature of man, its general features and its varieties. In order to forward the object he has chosen, he must have considered the different instruments for impressing mind, and the modes of applying them, and must know the properest moment for bringing them into action. In whatever light we consider virtue, whether we place it in the act or the disposition, its degree must be intimately connected with the degree of knowledge. No man can so much as love virtue sufficiently, who has not an acute and lively perception of its beauty, and its tendency to produce the most solid and permanent happiness....

We shall be more fully aware of the connection between virtue and knowledge, if we consider that the highest employment of virtue is to propagate itself. Virtue alone deserves to be considered as leading to true happiness, the happiness which is most solid and durable. Sensual pleasures are momentary; they fill a very short portion of our time with enjoyment, and leave long intervals of painful vacuity. They charm principally by their novelty; by repetition they first abate of their poignancy, and at last become little less than wearisome. It is perhaps partly to be ascribed to the high estimation in which sensual pleasures are held, that old age is so early and regular in its ravages. Our taste for these pleasures necessarily declines; with our taste our activity; and with our activity gradually crumble away the cheerfulness, the energy, and the lives, of those whose dependence was placed upon these resources. Even knowledge, and the enlargement of intellect, are poor, when unmixed with sentiments of benevolence and sympathy. Emotions are scarcely ever thrilling and electrical, without something of social feeling. When the mind expands in works of taste and imagination, it will usually be found that there is something moral in the cause which gives birth to this expansion; and science and abstraction will soon become cold, unless they derive new attractions from ideas of society. In proportion therefore to the virtue of the individual, will be the permanence of his cheerfulness, and the exquisiteness of his emotions. Add to which, benevolence is a resource which is never exhausted; but on the contrary, the more habitual are our patriotism and philanthropy, the more will they become invigorating and ardent.

It is also impossible that any situation can occur in which virtue cannot find room to expatiate. In society there is continual opportunity for its active employment. I cannot have intercourse with a human being, who may not be the better for that intercourse. If he be already just and virtuous, these qualities are improved by communication. If he be imperfect and erroneous, there must always be some prejudice I may contribute to destroy, some motive to delineate, some error to remove. If I be prejudiced and imperfect myself, it cannot however happen that my prejudices and imperfections shall be exactly coincident with his. I may therefore inform him of the truths that I know, and, even by the collision of prejudices, truth is elicited. It is impossible that I should strenuously apply myself to his improvement with sincere motives of benevolence, without some good being the result. Nor am I more at a loss in solitude. In solitude I may accumulate the materials of social benefit. No situation can be so desperate as to preclude these efforts. Voltaire, when shut up in the Bastille, and for aught he knew for life, deprived of the means either of writing or reading, arranged and in part executed the project of his Henriade.

All these reasonings are calculated to persuade us that the most precious boon we can bestow upon others is virtue, and that the highest employment of virtue is to propagate itself. But, as virtue is inseparably connected with knowledge in my own mind, so by knowledge only can it be imparted to others. How can the virtue we have just been contemplating be produced, but by infusing comprehensive views, and communicating energetic truths? Now that man alone is qualified to infuse these views, and communicate these truths, who is himself pervaded with them.

Let us suppose for a moment virtuous dispositions existing without knowledge or outrunning knowledge, the last of which is certainly possible; and we shall presently find how little such virtue is worthy to be propagated. The most generous views will, in such cases, frequently lead to the most nefarious actions. A Cranmer will be incited to the burning of heretics, and a Digby contrive the Gunpowder Treason. But, to leave these extreme instances: in all cases where mistaken virtue leads to cruel and tyrannical actions, the mind will be rendered discontented and morose by the actions it perpetrates. Truth, immortal and ever present truth is so powerful, that, in spite of all his prejudices, the upright man will suspect himself, when he resolves upon an action that is at war with the plainest principles of morality. He will become melancholy, dissatisfied and anxious. His firmness will degenerate into obstinacy, and his justice into inexorable severity. The further he pursues his system, the more erroneous will he become. The further he pursues it, the less will he be satisfied with it. As truth is an endless source of tranquillity and delight, error will be a prolific fountain of new mistakes and discontent.

As to the third point, which is most essential to the enquiry in which we are engaged, the tendency of truth to the improvement of our political institutions, there can be little room for scepticism or controversy. If politics be a science, investigation must be the means of unfolding it. If men resemble each other in more numerous and essential particulars than those in which they differ, if the best purposes that can be accomplished respecting them, be to make them free, virtuous and wise, there must be one best method of advancing these common purposes, one best mode of social existence deducible from the principles of their nature. If truth be one, there must be one code of truths on the subject of our reciprocal duties. Nor is investigation only the best mode of ascertaining the principles of political justice and happiness; it is also the best mode of introducing and establishing them. Discussion is the path that leads to discovery and demonstration. Motives ferment in the minds of great bodies of men, till their modes of society experience a variation, not less memorable than the variation of their sentiments. The more familiar the mind becomes with the ideas of which these motives consist, and the propositions that express them, the more irresistibly is it propelled to a general system of proceeding in correspondence with them.

Of the connection between understanding and virtue

...Thus far we have only been considering how impossible it is that eminent virtue should exist in a weak understanding; and it is surprising that such a proposition should ever have been contested. It is a curious question to examine, how far the converse of this proposition is true, and in what degree eminent talents are compatible with the absence of virtue.

From the arguments already adduced, it appears that virtuous desire is wholly inseparable from a strong and vivid perception of the nature and value of the object of virtue. Hence it seems most natural to conclude, that, though understanding, or strong percipient power, is the indispensible prerequisite of virtue, yet it is necessary that this power should be exercised upon this object, in order to its producing the desired effect. Thus it is in art. Without genius no man ever was a poet; but it is necessary that general capacity should have been directed to this particular channel, for poetical excellence to be the result.

There is however some difference between the two cases. Poetry is the business of a few, virtue and vice are the affair of all men. To every intellect that exists, one or other of these qualities must properly belong. It must be granted that, where every other circumstance is equal, that man will be most virtuous, whose understanding has been most actively employed in the study of virtue. But morality has been, in a certain degree, an object of attention to all men. No person ever failed, more or less, to apply the standard of just and unjust to his own actions and those of others; and this has, of course, been generally done with most ingenuity by men of the greatest capacity.

It must further be remembered, that a vicious conduct is always the result of narrow views. A man of powerful capacity, and extensive observation, is least likely to commit the mistake, either of feeling himself as the only object of importance in the universe, or of conceiving that his own advantage may best be promoted by trampling on that of others. Liberal accomplishments are surely, in some degree, connected with liberal principles. He, who takes into his view a whole nation, as the subjects of his operation, or the instruments of his greatness, may be expected to entertain some kindness for the whole. He, whose mind is habitually elevated to magnificent conceptions, is not likely to sink, without strong reluctance, into those sordid pursuits, which engross so large a portion of mankind.

But, though these general maxims must be admitted for true, and would incline us to hope for a constant union between eminent talents and great virtues, there are other considerations which present a strong drawback upon so agreeable an expectation. It is sufficiently evident that morality, in some degree, enters into the reflections of all mankind. But it is equally evident, that it may enter for more or for less; and that there will be men of the highest talents, who have their attention diverted to other objects, and by whom it will be meditated upon with less earnestness, than it may sometimes be by other men, who are, in a general view, their inferiors. The human mind is in some cases so tenacious of its errors, and so ingenious in the invention of a sophistry by which they may be vindicated, as to frustrate expectations of virtue, in other respects, the best founded.

From the whole of the subject it seems to appear, that men of talents, even when they are erroneous, are not destitute of virtue, and that there is a fulness of guilt of which they are incapable. There is no ingredient that so essentially contributes to a virtuous character, as a sense of justice. Philanthropy, as contradistinguished to justice, is rather an unreflecting feeling, than a rational principle. It leads to an absurd indulgence, which is frequently more injurious, than beneficial, even to the individual it proposes to favour. It leads to a blind partiality, inflicting calamity, without remorse, upon many perhaps, in order to promote the imagined interest of a few. But justice measures by one unalterable standard the claims of all, weighs their opposite pretensions, and seeks to diffuse happiness, because happiness is the fit and proper condition of a conscious being. Wherever therefore a strong sense of justice exists, it is common and reasonable to say, that in that mind exists considerable virtue, though the individual, from an unfortunate concurrence of circumstances, may, with all his great qualities, be the instrument of a very final portion of benefit. Can great intellectual power exist, without a strong sense of justice?

It has no doubt resulted from a train of speculation similar to this, that poetical readers have commonly remarked Milton's devil to be a being of considerable virtue. It must be admitted that his energies centred too much in personal regards. But why did he rebel against his maker? It was, as he himself informs us, because he saw no sufficient reason, for that extreme inequality of rank and power, which the creator assumed. It was because prescription and precedent form no adequate ground for implicit faith. After his fall, why did he still cherish the spirit of opposition? From a persuasion that he was hardly and injuriously treated. He was not discouraged by the apparent inequality of the contest: because a sense of reason and justice was stronger in his mind, than a sense of brute force; because he had much of the feelings of an Epictetus or a Cato, and little of those of a slave. He bore his torments with fortitude, because he disdained to be subdued by despotic power. He sought revenge, because he could not think with tameness of the unexpostulating authority that assumed to dispose of him. How beneficial and illustrious might the temper from which these qualities flowed, have been found, with a small diversity of situation!

Let us descend from these imaginary existences to real history. We shall find that even Cæsar and Alexander had their virtues. There is great reason to believe that, however, mistaken was their system of conduct, they imagined it reconcilable, and even conducive, to the general interest. If they had desired the general good more earnestly, they would have understood better how to promote it.

Upon the whole it appears, that great talents are great energies, and that great energies cannot flow but from a powerful sense of fitness and justice. A man of uncommon genius, is a man of high passions and lofty design; and our passions will be found, in the last analysis, to have their surest foundation in a sentiment of justice. If a man be of an aspiring and ambitious temper, it is because at present he finds himself out of his place, and wishes to be in it. Even the lover imagines, that his qualities, or his passion, give him a title superior to that of other men. If I accumulate wealth, it is because I think that the most rational plan of life cannot be secured without it; and, if I dedicate my energies to sensual pleasures, it is that I regard other pursuits as irrational and visionary. All our passions would die in the moment they were conceived were it not for this reinforcement. A man of quick resentment, of strong feelings, and who pertinaciously resists every thing that he regards as an unjust assumption, may be considered as having in him the seeds of eminence. Nor is it easily to be conceived, that such a man should not proceed, from a sense of justice, to some degree of benevolence; as Milton's hero felt real compassion and sympathy for his partners in misfortune....

46

Edmund Burke,
from *Reflections on the revolution in France* (1790)

History will record, that on the morning of the 6th of October 1789, the king and queen of France, after a day of confusion, alarm, dismay, and slaughter, lay down, under the pledged security of public faith, to indulge nature in a few hours of respite, and troubled melancholy repose. From this sleep the queen was first startled by the voice of the centinel at her door, who cried out to her, to save herself by flight – that this was the last proof of fidelity he could give – that they were upon him, and he was dead. Instantly he was cut down. A band of cruel ruffians and assassins, reeking with his blood, rushed into the chamber of the queen, and pierced with an hundred strokes of bayonets and poniards: the bed, from whence this persecuted woman had but just time to fly almost naked, and through ways unknown to the murderers had escaped to seek refuge at the feet of a king and husband, not secure in his own life for a moment.

This king, to say no more of him, and this queen, and their infant children (who once would have been the pride and hope of a great and generous people) were then forced to abandon the sanctuary of the most splendid palace in the world, which they left swimming in blood, polluted by massacre, and strewed with scattered limbs and mutilated carcasses. Thence they were conducted into the capital of their kingdom. Two had been selected from the unprovoked, unresisted, promiscuous slaughter, which was made of the gentlemen of birth and family who composed the king's body guard. These two gentlemen, with all the parade of an execution of justice, were cruelly and publicly dragged to the block, and beheaded in the great court of the palace. Their heads were stuck upon spears, and led the procession; whilst the royal captives who followed in the train were slowly moved along, amidst the horrid yells, and shrilling screams, and frantic dances, and infamous contumelies, and all the unutterable abominations of the furies of hell, in the abused shape of the vilest of women. After they had been made to taste, drop by drop, more than the bitterness of death, in the slow torture of a journey of twelve miles, protracted to six hours, they were, under a guard, composed of those very soldiers who had thus conducted them through this famous triumph, lodged in one of the old palaces of Paris, now converted into a Bastille for kings.

Is this a triumph to be consecrated at altars? to be commemorated with grateful thanksgiving? to be offered to the divine humanity with fervent prayer and enthusiastic ejaculation? – These Theban and Thracian Orgies, acted in France, and applauded only in the Old Jewry, I assure you, kindle prophetic enthusiasm in the minds but of very few people in this kingdom; although a saint and apostle, who may have revelations of his own, and who has so completely vanquished all the mean superstitions of the heart, may incline to think it pious and decorous to compare it with the entrance into the world of the Prince of Peace, proclaimed in an holy temple by a venerable sage, and not long before not worse announced by the voice of angels to the quiet innocence of shepherds.

At first I was at a loss to account for this fit of unguarded transport. I knew, indeed, that the sufferings of monarchs make a delicious repast to some sort of palates. There were reflections which might serve to keep this appetite within some bounds of temperance. But when I took one circumstance into my consideration, I was obliged to confess, that much allowance ought to be made for the Society, and that the temptation was too strong for common discretion; I mean, the circumstance of the Io Pæan of the triumph, the animating cry which called "for *all* the Bishops to be hanged on the lamp-posts," might well have brought forth a burst of enthusiasm on the foreseen consequences of this happy day. I allow to so much enthusiasm some little deviation from prudence. I allow this prophet to break forth into hymns of joy and thanksgiving on an event which appears like the precursor of the Millennium, and the projected fifth monarchy, in the destruction of all church establishments. There was, however (as in all human affairs there is) in the midst of this joy something to exercise the patience of these worthy gentlemen, and to try the long-suffering of their faith. The actual murder of the king and queen, and their child, was wanting to the other auspicious circumstances of this *"beautiful day."* The actual murder of the bishops, though called for by so many holy ejaculations, was also wanting. A group of regicide and sacrilegious slaughter, was indeed boldly sketched, but it was only sketched. It unhappily was left unfinished, in this great history-piece of the massacre of innocents. What hardy pencil of a great master, from the school of the rights of men, will finish it, is to be seen hereafter. The age has not yet the complete benefit of that diffusion of knowledge that has undermined superstition and error; and the king of France wants another object or two, to consign to oblivion, in consideration of all the good which is to arise from his own sufferings, and the patriotic crimes of an enlightened age.

Although this work of our new light and knowledge, did not go to the length, that in all probability it was intended it should be carried; yet I must think, that such treatment of any human creatures must be shocking to any but those who are made for accomplishing Revolutions. But I cannot stop here. Influenced by the inborn feelings of my nature, and not being illuminated by a single ray of this new-sprung modern light, I confess to you, Sir, that the exalted rank of the persons suffering, and particularly of the sex, the beauty, and the amiable qualities of the descendant of so many kings and emperors, with the tender age of royal infants, insensible only through infancy and innocence of the cruel outrages to which their parents were exposed, instead of being a subject of exultation, adds not a little to my sensibility on that most melancholy occasion.

I hear that the august person, who was the principal object of our preacher's triumph, though he supported himself, felt much on that shameful occasion. As a man, it became him to feel for his wife and his children, and the faithful guards of his person, that were massacred in cold blood about him; as a prince, it became him to feel for the strange and frightful transformation of his civilised subjects, and to be more grieved for them, than solicitous for himself. It derogates little from his fortitude, while it adds infinitely to the honour of his humanity. I am very sorry to say it, very sorry indeed, that such personages are in a situation in which it is not unbecoming in us to praise the virtues of the great.

I hear, and I rejoice to hear, that the great lady, the other object of the triumph, has borne that day (one is interested that beings made for suffering should suffer well) and that she bears all the succeeding days, that she bears the imprisonment of her husband, and her own captivity, and the exile of her friends, and the insulting adulation of addresses, and the whole weight of her accumulated wrongs, with a serene patience, in a manner suited to her rank and race, and becoming the offspring of a sovereign distinguished for her piety and her courage; that like her she has lofty sentiments; that she feels with the dignity of a Roman matron; that in the last extremity she will save herself from the last disgrace, and that if she must fall, she will fall by no ignoble hand.

It is now sixteen or seventeen years since I saw the queen of France, then the dauphiness, at Versailles; and surely never lighted on this orb, which she hardly seemed to touch, a more delightful vision. I saw her just above the horizon, decorating and cheering the elevated sphere she just began to move in, – glittering like the morning-star, full of life, and splendour, and joy. Oh! what a revolution! and what an heart must I have, to contemplate without emotion that elevation and that fall! Little did I dream that, when she added titles of veneration to those of enthusiastic, distant, respectful love, that she should ever be obliged to carry the sharp antidote against disgrace concealed in that bosom; little did I dream that I should have lived to see such disasters fallen upon her in a nation of gallant men, in a nation of men of honour and of cavaliers. I thought ten thousand swords must have leaped from their scabbards to avenge even a look that threatened her with insult. – But the age of chivalry is gone. – That of sophisters, economists, and calculators, has succeeded; and the glory of Europe is extinguished for ever. Never, never more, shall we behold that generous loyalty to rank and sex, that proud submission, that dignified obedience, that subordination of the heart, which kept alive, even in servitude itself, the spirit of an exalted freedom. The unbought grace of life, the cheap defence of nations, the nurse of manly sentiment and heroic enterprise is gone! It is gone, that sensibility of principle, that chastity of honour, which felt a stain like a wound, which inspired courage whilst it mitigated ferocity, which ennobled whatever it touched, and under which vice itself lost half its evil, by losing all its grossness.

This mixed system of opinion and sentiment had its origin in the ancient chivalry; and the principle, though varied in its appearance by the varying state of human affairs, subsisted and influenced through a long succession of generations, even to the time we live in. If it should ever be totally extinguished, the loss I fear will be great. It is this which has given its character to modern Europe. It is this which has distinguished it under all its forms of government, and distinguished it to its advantage, from the states of Asia, and possibly from those states which flourished in the most brilliant periods of the antique world. It was this, which, without confounding ranks, had produced a noble equality, and handed it down through all the gradations of social life. It was this opinion which mitigated kings into companions, and raised private men to be fellows with kings. Without force, or opposition, it subdued the fierceness of pride and power; it obliged sovereigns to submit to the soft collar of social esteem, compelled stern authority to submit to elegance, and gave a domination vanquisher of laws, to be subdued by manners.

But now all is to be changed. All the pleasing illusions, which made power gentle, and obedience liberal, which harmonised the different shades of life, and which, by a bland assimilation, incorporated into politics the sentiments which beautify and soften private society, are to be dissolved by this new conquering empire of light and reason. All the decent drapery of life is to be rudely torn off. All the superadded ideas, furnished from the wardrobe of a moral imagination, which the heart owns, and the understanding ratifies, as necessary to cover the defects of our naked shivering nature, and to raise it to dignity in our own estimation, are to be exploded as a ridiculous, absurd, and antiquated fashion.

On this scheme of things, a king is but a man; a queen is but a woman; a woman is but an animal; and an animal not of the highest order. All homage paid to the sex in general as such, and without distinct views, is to be regarded as romance and folly. Regicide, and parricide, and sacrilege, are but fictions of superstition, corrupting jurisprudence by destoying its simplicity. The murder of a king, or a queen, or a bishop, or a father, are only common homicide; and if the people are by any chance, or in any way gainers by it, a sort of homicide much the most pardonable, and into which we ought not to make too severe a scrutiny.

On the scheme of this barbarous philosophy, which is the offspring of cold hearts and muddy understandings, and which is as void of solid wisdom, as it is destitute of all taste and elegance, laws are to be supported only by their own terrors, and by the concern, which each individual may find in them, from his own private speculations, or can spare to them from his own private interests. In the groves of *their* academy, at the end of every visto, you see nothing but the gallows. Nothing is left which engages the affections on the part of the commonwealth. On the principles of this mechanic philosophy, our institutions can never be embodied, if I may use the expression, in persons; so as to create in us love, veneration, admiration, or attachment. But that sort of reason which banishes the affections is incapable of filling their place. These public affections, combined with manners, are required sometimes as supplements, sometimes as correctives, always as aids to law. The precept given by a wise man, as well as a great critic, for the construction of poems, is equally true as to states. *Non satis est pulchra esse poemata, dulcia sunto.* There ought to be a system of manners in every nation which a well-informed mind would be disposed to relish. To make us love our country, our country ought to be lovely.

But power, of some kind or other, will survive the shock in which manners and opinions perish; and it will find other and worse means for its support. The usurpation which, in order to subvert ancient institutions, has destroyed ancient principles, will hold power by arts similar to those by which it has acquired it. When the old feudal and chivalrous spirit of *fealty*, which, by freeing kings from fear, freed both kings and subjects from the precautions of tyranny, shall be extinct in the minds of men, plots and assassinations will be anticipated by preventive murder and preventive confiscation, and that long roll of grim and bloody maxims, which form the political code of all power, not standing on its own honour, and the honour of those who are to obey it. Kings will be tyrants from policy when subjects are rebels from principle....

It is not clear, whether in England we learned those grand and decorous principles, and manners, of which considerable traces yet remain, from you, or whether you took them from us. But to you, I think, we trace them best. You seem to me to be – *gentis incunabula nostræ.* France has always more or less influenced manners in England; and when your fountain is choked up and polluted, the stream will not run long, or not run clear with us, or perhaps with any nation. This gives all Europe, in my opinion, but too close and connected a concern in what is done in France. Excuse me, therefore, if I have dwelt too long on the atrocious spectacle of the sixth of October 1789, or have given too much scope to the reflections which have arisen in my mind on occasion of the most important of all revolutions, which may be dated from that day, I mean a revolution in sentiments, manners, and moral opinions. As things now stand, with every thing respectable destroyed without us, and an attempt to destroy within us every principle of respect, one is almost forced to apologise for harbouring the common feelings of men.

Why do I feel so differently from the Reverend Dr Price, and those of his lay flock, who will choose to adopt the sentiments of his discourse? – For this plain reason – because it is *natural* I should; because we are so made as to be affected at such spectacles with melancholy sentiments upon the unstable condition of moral prosperity, and, the tremendous uncertainty of human greatness; because in those natural feelings we learn great lessons; because in events like these our passions instruct our reason; because when kings are hurl'd from their thrones by the Supreme Director of this great drama, and become the objects of insult to the base, and of pity to the good, we behold such disasters in the moral, as we should behold a miracle in the physical order of things. We are alarmed into reflection; our minds (as it has long since been observed) are purified by terror and pity; our weak unthinking pride is humbled, under the dispensations of a mysterious wisdom. – Some tears might be drawn from me, if such a spectacle were exhibited on the stage. I should be truly ashamed of finding in myself that superficial, theatric sense of painted distress, whilst I could exult over it in real life. With such a perverted mind, I could never venture to show my face at a tragedy. People would think the tears that Garrick formerly, or that Siddons not long since, have extorted from me, were the tears of hypocrisy; I should know them to be the tears of folly.

Indeed the theatre is a better school of moral sentiments than churches, where the feelings of humanity are thus outraged. Poets, who have to deal with an audience not yet graduated in the school of the rights of men, and who must apply themselves to the moral constitution of the heart, would not dare to produce such a triumph as a matter of exultation. There, where men follow their natural impulses, they would not bear the odious maxims of a Machiavellian policy, whether applied to the attainment of monarchical or democratic tyranny. They would reject them on the modern, as they once did on the ancient stage, where they could not bear even the hypothetical proposition of such wickedness in the mouth of a personated tyrant, though suitable to the character he sustained. No theatric audience in Athens would bear what has been borne, in the midst of the real tragedy of this triumphal day; a principal actor weighing, as it were in scales hung in a shop of horrors, – so much actual crime against so much contingent advantage, – and after putting in and out weights, declaring that the balance was on the side of the advantages. They would not bear to see the crimes of new democracy posted as in a ledger against the crimes of old despotism, and the book-keepers of politics finding democracy still in debt, but by no means unable or unwilling to pay the balance. In the theatre, the first intuitive glance, without any elaborate process of reasoning, would show, that this method of political computation, would justify every extent of crime. They would see, that on these principles, even where the very worst acts were not perpetrated, it was owing rather to the fortune of the conspirators than to their parsimony in the expenditure of treachery and blood. They would soon see, that criminal means once tolerated are soon preferred. They present a shorter cut to the object than through the highway of the moral virtues. Justifying perfidy and murder for public benefit, public benefit would soon become the pretext, and perfidy and murder the end; until rapacity, malice, revenge, and fear more dreadful than revenge, could satiate their insatiable appetites. Such must be the consequences of losing in the splendour of these triumphs of the rights of men, all natural sense of wrong and right.

47

Edmund Burke,
from *A letter from the right honourable Edmund Burke to a noble Lord* (1796)

My Lord, it is a subject of aweful meditation. Before this of France, the annals of all time have not furnished an instance of a *complete* revolution. That revolution seems to have extended even to the constitution of the mind of man. It has this of wonderful in it, that it resembles what Lord Verulam says of the operations of nature: It was perfect, not only in all its elements and principles, but in all its members and its organs from the very beginning. The moral scheme of France furnishes the only pattern ever known, which they who admire will *instantly* resemble. It is indeed an inexhaustible repertory of one kind of example. In my wretched condition, though hardly to be classed with the living, I am not safe from them. They have tigers to fall upon animated strength. They have hyenas to prey upon carcasses. The national menagerie is collected by the first physiologists of the time; and it is defective in no description of savage nature. They pursue, even such as me, into the obscurest retreats, and haul them before their revolutionary tribunals. Neither sex, nor age – not the sanctuary of the tomb is sacred to them. They have so determined a hatred to all privileged orders, that they deny even to the departed, the sad immunities of the grave. They are not wholly without an object. Their turpitude purveys to their malice; and they unplumb the dead for bullets to assassinate the living. If all revolutionists were not proof against all caution, I should recommend it to their consideration, that no persons were ever known in history, either sacred or profane, to vex the sepulchre, and by their sorceries, to call up the prophetic dead, with any other event, than the prediction of their own disastrous fate. — "Leave me, oh leave me to repose!"...

...I knew that there is a manifest marked distinction, which ill men, with ill designs, or weak men incapable of any design, will constantly be confounding, that is, a marked distinction between Change and Reformation. The former alters the substance of the objects themselves; and gets rid of all their essential good, as well as of all the accidental evil annexed to them. Change is novelty; and whether it is to operate any one of the effects of reformation at all, or whether it may not contradict the very principle upon which reformation is desired, cannot be certainly known beforehand. Reform is, not a change in the substance, or in the primary modification of the object, but a direct application of a remedy to the grievance complained of. So far as that is removed, all is sure. It stops there; and if it fails, the substance which underwent the operation, at the very worst, is but where it was.

All this, in effect, I think, but am not sure, I have said elsewhere. It cannot at this time be too often repeated; line upon line; precept upon precept; until it comes into the currency of a proverb, *To innovate is not to reform.* The French revolutionists complained of every thing; they refused to reform any thing; and they left nothing, no, nothing at all *unchanged.* The consequences are *before* us, – not in remote history; not in future prognostication: they are about us; they are upon us. They shake the public security; they menace private enjoyment. They dwarf the growth of the young; they break the quiet of the old. If we travel, they stop our way. They infest us in town; they pursue us to the country. Our business is interrupted; our repose is troubled; our pleasures are saddened; our very studies are poisoned and perverted, and knowledge is rendered worse than ignorance, by the enormous evils of this dreadful innovation. The revolution harpies of France, sprung from night and hell, or from that chaotic anarchy, which generates equivocally "all monstrous, all prodigious things," cuckoo-like, adulterously lay their eggs, and brood over, and hatch them in the nest of every neighbouring state. These obscene harpies, who deck themselves, in I know not what divine attributes, but who in reality are foul and ravenous birds of prey (both mothers and daughters) flutter over our heads, and souse down upon our tables, and leave nothing unrent, unrifled, unravaged, or unpolluted with the slime of their filthy offal.*

If his Grace can contemplate the result of this complete innovation, or, as some friends of his will call it *reform,* in the whole body of its solidity and compound mass, at which, as Hamlet says, the face of Heaven glows with horror and indignation, and which, in truth, makes every reflecting mind, and every feeling heart, perfectly thought-sick, without a thorough abhorrence of every thing they say, and every thing they do, I am amazed at the morbid strength, or the natural infirmity of his mind.

It was then not my love, but my hatred to innovation, that produced my Plan of Reform.

---

* Tristius haud illis monstrum, nec saevior ulla
Pestis, et ira Deum Stygiis sese extulit undis,
Virginei volucrum vultus; foedissima ventris
Proluvies; uncaeque manus; et pallida semper
Ora fame.
Here the Poet breaks the line, because he (and that He is Virgil) had not verse or language to describe that monster even as he had conceived her. Had he lived to our time, he would have been more overpowered with the reality than he was with the imagination. Virgil only knew the horror of the times before him. Had he lived to see the Revolutionists and Constitutionalists of France, he would have had more horrid and disgusting features of his harpies to describe, and more frequent failures in the attempt to describe them.

48

Mary Wollstonecraft,
from *A vindication of the rights of men*
(1790)

Had you been in a philosophising mood, had your heart or your reason been at home, you might have been convinced, by ocular demonstration, that madness is only the absence of reason. – The ruling angel leaving its seat, wild anarchy ensues. You would have seen that the uncontrolled imagination often pursues the most regular course in its most daring flight; and that the eccentricities are boldly relieved when judgment no longer officiously arranges the sentiments, by bringing them to the test of principles. You would have seen every thing out of nature in that strange chaos of levity and ferocity, and of all sorts of follies jumbled together. You would have seen in that monstrous tragi-comic scene the most opposite passions necessarily succeed, and sometimes mix with each other in the mind; alternate contempt and indignation; alternate laughter and tears; alternate scorn and horror – This is a true picture of that chaotic state of mind, called madness; when reason gone, we know not where, the wild elements of passion clash, and all is horror and confusion. You might have heard the best turned conceits, flash following flash, and doubted whether the rhapsody was not eloquent, if it had not been delivered in an equivocal language, neither verse nor prose, if the sparkling periods had not stood alone, wanting force because they wanted concatenation.

It is a proverbial observation, that a very thin partition divides wit and madness. Poetry therefore naturally addresses the fancy, and the language of passion is with great felicity borrowed from the heightened picture which the imagination draws of sensible objects concentred by impassioned reflection. And, during this 'fine frenzy,' reason has no right to rein-in the imagination, unless to prevent the introduction of supernumerary images; if the passion is real, the head will not be ransacked for stale tropes and cold rodomontade. I now speak of the genuine enthusiasm of genius, which, perhaps, seldom appears, but in the infancy of civilisation; for as this light becomes more luminous reason clips the wing of fancy – the youth becomes the man.

Whether the glory of Europe is set, I shall not now enquire; but probably the spirit of romance and chivalry is in the wane; and reason will gain by its extinction.

From observing several cold romantic characters I have been led to confine the term romantic to one definition – false, or rather artificial, feelings. Works of genius are read with a prepossession in their favour, and sentiments imitated, because they were fashionable and pretty, and not because they were forcibly felt.

In modern poetry the understanding and memory often fabricate the pretended effusions of the heart, and romance destroys all simplicity; which, in works of taste, is but a synonymous word for truth. This romantic spirit has extended to our prose, and scattered artificial flowers over the most barren heath; or a mixture of verse and prose producing the strangest incongruities. The turgid bombast of some of your periods fully proves these assertions; for when the heart speaks we are seldom shocked by hyperbole, or dry raptures....

Reading your *Reflections* warily over, it has continually and forcibly struck me, that had you been a Frenchman, you would have been, in spite of your respect for rank and antiquity, a violent revolutionist; and deceived, as you now probably are, by the passions that cloud your reason, have termed your romantic enthusiasm an enlightened love of your country, a benevolent respect for the rights of men. Your imagination would have taken fire, and have found arguments, full as ingenious as those you now offer, to prove that the constitution, of which so few pillars remained, that constitution which time had almost obliterated, was not a model sufficiently noble to deserve close adherence. And, for the English constitution, you might not have had such a profound veneration as you have lately acquired; nay, it is not impossible that you might have entertained the same opinion of the English Parliament, that you professed to have during the American war.

Another observation which, by frequently occurring, has almost grown into a conviction, is simply this, that had the English in general reprobated the French revolution, you would have stood forth alone, and been the avowed Goliath of liberty. But, not liking to see so many brothers near the throne of fame, you have turned the current of your passions, and consequently of your reasoning, another way. Had Dr Price's sermon not lighted some sparks very like envy in your bosom, I shrewdly suspect that he would have been treated with more candour; nor is it charitable to suppose that any thing but personal pique and hurt vanity could have dictated such bitter sarcasms and reiterated expressions of contempt as occur in your *Reflections*.

But without fixed principles even goodness of heart is no security from inconsistency, and mild affectionate sensibility only renders a man more ingeniously cruel, when the pangs of hurt vanity are mistaken for virtuous indignation, and the gall of bitterness for the milk of Christian charity.

Where is the dignity, the infallibility of sensibility, in the fair ladies, whom, if the voice of rumour is to be credited, the captive negroes curse in all the agony of bodily pain, for the unheard of tortures they invent? It is probable that some of them, after the sight of a flagellation, compose their ruffled spirits and exercise their tender feelings by the perusal of the last imported novel. – How true these tears are to nature, I leave you to determine. But these ladies may have read your *Enquiry concerning the origin of our ideas of the Sublime and Beautiful*, and, convinced by your arguments, may have laboured to be pretty, by counterfeiting weakness.

You may have convinced them that *littleness* and *weakness* are the very essence of beauty; and that the Supreme Being, in giving women beauty in the most supereminent degree, seemed to command them, by the powerful voice of Nature, not to cultivate the moral virtues that might chance to excite respect, and interfere with the pleasing sensations they were created to inspire. Thus confining truth, fortitude, and humanity, within the rigid pale of manly morals, they might justly argue, that to be loved, woman's high end and distinction! they should "learn to lisp, to totter in their walk, and nickname God's creatures." Never, they might repeat after you, was any man, much less a woman, rendered amiable by the force of those exalted qualities, fortitude, justice, wisdom, and truth; and thus forewarned of the sacrifice they must make to those austere, unnatural virtues, they would be authorised to turn all their attention to their persons, systematically neglecting morals to secure beauty. – Some rational old woman indeed might chance to stumble at this doctrine, and hint, that in avoiding atheism you had not steered clear of the mussulman's creed; but you could readily exculpate yourself by turning the charge on Nature, who made our idea of beauty independent of reason. Nor would it be necessary for you to recollect, that if virtue has any other foundation than worldly utility, you have clearly proved that one half of the human species, at least, have not souls; and that Nature, by making women *little, smooth, delicate, fair* creatures, never designed that they should exercise their reason to acquire the virtues that produce opposite, if not contradictory, feelings. The affection they excite, to be uniform and perfect, should not be tinctured with the respect which moral virtues inspire, lest pain should be blended with pleasure, and admiration disturb the soft intimacy of love. This laxity of morals in the female world is certainly more captivating to a libertine imagination than the cold arguments of reason, that give no sex to virtue. If beautiful weakness be interwoven in a woman's frame, if the chief business of her life be (as you insinuate) to inspire love, and Nature has made an eternal distinction between the qualities that dignify a rational being and this animal perfection, her duty and happiness in this life must clash with any preparation for a more exalted state. So that Plato and Milton were grossly mistaken in asserting that human love led to heavenly, and was only an exaltation of the same affection; for the love of the Deity, which is mixed with the most profound reverence, must be love of perfection, and not compassion for weakness.

To say the truth, I not only tremble for the souls of women, but for the good natured man, whom every one loves. The *amiable* weakness of his mind is a strong argument against its immateriality, and seems to prove that beauty relaxes the *solids* of the soul as well as the body.

It follows then immediately, from your own reasoning, that respect and love are antagonist principles; and that, if we really wish to render men more virtuous, we must endeavour to banish all enervating modifications of beauty from civil society. We must, to carry your argument a little further, return to the Spartan regulations, and settle the virtues of men on the stern foundation of mortification and self-denial; for any attempt to civilise the heart, to make it humane by implanting reasonable principles, is a mere philosophic dream. If refinement inevitably lessens respect for virtue, by rendering beauty, the grand tempter, more seductive; if these relaxing feelings are incompatible with the nervous exertions of morality, the sun of Europe is not set; it begins to dawn, when cold metaphysicians try to make the head give laws to the heart.

But should experience prove that there is a beauty in virtue, a charm in order, which necessarily implies exertion, a depraved sensual taste may give way to a more manly one – and *melting* feelings to rational satisfactions. Both may be equally natural to man; the test is their moral difference, and that point reason alone can decide.

Such a glorious change can only be produced by liberty. Inequality of rank must ever impede the growth of virtue, by vitiating the mind that submits or domineers; that is ever employed to procure nourishment for the body, or amusement for the mind. And if this grand example be set by an assembly of unlettered clowns, if they can produce a crisis that may involve the fate of Europe, and 'more than Europe,' you must allow us to respect unsophisticated reason, and reverence the active exertions that were not relaxed by a fastidious respect for the beauty of rank, or a dread of the deformity produced by any *void* in the social structure....

It may be confidently asserted that no man chooses evil, because it is evil; he only mistakes it for happiness, the good he seeks. And the desire of rectifying these mistakes, is the noble ambition of an enlightened understanding, the impulse of feelings that Philosophy invigorates. To endeavour to make unhappy men resigned to their fate, is the tender endeavour of short-sighted benevolence, of transient yearnings of humanity; but to labour to increase human happiness by extirpating error, is a masculine godlike affection. This remark may be carried still further. Men who possess uncommon sensibility, whose quick emotions show how closely the eye and heart are connected, soon forget the most forcible sensations. Not tarrying long enough in the brain to be subject to reflection, the next sensations, of course, obliterate them. Memory, however, treasures up these proofs of native goodness; and the being who is not spurred on to any virtuous act, still thinks itself of consequence, and boasts of its feelings. Why? Because the sight of distress, or an affecting narrative, made its blood flow with more velocity, and the heart, literally speaking, beat with sympathetic emotion. We ought to beware of confounding mechanical instinctive sensations with emotions that reason deepens, and justly terms the feelings of *humanity*. This word discriminates the active exertions of virtue from the vague declamation of sensibility.

The declaration of the National Assembly, when they recognised the rights of men, was calculated to touch the humane heart – the downfall of the clergy

298   *Part VI: From the picturesque to the political*

clergy, to agitate the pupil of impulse. On the watch to find fault, faults met your prying eye; a different prepossession might have produced a different conviction.

When we read a book that supports our favourite opinions, how eagerly do we suck in the doctrines, and suffer our minds placidly to reflect the images that illustrate the tenets we have previously embraced. We indolently acquiesce in the conclusion, and our spirit animates and corrects the various subjects. But when, on the contrary, we peruse a skilful writer, with whom we do not coincide in opinion, how attentive is the mind to detect fallacy. And this suspicious coolness often prevents our being carried away by a stream of natural eloquence, which the prejudiced mind terms declamation – a pomp of words! We never allow ourselves to be warmed; and, after contending with the writer, are more confirmed in our opinion; as much, perhaps, from a spirit of contradiction as from reason. A lively imagination is ever in danger of being betrayed into error by favourite opinions, which it almost personifies, the more effectually to intoxicate the understanding. Always tending to extremes, truth is left behind in the heat of the chase, and things are viewed as positively good, or bad, though they wear an equivocal face.

Some celebrated writers have supposed that wit and judgment were incompatible; opposite qualities, that, in a kind of elementary strife, destroyed each other: and many men of wit have endeavoured to prove that they were mistaken. Much may be adduced by wits and metaphysicians on both sides of the question. But, from experience, I am apt to believe that they do weaken each other, and that great quickness of comprehension, and facile association of ideas, naturally preclude profundity of research. Wit is often a lucky hit; the result of a momentary inspiration. We know not whence it comes, and it blows where it lists. The operations of judgment, on the contrary, are cool and circumspect; and coolness and deliberation are great enemies to enthusiasm. If wit is of so fine a spirit, that it almost evaporates when translated into another language, why may not the temperature have an influence over it? This remark may be thought derogatory to the inferior qualities of the mind: but it is not a hasty one; and I mention it as a prelude to a conclusion I have frequently drawn, that the cultivation of reason damps fancy. The blessings of Heaven lie on each side; we must choose, if we wish to attain any degree of superiority, and not lose our lives in laborious idleness. If we mean to build our knowledge or happiness on a rational basis, we must learn to distinguish the *possible*, and not fight against the stream. And if we are careful to guard ourselves from imaginary sorrows and vain fears, we must also resign many enchanting illusions: for shallow must be the discernment which fails to discover that raptures and ecstasies arise from error. – Whether it will always be so, is not now to be discussed; suffice it to observe, that Truth is seldom arrayed by the Graces; and if she charms, it is only by inspiring a sober satisfaction, which takes its rise from a calm contemplation of proportion and simplicity. But, though it is allowed that one man has by nature more fancy than another, in each individual there is a springtide when fancy should govern and amalgamate materials for the understanding; and a graver period, when those materials should be employed by the judgment. For example, I am inclined to have a better opinion of the heart of an *old* man, who speaks of Sterne as his favourite author, than of his understanding. There are times and seasons for all things: and moralists appear to me to err, when they would confound the gaiety of youth with the seriousness of age; for the virtues of age look not only more imposing, but more natural, when they appear rather rigid. He who has not exercised his judgment to curb his imagination during the meridian of life, becomes, in its decline, too often the prey of childish feelings. Age demands respect; youth love: if this order is disturbed, the emotions are not pure; and when love for a man in his grand climacteric takes place of respect, it, generally speaking, borders on contempt. Judgment is sublime, wit beautiful; and, according to your own theory, they cannot exist together without impairing each other's power. The predominancy of the latter, in your endless Reflections, should lead hasty readers to suspect that it may, in a great degree, exclude the former.

49

Helen Maria Williams,
from *Letters written in France* (1790)

Letter II

I promised to send you a description of the federation: but it is not to be described! One must have been present, to form any judgment of a scene, the sublimity of which depended much less on its external magnificence than on the effect it produced on the minds of the spectators. "The people, sure, the people were the sight!" I may tell you of pavillions, of triumphal arches, of altars on which incense was burnt, of two hundred thousand men walking in procession; but how am I to give you an adequate idea of the behaviour of the spectators? How am I to paint the impetuous feelings of that immense, that exulting multitude? Half a million of people assembled at a spectacle, which furnished every image that can elevate the mind of man; which connected the enthusiasm of moral sentiment with the solemn pomp of religious ceremonies; which addressed itself at once to the imagination, the understanding, and the heart!...

You will not suspect that I was an indifferent witness of such a scene. Oh no! this was not a time in which the distinctions of country were remembered. It was the triumph of human kind; it was man asserting the noblest privileges of his nature; and it required but the common feelings of humanity to become in that moment a citizen of the world. For myself, I acknowledge that my heart caught with enthusiasm the general sympathy; my eyes were filled with tears; and I shall never forget the sensations of that day, "while memory holds her seat in my bosom."...

Letter IX

Yesterday I received your letter, in which you accuse me of describing with too much enthusiasm the public rejoicings in France, and prophesy that I shall return to my own country a fierce republican. In answer to these accusations, I shall only observe, that it is very difficult, with common sensibility, to avoid sympathizing in general happiness. My love of the French revolution, is the natural result of this sympathy, and therefore my political creed is entirely an affair of the heart; for I have not been so absurd as to consult my head upon matters of which it is so incapable of judging. If I were at Rome, you would not be surprised to hear that I had visited, with the warmest reverence, every spot where any relics of her ancient grandeur could be traced; that I had flown to the capitol, that I had kissed the earth on which the Roman senate sat in council: and can you then expect me to have seen the Federation at the Champ de Mars, and the National Assembly of France, with indifference? Before you insist that I ought to have done so, point out to me, in the page of Roman history, a spectacle more solemn, more affecting, than the Champ de Mars exhibited, or more magnanimous, more noble efforts in the cause of liberty than have been made by the National Assembly....

...Upon the whole, liberty appears in France adorned with the freshness of youth, and is loved with the ardour of passion. In England she is seen in her matron state, and, like other ladies at that period, is beheld with sober veneration.

With respect to myself, I must acknowledge, that, in my admiration of the revolution in France, I blend the feelings of private friendship with my sympathy in public blessings; since the old constitution is connected in my mind with the image of a friend confined in the gloomy recesses of a dungeon, and pining in hopeless captivity; while, with the new constitution, I unite the soothing idea of his return to prosperity, honours, and happiness.

Letter X

We have been driving at a furious rate, for several days past, through the city of Paris, which I think bears the same resemblance to London (if you will allow me the indulgence of a simile) that the grand natural objects in a rude and barren country bear to the tame but regular beauties of a scene rich with cultivation. The streets of Paris are narrow, dark, and dirty; but we are repaid for this by noble edifices, which powerfully interest the attention. The streets of London are broad, airy, light, and elegant; but I need not tell you that they lead scarcely to any edifices at which foreigners do not look with contempt. London has, therefore, most of the beautiful, and Paris of the sublime, according to Mr Burke's definition of these qualities; for I assure you a sensation of terror is not wanting to the sublimity of Paris, while the coachman drives through the streets with the impetuosity of a Frenchman, and one expects every step the horses take will be fatal to the foot-passengers,...who are heard exclaiming, "Que les rues de Paris sont aristocrates." By the way, *aristocracie*, and *à la nation*, are become cant terms, which, as *Sterne* said of *tant pis*, and *tant mieux*, may now be considered as two of the great hinges in French conversation. Every thing tiresome or unpleasant, "c'est une aristocracie!" and every thing charming and agreeable is, "à la nation."...

As we came out of La Maison de Ville, we were shown, immediately opposite, the far-famed lanterne,* at which, for want of a gallows, the first victims

* The lamp-iron.

of popular fury were sacrificed. I own that the sight of La Lanterne chilled the blood within my veins. At that moment, for the first time, I lamented the revolution; and, forgetting the imprudence, or the guilt, of those unfortunate men, could only reflect with horror on the dreadful expiation they had made. I painted in my imagination the agonies of their families and friends, nor could I for a considerable time chase these gloomy images from my thoughts.

It is for ever to be regretted, that so dark a shade of ferocious revenge was thrown across the glories of the revolution. But, alas! where do the records of history point out a revolution unstained by some actions of barbarity? When do the passions of human nature rise to that pitch which produces great events, without wandering into some irregularities? If the French revolution should cost no farther bloodshed, it must be allowed, notwithstanding a few shocking instances of public vengeance, that the liberty of twenty-four millions of people will have been purchased at a far cheaper rate than could ever have been expected from the former experience of the world.

Letter XXVI

...I hear of nothing but crimes, assassinations, torture, and death. I am told that every day witnesses a conspiracy; that every town is the scene of a massacre; that every street is blackened with a gallows, and every highway deluged with blood. I hear these things, and repeat to myself, is this the picture of France? Are these the images of that universal joy, which called tears into my eyes, and made my heart throb with sympathy? – To me, the land which these mighty magicians have suddenly covered with darkness, where, waving their evil wand, they have reared the dismal scaffold, have clotted the knife of the assassin with gore, have called forth the shriek of despair, and the agony of torture; to me, this land of desolation appeared dressed in additional beauty beneath the genial smile of liberty. The woods seemed to cast a more refreshing shade, and the lawns to wear a brighter verdure, while the carols of freedom burst from the cottage of the peasant, and the voice of joy resounded on the hill, and in the valley.

Must I be told that my mind is perverted, that I am become dead to all sensations of sympathy, because I do not weep with those who have lost a part of their superfluities, rather than rejoice that the oppressed are protected, that the wronged are redressed, that the captive is set at liberty, and that the poor have bread? Did the universal parent of the human race, implant the feelings of pity in the heart, that they should be confined to the artificial wants of vanity, the ideal deprivations of greatness; that they should be fixed beneath the dome of the palace, or locked within the gate of the chateau; without extending one commiserating sigh to the wretched hamlet, as if its famished inhabitants, though not ennobled by *man*, did not bear, at least, the ensigns of nobility stamped on our nature by God?...

Helen Maria Williams,
from *A tour in Switzerland* (1798)

Chapter IV

... It was not without the most powerful emotion that, for the first time, I cast my eyes on that solemn, that majestic vision, the Alps! – how often had the idea of those stupendous mountains filled my heart with enthusiastic awe! – so long, so eagerly, had I desired to contemplate that scene of wonders, that I was unable to trace when first the wish was awakened in my bosom – it seemed from childhood to have made a part of my existence – I longed to bid adieu to the gayly-peopled landscapes of Zurich, and wander amidst those regions of mysterious sublimity, the solitudes of nature, where her eternal laws seem at all seasons to forbid more than the temporary visits of man, and where, sometimes, the dangerous passes to her frozen summits are inflexibly barred against mortal footsteps. The pleasure arising from the varying forms of smiling beauty with which we were surrounded, became a cold sensation, while expectation hung upon those vast gigantic shapes, that half-seen chaos which excited the stronger feelings of wonder, mingled with admiration. But I was obliged, with whatever regret, to relinquish for the present a nearer view of those tremendous objects, since private affairs left me only sufficient leisure to visit the cataract of the Rhine before I returned to Basle; whence, however, I soothed myself with the hope of being soon able to depart in search of the terrific scenes of the Alps, and the rich luxuriant graces of the Italian valleys of Switzerland. In the mean time we passed happily through Zurich, in our way to Schaffhausen, for although I had been assured that the cataract of the Rhine was "but a fall of water," it had excited so tormenting a curiosity, that I found I should be incapable of seeing any thing else with pleasure or advantage, till I had once gazed upon that object.

When we reached the summit of the hill which leads to the fall of the Rhine, we alighted from the carriage, and walked down the steep bank, whence I saw the river rolling turbulently over its bed of rocks, and heard the noise of the torrent, towards which we were descending, increasing as we drew near. My heart swelled with expectation – our path, as if formed to give the scene its full effect, concealed for some time the river from our view; till we reached a wooden balcony, projecting on the edge of the water, and whence, just sheltered from the torrent, it bursts in all its overwhelming wonders on the astonished sight. That stupendous cataract, rushing with wild impetuosity over those broken, unequal rocks, which, lifting up their sharp points amidst its sea of foam, disturb its headlong course, multiply its falls, and make the afflicted waters roar – that cadence of tumultuous sound, which had never till now struck upon my ear – those long feathery surges, giving the element a new aspect – that spray rising into clouds of vapour, and reflecting the prismatic colours, while it disperses itself over the hills – never, never can I forget the sensations of that moment! when with a sort of annihilation of self, with every part impression erased from my memory, I felt as if my heart were bursting with emotions too strong to be sustained. – Oh, majestic torrent! which hast conveyed a new image of nature to my soul, the moments I have passed in contemplating thy sublimity will form an epoch in my short span! – thy course is coeval with time, and thou wilt rush down thy rocky walls when this bosom, which throbs with admiration of thy greatness, shall beat no longer!

What an effort does it require to leave, after a transient glimpse, a scene on which, while we meditate, we can take no account of time! its narrow limits seem too confined for the expanded spirit; such objects appear to belong to immortality; they call the musing mind from all its little cares and vanities, to higher destinies and regions, more congenial than this world to the feelings they excite. I had been often summoned by my fellow-travellers to depart, had often repeated "but one moment more," and many "moments more" had elapsed, before I could resolve to tear myself from the balcony.

We crossed the river, below the fall, in a boat, and had leisure to observe the surrounding scenery. The cataract, however, had for me a sort of fascinating power, which, if I withdrew my eyes for a moment, again fastened them on its impetuous waters. In the back-ground of the torrent a bare mountain lifts its head encircled with its blue vapours; on the right rises a steep cliff, of an enormous height, covered with wood, and upon its summit stands the Castle of Laussen, with its frowning towers, and encircled with its crannied wall; on the left, human industry has seized upon a slender thread of this mighty torrent in its fall, and made it subservient to the purposes of commerce. Foundries, mills, and wheels, are erected on the edge of the river, and a portion of the vast basin into which the cataract falls is confined by a dyke, which preserves the warehouses and the neighbouring huts from its inundations. Sheltered within this little nook, and accustomed to the neighbourhood of the torrent, the boatman unloads his merchandise, and the artisan pursues his toil, regardless of the falling river, and inattentive to those thundering sounds which seem calculated to suspend all human activity in solemn and awful astonishment; while the imagination of the spectator is struck with the comparative littleness of fleeting man, busy with his trivial occupations, contrasted with the view of nature in all her vast, eternal, uncontrollable grandeur....

Chapter XI

After winding for some time among these awful scenes, of which no painting can give an adequate description, and of which an imagination the most pregnant in sublime horrors could form but a very imperfect idea, we came within the sound of these cataracts of the Reuss which announced our approach towards another operation of Satanic power, called the Devil's Bridge. We were more struck with the august drapery of this supernatural work, than with the work itself. It seemed less marvellous than expectation had pictured it, and we were perhaps the more disappointed, as we remembered that "the wonderous art pontifical," was a part of architecture with which his infernal majesty was perfectly well acquainted; and the rocks of the valley of Schellenen were certainly as solid foundations for bridge building as "the aggregated soil solid, or flimsy," which was collected amidst the waste of chaos, and crowded drove "from each side shoaling towards the mouth of hell."*

On this spot we loitered for some time to contemplate the stupendous and terrific scenery. The mountainous rocks lifted their heads abrupt, and appeared to fix the limits of our progress at this point, unless we could climb the mighty torrent which was struggling impetuously for passage under our feet, after precipitating its afflicted waters with tremendous roar in successive cascades over the disjointed rocks, and filling the atmosphere with its foam.

Separating ourselves with reluctance from these objects of overwhelming greatness, we turned an angle of the mountain at the end of the bridge, and proceeded along a way of difficult ascent, which led to a rock that seemed inflexibly to bar our passage. A bridge fastened to this rock by iron work, and suspended over the torrent, was formerly the only means of passing, but numerous accidents led the government to seek another outlet. The rock being too high to climb, and too weighty to remove, the engineer took the middle way, and bored a hole in the solid mass two hundred feet along, and about ten or twelve feet broad and high, through which he carried the road. The entrance into this subterranean passage is almost dark, and the little light that penetrates through a crevice in the rock, serves only to make its obscurity more visible. Filled with powerful images of the terrible and sublime, from the enormous objects which I had been contemplating for some hours past, objects, the forms of which were new to my imagination, it was not without a feeling of reluctance that I plunged into this scene of night, whose thick gloom heightened every sensation of terror.

After passing through this cavern, the view which suddenly unfolded itself appeared rather a gay illusion of the fancy than real nature. No magical wand was ever fabled to shift more instantaneously the scene, or call up forms of more striking contrast to those on which we had gazed. On the other side of the cavern we seemed amidst the chaos or the overthrow of nature; on this we beheld her dressed in all the loveliness of infancy or renovation, with every

* *Paradise Lost*, Book X.

charm of soft and tranquil beauty. The rugged and stony interstices between the mountain and the road were here changed into smooth and verdant paths; the abrupt precipice and shagged rock were metamorphosed into gently sloping declivities; the barren and monotonous desert was transformed into a fertile and smiling plain. The long resounding cataract, struggling through the huge masses of granite, here became a calm and limpid current, gliding over fine beds of sand with gentle murmurs, as if reluctant to leave that enchanting abode....

Chapter XL

...Whether the French Republic will accede to this invitation, and render the Pays de Vaud independent of Berne, is a secret which the book of destiny will perhaps ere long unfold.

In the mean time, it is natural to conclude, that the principles of that mighty revolution which have already diffused themselves over remote regions of the globe, cannot fail to expand in those countries which are placed immediately within their influence. Since the period of the French revolution, ages have flitted before our eyes, and we have risen suddenly, like the offspring of Deucalion, from infancy to manhood, not without indications it must be confessed, of the hardened origin whence we sprung. Like the traveller, who from the scorching plains, climbs the rocks that lead him to the regions of eternal snow, and finds that in the space of a few hours he has passed through every successive latitude, from burning heat to the confines of the frozen pole, the journey of months; so the human mind, placed within the sphere of the French revolution, has bounded over the ruggedness of slow metaphysical researches, and reached at once, with an incredible effort, the highest probable attainments of political discovery....

Sources and further reading

Sources Part I

Dionysius Longinus
Text: *Dionysius Longinus on the sublime: translated from the Greek, with notes and observations, and some account of the life, writings, and character of the author. By William Smith, ... The second edition, corrected and improved* (London, 1743), pp. 2-3; 14-15; 16; 18-20; 21-24; 25; 27; 27-29; 38-39; 84-86; 92-93; 95-96.
Reprints: Oxford: Clarendon Press, 1964, with commentary by D. A. Russell.
Further reading: Alfred Rosenberg, *Longinus in England bis zum Ende des 18 Jahrhunderts* (Berlin: Meyer and Muller, 1917); T.R. Henn, *Longinus and English criticism* (Cambridge: Cambridge University Press, 1934); Elizabeth Nitchie, 'Longinus and later literary criticism', *Classical Weekly*, 27, 16 (1934), 121-6; 129-36, and 'Longinus and the theory of poetic imitation in seventeenth and eighteenth-century England', *SP*, 32 (1935), 580-97; Cora Lee Beers, 'Longinus and the disintegration of English neo-classicism', Stanford PhD, 1940; Elder Olson, 'The argument of Longinus "On the sublime"', *MP*, 39 (1942), 225-58; Samuel Holt Monk, *The sublime: a study of critical theories in XVIII-century England* (Ann Arbor: University of Michigan Press, 1960), esp. pp. 10-28; John Arthos, *Dante, Michelangelo and Milton* (London: Routledge and Kegan Paul, 1963); Gustavo Costa, 'Longinus's Treatise on the sublime in the age of Arcadia', *Nouvelles de la Republique des Lettres*, 1 (1981), 65-86; Neil Hertz, *The end of the line: essays on psychoanalysis and the sublime* (New York: Columbia University Press, 1985), pp. 1-20; Suzanne Guerlac, 'Longinus and the subject of the sublime', *NLH*, 16, 2 (1985), 275-89; Frances Ferguson, 'A commentary on Suzanne Guerlac's "Longinus and the subject of the sublime"', *NLH*, 16, 2 (1985), 291-7; Penelope Murray, 'Poetic genius and its classical origins', in *Genius: the history of an idea*, ed. Penelope Murray (Oxford: Basil Blackwell, 1989), pp. 9-31; Suzanne Guerlac, *The impersonal sublime* (Stanford: Stanford University Press, 1990), pp. 1-12; Frances Ferguson, *Solitude and the sublime* (London: Routledge, 1992).
There is a synoptic overview of Longinus criticism in Theodore E. Wood, *The word 'sublime' and its context 1650-1760* (The Hague: Mouton, 1972), esp. pp. 15-48, as well as useful guides in the bibliography of D.A. Russell's translation *"Longinus" on the sublime* (Oxford: Clarendon Press, 1965).

John Dennis
Text: *Remarks on a book entitled Prince Arthur, an heroic poem. With some general critical observations, and several new remarks upon Virgil* (London, 1696), pp. iii-viii. Text: *The advancement and reformation of modern poetry* (London, 1701), pp. 23-27; 45-47. Text: *The grounds of criticism in poetry* (London, 1704), pp. 15-18; 69-70; 76-79; 85-93.
Reprints: *The grounds of criticism in poetry* (Menston, 1971); *The critical works of John Dennis*, ed. E. N. Hooker, 2 vols. (Baltimore: Johns Hopkins University Press, 1939).
Further reading: T. E. B. Wood, "Dennis on the sublime" in *The word 'sublime' and its context 1650-1760* (The Hague: Mouton, 1972), pp. 169-88; Paul J. Korshin, *From concord to dissent: major themes in English poetic theory, 1640-1700* (Menston: The Scolar Press, 1975); W. P. Albrecht, *The sublime pleasures of tragedy: a study of critical theory from Dennis to Keats* (Lawrence, Kansas: University of Kansas Press, 1975); Jeffrey Barnouw, 'The morality of the sublime: to John Dennis', *Comparative Literature*, 35, 1 (1983), 21-42; Patricia Phillips, *The adventurous muse: theories of originality in English poetics, 1650-1760* (Uppsala: University of Uppsala, 1984); David M. Wheeler, 'John Dennis and the religious sublime', *College Language Association Journal*, 30, 2 (1986), 210-18.

Sir Richard Blackmore
Text: *Essays upon several subjects* (London, 1716), pp. 33-37; 94-97.

307

Reprints: New York: Garland Publishing, 1971.

Further reading: Theodore McGuinness Moore, 'Longinus and classical rhetoric' in his 'The background of Edmund Burke's theory of the sublime', PhD, Cornell, 1933, pp. 22-71; A. Rosenberg, *Sir Richard Blackmore: a poet and physician of the augustan age* (Lincoln: University of Nebraska, 1953).

Tamworth Reresby
Text: *A miscellany of ingenious thoughts,...* (London, 1721), pp. 26-28.
Reprints: New York: Garland Publishing, 1971.

Jonathan Richardson, the elder
Text: *An essay on the theory of painting. The second edition, enlarg'd and corrected* (London, 1725), pp. 227-28; 235-36; 244-45; 255-60; 261-63.
Reprints: Menston: Scolar Press, 1971.
Further reading: G.W. Snelgrove, 'The work and theories of Jonathan Richardson', PhD, Courtauld Institute of Art, 1936; S. H. Monk, *op. cit*, pp. 174-8; Laurence Lipking, 'The uncomplicated Richardson', in *The ordering of the arts in eighteenth-century England* (Princeton: Princeton University Press, 1970), pp. 109-26; Johannes Dobai, *Die Kunstliteratur das Klassizismus und der Romantik in England*, 2 vols. (Bern: Benteli Verlag, 1974-), I, 633-49.

Thomas Stackhouse
Text: *Reflections on the nature and property of languages in general,...* (London, 1731), pp. 133-40.
Reprints: Menston: Scolar Press, 1968. ˙

Hildebrand Jacob
Text: *The works of Hildebrand Jacob, Esq;...* (London, 1735), pp. 421-26.
Further reading: S. H. Monk, *op. cit.* pp. 60-2.

Joseph Trapp
Text: *Lectures on poetry. Read in the schools of natural philosophy at Oxford. Translated from the latin, with additional notes* (London, 1742), pp. 115; 125-26; 147-48.
Reprints: Hildesheim: Georg Olms, 1969.
Further reading: Vincent Freimarch, 'Joseph Trapp's advanced conception of metaphor', *PQ*, 29, (1950), 413-416.

Sources Part II

Joseph Addison
Text: *The Spectator*, 8 vols. (London, 1712-1715), VI, 88-91; 95-97; 98-101; 117-19; 121-25; VII, 83-85. Text: *A discourse on antient and modern learning* (London, 1734), pp. 17-20; 21-23.
Reprints: *A discourse on ancient learning* in *The miscellaneous works of J. Addison*, ed. A. L. Guthkelch, 2 vols. London: G. Bell and Sons, 1914, II, 449-63. *The Spectator*, ed. D. F. Bond, 5 vols. Oxford: Clarendon Press, 1965.
Further reading: Clarence D. Thorpe, 'Addison and Hutcheson on the imagination', *ELH*, 2 (1935), 215-34; Clarence D. Thorpe, 'Addison's theory of the imagination as "perceptive response"', *PMASAL*, 21 (1935), 509-30; Clarence D. Thorpe, 'Addison and some of his predecessors on "novelty"', in R. F. Jones and others writing in his honour, *The seventeenth century: studies in the history of English thought and literature from Bacon to Pope* (Stanford: Stanford University Press, 1951), pp. 318-29; Lee Elioseff, *The cultural milieu of Addison's literary criticism* (Austin: University of Texas Press, 1963); Neil Saccamano, 'The sublime force of words in Addison's "Pleasures"', *ELH*, 58, 1 (1991), 83-106; Masahiro Hamashita, 'Genealogy of the aesthetics of the sublime: to Addison and Shaftesbury', *KCS*, 38 (1992), 105-27.

Anthony Ashley Cooper, Third Earl of Shaftesbury
Text: *Characteristicks of men, manners, opinions, times. The second edition corrected*, 3 vols. (London, 1714), II, 343-47; 366-74; 388-91; 400-405.
Reprints: *Standard edition: complete works, selected letters and posthumous writings in English with parallel German translation*, edited, translated and commented by Gerd Hemmerich and Wolfram Benda, Stuttgart-Bad Canstatt, 1981, II.1; Farnborough: Gregg International, 1968; ed. John M. Robertson, with an introduction by Stanley Green, Indianapolis: Library of Liberal Arts, 1964.

Further reading: R. L. Brett, *The Third Earl of Shaftesbury: a study in eighteenth-century literary theory* (London: Thomas Hutchinson, 1951); Marjorie Hope Nicolson, *Mountain gloom and mountain glory* (Ithaca: Cornell University Press, 1959); E. L. Tuveson, *The imagination as a means of grace: Locke and the aesthetics of romanticism* (Berkeley: University of California Press, 1960); Robert W. Uphaus, 'Shaftesbury on art: the rhapsodic aesthetic', *JAAC*, 27 (1969), 341-8; Pat Rogers, 'Shaftesbury and the aesthetics of rhapsody', *BJA*, 12 (1972), 244-57; John Barrell, *The political theory of painting from Reynolds to Hazlitt* (New Haven: Yale University Press, 1986), pp. 1-69; Gloria Flaherty, 'Transport, ecstasy, and enthusiasm', in Georgia Cowart, ed., *French Musical Thought, 1600-1800* (Ann Arbor: UMI Research Publications, 1990), pp. 81-93.

Henry Needler
Text: *The works of Mr. Henry Needler*, [Ed. William Duncombe] (London, 1724), pp. 71-79; 94-99.
    Further reading: Herbert Drennon, 'Henry Needler and Shaftesbury', *PMLA*, 46 (1931), 1095-1106; Alfred Owen Aldridge, 'Henry Needler's knowledge of Shaftesbury', *MLN*, 62 (1947), 264-7.

Mark Akenside
Text: Samuel Johnson, *The lives of the most eminent English poets, with critical observations on their works. With notes corrective and explanatory by Peter Cunningham*, 3 vols. (London, 1854), III, 385-86. Text: *The pleasures of the imagination. A poem.* (London, 1744), pp. 102n-104n.
    Further reading: Alfred Owen Aldridge, 'Akenside and imagination', *SP*, 42 (1945), 769-92; John Norton, 'Akenside's *The pleasures of the imagination*: an exercise in poetics', *ECS*, 3 (1970).

John Baillie
Text: *An essay on the sublime* (London, 1747), pp. 1-41 (complete).
    Reprints: Los Angeles: Augustan Reprint Society, William Andrews Clark Memorial Library, 1954, with an introduction by S. H. Monk.
    Further reading: A. O. Wlecke, *Wordsworth and the sublime* (Berkeley: University of California Press, 1973), pp. 48-62.

David Hartley
Text: *Observations on man, his frame, his duty, and his expectations*, 2 vols. (London, 1749), I, 418-25.
    Reprints: Hildesheim: Georg Olms, 1967, 2 vols; Gainesville: Scholars Facsimiles and Reprints, 1966, with an introduction by Theodore L. Huguelet.
    Further reading: Gordon McKenzie, *Critical responsiveness: a study of the psychological current in later eighteenth-century criticism* (Berkeley: University of California Press, 1949).

Robert Lowth
Text: *Lectures on the sacred poetry of the Hebrews, translated from the Latin... by G. Gregory*, 2 vols. (London, 1787), I, 307-9; 346-9; 365-76.
    Reprints: Hildesheim: Georg Olms, 1969, with an introduction by Vincent Freimarck; New York: Garland Press, 1971.
    Further reading: Stephen Prickett, 'Poetry and prophecy: Bishop Lowth and the Hebrew Scriptures in eighteenth century England', in Jasper David, ed., *Images of belief in literature* (New York: St. Martin's Press, 1984); Murray Roston, *Prophet and poet: the bible and the growth of romanticism*, (London: Faber & Faber, 1965).

Samuel Johnson
Text: *A dictionary of the English language: in which words are deduced from their originals, and illustrated in their different significations...* (London, 1755).
    Further reading: Jean H. Hagstrum, *Samuel Johnson's literary criticism* (Chicago: University of Chicago Press, 1967), pp. 129-52; Jonathan Arac, 'The media of sublimity: Johnson and Lamb on King Lear', *Studies in Romanticism*, 26, 2 (1987), 209-20.

Edward Young
Text: *Conjectures on original composition....* (London, 1759), pp. 9-14; 25-31.
    Reprints: Menston: Scolar Press, 1966; ed. Edith J. Morley, Manchester: Manchester University Press, 1918.

James Burgh
Text: *The art of speaking...* (London, 1761), pp. 28-30.
   Further reading: W. M. Parrish, 'The burglarizing of Burgh, or the case of the purloined passions', *OJS*, 38 (1952), 431-4; Donald E. Harris, 'James Burgh and the art of speaking', *SM*, 24, (1957), 275-84; W. S. Howells, *Eighteenth-century British logic and rhetoric* (Princeton: Princeton University Press, 1971), pp. 244-6.

Joseph Priestley
Text: *A course of lectures on oratory and criticism* (London, 1777), pp. 151-52; 154-63.
   Reprints: Carbondale: Southern Illinois University Press, 1965 ed. V. M. Bevilacqua and R. Murphy; Menston: Scolar Press, 1968.
   Further reading: Dahney Townsend, 'The aesthetics of Joseph Priestley', *JAAC*, 51, 4 (1993), 561-72.

Frances Reynolds
Text: *An enquiry concerning the principles of taste, and of the origin of our ideas of beauty, &c* (London, 1785), pp. 1-7; 17-19.
   Reprints: Los Angeles: Augustan Reprint Society, William Andrews Clark Memorial Library, 1951, with an introduction by James L. Clifford.

Sources Part III

Edmund Burke
Text: *A philosophical enquiry into the origin of our ideas of the sublime and beautiful. The second edition. With an introductory discourse concerning taste* (London 1759), pp. 58-60; 84-87; 95-96; 96-98; 101-103; 103-110; 110-20; 124; 237-39; 334-42.
   Reprints: ed. James T. Boulton, London: Routledge and Kegan Paul, 1958; Menston: Scolar Press, 1970.
   Further reading: Herbert A. Wichelns, 'Burke's essay on the sublime and its reviewers', *JEGP*, 21 (1922); Theodore Moore, 'The background of Edmund Burke's theory of the sublime 1660-1759', PhD, Cornell, 1933; Walter John Hipple Jr, *The beautiful, the sublime & the picturesque in eighteenth-century British aesthetic theory* (Carbondale: The Southern Illinois University Press, 1957), pp. 83-98; J. T. Boulton, introduction to edition above; pp. 645-61; Frances Ferguson, 'Legislating the sublime', in Ralph Cohen, ed., *Studies in eighteenth century British art and aesthetics* (Berkeley: University of California Press, 1995), pp. 128-47; Steven H. Browne, 'Aesthetics and the heteromony of rhetorical judgment', *Rhetoric Society Quarterly*, 18, 2 (1988), 141-52; Steven Cresap, 'Sublime politics: on the uses of an aesthetics of terror', *Clio*, 19, 2 (1990), 111-25; Frances Ferguson, *Solitude and the sublime* (London: Routledge, 1992); Carsten Zelle, 'Beauty and horror: on the dichotomy of beauty and the sublime in eighteenth-century aesthetics', *SVEC*, 305 (1992), 1542-45; Tom Furniss, *Edmund Burke's aesthetic ideology* (Cambridge: Cambridge University Press, 1993).

John Lawson
Text: *Lectures concerning oratory. Delivered in Trinity College Dublin* (Dublin, 1758), pp. 247-53.
   Reprints: Menston: Scolar Press, 1969.
   Further reading: W. S. Howells, *Eighteenth-century British logic and rhetoric* (Princeton: Princeton University Press, 1971), pp. 616-31.

James Usher
Text: *Clio; or a discourse on taste. Addressed to a young lady. The second edition, with large additions* (London, 1769), pp. 102-36.
   Further reading: S. H. Monk, *op. cit.*, pp. 142-5.

Sources Part IV

Thomas Blackwell
Text: *An enquiry into the life and writings of Homer* (London, 1735), pp. 22-28.
   Reprints: 2nd edn, Hildesheim: Georg Olms, 1976.
   Further reading: Lois Whitney, 'Thomas Blackwell, a disciple of Shaftesbury', *PQ*, 5, (1926),

196-211; B. H. Stern, *The rise of romantic hellenism in English literature, 1732-1786*, (Menasha, Wisconsin: Banta Press, 1940); Kirsti Simonsouri, *Homer's original genius: eighteenth-century notions of the early Greek epic (1688-1798)* (Cambridge: Cambridge University Press, 1979); Gregory Hollingshead, 'Berkeley, Blackwell, and Blackwell's Homer', *Scottish Literary Journal*, 11, 1 (1984), 20-35.

David Fordyce

Text: *Theodorus: a dialogue concerning the art of preaching*, [Ed. James Fordyce] (London, 1752), pp. 68-70; 122-23; 131; 134-135; 147-48.

Alexander Gerard

Text: *An essay on taste...* (London, 1759), pp. 13-25; 26-27; 28-30.
Reprints: 1st edn, Menston: Scolar Press, 1971; 3rd edn containing a fourth part to the Essay, 'Of the standard of taste', with introduction by W. J. Hipple Jr, Gainesville: Scholars Facsimiles and Reprints, 1963.
Further reading: James McCosh, *The Scottish philosophy from Hutcheson to Hamilton* (London, 1875); Marjorie Greene, 'Gerard's *Essay on taste*', *MP*, 41 (1943), 45-58; W. J. Hipple Jr, *The beautiful, the sublime and the picturesque* (Carbondale: Southern Illinois University Press, 1957), pp. 67-82; Morton J. Cauvel, 'The critic "blest with a poet's fire": Alexander Gerard's interpretation of genius, taste and aesthetic criticism', PhD, Bryn Mawr, 1963; James Engell, *The creative imagination* (Cambridge, Mass.: Harvard University Press, 1981), pp. 78-84.

William Duff

Text: *An essay on original genius, and its various modes of exertion in philosophy and the fine arts, particularly in poetry* (London, 1767), pp. 150-56; 162-72; 176-77; 178-79.
Reprints: ed. with introduction by J. L. Mahoney, Gainesville: Scholars Facsimiles and Reprints, 1964.
Further reading: James Engell, *The creative imagination: enlightenment to romanticism* (Cambridge, Mass.: Harvard University Press, 1981), pp. 84-7.

Thomas Reid

Text: *Essays on the intellectual powers of man* (Edinburgh, 1785), pp. 729-32.
Reprints: Menston: Scolar Press, 1971; Cambridge, Mass.: MIT Press, 1969, with introduction by Baruch Brody.
Further reading: D. D. Robbins, 'The aesthetics of Thomas Reid', *JAAC*, 5, (1942), 20-41. Selwyn Alfred Grave, *The Scottish philosophy of common sense* (Oxford: Oxford University Press, 1960); Norman Daniels, *Thomas Reid's 'inquiry': the geometry of visibles and the case for realism* (Stanford: Stanford University Press, 1974); Roger D. Gallie, *Thomas Reid and 'the way of ideas'* (Boston: Kluwer Academic, 1989); Peter Jones, ed., *The 'science of man' in the Scottish enlightenment: Hume, Reid and their contemporaries* (Edinburgh: Edinburgh University Press, 1989); Peter Kivy, 'On the significance of Reid in the history of aesthetics', in Melvin Dalgarno and Eric Matthews, eds., *The philosophy of Thomas Reid* (Boston: Kluwer Academic, 1989), pp. 307-28; and the introduction by Knud Haakonssen to his edition of *Thomas Reid: practical ethics* (Princeton: Princeton University Press, 1990).

James Beattie

Text: *Dissertations moral and critical...*(London, 1783), pp. 605-31; 639; 641-45; 647; 655.
Reprints: Stuttgard-Bad Caanstatt: Friedrich Fromann Verlag, 1970; vol. III of *The philosophical works*.
Further reading: Vincent M. Bevilacqua, 'James Beattie's theory of rhetoric', *SM*, 34 (1967), 109-24; Karen Kloth, *James Beatties asthetische Theorien: ihre Zusammenhange mit der Aberdeener Schulphilosophie* (Munchen: Wilhelm Fink, 1974).

Sources part V

David Hume

Text: *A treatise of human nature: being an attempt to introduce the experimental method of reasoning into moral subjects*, 3 vols. (London, 1739-40), II, 279-89; III, 242-47; 256-61.
Reprints: ed. L. A. Selby-Bigge, second edition, Oxford: Clarendon Press, 1978).
Further reading: T. E. Jessop, *A bibliography of Hume and of Scottish philosophy from*

Hutcheson to Lord Balfour (London, 1938; revd 1972); M. Kallich, 'The associationist criticism of F. Hutcheson and D. Hume', *Studies in Philosophy*, 43 (1946), 644-67; Charles E. Noyes, 'Aesthetic theory and literary criticism in the works of David Hume', PhD, University of Texas, 1950; Ralph Cohen, 'David Hume's experimental method and the theory of taste', *ELH*, 25 (1958); Peter Jones, 'Hume's aesthetics reassessed', *PQ*, 26 (1976), 48-62; C. W. Korsmeyer, 'Hume and the foundations of taste', *JAAC*, 35 (1976), 201-15; Peter Jones, *Hume's sentiments: their Ciceronian and French context* (Edinburgh: Edinburgh University Press, 1982); and Peter Kivy, 'Hume's neighbour's wife: an essay on the evolution of Hume's aesthetics', *BJA*, 24 (1984); Jerome C. Christensen, *Practicing enlightenment* (Madison: University of Wisconsin Press, 1986); Frans De Bruyn, 'Hooking the Leviathan: the eclipse of the heroic and the emergence of the sublime in eighteenth-century British literature', *The Eighteenth Century: Theory and Interpretation*, 28, 3 (1987), 195-215; Peter Jones, 'Hume and the beginnings of modern aesthetics', in Peter Jones ed., *The 'Science of Man' in the Scottish enlightenment* (Edinburgh: Edinburgh University Press, 1989), pp. 54-67; Donald T. Siebert, 'The sentimental sublime in Hume's History of England', *RES*, 40, 159 (1989), 352-72.

Hugh Blair
Text: *A critical dissertation on the poems of Ossian, son of Fingal* (London, 1763), pp. 1-4; 20-22; 68-71; 74. Text: *Lectures on rhetoric and belles lettres*, 2 vols. (London, 1783), I, 45-49; 50; 51-52; 53-56; 57-61; 63; 65; 66-67; 68-72; 75-77; 78.
    Reprints: *Lectures*, ed. H. F. Harding, 2 vols. Carbondale: Southern Illinois University Press, 1965.
    Further reading: Robert Morell Schmitz, *Hugh Blair*, (New York: King's Crown Press, 1948); H. Cohen, 'Hugh Blair's theory of taste', *QJS*, 44 (October, 1958), 264-74; V. Bevilacqua, 'Philosophical assumptions underlying Hugh Blair's lectures on rhetoric and belles lettres', *WS*, 31, (1967); and on Ossian, R.W. Chapman, 'Blair on Ossian', *RES*, 7 (1931).

Henry Home, Lord Kames
Text: *Elements of criticism. The third edition. With additions and improvements*, 2 vols. (Edinburgh, 1765), I, 199-206; 208-13; 215-17; 218; 219-21; 225-26; 227-29; 234-35; 235-36.
    Reprints: First edition, ed. R. Voitle, Hildesheim: Georg Olms, 1969.
    Further reading: Helen Whitcomb Randall, *The critical theory of Lord Kames* (Northampton: Smith College Studies in Modern Languages, 1940-1); Vincent M. Bevilacqua, 'The rhetorical theory of Henry Home, Lord Kames', PhD, University of Illinois, 1961; Loomis Caryl Irish, 'Human nature and the arts: the aesthetic theory of Henry Home, Lord Kames', PhD, Columbia University, 1961; Arthur E. McGuinness Jr, 'The influence of David Hume's critical theory on Lord Kames's *Elements of criticism*', PhD, University of Wisconsin, 1964; Arthur E. McGuinness Jr, *Henry Home, Lord Kames* (New York: Twayne Publishers, 1970).

Adam Smith
Text: *Essays on philosophical subjects* [Ed. Joseph Black and James Hutton] (London, 1795), pp. 3-4; 4-5; 5-8; 10-17; 20-22; 23-26. Text: *The theory of moral sentiments;...The sixth edition, with considerable additions and corrections*, 2 vols. (London, 1790), I, 44; 47-49; 247-49; 374-79; 466-69; II, 126-27; 159-62; 300-33.
    Reprints: *Essays on philosophical subjects*, ed. W. P. D. Wightman and J. C. Bryce, Oxford: Clarendon Press, 1980. *The theory of moral sentiments*, ed. D. D. Raphael and A. L. MacFie, Oxford: Clarendon Press, 1976.
    Further reading: Walter Jackson Bate, 'The sympathetic imagination in eighteenth-century criticism', *ELH*, 12 (1945), 144-64; H. F. Thomson, 'Adam Smith's philosophy of science', *QJE*, 79 (1965); James S. Malek, 'Adam Smith's contribution to eighteenth-century British aesthetics', *JAAC*, 31 (1972), 49-54; Andrew S. Skinner and Thomas Wilson, eds., *Essays on Adam Smith* (Oxford: Clarendon Press, 1975); M. L. Myers, 'Adam Smith as critic of ideas', *JHI*, 36 (1975), 281-96; David Marshall, 'Adam Smith and the theatricality of moral sentiments', *CI*, 10 (1984), 592-613; Elizabeth A. Bohls, 'Disinterestedness and denial of the particular: Locke, Adam Smith and the subject of aesthetics', in Paul Mattick Jr., ed., *Eighteenth-century aesthetics and the reconstruction of art* (Cambridge: Cambridge University Press, 1993), pp. 16-51.

Adam Ferguson
Text: *An essay on the history of civil society* (Edinburgh, 1767), pp. 9-13; 44-46; 328-34; 335-37; 338; 339-41; 345-46.
    Reprints: New York: Garland Press, 1971; ed. Duncan Forbes, Edinburgh: Edinburgh University Press, 1966.

Further reading: John Small, *Biographical sketch of Adam Ferguson* (Edinburgh, 1864); David Kettler, *The social and political thought of Adam Ferguson* (Ohio: Ohio State University Press, 1965).

Sources Part VI

Sir William Chambers
Text: *A dissertation on oriental gardening* (London, 1772), pp. 35-40; 44-46.
Reprints: Farnborough: Gregg International, 1972; with an introduction by J. Harris.
Further reading: R. C. Bald, 'Sir William Chambers and the Chinese garden', *JHI*, 11, 3 (June, 1950), 287-320; Eileen Harris, 'Designs of Chinese buildings', in John Harris, *Sir William Chambers* (London: Zwemmer, 1970); Patrick Conner, 'China and the landscape garden: reports, engravings, and misconceptions', *Art History*, 2, 4 (December 1979), 429-40; Jurgis Baltrusaitis, *Aberrations: an essay on the legend of forms* (Cambridge, Mass: MIT Press, 1989), pp. 162-82. On Chambers and Burke: Eileen Harris, 'Burke and Chambers on the sublime and beautiful', in *Essays in the history of architecture presented to Rudolf Wittkower* (London: Phaidon, 1967), pp. 207-13.

Uvedale Price
Text: *An Essay on the picturesque as compared with the sublime and beautiful;...* (London, 1794), pp. 34; 39-40; 43-46; 76-77; 80-88.
Reprints: 3rd edn, 3 vols. Farnborough: Gregg International, 1971.
Further reading: Christopher Hussey, *The picturesque* (London: Cass and Co, 1927), esp. pp. 171-85; Samuel Kliger, 'Whig aesthetics: a phase of eighteenth-century taste', *ELH*, 16 (1949), esp 141-3; John Dixon Hunt, *The figure in the landscape* (Baltimore: John Hopkins University Press, 1976), pp. 191-5; David Jacques, *Georgian gardens: the reign of nature* (London: Batsford, 1983), pp. 150-6; Ann Bermingham, *Landscape and ideology* (Berkeley: University of California Press, 1986), esp. pp. 66-70; Malcolm Andrews, *The search for the picturesque* (Stanford: Stanford University Press, 1989); Sidney K. Robinson, *Inquiry into the picturesque* (Chicago: University of Chicago Press, 1991); Andrew Ballantyne 'Genealogy of the picturesque', *BJA*, 32 (1992), 320-29; Stephen Copley and Peter Garside, eds., *The politics of the picturesque* (Cambridge: Cambridge University Press, 1994).

William Marshall
Text: *A review of The landscape, a didactic poem,...* (London, 1795), pp. 272-75.
Further reading: David Jacques, *Georgian gardens: the reign of nature* (London: Batsford, 1983), pp. 110-18.

William Godwin
Text: *The history of the life of William Pitt, Earl of Chatham* (London, 1783), pp. 297-301.
Text: *Enquiry concerning political justice, and its influence on morals and happiness. The third edition corrected*, 2 vols. (London, 1798), I, 308-15; 320-25.
Reprints: Toronto: Toronto University Press, 1946, ed. F. E. L. Priestley; *Collected novels and writings*, ed. Mark Philip, 8 vols. London: William Pickering, 1992.
Further reading: D. H. Monro, *Godwin's moral philosophy* (Oxford: Clarendon Press, 1953); B. R. Pollin, *Education and enlightenment in the thought of William Godwin* (New York: Las Americas, 1962); David McCracken, 'Godwin's literary theory: the alliance between fiction and political philosophy', *PQ*, 49, (1970), 113-33; M. Fitzpatrick, 'William Godwin and the rational dissenters', *Price-Priestley Newsletter*, 3 (1979), 4-28; Marilyn Butler, 'Godwin, Burke, and Caleb Williams', *Essays in Criticism*, 32, 3 (1982), 237-57; J. A. Hone, *For the cause of truth: radicalism in London 1796-1802* (Oxford: Clarendon Press, 1982); Mark Philip, *Godwin's political justice* (London: Duckworth, 1986).

Edmund Burke
Text: *Reflections on the revolution in France, and on the proceedings in certain societies in London relative to that event....* (London, 1790), pp. 95-103; 105-116; 118-21; 231-32; 245-52.
Text: *A letter from the right honourable Edmund Burke to a noble lord,...* (London, 1791), pp. 3-5; 19-22.
Reprints: *The writings and speeches of Edmund Burke. Vol. 8, The French Revolution 1790-1794*, ed. L. G. Mitchell, Oxford: Clarendon Press, 1989, *Vol. 9, The Revolutionary War 1794-1797*, ed. R. B. McDowell, Oxford: Clarendon Press, 1991.

Further reading: Neal Wood, 'The aesthetic dimension of Burke's political thought', *Journal of British Studies*, 4 (1964), 41-64; Peter H. Melvin, 'Burke on theatricality and revolution', *JHI*, 36 (1975), 447-68; R. T. Allen, 'The state and civil society as objects of aesthetic appreciation', *BJA*, 16, 3 (1976), 237-42; Ronald Paulson, 'Burke's sublime and the representation of revolution', in Perez Zagorin, ed., *Culture and politics from puritanism to the enlightenment* (Berkeley: University of California Press, 1980), pp. 241-69; James K. Chandler, *Wordsworth's second nature: A study of the poetry and politics* (Chicago: Chicago University Press, 1984), pp. 62-77; Craig Howes, 'Burke, Poe, and "Usher": the sublime and rising woman', *ESO: A Journal of the American Renaissance*, 31, 3 (1985), 173-89; Steven Blakemore, *Burke and the fall of language: the French revolution as linguistic event* (London: University Press of New England, 1988); John Turner, 'Burke, Paine, and the nature of language', *Yearbook of English Studies*, 19 (1989), 36-53; Arnd Bohm, 'The politics of the sublime: Burke and Klopstock', *SVEC*, 305 (1992), 1531-34.

Mary Wollstonecraft
Text: *A vindication of the rights of man, in a letter to the right honourable Edmund Burke; occasioned by his Reflections on the revolution in France. Second edition* (London, 1790), pp. 62-66; 109-17; 135-42.

Reprints: Gainesville: Scholars Facsimiles and Reprints, 1960. *The works*, ed. Janet Todd and Marilyn Butler, 7 vols. London: William Pickering, 1989.

Further reading: Mitzi Myers, 'Politics from the outside: Mary Wollstone-craft's first vindication', *Studies in Eighteenth-Century Culture*, 6 (1977), 113-32.

Helen Maria Williams
Text: *Letters written in France, in the summer 1790, ...* (London, 1790), pp. 5-6; 13-14; 66-67; 71-72; 73-74; 80-82; 217-19. Text: *A tour in Switzerland; ...* (London, 1798), pp. 57-53; 160-164; 270-271.

Reprints: *Letters*: Oxford: Woodstock Books, 1989.

Further reading: L. D. Woodward, *Une adhérente anglaise de la révolution française Helène-Maria Williams et ses amis* (Paris, 1930); M. Ray Adams, 'Helen Maria Williams and the French revolution', in G. L. Griggs, ed., *Wordsworth and Coleridge: Studies in honor of G. M. Harpur*, (Princeton: Princeton University Press, 1939); Julie Ellison, 'Redoubled feeling: politics, sentiment and the sublime in Williams and Wollstonecraft', *Studies in Eighteenth-Century Culture*, 20 (1990), 197-215; Matthew Bray, 'Helen Maria Williams and Edmund Burke: radical critique and complicity', *Eighteenth-Century Life*, 16, 2 (1992), 1-24.

Lightning Source UK Ltd.
Milton Keynes UK
UKOW03f1815220514

232149UK00001B/44/P